FROM CONSTANTINE TO JULIAN

The reign of Constantine, the first Christian Emperor, is both a major turning point in world history and a source of controversy. The adoption of Christianity as the religion of the Roman State gave a major stimulus to Christian writings. The work of Christian propagandists, such as Lactantius and Eusebius, has long been relied on for information. The fact that writing in the pagan tradition continued to thrive has often been ignored.

From Constantine to Julian redresses the balance, providing translations of key pagan historical writings and panegyric as well as Byzantine hagiographies. It includes the *Origo Constantini*, an anonymous life of Constantine, Libanius' *Oratio* LIX, and the *Artemii passio*. Each text is accompanied by an introduction and a detailed commentary.

This sourcebook illuminates the history of Constantine's reign. It explores the Constaninian process of myth-making and shows how the pagan sources help balance the biased Christian accounts. This book is essential reading for undergraduates and research scholars.

Samuel N. C. Lieu is Professor of Ancient History at Macquarie University, New South Wales, Australia. **Dominic Montserrat** is Lecturer in Classics at the University of Warwick.

FROM CONSTANTINE TO JULIAN: PAGAN AND BYZANTINE VIEWS

A Source History

Edited by
Samuel N. C. Lieu and
Dominic Montserrat

London and New York

First published 1996
by Routledge
11 New Fetter Lane, London EC4P 4EE

Simultaneously published in the USA and Canada
by Routledge
29 West 35th Street, New York, NY 10001

© 1996 Samuel N. C. Lieu and Dominic Montserrat

Typeset in Garamond by
Ponting–Green Publishing Services, Chesham, Bucks
Printed and bound in Great Britain by
Clays Ltd, St Ives PLC

British Library Cataloguing in Publication Data
A catalogue record for this book is available from
the British Library

Library of Congress Cataloguing in Publication Data
A catalogue record for this book has been requested

ISBN 0–415–09335–X
0–415–09336–8 (pbk)

CONTENTS

v

CONTENTS

PREFACE

The Centre for Research in East Roman Studies at the University of Warwick was created in 1991 to co-ordinate a number of existing research projects which concern the history and archaeology of the Roman East. A new project adopted at the time of the launch was the investigation of pagan, Christian and Byzantine sources on the reign of Constantine. The result was a number of seminars based on the *Vita Constantini* of Eusebius, augmented by various translation projects on individual sources. The present first volume of the Centre's monograph series reflects some of these activities. Though the book is entitled *From Constantine to Julian*, its main focus is on the reign of Constantine and that of his sons. The choice of the sources is decided partly by their importance to the political history of the period and partly by their general unavailability in English translation. Only the first text, the *Origo Constantini*, has been translated before, but the translation of J. C. Rolfe, though much used, is generally regarded as highly unsatisfactory and the accompanying commentary offers virtually no help to the research scholar. The remaining texts in the volume, to the best of our knowledge, have never before been published in English translation.

The editors would wish, first and foremost, to thank the translators: Dr Jane Stevenson, Research Fellow in British and Comparative Cultural Studies, Warwick University; Mark Vermes, Research Officer, *Corpus Fontium Manichaeorum* project based at the Centre; Frank Beetham, Honorary Lecturer in Classics, Birmingham University; and Michael Dodgeon, Classics Master, Solihull School. Mark Vermes also gave considerable assistance with the proof-reading. They would also like to thank Richard Stoneman for his interest and patience, and the staff of the Joint Library of the Hellenic and Roman Societies for their unfailing support, especially in fetching rare items (essential for the commentaries) from the basement of the Library on a regular basis. Sam Lieu would like to thank Prof. Tim Barnes (Toronto) for much helpful discussion on many aspects of the reign of Constantine and to thank him and Stella for their generous hospitality. He would also like to thank the British Academy for a small research grant for work on the *Artemii passio* as a source for the history of the fourth century. A fuller version of the introduction to Chapter 5 will appear in *Byzantine and Modern Greek Studies* (Birmingham).

LIST OF ABBREVIATIONS
AND PRIMARY SOURCES

AB   *Analecta Bollandiana* (Paris and Brussels, 1882–).
AE   *Année Épigraphique* (Paris, 1888–).
Agathias
         Historiae, ed. R. Keydell, CFHB 2 (Berlin, 1967). Eng.
         trans. J. D. Frendo, *Agathias: The Histories*, CFHB 2A
         (Berlin, 1975).
Ambros., *De obitu Theod.*
         Ambrosius, *De obitu Theodosii oratio, PL* 16. 1445–68.
Amm.   Ammianus Marcellinus, *Res gestae*, ed. W. Seyfarth, 2
         vols (Leipzig, 1978). Eng. trans. J. C. Rolfe, LCL, 3 vols
         (1935–52).
Anon. Vales.
         Anonymus Valesianus, ed. and trans. J. C. Rolfe, in LCL
         Ammianus Marcellinus (iii, 1939) 508–69.
AP   *Artemii passio*, ed. P. B. Kotter, *Die Schriften des
         Johannes von Damaskos*, V (Berlin, 1988) 185–245, see
         also partial edition by J. Bidez in his GCS edn of
         Philostorgius (below).
Athan., *Apol. ad Const.*
         Athanasius, *Apologia ad Constantium imperatorem*, ed.
         W. Bright, *Athanasius' Historical Works* (Oxford, 1881)
         130–57. Eng. trans. M. Atkinson in NPNF *Athanasius*,
         236–53.
——, *Apol. c. Ar.*
         Athanasius, *Apologia contra Arianos*, ed. Bright, *op. cit.*,
         11–104. Eng. trans. M. Atkinson and rev. A. Robertson
         in NPNF *Athanasius*, 97–148.
——, *De synod.*
         Athanasius, *Epistula de synodis Arimini in Italia et*

Seleuciae in Isauria celebratis, ed. Bright, *op. cit.*,
145–306. Eng. trans. J. H. Newman and rev. A.
Robertson in NPNF *Athanasius*, 448–80.

——, *Ep. encycl.*

Athanasius, *Epistula ad episcopos encyclica*, ed. Bright,
op. cit., 1–10. Eng. trans. M. Atkinson in NPNF
Athanasius, 91–96.

——, *Fest. Letters*

Athanasius, *Festal Letters and Index*, trans. from the
Syriac by J. Payne Smith in NPNF *Athanasius*, 500–80.

——, *Hist. Ar.*

Athanasius, *Historia Arianorum ad monachos*, ed. H.-G.
Opitz, *Athanasius Werke*, II (Berlin, 1940–41) 183–230.
Eng. trans. M. Atkinson in NPNF *Athanasius*, 266–302.

Aur. Vict., *Caes.*

Aurelius Victor, *Liber de Caesaribus*, ed. F. Pichelmayr,
Sextus Aurelius Victor (Leipzig, 1911). Eng. trans. Bird,
1994: 1–54.

[Aur. Vict.], *Epit.* see under *epit.*

Aus., *Mosella*

Ausonius, *Mosella*, ed. and trans. H. G. Evelyn White,
LCL *Ausonius* ii (1919) 224–67.

BHG   *Bibliotheca Hagiographica Graeca*, 3rd edn, ed. F.
Halkin, 3 vols (Brussels, 1957).

BNgJ   *Byzantinisch-Neugriechische Jahrbücher.*

CCSL   Corpus Christianorum, Series Latina (Turnhout, 1967–).

Cedren., *Comp. hist.*

Cedrenus, *Compendium historiarum*, ed. I. Bekker,
2 vols, CSHB, 1838–39.

CFHB   Corpus Fontium Historiae Byzantinae (Washington,
DC etc., 1967–).

Chron. an. 354

Chronographus anni CCCLIIII, ed. T. Mommsen,
Chronica minora, MGH (Auct. Ant.) IX (Berlin, 1892)
14–153.

Chron. Pasch.

Chronicon Paschale, ed. L. Dindorf, 2 vols, CSHB,
1832. Eng. trans. M. and M. Whitby, *Chronicon
Paschale 284–628 A.D.*, Translated Texts for Historians
7 (Liverpool, 1989).

Chron. Ps.-Symeon
> La règne de Constantin d'après la Chronique inédite du
> Pseudo-Syméon, ed. F. Halkin, *Byzantion*, 29–30
> (1959–60) 7–27.

Chrys., *De S. Babyla*
> Ioannes Chrysostomus, *De sancto Babyla contra
> Julianum et Gentiles*, *PG* 50.533–79. Eng. trans. of
> XIV/75–XIX/109 by M. Morgan, in Lieu, 1989: 59–79,
> of the whole discourse by M. Shatkin in *Saint John
> Chrysostom Apologist*, Fathers of the Church, vol. 73
> (Washington DC, 1984) 75–152.

CIL *Corpus Inscriptionum Latinarum* (Berlin, 1863–).

CJ *Codex Justinianus*, ed. P. Krüger, Corpus Iuris Civilis,
vol. 2 (Berlin, 1929).

Cons. Const.
> *Consularia Constantinopolitana*, ed. Th. Mommsen,
> MGH, Auct. Ant. 9 (1892) 205–47.

Constantinus (Imp.)
> *Oratio ad sanctorum coetum*, ed. I. Heikel, GCS 7
> (Eusebius Werke 1, Berlin, 1902) 149–92. Eng. trans. E.
> C. Richardson, NPNF *Eusebius*, 561–80.

CPG *Clavis Patrum Graecorum*, ed. M. Geerard (Turnhout,
1974–, 4 vols to date).

CSCO Corpus Scriptorum Christianorum Orientalium (Paris,
Louvain etc., 1903–).

CSHB Corpus Scriptorum Historiae Byzantinae, 49 vols
(Bonn, 1828–78).

CT *Codex Theodosianus*, ed. T. Mommsen and E. Meyer
(Berlin, 1905). Eng. trans. Clyde Pharr *et al.*, *The
Theodosian Code* (Princeton, 1952).

Dexippus
> *Chron.* ΧΡΟΝΙΚΗ ΙΣΤΟΡΙΑ, ed. F. Jakoby, *FGrH*
> IIA, 463–66.
> *Scythica* ΣΚΥΘΙΚΑ, ed. *idem*, *op. cit.*, 467–75.

ELF see under Jul., *ELF*.
Epiph., *Haer.*
> Epiphanius, *De haeresibus (Panarion)*, ed. K. Holl, GCS
> 25, 31 and 37 (Leipzig, 1915–33), rev. J. Dummer, vols 2 and
> 3 (Berlin, 1980–85). Eng. trans. F. Williams, *The Panarion
> of Epiphanius of Salamis*, 2 vols (Leiden, 1987–94).

epit.   [Aurelius Victor], *Epitome de Caesaribus*,
            ed. F. Pichelmayr in *Sextus Aurelius Victor*, 133–76.
Eunap., *Frag.*
            Eunapius, *Fragmenta historiae*, ed. and trans. R. C.
            Blockley, *The Fragmentary Classicising Historians of
            the Later Roman empire*, vol. 2 (Liverpool, 1983) 2–127.
——, *Vit. soph.*
            Vitae sophistarum, ed. C. Giangrande (Rome,
            1956). Eng. trans. W. C. Wright in *Philostratus and
            Eunapius, The Lives of the Sophists*, LCL, 1922.
Eus., *H. e.*
            Eusebius, *Historia ecclesiastica*, ed. E. Schwartz,
            GCS IX/1–3 (Leipzig, 1903–9). Eng. trans. H. J. Lawlor
            and J. R. L. Oulton, *Eusebius etc., The Ecclesiastical
            History etc.*, 2 vols (London, 1927–28).
——, *V. C.*
            Vita Constantini, ed. F. Winkelmann, GCS (Berlin,
            1975). Eng. trans. E. C. Richardson, NPNF, 2nd ser., I,
            481–559. New trans. A. M. Cameron and S. G. Hall is in
            preparation.
Eugenii et Macarii passio (*BHG* 2126), ed. F. Halkin, 'La passion
            grecque des saints Eugène et Macaire', *AB*, 78 (1964)
            43–52.
Eutr.   Eutropius, *Breviarium ab urbe condita*, ed. F. Ruehl
            (Stuttgart, 1975). Eng. trans. Bird, 1993: 1–70.
Evagr., *H. e.*
            Evagrius, *Historia ecclesiastica*, ed. J. Bidez and
            L. Parmentier (London, 1898). Eng. trans. *anon.*,
            Theodoret and Evagrius, Bohn's Ecclesiastical Library
            (London, 1851).
Expositio totius mundi et gentium, ed. J. Rougé, SC 124
            (Paris, 1966).
Festus, Brev.
            Festus, *Breviarium*, ed. J. W. Eadie (London, 1967).
FIRA I   *Fontes iuris Romani anteiustiniani*, ed. S. Riccobono,
            vol. 1 (Florence, 1968).
Firmicus Maternus, *De errore*
            Julius Firmicus Maternus, *De errore profanarum
            religionum*, ed. and trans. G. Heuten (Brussels, 1938).
FGrH   *Fragmente der griechischen Historiker*, ed. F. Jacoby
            et al. (Leiden, 1923–).

FHG   *Fragmenta Historicorum Graecorum*, ed. C. Müller, 5 vols (Paris, 1841–70).

GCS   *Die griechischen christlichen Schriftsteller der ersten Jahrhunderte* (Leipzig, 1897–1941; Berlin and Leipzig, 1953; Berlin,1954–).

Georg. Mon.
    Georgius Monachus, *Chronicon*, ed. C. de Boor, rev. P. Wirth (Stuttgart, 1978).

Greg. Naz., *Or.*
    Gregorius Nazianzenus, *Orationes* IV–V (*contra Julianum*), ed. and trans. J. Bernardi (SC 309, 1983). Eng. trans. C. W. King in *Julian the Emperor* (London, 1888) 1–121.

Hesychius Illustrius, Πάτρια Κωνσταντινουπόλεως, ed. T. Preger, *Scriptores Originum Constantinopolitanarum*, I (Leipzig, 1901) 1–18.

Hieron., *Chron.*
    Hieronymus (Jerome), *Chronicon*, ed. R. Helm, GCS 47 (= *Eusebius Werke*, VII, Berlin, 1956).

Hist. Aceph.
    Historia Acephala (*Chronicon Acephalum*), ed. A. Martin, *Histoire 'Acéphale' et Index syriaque des lettres festales d'Athanase d'Alexandrie*, SC 317. See also *PG* 26.1443–50. Eng. trans. A. Robertson, NPNF *Athanasius*, 495–99.

Hydatius, *Chron.*
    Chronicon, ed. and trans. R. W. Burgess, *The Chronicle of Hydatius and the Consularia Constantinopolitana* (Oxford, 1993).

——, *Des. cons.*
    Descriptio consulum, PL 51.894–914.

Iamb., *v. P.*
    Iamblichus, *De vita Pythagorica*, ed. A. Nauck (Leipzig, 1884). Eng. trans. G. Clark, *Iamblichus: On the Pythagorean Life*, Translated Texts for Historians 8 (Liverpool, 1989).

ILS   H. Dessau, *Inscriptiones Latinae Selectae* (Berlin, 1892–1916).

Ioh. Ant.
    Joannes Antiochenus, *Fragmenta historiae*, in *FHG* IV, 535–622.

Ioh. Lyd., *De mag.*

> Joannes (Laurentius) Lydus, *Liber de magistratibus populi Romani*, ed. and trans. A. Bandy, *On Powers, or the Magistracies of the Roman State* (Philadelphia, 1983).

Iord., *Get.*

> Iordanes, *Getica*, ed. Th. Mommsen, MGH Auct. Ant. (Berlin, 1882). Eng. trans. C. Mierow, *Jordanes: The Gothic History* (New Jersey, 1915).

JHS   *Journal of Hellenic Studies* (London, 1880–).

JRS   *Journal of Roman Studies* (London, 1910–).

Jul., *Caes.*

> Julian, *De Caesaribus*, ed. C. Lacombrade, *L'empereur Julien*: Oeuvres complètes, II/2 (Paris, 1964) 32–71. Eng. trans. W. C. Wright, LCL *Julian* ii, (1913) 345–415.

——, *ELF*

> Julian, *Imp. Caesaris Flavii Claudii Iuliani epistulae leges poemata fragmenta varia*, ed. J. Bidez and F. Cumont (Paris and Oxford, 1922). Eng. trans. of the letters, *op. cit.*, iii.

——, *Ep. ad Ath.*

> Julian, *Epistula ad Athenienses*, ed. and trans. J. Bidez in *L'empereur Julien: Oeuvres complètes*, I/1 (Paris, 1932) 213–35. Eng. trans. Wright, *op. cit.*, ii, 243–91.

——, *Misop.*

> Julian, *Misopogon*, ed. Ch. Lacombrade in *L'empereur Julien etc.*, II/2 (1964) 156–99. Eng. trans. Wright, *op. cit.*, ii, 421–511.

——, *Or.*

> Julian, *Orationes*, ed. Bidez, *op. cit.*, 10–206, and G. Rochefort in *L'empereur Julien etc.* II/1 (1963) 103–73 and Lacombrade, *op. cit.* II/2, 100–38. Eng. trans. Wright, *op. cit.*, i and ii, 5–197.

Lact., *Mort. pers.*

> Lactantius, *De mortibus persecutorum*, ed. and trans. J. L. Creed (Oxford, 1985).

LCL   Loeb Classical Library (London and Cambridge, Mass., 1912–).

Leo   Grammaticus, *Chronographia*, ed. I. Bekker, CSHB 45 (Bonn, 1842).

Lib., *Ep.*

> Libanius, *Epistulae*, 2 vols, ed. R. Foerster (Leipzig, 1921). Eng. trans. A. F. Norman of a selection which will contain nearly all the letters to Julian, LCL, Libanius, *Autobiography*. See also Fatouros and Krischer, 1980.

——, *Or.*

> Libanius, *Orationes*, ed. R. Foerster, 4 vols (Leipzig, 1903–8). Eng. trans. of *Or.* I, A. F. Norman, *Libanius' Autobiography* (Oxford, 1965); of *Or.* XII–XVIII and XXIV (the Julianic Orations), A. F. Norman in LCL, Lib., i; of *Or.* XI (*In Praise of Antioch*) by Downey, 1959.

MA *Miracula Artemii*, ed. A. Papadopoulos-Kerameus, *Varia Graeca Sacra*, in Zapiski istoriko-philologicheskago Phakul'teta imperatorskago S.-Peterburgskago Universiteta, Chast XCV (St Petersburg, 1909) 1–79. Eng. trans. by an international team is in preparation.

Malalas, *Chronographia*, ed. L. Dindorf, CSHB, 1831. Eng. trans. E. Jeffreys, *The Chronicle of John Malalas*, Byzantina Australiensia 4 (Melbourne, 1986).

Men. Rhet.

> Menander Rhetor, ed. and trans. D. Russell and N. G. Wilson (Oxford, 1981).

MGH Monumenta Germaniae Historica (Berlin, 1877–1919) (Auct. ant. = Auctores antiquissimi).

Niceph., *H. e.*

> Nicephorus Callistus ('Xanthopoulos'), *Historia ecclesiastica*, PG 145.559–1332, 146 and 147.449–634.

NPNF The Writings of the Nicene and Post-Nicene Fathers (New York, 1887–92 and Oxford, 1890–1900).

ODB *Oxford Dictionary of Byzantium*, 3 vols (Oxford, 1991).

Optatianus, *Carm.*

> *Publilii Optatiani Porfyrii carmina*, ed. J. Polara, 2 vols (Turin, 1981).

Or. ad s. coetum. See under Constantinus.

Oros. *Adv. pag.*

> Orosius, *Historia adversus paganos*, ed. C. Zangemeister (Leipzig, 1889), trans. R. J. Deferrari, *The Seven Books of History Against the Pagans*, Fathers of the Church, vol. 50 (Washington DC, 1964).

(Pachomius) *Vita prima Graeca*, ed. F. Halkin, in *Sancti Pachomii vitae Graecae* (Brussels, 1932) 1–96. Eng. trans. A. Veilleux, 'The First Greek Life', in *Pachomian Koinonia, Vol. 1, The Life of Saint Pachomius and his Disciples*, Cistercian Studies XLV (Kalamazoo, 1980) 297–407.

——, 'The Bohairic Life of Pachomius', trans. Veilleux, *ibid.*, 23–266.

Pan. Lat.
    Panegyrici Latini, ed. E. Galletier, Panégyriques latins, 3 vols (Paris, 1949–55).

Pass. Eusign.
    Passio Eusignii (*BHG* 639) ed. P. Devos, Une recension nouvelle de la passion grecque *BHG* 639 de Saint Eusignios, *AB*, 100 (1982) 209–28. (Appendix to Coquin and Lucchesi, 1982.)

Pat. Const.
    Patria Constantinoupoleos, ed. Preger, *Scriptores origenum Constantinopolitanum*, ii (Leipzig, 1907).

Pet. Patric.
    Petrus Patricius, *Fragmenta historiae*, *FHG* iv, 181–91.

Petrus Diaconus
    Liber de locis sanctis, ed. R. Weber, CCSL 175, 93–103.

PG   *Patrologiae Cursus Completus, Series Graeco-Latina*, ed. J. P. Migne, 162 vols (Paris, 1857–66).

Philost., *H. e.*
    Philostorgius, *Historia ecclesiastica*, ed. J. Bidez and rev. J. Winkelmann, GCS, 1972. Eng. trans. of the summary of Photius by E. Walford in *Sozomen and Philostorgius*, Bohn's Ecclesiastical Library (London, 1855) 429–528. (New trans. by A. Emmett Nobbs is forthcoming.)

Phot., *Bibl.*
    Photius, *Bibliotheca*, ed. P. Henry, 8 vols (Paris, 1959–77). Eng. trans. codd. 1–165 only by J. H. Freese, *The Library of Photius*, vol. 1 (London, 1920).

PL   *Patrologiae Cursus Completus, Series Latina*, ed. J. P. Migne *et al.*, 221 vols (Paris, 1844–64).

PLRE, i
    A. H. M. Jones, J. R. Martindale and J. Morris (eds), *The Prosopography of the Later Roman Empire*, vol. 1 (Cambridge, 1971).

Polemius Silvius, *Laterculus, I. Nomina omnium principum Romanorum*, ed. Th. Mommsen, MGH, Auct. Ant. IX (Berlin, 1902) 520–23.

POxy.VIII
    The Oxyrhynchus Papyri Part VIII, ed. A. S. Hunt (London, 1911).

PPO   Praefectus Praetorio (Praetorian Prefect).

Procop., *Pers.*
    Procopius of Caesarea, *History of the Wars I: The Persian War*, Eng. trans. H. B. Dewing, LCL *Procopius* (i, 1971).

PW   A. Pauly (ed.), *Real-Encyclopädie der klassischen Altertumswissenschaft*, ed. G. Wissowa (Stuttgart, 1893–).

RIC   *Roman Imperial Coinage*, ed. H. Mattingly *et al.*, (London, 1923–).

RQA
    Römische Quartalschrift für die christliche Altertumskunde und für Kirchengeschichte (Rome, 1887–).

Ruf., *H. e.*
    Rufinus, *Historia ecclesiastica*, ed. E. Schwartz, GCS (= *Eusebius Werke*, II/2, Leipzig, 1908) 960–1040.

SC   Sources Chrétiennes (Paris, 1940–).

SHA   *Scriptores Historiae Augustae*, LCL *SHA* iii, ed. and trans. D. Magie (1932).

——, *Claud.*
    Divus Claudius, ibid. 152–91.

——, *Gall.*
    Gallieni duo, ibid. 16–63.

——, *Tyr. trig.*
    Tyranni triginta, ibid. 64–151.

Soc., *H. e.*
    Socrates, *Historia ecclesiastica*, ed. R. Hussey, 3 vols (Oxford, 1853). Eng. trans. A. C. Zenos in NPNF, *Socrates and Sozomen*, 1–178.

Soz., *H. e*
    Sozomenus, *Historia ecclesiastica*, ed. J. Bidez and rev. G. C. Hansen, GCS 50 (Berlin, 1960). Eng. trans. C. D. Hartranft in NPNF, *Socrates and Sozomen*, 239–427.

Synax. Cpol.
    Synaxarium Constantinopolitanum, ed. H. Delehaye, *Propylaeum ad acta sanctorum novembris* (Brussels, 1902).

Thdt., *H. e.*

> Theodoretus, *Historia ecclesiastica*, ed. L. Parmentier and rev. F. Scheidweiler, GCS 44 (1954). Eng. trans. (N.B. with different chapter divisions) B. Jackson in NPNF, *Theodoret and Gennadius*, 33–159.

Theophylactus Bulgariae, *Historia martyrium XV martyrum*, *PG* 126.151–221.

Thphn., *Chron.*

> Theophanes, *Chronographia*, ed. C. de Boor, 2 vols (Leipzig, 1883–85). Eng. trans. by R. Scott and C. Mango is in progress.

TU   Texte und Untersuchungen zur Geschichte der altchristlichen Literatur (Leipzig and Berlin).

V. Metroph.

> *Vita Metrophani et Alexandri* (BHG 1279), ed. F. Winkelmann, *AB*, 100 (1982) 147–83.

Zon.   Zonaras, *Annales*, ed. M. Pinder *et al.*, 3 vols, CSHB, 1841–97. Eng. trans. of Bks XII–XIII by Di Maio, 1977: 1–60.

Zos.   Zosimus, *Historia nova*, ed. L. Mendelssohn (Leipzig, 1887). Eng. trans. R. T. Ridley, *Zosimus: New History*, Byzantina Australiensia 2 (Canberra, 1982).

ZPE   *Zeitschrift für Papyrologie und Epigraphik* (Bonn).

CHRONOLOGY OF THE MAIN EVENTS

272 or 273 A.D.	Birth of Constantine at Naissus.
285	Diocletian defeated Carinus at the Battle of the River Margus.
293	Constantius Chlorus appointed Caesar.
303 (23 Feb.)	Beginning of the Great Persecution.
305	(1 May) Abdication of Diocletian and Maximianus Herculius at Nicomedia, Galerius and Constantius Chlorus made emperors, Severus and Maximinus Daia made Caesars, flight of Constantine to Britain via Bonnonia.
306 (25 July)	Death of Constantius Chlorus at York and proclamation of Constantine as Caesar.
307	Maximianus returned to political life. Defeat and death of Severus.
308	Conference at Carnuntum, Licinius became emperor.
310	'Revolt' and death of Maximianus Herculius.
311	Maxentius reconquered North Africa.
312 (28 Oct.)	Defeat and death of Maxentius at the Battle of Milvian Bridge.
313	Conference between Constantine and Licinius at Milan. Edict of Nicomedia (commonly referred to as the 'Edict of Milan'). Maximinus Daia defeated and killed by Licinius.
[314	First war between Constantine and Licinius (traditional dating)].
316	First war between Constantine and Licinius (new dating), defeat of Licinius at the Battle of Cibalae (8 Oct.) and Constantine gained Licinius'

	European territories (except Thrace).
317	Crispus, Constantine II and Licinianus made Caesars.
322–323	Constantine campaigned on lower Danube.
324	Second war between Constantine and Licinius, Battle of Hadrianople (3 Jul.), Battle of Chrysopolis (18 Sept.).
	Constantine sole emperor. Byzantium chosen as new capital; Constantius II made Caesar.
325	Council of Nicaea.
326	Execution of Crispus and 'murder' of Fausta.
326–329	Constantine campaigned on Danube.
328	Athanasius installed as bishop of Alexandria.
330 (11 May)	Inauguration of Constantinople.
331	Confiscation of temple treasures.
332 (May?)	Birth of Flavius Claudius Julianus at Constantinople.
333	Constans made Caesar.
337 (22 May)	Death of Constantine the Great.
337 (July?)	Massacre by the soldiers of the male descendants of Constantius Chlorus.
337 (Aug. or early Sept.	Meeting of Constantine II, Constantius II and Constans at Viminacium.
337 or 338	First siege of Nisibis.
340	Constantine II defeated and killed by the forces of Constans.
341	Council of Antioch.
341/2	Gallus and Julian at Macellum.
343	Council of Serdica.
344 (summer)	Both Romans and Persians suffered heavy casualties at the Battle of Singara.
344 (late summer/ autumn)	Libanius delivered his *Basilikos Logos*.
346	Second siege of Nisibis.
350	Usurpation of Magnentius and death of Constans. Third siege of Nisibis.
351 (March)	Gallus made Caesar by Constantius.
351 (28 Sept.)	Magnentius defeated by Constantius at Mursa.
353 (Aug.)	Death of Magnentius.
354	Gallus executed for maladministration.
355	Revolt of Silvanus.

355 (May)	Julian granted permission to study in Athens.
355 (6 Nov.)	Julian proclaimed Caesar at Milan. He also married Helena, the sister of Constantius.
355 (1 Dec.)	Julian sent to Gaul.
356 (1 Jan.)	Julian received his insignia as consul.
356 (summer)	Julian's first campaign in Gaul (mainly against the Alamanni).
357 (summer)	Julian's second campaign in Gaul. He won a major victory at the Battle of Strasbourg (25 Aug.).
358 (summer)	Julian's third campaign in Gaul, victories over the Salian Franks and the Chamavi.
358 (24 Aug.)	Nicomedia destroyed by an earthquake.
359 (spring)	Shapur II entered Mesopotamia.
359 (spring)	Julian's fourth campaign in Gaul.
359 (Oct.)	Amida fell to Shapur after a long siege of seventy-three days.
360 (Feb.)	Julian proclaimed emperor at Paris by the troops who refused to be transferred to the eastern frontier.
360 (June–Aug.)	Julian's campaign against the Attuarian Franks.
361 (end of June)	Aquileia occupied by troops loyal to Constantius and besieged within a month by Julian's forces.
361 (end of Oct.)	Constantius left Antioch to confront Julian.
361 (3 Nov.)	Constantius died at Mopsucrena.
361 (11 Dec.)	Julian entered Constantinople.
362 (July–March 363)	Julian at Antioch.
363	Julian's Persian expedition and death.

INTRODUCTION
Pagan and Byzantine historical writing on the reign of Constantine

Sam Lieu

THE LATIN HISTORIANS AND EPITOMATORS
OF LATE ANTIQUITY

In the annals of late Roman secular historiography, the figure of Ammianus Marcellinus towers over all other secular historians of his age. His *Res gestae* – the product of an eventful military career in several spheres of operations under two emperors and years of assiduous research in Rome – was intended to be a continuation of the work of Tacitus down to his own times (i.e. 96–378 A.D.). The first thirteen books of this monumental work, covering the period from Nerva to the revolt of Magnentius under Constantius II (96–353 A.D.), have sadly vanished without trace, save for a few cross-references to them in the surviving books. Although the coverage of this early period could not have been as extensive as that of his own times – the eighteen extant books cover a period of only twenty-five years (cf. Matthews, 1989: 29–30) – the loss of the books covering the history after the mid-third century is nevertheless grievous, as the works of the main historians of the third century like Dio Cassius and Herodian, all written in Greek, did not go beyond the Severan dynasty and the one important historical work which covers the period of the Gothic invasion of the late 260s, the *Chronica* of the Athenian Dexippus, has survived only in fragments. Moreover, Ammianus' penchant for accuracy, his excellent understanding of Roman political life, his personal experience of military matters and his even-handed treatment of religious matters would have made him a unique authority on the reigns of Diocletian and Constantine, a period which witnessed profound political and religious change. The work would also have acted as a valuable counterweight to those of

1

the emergent ranks of Christian historians (see below, Appendix) whose interest in political events was often restricted to ways in which they affected the relationship between the imperial government and the Christian Church.

Ammianus, however, was not the only secular Latin historian of his time. Two of his contemporaries, Sextus Aurelius Victor and Eutropius, the former a distinguished imperial servant from Africa (Victor Afer) and supporter of Julian, the latter a companion-in-arms of Ammianus, wrote epitomes of Roman history down to the fourth century. (Cf. Den Boer, 1972: 19–172, Bird, 1984: *passim* and Günther, 1990: 214–15.) There is considerable similarity in their accounts of the events of the third century as both epitomators drew material from a lost common source (the so-called *Kaisergeschichte* – see below) – a source which Ammianus may also have utilised. Both works reflect the dominant Latin historiographical style of their time with a distinct tendency towards brief coverage of a long time-span and concentrating on military and, to a lesser extent, political happenings. Religious affairs were given such short shrift that the reader is hardly aware of the great changes in Church and State relations so obvious to the Christian historians like Eusebius (see e.g. *V. C.* III,15,2). For Victor, Constantine was a Roman emperor like any other who had gone before him. He was victorious in civil war and was a capable administrator. Victor's coverage of events leaps from the final end of the civil wars in 324 to Constantine's death in 327 with the briefest of mentions and the vaguest of allusions to some of the most significant events in the Christianisation of the Empire, such as Constantine's patronage for the Christian Church and the founding of a new Christian capital:

> Thus the State began to be governed by the power of one man, Constantine's children retaining their title Caesar in various forms; it is at this moment that the insignia of this rank were conferred on our emperor Constantius. 11. When the eldest had, for reasons unknown, perished condemned by his father, Calocerus, herdsman of a troupe of camels, suddenly seized the island of Cyprus like a madman, with the pretext of ruling it. 12. When he had been tortured as were slaves or brigands, for that was legal, Constantine turned his noble spirit away from political struggles by founding a city, developing religious beliefs and reorganising the army. 13. During this time the populations of Goths and Sarmatians are annihilated, and

Constans, the youngest of all his sons, becomes Caesar. 14. Some astonishing wonders proclaimed that he would be the cause of upheavals in the State: in fact, on the night which followed the day of his accession, the sky seemed to burn with continual fire. 15. About two years had elapsed since this event, when Constantine, with the keen approval of the soldiers, imposed as Caesar the son of his brother, named Dalmatius after his father. 16. Thus in the thirty-second year of his reign, when he had ruled the entire world for thirteen years, he died at the age of sixty-two, while marching against the Persians, who had reopened hostilities. He died in a region named Achyrona near Nicomedia; the star fatal to empires, called the comet, had predicted this death.

(Aurelius Victor, *Caes.* 41,10–16)

Eutropius, on the other hand, shows greater awareness of the enormous changes in Roman society brought about by Constantine's voluminous legislation (much of which was in favour of Christianity and granted special privileges to the Church) in his overall assessment of the character and achievements of an emperor who above all was fortunate in civil wars:

He who in the springtime of his reign could have been compared to the best of princes, finished up by resembling the mediocre ones. Innumerable brilliant physical and moral qualities were seen to shine in him; he had a keen taste for military glory, good fortune in battle which in no way outdid his tenacity. It was thus after the civil war that he again conquered the Goths in numerous battles, finally made peace with them and brought upon himself the immense gratitude of the barbarian nations through his good deeds. He was devoted to fine arts and cultural studies, and keen to earn public affection, which he sought on every occasion by his generosity and [*mores*] affability. If he appeared indifferent towards some of his friends, he was excessively devoted to others, seizing every opportunity for increasing their wealth or glory. 8. He made many laws, some founded on goodwill and equity, most of them futile, some harsh. He was the first to devote all his efforts to raise the city which bore his name to such heights that it emulated Rome.

(Eutropius, *Breviarium ab urbe condita* X,7–8)

3

The epitomes or *breviaria* undoubtedly filled a gap in the reading matter of the senatorial aristocracy which remained largely pagan until the reign of Theodosius. The epitomes served to remind them of Rome's lengthy (and in part glorious) history and also of the events of the more immediate past which were not covered by any major historian – hence the justification for the 'compilation' of the semi-fictional *'Scriptores historiae Augustae'* in the reign of Theodosius. That the work of Eutropius clearly filled a major gap is evident from its early translation into Greek by Paenius (*c.* 380) and in that language it became a source much used by later Byzantine historians. However, in the West, the work which was dedicated to Valens might have proved too long for a busy emperor, and another civil servant, Rufus Festus (ed. Eadie, 1967), was commissioned to produce an even shorter epitome. Festus had a specialist's interest in foreign wars and diplomatic relations and this is disproportionately reflected in his epitome which, though valuable on Romano-Parthian and Sassanian relations (cf. Dodgeon and Lieu, 1991: 126–67, 159, 188 and 248–49), is almost valueless on the non-diplomatic events of the fourth century. The preference for brevity and salaciousness may explain why the first fourteen books of Ammianus, the only known major Latin historical work on the third and early fourth century, have not survived – the loss is so total that we do not possess a single quotation from sources other than the surviving books of Ammianus.

From the same stable as Aurelius Victor and Eutropius comes the anonymous author of the *Epitome de caesaribus* – a work which covers the same period as that of Aurelius Victor and is preserved in the same Aurelian *corpus*; but the narrative also goes down to the end of the reign of Theodosius, while that of Victor stops before the rise of Julian. The work draws material from sources different from those of Victor for the events of the fourth century. (Cf. Schlumberger, 1974: 188–207, Barnes, 1976b: 264–65 and Günther, 1990: 216–17.) On Constantine the emphasis of its narrative is, like that of Victor, on the civil wars, but on the non-military events of the reign the anonymous author pulled no punches in his attack on the emperor, his criticisms prefiguring those of the Greek historian Zosimus (see below):

> Through his extraordinary luck in battles, Constantine had gained control of the whole of the Roman empire, and at the suggestion of his wife Fausta, so people think, he ordered the

murder of his son Crispus. Next he had his own wife Fausta thrown into hot baths and killed, since his mother Helena was chiding him through excessive grief for her grandson. He was in fact more greedy for praise than can be imagined. He was in the habit of calling Trajan 'grass on the wall' because of his inscriptions written on many buildings. He built a bridge over the Danube. He wore the garb of kings adorned with jewels and on his head a diadem continually. However, he was very useful in many areas. He quashed intrigues by severe laws and nurtured the arts, particularly literature. He himself would read, write, ponder and listen to delegations and complaints from the provinces. He confirmed his children and his nephew Delmatius as Caesars. Having lived for sixty-three years, half of them in such a way that he reigned alone for thirteen, he perished from an illness. He preferred to use mockery rather than flattery. Hence in common parlance he was called 'Bull-neck' and described as most excellent for ten years, a bandit for the next twelve, and for the last ten an orphan because of his excessive profligacy. His body was buried in Byzantium which became known as Constantinople. After his death Delmatius was murdered by the army.

(*Epit.* 41,11–18)

Constantine's nickname of 'Bullneck' is found in Latin only in this source but it re-emerges in later Byzantine historians (e. g. *Chron. Ps.-Symeon*, 1, ed. Halkin, p. 11 and Cedrenus, pp. 472,22–573,1) and might have been transmitted in a now lost contemporary Greek source like Praxagoras or Bemarchius or the lost portions of the *Universal History* of Eunapius (see below).

The success of the *breviaria* as a popular genre of historical writing was such that it was even appreciated by no less important a Christian writer than Augustine. When the pagans blamed the abandonment of the ancestral gods by the Christians as the cause of the fall of the city of Rome in 410, Augustine replied with his monumental *City of God* which includes a Christian interpretation of the history of Rome. He also asked one of his younger friends, Paulus Orosius, to compile a Christian *breviarium* of Roman history. Orosius' *Historia contra paganos* in seven books was a work in the tradition of Victor and Eutropius. The overview which he gives of Roman history down to 378 exhibits all the characteristics of pagan Latin historiography of his time. On the reign of Constantine its coverage of events is meagre, and he deliberately avoids tackling controversial issues such as Constantine's religious policy, presumably to avoid showing the support given to the Arians by the Emperor towards the end of his life. (On the *Origo Constantini* and the *Panegyrici Latini* see below, pp. **39–43** and **66–77** respectively.)

Historical writing and annalistic compilation once more became favourite pastimes among members of a number of pagan senatorial families in Rome under Theodosius, and it was in the late fourth century that the epitome to the last books of Livy was compiled by the scion of a distinguished senatorial family, Flavianus Nicomachus (PPO Italiae 431–32, cf. *PLRE*, i, Flavianus 14) – an epitomisation the success of which may have inadvertently caused the full versions of these books of Livy to go out of circulation. An antecedent of his and namesake (cos. 394, *PLRE*, i, Flavianus 15) is lauded in an inscription set up probably in 394 (*CIL* VI 1782 = Dessau 2947) as the author or compiler of certain *annales* – a work which was dedicated to Theodosius. Little is known of this work. The title seems to suggest that it might have been modelled on the work of Tacitus and, like the work of Ammianus, was a continuation of the work of the great historian. In the Life of Aurelian (27,2–6) in the semi-fictional *Scriptores historiae Augustae* – the likely product of a light-hearted member of the late Roman senatorial class interested in historical writing – part of a letter from Zenobia to Aurelian is cited from the work of a certain Nicomachus (*FGrH* 215F, cf. Dodgeon and Lieu, 1991: 96–97), and if the citation is not fictitious the *Annales* of Nicomachus Flavianus will have covered the period of imperial history after the work of Tacitus. Though nothing more is known of this work, it is the putative source among many modern scholars of the events of the third and fourth century, and has even been suggested as a source for Ammianus which cannot easily be proven as we possess no *terminus ante quem* for the publication of the work of Nicomachus Flavianus. One argument for the *Annales* as a major lost source for the Constantinian period rests on the detailed knowledge shown by Zosimus (and his source Eunapius) (see below) on the events in Rome subsequent to the execution of Crispus, presupposing a senatorial source. (Cf. Paschoud, 1971: lv and 220.) However, as we possess no *nominatim* quotation from the work covering the Constantinian period, this can be no more than a scholarly conjecture. (Cf. Zecchini, 1993: 51–64.)

INTRODUCTION

THE GREEK PAGAN HISTORIANS

In the Greek East where there was a stronger and less interrupted historiographical tradition than there was in the Latin West, the reign of Constantine was the subject of a historical work in two books in Greek by the young Athenian historian Praxagoras, but it has only survived in the form of a short summary by the Patriarch Photius:

I have read the *History of Constantine the Great* of Praxagoras the Athenian in two volumes. In it he relates that Constantius, Constantine's father, ruled over Britain, Maximianus ruled over Rome, the rest of Italy and Sicily, the other Maximianus [i.e. Galerius] over Greece, Macedonia, Asia Minor and Thrace. The oldest of all of them, Diocletian, was the governor of Bithynia, Arabia, Libya and the flood-plain of the Nile.

2. Constantine was sent by his father to Diocletian in Nicomedia, in order to receive his education; there, says the author, was Maximianus [i.e. Galerius], the ruler of Asia Minor who began to set snares for the young prince. He pitted the youth against a ferocious lion and Constantine got the better of the wild beast and killed it, then he became aware of the plotting and fled back to his father. 3. When the latter died, the young man succeeded to the emperorship; as soon as he was established there he subdued the Celts and Germans, who were neighbouring barbarian tribes. 4. He learned that Maxentius was governing his subjects with violence and harshness (this Maxentius had become the master of Rome after Maximianus). He embarked on a campaign against him in order to make him pay for his injustice towards his subjects; he defeated him and forced him to flee. In his flight, Maxentius met the kind of death that he himself had often thought up in order to destroy his enemies, and he fell into the ditch that he had dug. Some Romans cut off his head, stuck it on a pole and walked with it through the city.

This part of the empire submitted spontaneously and joyfully to Constantine. 5. He had learned that Licinius was also treating his subjects with inhuman cruelty. (This Licinius was ruling over the territory governed by Maximianus [i.e. Galerius], who had brought about Constantine's ordeal with the lion, and who was now dead.) Unable to tolerate this unbearable treatment of his fellow citizens, Constantine undertook an expedition against

7

him in order to make him exchange his tyrannical ways for a sovereign's attitude.

Licinius took fright on hearing of the emperor's expedition and masked his cruelty beneath a kindly appearance; he swore to be good to those for whom he was responsible, and not to violate the treaties already concluded. 6. That is why the emperor refrained from waging war on him at that time; but later on, as wickedness cannot cease its effects, he broke his oaths and gave way utterly to his evil nature. Constantine overwhelmed him in harsh battles, then trapped and laid siege to him in Nicomedia; from there, he escaped to the emperor like a suppliant and lost his sovereign authority. Thus it was that Constantine the Great, at the time when the great empire was seeking a worthy leader, gathered together the above territories under his command. In fact he retained the paternal domain through inheritance, Rome through having overthrown Maximianus [i.e. Maxentius], Greece, Macedonia and Asia Minor through having divested Licinius of his power, as described. Furthermore, he assumed authority over the rest of the territory where Diocletian had been master, for Licinius also held this domain which he had taken in battle from Maximianus, Diocletian's successor. 7. Therefore, having gained control and displayed the whole empire to be united, he founded Byzantium, which was renamed after him. 8. And Praxagoras, despite his pagan religion, declares that through his many virtues, his personality and all his successes, the emperor Constantine eclipsed the memory of all those who had ruled before him.

His two volumes end thus.

9. According to Praxagoras himself, he was twenty-one years old when he wrote this book. 10. He also wrote two other books *On the Kings of Athens*, written when he was eighteen. He wrote another six books on Alexander, king of Macedonia, at the age of thirty.

11. His style is clear and pleasant, a little less energetic than it should be. He wrote in the Ionian dialect.

(*FGrH* 219)

Praxagoras wrote shortly after the death of Constantine in 337 and the concluding words of his work as given by Photius show that he treated the reign sympathetically in spite of his not being a Christian. (Cf. Gerland, 1937: 37.) Photius also shows that the main emphasis

INTRODUCTION

of the work was on the political events of the reign, especially of
the civil wars. Such equanimity shown by a pagan author appears to
suggest that the religious policy of Constantine had yet to make any
major impact on pagan attitudes towards his posthumous reputation.
Another pagan *literatus* who made the reign of Constantine the
subject of a history in ten books was Bemarchius (*Suda*, K259, ed.
Adler, I, 469,18–20 = *FGrH* 220). This sophist, who set himself up
as rival to the more famous orator Libanius (see below), was said to
have been a staunch supporter of Constantius II who was a scourge
of pagans. This Bemarchius also discoursed at length on the great
church at Antioch which was completed by that same emperor in
341 (Lib., *Or.* I,39) – a task which would have been more appropriately performed by a Christian panegyrist like Eusebius. Sadly,
no citation from his *laus* or summary of his history has come down
to us, but we may assume from his close links to the royal house that
he might not have been entirely unsympathetic to the founder of the
dynasty.

The work of the major universal historian Dexippus who flourished in the third century was continued by the pagan sophist
Eunapius of Sardis (*fl.* mid 4th–early 5th century). Writing after the
pagan revival of Julian and the Christian backlash which followed,
Eunapius was much more critical of the deeds of Constantine.
According to Photius (Phot., *Bibl.*, cod. 77) who read the 'second
edition' of the history of Eunapius, the work covered the period from
the death of Claudius Gothicus to the reign of Arcadius and
Honorius (i.e. 270–404). The work did not survive the condemnation
of Christian authorities intact because of its vilification of Constantine (see below) and much of what is known of the work comes
from references to it in the best preserved work of Eunapius, the
Lives of Sophists – a collection of lives of men of letters (*Vitae
sophistarum*) the majority of whom were pagans. (For references to
the *History*, see e.g. *Vit. soph.* §§472, 476, 480, 482 and 493). The fact
that he should have chosen to continue the work of Dexippus may
well indicate the lack of a major historical work in Greek covering
the period of the Tetrarchy and Constantine. By linking his work
with a major work of pagan historiography, Eunapius was also
consciously continuing a historiographical tradition which would
enable him to focus on the traditional merits of his hero the emperor
Julian who attempted to revive pagan worship and ancient values.
(Cf. Blockley, 1981: 7.) Eunapius' *History* is often said to have dealt
with events as late as 395, since there is an apparent cross-reference

9

to it in the *Lives* when describing Alaric's attack upon Greece in that year (§476) and another on the death of Hilarius, the sophist and painter, during the invasion (§482). The death of Theodosius would have been a convenient point at which to end, and thus the latest parts would have been composed not long after 395. However, Barnes (1976b: 266) has pointed out that the the first of the two references should be understood as the author's intention to speak about the impending disasters in his *History* and the relevant clause does not cover the mention of Alaric. Similarly, the second reference gives more precisely the impression that the fuller account of the death of Hilarius in his *History* has not yet been written. It is therefore possible for the first edition of the *History* or parts of it to have been published before 390 and therefore early enough to be a source both to Ammianus and the anonymous author of the *Epitome de Caesaribus*. (Cf. Blockley, 1981: 4.)

Eunapius completed his *Lives of the Sophists* some time after 395 and followed it with the extended version of the *Histories* which he already had in mind when he was composing the *Lives* (§482). The last dateable event among the surviving fragments was the execution of Fravitta which took place after Pulcheria had become Augusta on 4 July 414 (fr. 87). (Cf. Buck, 1977: 236.) The two versions were both still in circulation in the time of Photius:

He wrote two volumes, covering the same period. In the first, he bespatters with abuse the pure faith of us Christians, glorifies the pagan superstition, and makes many attacks on the pious emperors. In the second volume, which he calls a 'new edition', he has cut out the insults and brutal abuse which he had showered upon Christian piety, and having connected the rest of the body of the work, calls it, as we have said, a 'new edition', although it still shows considerable traces of the original frenzy. We have come across old copies of both editions, both in separate volumes and combined, and, having read both, are in a position to estimate the difference. The result is that in the new edition many passages, owing to the omissions, are mutilated and obscure, although generally the author shows a great regard for clearness. Somehow or other in this second edition he has not connected the narrative with due regard to the omissions, and so has spoiled the meaning.

(Photius, *Bibl.*, cod. 77)

The anti-Constantinian stance of the work is probably the main cause for both versions not to have survived Byzantine scholarly censorship. Some of Eunapius' negative comments on the reign of the first Christian emperor could be flavoured from his main surviving work, the *Lives of the Sophists*. On the founding of the capital city, for instance, Eunapius comments in his *Vita* of Sopater, a pagan who for a while found favour with Constantine:

> For Constantinople, originally called Byzantium, in distant times used to furnish the Athenians with a regular supply of corn, and an enormous quantity was imported thence. But in our times neither the great fleet of merchant vessels from Egypt and from all Asia, nor the abundance of corn that is contributed from Syria and Phoenicia and the other nations as the payment of tribute, can suffice to satisfy the intoxicated multitude which Constantine transported to Byzantium by emptying other cities, and established near him because he loved to be applauded in the theatres by men so drunk that his name should be in their mouths, though so stupid were they that they could hardly pronounce the word.
>
> (Eunapius, *Vit. soph.* §462, trans. Wright)

Sopater of Apamea was a disciple of Iamblichus and had for a time been the head of the school of Plotinus. He came to the court at a time when the emperor was said to be open to new religious and philosophical ideas, and he was welcomed by Constantine. He tried to wean Constantine away from Christianity by the force of his learned arguments and in so doing won many enemies. Later, when a famine broke out in Constantinople because of adverse winds, the crowds clamoured for a scapegoat and Sopater, who was accused of having detained the corn-fleet by a magical spell, was executed at the instigation of the Praetorian Prefect Ablabius, a close friend of Constantine and a Christian. Eunapius saw the execution of Sopater as the main cause of Constantine's death which took place shortly afterwards. Ablabius himself would later be executed in cold blood at the orders of Constantius II. This account of Constantine's favouring of pagan philosophers towards the end of his reign (between 330 and 337) when he was already fully immersed in the politics of the Christian Church is wholly glossed over in the Christian sources on the reign.

Eunapius' work may have been the source for the early life of Constantine by the anonymus compiler of the Latin *Epitome de*

Caesaribus because of unmistakeable verbal similarities. (see above, see also Blockley, 1983: 14, frags 7–8.) More significant is the fact that the *History* of Eunapius was extensively used as a principal source by the early Byzantine pagan historian and civil servant Zosimus (*fl.* late 5th century) for his work commonly known as the *Historia nova*. Little or nothing is known about Zosimus except that he held the rank of *advocatus fisci* and according to Photius his work is heavily dependent on that of Eunapius:

> It may be said that Zosimus did not himself write the history, but that he copied that of Eunapius, from which it only differs in brevity and in being less abusive of Stilicho. In other respects his account is much the same, especially in the attacks upon Christian emperors. I think that both these authors brought out new editions, although I have not seen the first edition, but it may be conjectured from the title of the 'new edition', which I have read, that, like Eunapius, he published a second edition. He is clearer and more concise, as we have said, than Eunapius, and rarely employs figures of speech.
>
> (Photius, *Bibl.*, cod. 98)

The *Historia nova* covers the period *c.* 200–410 but with an unfortunate lacuna on the reign of Diocletian. We may assume that the far from laudatory depiction of Constantine in the *Historia nova* is a direct reflection of his source and for this reason the works of Eunapius and Zosimus have to be assessed together. In his *Lives of the Sophists* Eunapius appears to make a distinction between his *History* and what he had written concerning Constantine and especially Julian. That the work contains a panegyrical account of the reign of Julian could be easily pieced together from the *nominatim* citations of the work. His account of the life of Constantine might have been a conscious attempt to counter the more eulogistic endeavours of Praxagoras and Bemarchius. It is possible that these two so-called 'biographies' actually formed two thematic parts of Eunapius' *History* and were not circulated as separate works as some scholars have alleged (cf. Chalmers, 1953: 165–70). In the extant introduction to the *History* the author claims that he has arranged the material by individual reigns rather than slavishly adhering to a strict chronological framework by dividing the narrative into Olympiads as Dexippus had done (frag. 3, ed. Blockley, 1983: 7–10). Thus the section dealing with the reign of Constantine probably contained much material more appropriate for biography, such as that concerning his early life and career. Some of this biographical treatment within the thematic framework of the *History* can be detected in Book II of the *Historia nova* of Zosimus. Ch. 8 gives an account of the origin and early life of Constantine. Chs 9–28 are a chronological account of his civil wars from his proclamation in Britain to the final defeat of Licinius, and this is followed by a topical treatment of his deeds as sole ruler until his death in Ch. 39. (Cf. Buck, 1977: 244–45.)

For Eunapius, and even more so for Zosimus, writing after the sack of Rome by the Visigoths under Alaric, the reign of Constantine marks a decisive turn for the worse in Rome's fortunes. The blame for this irreversible decline he pins decisively on Constantine's deceitful character which he saw as the dominant factor in his actions, including both his religious and administrative reforms. It was undoubtedly the negative depiction of Constantine in the *History* which caused the compiler of the Byzantine lexicon, the *Suda*, to issue this terse warning in his brief article on Constantine:

> Constantine, the great emperor. There is much nonsense written about him by Eunapius and this I have passed over out of respect for the man.
>
> (Suda, K 2285)

The reign of Constantine occupies much of the second book of the *Historia nova* of Zosimus. There is a gap in the extant manuscripts of the work following the accession of Carinus, and Book II opens in the middle of a description of the Secular Games, about twenty years into the reign of Diocletian. The treatment of the games, which were held once every 100 or 110 years as a religous ceremony to celebrate the beginning of the new 'century' or 'age', is very detailed. In Zosimus' view, there is a clear connection between the observance of traditional religious practices and the welfare of the empire. He notes that the last time the games were celebrated was during the reign of Septimius Severus in 204. The conclusion therefore that a link existed between the non-observance of the religious rites associated with the games and subsequent imperial decline was irrefutable:

> Therefore, as the oracle says and the truth bears out, for as long as all these rites were duly accomplished the Roman empire remained intact and they continued to dominate over the whole of our world, as one might say; but when the feast was neglected after Diocletian had abdicated from imperial power,

the empire gradually fell into ruins and a large part of it was imperceptibly invaded by the barbarians, as events themselves have shown us; I also wish to demonstrate the truth of my assertion through chronological considerations. 2. Indeed, from the time of the consulate of Chilonius and Libonius during which Severus celebrated the Secular Games, until the year in which Diocletian was consul for the ninth time and Maximian for the eighth, 101 years elapsed; it was then that Diocletian went from being emperor to being an ordinary individual, and Maximian did likewise; whereas when Constantine and Licinius were already consuls for the third time, the 110-year period came to an end, and it was then necessary to celebrate the feast according to the established custom; but since this was not done, it was certainly due to fate that the catastrophic state occurred by which we are now overwhelmed.

(Zosimus, *Historia nova* II,7,1–2)

Zosimus (and almost certainly Eunapius) spared no blushes over the illegitimacy of Constantine. The product of such a union is thus stamped with impiety – one of Constantine's dominant characteristics – and Zosimus would later place great emphasis on legitimacy as an issue of succession and one which might have led to the death of Crispus (see below):

Now Diocletian died three years later, and those who were already emperors, Constantius and Maximianus Galerius, appointed Severus and Maximinus as Caesars, and entrusted Italy to Severus, and the Eastern territories to Maximinus who was the son of Galerius' sister. 2. The situation at that time was generally favourable and the intention of barbarians everywhere, as a result of previous successful expeditions, was to remain at peace; Constantine, born of the relationship between an ignoble woman and the emperor Constantius, who was not her lawful husband, was already obsessed with the idea of imperial power and, filled with a desire which increased after Severus and Maximinus had obtained the rank of Caesar, decided to leave the place in which he was staying just then, and go to his father Constantius, who was in the transalpine provinces and had been settled for a considerable time in Britain. 3. Since he feared being stopped sooner or later in his flight (indeed his desire to seize imperial power had long been clear to many), he mutilated the horses which were maintained

14

at State expense when he reached each staging-post, and left them useless, and used the next horses that were stabled; acting in the same way at every stage of the journey, he prevented the advance of his pursuers while he himself approached the provinces where his father lived.

(Zosimus, *Historia nova* II,8)

The issue of illegitimacy resurfaces at the proclamation of Constantine by the army – the soldiers proclaimed Constantine emperor because they felt that none of Constantius Chlorus' *legitimate* heirs was fit to rule, thereby confirming Constantine's status as a bastard. This is reinforced by Maxentius' resentment at the proclamation: he 'the son of Maximianus Herculius thought it intolerable that Constantine, born of an ignoble woman, should achieve his ambition, whereas he, son of so remarkable an emperor, remained at the whim of chance while others exercised his father's power' (II,9,2). The soldiers wanted Constantine not because of his ability to command but because of his fine looks and particularly because of his liberality with donatives (II,9,1).

The contest between Constantine and Maxentius was cast in an entirely traditional historiographical mode with no place for divine interference of a Christian variety. Constantine's only contact with the supernatural was to order his troops into battle formation when he saw a large flock of owls settle on the walls of Rome (II,16,2). It matters little that Constantine was too far from Rome to have seen this ill omen. The episode of the owls, only found in Zosimus, is probably an invention of Eunapius' sources intended to counter Christian stories of Constantine's visions. (Cf. Paschoud, 1971: 206, n. 26 and Buck, 1977: 301–2):

The event revealed the truth: in fact when Maxentius brought his army out before the city of Rome and crossed the bridge which he himself had built, a numberless crowd of screech owls landed on the wall and covered it; when Constantine saw this he instructed his forces to form battle lines; when the armies were in position face to face, flank against flank, Constantine sent his cavalry forward which advanced and defeated the enemy horsemen.

(Zosimus, *Historia nova* II,16,2)

Licinius, much vilified as a persecutor in Christian sources (Eus., *H. e.* X,8,5 and *V. C.* I,50,1), is depicted by Zosimus as the first of

Constantine's opponents to be cast in the role of victim. The outbreak of hostilities between the two in 316 is seen in an entirely different light, namely as part of Constantine's ambition to seize a part of Licinius' territory (II,18,1, cf. *Anon. Vales.* V (15), see below, p. **45**). The blame for the renewal of the war was also placed on Constantine – it was a planned campaign and only the invasions by Sarmatians prevented Constantine from attacking his rival earlier (II,22,1). Constantine the eventual victor then exhibited one of the worst traits of his character, namely perjury:

> Constantine also laid siege to Licinius at Nicomedia. The latter lost hope, for he knew that that he did not have sufficient forces available to fight; having left the city he assumed a supplicant's demeanour towards Constantine and, having brought the purple to him, proclaimed him emperor and master, demanding pardon for the past. 2. In fact he was confident of remaining alive, as his wife had received Constantine's oath to this effect; but Constantine handed Martinius over to the guards, so that they might put him to death; as for Licinius, having sent him to Thessalonica to live there in safety, he soon broke his word (as was usual for him) and took his life by hanging.
>
> (Zosimus, *Historia nova* II,28)

Constantine's perjury was particularly offensive in view of the fact that Licinius' wife was a half-sister of Contantine (II,17,2). To blatant ambition and perjury would later be added impiety through a crime which marks the final downturn in Zosimus' assessment of Constantine's character:

> When all the power was in Constantine's hands alone, he no longer concealed his natural wickedness, but took the liberty of acting exactly as he pleased in every respect; he still celebrated the ancestral rites, not through respect, but out of advantage; it is why he also obeyed the soothsayers, his experience of whom being that they had foretold the truth about all his successes; when he arrived in Rome full of conceit, he thought it necessary to instil his impiety into his own household. 2. In fact his son Crispus, who, as I have already said, had been considered worthy of the rank of Caesar, and had been suspected of having a liaison with his mother, Fausta, he put to death without any regard for the laws of nature. Since Helena, Constantine's mother, was indignant at such violence

and could not accept the young man's murder, Constantine, as if to console her, brought her a cure for this evil which was worse than the evil itself; having ordered an extremely hot bath to be heated, he placed Fausta in it, only taking her out when she was dead. 3. As he had these crimes on his conscience, and, moreover, had paid no attention to his promises, he went to find the priests and asked them for expiatory sacrifices for his misdeeds; the latter had replied that no method of expiation existed which was effective enough to cleanse such impieties, when an Egyptian, having arrived in Rome from Spain and made the acquaintance of the palace women, met with Constantine and stated strongly that the Christian belief destroyed all sins and included the promise that unbelievers who were converted would immediately be purged of all crimes. 4. Having received this explanation very favourably, Constantine detached himself from the ancestral rites, accepted the Egyptian's suggestion, and entered the ways of impiety by despising divination. Since through divination many successes had been predicted to him and been fulfilled, he feared that the future might also be revealed to others who might make enquiries about some point in a spirit of hostility towards him, and on the basis of this prejudice was determined to bring an end to these practices. 5. When the traditional feast-day arrived, during the course of which the army had to climb up to the Capitol and carry out the traditional rites, Constantine feared the soldiers and took part in the celebration; but when the Egyptian sent an apparition which unreservedly condemned this ascent of the Capitol, he withdrew from the holy ceremony and aroused the hatred of the Senate and people.

(Zosimus, *Historia nova* II,29)

Zosimus' source for this sordid episode is almost certainly Eunapius who probably also named Sopater as one of the pagan priests consulted by Constantine. (Cf. Soz., *H. e.* I,5,2.) The Christian priest from Spain was probably Hosius of Cordoba, the theologian much used by Constantine for probing into the Arian controversy. According to a late Byzantine source which drew probably on now lost material (Codinus, *De signo*, pp. 62–63, CSHB) an expression of Constantine's grief was the erection afterwards of a statue of Crispus in pure silver with the inscription 'My unjustly treated son'. The association of the crime with Constantine turning to Christianity for remission was certainly strong in pagan thinking and was lampooned by his nephew Julian the Apostate in his satire in which the *mores* of his imperial predecessors were paired with Olympian deities (*Caes.* 336B):

> As for Constantine, he could not discover among the gods the model of his own career, but when he caught sight of Pleasure who was not far off, he ran to her. She received him tenderly and embraced him, then after dressing him in raiment of many colours and otherwise making him beautiful, she led him away to Perdition. There too he found Jesus, who had taken up his abode with her and harangued all comers: 'Whosoever is an adulterer, whosoever is a murderer, whosoever is accursed and wicked, let him be of good cheer and come; for I will wash him in this water and at once make him clean, and, if he falls into the same sins again, I will allow him to smite his breast and strike his head and come clean.' To him Constantine came gladly, when he had conducted his sons forth from the assembly of the gods. But the avenging deities none the less punished both him and them for their impiety, and exacted the penalty for the shedding of the blood of their kindred, until Zeus made them desist for the sake of Claudius [i.e. Gothicus] and Constantius [i.e. Chlorus].
>
> (Julian, *Caes.* 336B, trans. Wright, revised)

The *Caesares* was composed *after* Julian had become sole emperor upon the death of Constantius II and after he had begun his programme to revive paganism. Earlier in his career, Julian had given Constantine fulsome praise for his liberality and his popularity as a ruler in his panegyric on his cousin Constantius II (*Or.* I,5, pp. 16–17, Bidez = 6c–8d).

Many Christians clearly found Eunapius' version of the pagan legend of conversion of Constantine to Christianity disturbing and the Church historian Sozomen was impelled to refute it on the grounds that Crispus did not die until the twentieth year of the reign, i.e. long after his conversion, and until then complete harmony between father and son could be shown by the many laws issued in both their names. Moreover, it was generally accepted (among Christians that is) that Constantine's conversion had taken place before his war against Maxentius and it was unlikely that he would have encountered Sopater in Gaul or Britain (Soz., *H. e.* I,5,2–3). Zosimus' version of the same legend was opposed by another Church historian Evagrius (III,40–41, pp. 139–40), who drew attention to Eusebius' remarks on the mildness of Constantine's character and to the positive remarks on Crispus in the same work – remarks which only prove that the *Ecclesiastical History* of Eusebius was completed before 306. To maintain that Constantine could not have executed Crispus was clearly overstepping the mark.

The founding of the city of Constantinople, seen by many Christians as Constantine's desire to create a Christian capital shorn of Rome's pagan past, is given a more sinister explanation by Eunapius and Zosimus:

Since he could not bear to be thus accused by practically everyone, he looked for a city equal in stature to Rome where he would have to build a palace; finding himself between Troy and ancient Ilion, he found a place suitable for building a city, laid some foundations and erected part of a wall up to a certain height, which those sailing towards the Hellespont can still see today; but he changed his mind, abandoned this unfinished project, and went to Byzantium. 2. Full of admiration for the city's site, he decided to enlarge it considerably and give himself the scope which is appropriate for an imperial residence. In fact this city is on a hill and occupies a part of the isthmus which stretches past what is known as the Horn and the Propontis. It had of old its gate which completed the porticoes which the emperor Severus had built when he had desisted from his antagonism against the inhabitants of Byzantium, which was due to the fact that they had given asylum to his enemy Niger. 3. The wall was built across the western part of the hillside as far as the temple of Aphrodite and to the sea opposite Chrysopolis, descending similarly from the northern slope of the hill as far as the port called Arsenal, and beyond that as far as the sea which is situated exactly below the channel though which one goes towards the Euxine Sea; to the sea this strait is about 300 stades in length. 4. This was the extent of the city in ancient times; as for Constantine, when he had built a circular forum in the place where the gate was previously situated, and had surrounded it with porticoes on two levels, he placed two huge corridors of Proconnesian marble opposite one another, through which it is possible to enter the porticoes of Severus and leave the old city. Since he wanted to make the city very much larger, he surrounded it with a wall fifteen stades beyond the old one, which cut off the isthmus from sea to sea.

(Zosimus, *Historia nova* II,30)

As noted above, to satisfy his pride and love of flattery, Constantine, according to Eunapius (*V. soph.* §462, see above), transported masses of people to his city – so that he could be praised by the drunken mob in the theatre. Zosimus' criticism of the foundation was based less on Constantine's character but more on the physical limitations of the earliest urban constructions:

While he was not engaged in war and leading an easy life, he distributed food to the people of Byzantium at the expense of the State, from which it has continued to benefit to this day; he squandered public money on numerous useless buildings and put up some which fell down shortly afterwards: hastily constructed, they lacked stability. He also overturned customs which had been established for a long time.

(Zosimus, *Historia nova* II,32,1)

The established customs were overturned through administrative reforms, and Zosimus took pains to avoid mentioning those which favoured Christianity and instead concentrated on those the adverse effects of which could be strongly felt in his own time:

33 Now Constantine, altering what was perfectly well established, divided what was one person's responsibility into four; to one of the prefects he assigned the whole of Egypt up to the Pentapolis of Libya, and the East as far as Mesopotamia, and in addition Cilicia, Cappadocia and Armenia as well as the entire coast from Pamphylia as far as Trebizond and the guard posts situated near Phasis, entrusting to the same man the areas of Thrace bordering on Moesia as far as Asemos, and on Rhodope as far as the city of Toperos, also Cyprus and the islands of the Cyclades except for Lemnos, Imbros and Samothrace. 2. To the second prefect, Macedonia, Thessaly, Crete, Greece and its surrounding islands, both the Epiruses, in addition Illyria, Dacia, the Triballi, Pannonia as far as Valeria, and in addition, upper Moesia; to the third he gave the whole of Italy and Sicily and their neighbouring islands, as well as Sardinia, Corsica and Africa from the Syrtes to Mauretania Caesariensis; to the fourth he gave Transalpine Gaul, Spain and the British Isles. 3. Having thus divided up the Praetorian

Prefecture, he applied himself to weakening it still further by other means. Indeed, when the soldiers everywhere were led not only by centurions and tribunes, but also by men called 'dux', who carried out a general's function in each garrison, Constantine, having created some 'masters', those of cavalry and infantry, and invested them with the power of lining up the army for battle and of inflicting punishment on miscreants, deprived the prefects of this prerogative. 4. The consequences of this were disastrous, in peacetime as in war, as I shall very soon relate: since the prefects everywhere used to raise taxes through their subordinates and use these revenues to maintain the army, and also had authority over the soldiers to inflict punishment as they saw fit according to their misdeeds, the soldiers had good reason not to forget that the man who ensured their upkeep also punished the guilty ones, and in no way dared to act outside the bounds, through fear of being deprived of rations and swiftly punished. 5. Now, since it is one person who issues the rations to the army and another who issues orders, they get away with everything they can, besides which most of the provisions go to the use of the general and his subordinate officers.

34 Constantine took yet another measure, which allowed the barbarians to go unresisted into territory under Roman domination. Since, due to Diocletian's foresight, according to the method which I explained earlier, the Roman empire was closed in on all its frontiers by cities, fortified positions and towers, and the whole army had its encampments in such places, it was impossible for the barbarians to find a way in, seeing that there were forces everywhere prepared to resist and capable of driving back assailants. 2. Now, abolishing this security and withdrawing most of his soldiers from the frontiers, Constantine installed them in the cities which had no need of protection, and deprived of help those who were threatened by the barbarians, imposed upon peaceful towns the disturbances which soldiers cause, which led to them being for the most part deserted, and allowed the soldiers to become soft through watching entertainments and leading a comfortable life. In short he sowed the seeds of the ruination of the State which still affects us today, and of which he himself was the source.

(Zosimus, *Historia nova* II,33–34)

Above all Constantine was remembered for the introduction of the highly unpopular sales tax, the *chrysargyron*. Unlike the *capitatio* and *iugatio* system of the Tetrarchy which was based on fixed assessment-units and therefore taxed potential wealth rather than actual production, the *chrysargyron* was a tax on economic activity and netted those whose income was not dependent on property and agriculture:

Having accomplished this, Constantine continued to squander the revenue from the taxes by making gifts, not to those in need of them, but to unworthy and useless people, becoming unbearable to the taxpayers and enriching individuals incapable of providing the least service: in fact he considered prodigality to be a point of honour. 2. It was he who also imposed the payment of gold and silver upon those who, everywhere in the world, engaged in commerce and upon those who offered all kinds of objects for sale in the towns, and upon the humblest also, without even allowing the wretched prostitutes to escape this tax, so much so that when the end of the four-year period was approaching, and the amount was due, tears and lamentations could be seen in all the cities and, when the term had expired, whiplashes and tortures were inflicted on the limbs of those who could not afford the burden of a fine because of their extreme poverty. 3. From then on, mothers sold their children and fathers sent their daughters to brothels, using their labours to scrape together in their desperation the money for those who collected the *chrysargyron*. Since Constantine also wished to find some way of afflicting those in fortunate situations, of all those whom he called upon to accept praetorian rank, he also demanded a considerable sum of money with this honour as a pretext. 4. When those responsible for carrying out this duty came into the towns, one could then see each person fleeing to reside elsewhere, in the fear that he might receive this rank at the expense of his fortune. Furthermore, he took an inventory of the property of the *clarissimi*, imposing on them a tax to which he himself gave the name of *follis*. He drained the towns dry with such taxes; this demand being in fact maintained for a long time, even after Constantine, and the wealth of the towns having been dissipated little by little, most of them have become empty of inhabitants.

(Zosimus, *Historia nova* II,38)

Despite the negative assessment of his character and his ability as an emperor, nowhere in his account does Zosimus accuse Constantine of cowardice, and he even commended Constantine for his personal bravery in spearheading a daring raid on the forces of Licinius prior to the battle near Byzantium (II,22,6). It was after he had triumphed over all his rivals in the civil wars that Constantine lapsed into naked tyranny and soft living. The result was an end to successful wars (II,31,3). Zosimus (probably following his source Eunapius) did not consider the settlements made with barbarians as victories and ignored the fact that towards the end of his reign Constantine delegated the main military commands, especially that of the eastern frontier, to his sons.

THE BYZANTINE HISTORIANS ON CONSTANTINE

The negative account of Constantine's reign in the *Historia nova* of Zosimus is by far the most detailed surviving treatment by a pagan historian. That it was compiled in early Byzantium under Christian rulers is indeed remarkable. It demonstrates clearly the extent to which secular history, as distinct from Church history, was still governed by traditional values and its main practitioners were pagan men of letters. As we have seen, Zosimus' account provoked a strong reaction from the Church historian Evagrius who defended the actions and reforms (including the unpopular *chrysargyron*) of the first Christian emperor by citing the Church historian Eusebius. In the following century, Joannes Lydus (*fl.* late 5th–mid 6th century), a civil servant and antiquarian under Justinian, included material of an antiquarian nature on the foundation of Constantinople in the third book of his work on the Roman calendar (*Liber de mensibus*) (cf. Burch, 1927: 76–104 and Maas, 1992: 53–66) but few of his contemporaries, not even Procopius, the great historian of the reign of Justinian, showed much interest in the reign of Constantine. This may seem surprising as one would expect the reign of the founder of Constantinople, which was to become the capital of a new Christian Roman empire in the East, to feature prominently in the annals of Byzantine historians and chroniclers. However, the earliest Byzantine sources on Constantine are not exceptionally detailed, reflecting the ambiguous position of an emperor who towards the end of his life showed distinct favour towards the heretical Arians. A combined process of official censorship and general avoidance of the political history of the reign by pagan and Christian intellectuals had clearly left few historical details for incorporation. Already by the end of the fourth century, John Chrysostom, the great ecclesiastical writer of Antioch and later Patriarch of Constantinople (c. 347–407) lamented that by his time the greater part of the emperor's deeds were forgotten (*PG* 49.216), and Chrysostom's evidence is supported by other sources testifying to an early confusion between the various members of the Constantinian dynasty with similar sounding names – a state of affairs which would persist throughout most of the Middle Ages. (Cf. Linder, 1975: 46.) A good example of the neglect is the woefully inadequate treatment of the reign by two of the earliest surviving Byzantine chronicles. Joannes Malalas, another Antiochene and author of the oldest extant world chronicle, devoted a part of Book XIII of his work to Constantine. (Cf. Rochow, 1990: 194–95.) The account contains valuable material on the foundation of Constantinople and on the emperor's building programme and administrative changes, especially in the eastern part of the empire, but gives no chronological coverage of the main events of the reign. It does, however, contain one of the earliest witnesses in Greek historical writing to the legend that Constantine was not baptised on his death bed by an Arian bishop but that he had been baptised by Pope Sylvester at Rome after his victory over barbarians (sic!) and after seeing the sign of the cross in the sky (XIII,317,12–13, cf. Scott, 1994: 59 and see below). Similarly brief is the anonymous Constantinople-based *Chronicon paschale* which is valuable for its treatment of the reign only on matters of chronology and for providing us with a consular *fasti*.

Between the eighth and tenth centuries, Constantine and his mother Helena who were saints of the Eastern Church, became central figures in a host of legends. These sometimes incorporate historical material drawn from more contemporary sources – some, like the work of the Arian ecclesiastical historian Philostorgius, is now lost to us, but on the whole they reflect the political expectations and pietistic ideals of early Byzantium. (See below, pp. **97–146**.) These legends which developed from the seventh century onwards filled the gaping void left by the shortage of reliable historical and especially biographical material on the emperor. An important ingredient of the legend, namely the baptism of Constantine in Rome by Pope Sylvester shortly after his victory over Maxentius, features in the *Chronographia* of Theophanes, one of the first major historical works to emerge at the end of the Iconoclastic period (early 9th century). The legendary material becomes even more dominant as we enter the great period of Byzantine chronicles. In the works of Georgius Monachus (mid–late 9th century), Georgius Cedrenus (11th century) and Ioannes Zonaras (12th century), as well as the compilatory *Historia ecclesiastica* of Nicephorus Callistus Xanthopulus (*c.* 1256–*c.* 1335), the legendary material is so closely woven into the historical narrative that it is easy for the former to be regarded as having been derived from earlier (i.e. pre-7th-century) sources. (See e.g. Drijvers, 1992: 17, n. 43. See also below, pp. 102–6.)

Of the later Byzantine historians whose works cover the reign of Constantine, Ioannes Zonaras deserves special mention. His major work, commonly entitled *Epitome of (Roman) History*, is a digest of Roman and Byzantine history from the foundation of the city of Rome to the history of his own time (down to 1118) on a grand scale. His main source for much of the Republican and Imperial period is the *Roman History* of the great senatorial historian Dio Cassius (*cos. suf.* 205). For the fourth century he drew material from Eusebius, Zosimus, John of Antioch (*fl.* 7th century) and, more significantly, Philostorgius. The freedom to use material from a pagan and an erstwhile heretical source without qualification or apology (or acknowledgement) by an orthodox Christian reflects the dearth of good source material in Greek on political events of the reign of Constantine and of those of his sons. The need to use Philostorgius for this period was already apparent in the ninth century (?) when a substantial life of the martyr Artemius (see below, pp. 210–62) was compiled. The arrangement of material on the reign of Constantine is worthy of comment at length as it shows a clear attempt to combine late Roman pagan and Christian traditions of historiography as well as those legendary elements from Byzantine hagiographical writings on Constantine and Helena which had had become accepted as historical facts.

Zonaras' account of the period after the abdication of Diocletian draws upon Eusebius (*H. e.*) and Zosimus. It is inconceivable that he could have read Lactantius, and the detailed knowledge he exhibits on the conflict between Galerius and Maxentius and on the fate of Maximianus Herculius must have been derived from at least one major Greek source which is now lost to us (John of Antioch?). His description of the tyrants (i.e. Galerius and Maxentius) is typical of the Church historians – namely, they met their wretched ends not because they misunderstood auguries or failed to observe the Secular

Games, but because of their licentious behaviour and their persecution of the Christians (XII,33, ii, 619,22–621,13). Constantine was adjudged the most suitable successor not because of his liberality towards the army or the interference of tribal kings, but because it was part of God's design for the destruction of tyrants, and an angel was said to have stood symbolically by the bedside to seal the arrangement (XII,33, ii, 622,15–623,8). At this point Zonaras introduces his account of Constantine's early life in which he recounts an incident in the Sarmatian campaign in which he served as an officer cadet under Galerius (XII,33, ii, 623,12–16). A parallel to this is found only in a fourth-century pagan Latin source, the *Anonymus Valesianus pars prior* (*Origo Constantini*). (See below, pp. **50–51**.) The common source for this might have been the now lost panegyrical history of Constantine by Praxagoras (see above). On the lineage of Constantine, Zonaras reported on the disagreement in the sources on whether Helena was the wife or mistress of Constantius Chlorus. The influence of hagiography which stressed the semimiraculous, the romantic and the extramarital element in the conception of Constantine (see below, pp. **108–10**) had given respectability to the humble origin of Helena and the illegitimate nature of their liaison:

> Constantius sired him through the blessed Helena about whom the historians have no agreement. Some maintain that she was legitimately married to Constantius and was repudiated by him when, as stated above, Maximianus Herculius betrothed his own daughter Theodora to him and made him Caesar. Others insinuate that she was not legally married to him but the side-interest of his erotic desires and Constantine was conceived out of their affair.
>
> (Zonaras, *Annales* XIII,1,4)

The account given by Zonaras of Constantine's civil war with Maxentius and with Licinius is much more factually correct and informative than the highly stylized and opaque accounts given by Eusebius and the other Church historians, although Zonaras was certainly familiar with the *Ecclesiastical History* of Eusebius (XIII,1,6–29). For Constantine's second conflict with Licinius (XIII,1,21–26), Zonaras' main source is almost certainly Zosimus. The chronicler then departs from his reliable sources as he follows the example already set by an earlier chronicler, George the Monk, in telling the story, albeit in an extremely abridged form, of the baptism of Constantine by Pope Sylvester. The best known version of the *Actus Sylvestri* is in Latin and precedes the text of one of the most famous medieval forgeries, namely the *Donatio Constantini* in which a grateful Constantine granted secular supremacy to the papacy in Italy. The *Actus* was most likely to have originated in Rome between the late fourth and early fifth century as it was mentioned in the Gelasian Decretals and its contents appear to be known to the compiler of the Book of the Popes (*Liber pontificalis* 34, 1–2, p. 170, ed. Duchesne). (Cf. Pohlkamp, 1988: 416.) The version of the *Actus* given by the Byzantine hagiographers and historians gives the impression of having been derived from a source which originated in the city of Rome although there are strong arguments for an Eastern (i.e. Greek or Syriac) origin. In the version of the legend told by George the Monk (IX,1, ii, 490,18–491,11, den Boor) and by one of the Byzantine lives of Constantine (*BHG* 365, 4, 547,21–548,7, Opitz), Pope Sylvester came into prominence through taming with special spells a dragon which lurked in the depths of the city of Rome and was molesting the miserable populace with his foul breath. (On the Latin version of the story see Pohlkamp, 1983: 11.) Sylvester was forced into hiding by the Diocletianic persecutions but was summoned from his place of refuge – a place called Serapte (Greek: Serapis!) which was afterwards identified with Soracte near Rome – by Constantine. Although he had been led to victory by the sign of the Cross, he was nevertheless cajoled by his wife called Maximiana in Latin, the daughter of Diocletian (*sic*), to instigate a persecution of the Christians. (Constantine's wife after 307 was Flavia *Maxima* Fausta, the younger daughter of Maximianus Herculius.) The persecutor was soon afflicted by elephantiac leprosy (*sic*!) and his pagan priests advised bathing in a pool of blood of infants – i.e. a pagan caricature of Christian baptism. Children were duly rounded up. But, troubled by their wailing, Constantine relented and sent them home. That same night the saints Peter and Paul appeared to him, promising as recompense for his humane gesture cure from his hideous illness if he would seek out Sylvester and follow his commands. When summoned to the emperor's presence, Sylvester showed him likenesses of Peter and Paul and these were duly recognised by Constantine as those who had appeared to him. He was then given Christian instruction and after a solemn fast, was baptised in the Lateran palace. A bright light was seen when he entered the water and he was instantly healed. This was followed by a flood of legislation against paganism and in favour of

Christianity. A week after his baptism, Constantine also began the construction of a church in the Lateran palace. The miraculous healing of monarchs with seemingly incurable diseases through conversion is hardly a novel motif in Judaeo-Christian literature. Naaman the Syrian was cured of his leprosy by the prophet Elijah, and a legend which gained prominence during the reign of Constantine relates the conversion of Abgar the Black who was Emir of Edessa at the time of Tiberius who was said to have been baptised by a special envoy of Jesus (Adda in earlier and Thomas in later versions of the story) who also cured him of a royal disease (elephantiasis?) (Eus., *H. e.* I,13). The account of Constantine's baptism in the *Actus Sylvestri* may have been modelled on such missionary accounts, but the legend also echoes in part pagan accounts of Constantine's desperate desire after 306 to seek remission through baptism for the sin of murdering his son and wife. (Cf. Fowden, 1994: 166–68.)

Meanwhile, Helena, his mother, then living in Bithynia, wrote approvingly of her son's conversion from paganism but urged him to adopt Judaism instead. To give her the benefit of the doubt, a public disputation took place on 13 August 315 before the emperor and his mother between twelve rabbis and Pope Sylvester, with two pagans as judges. The high point of the debate was when the rabbis caused a bull to die by whispering the name Jehovah into its ear but Sylvester was able to restore it to life by uttering the name of Jesus Christ. Helena was so astonished by this that she instantly accepted the Christian faith. Zonaras omitted the entire dialogue which is extensively cited in *BHG* 365 (5–6, Opitz) and the chronicle of George the Monk (XI,1, ii, pp. 491,17–499,7), and gives only the trial of strength over the bull. He then tells us about the conversion and baptism of Helena as well as her travels in the Holy Land with Sylvester, in the course of which she discovered relics of the True Cross (XIII,2,34–35). Zonaras gave none of the details surrounding the discovery which are readily found in hagiographical literature (see below, pp. 134–38) and the mention of Helena being accompanied by Sylvester is probably unique to the version of the *Actus Sylvestri* which he used as his source.

The death of Fausta is treated by Zonaras as a just punishment for a scheming and vengeful wife who was jilted by her stepson. It is worth noting that in the *Epitome*, the account of the founding of Constantinople follows upon the Fausta episode after a brief reference to Constantine's victory against the Sarmatians. The chronological proximity of the two events clearly cannot be denied and the linking of the two by pagan historians like Eunapius and Zosimus was therefore inevitable. The brief reference to the victory against the Sarmatians and Goths is needed to counter the pagan propaganda that Constantine won no more major wars after he had triumphed over Licinius and thereupon gave himself over to soft living (Zos. II,31,3). Constantinople, according to Zonaras, was founded by Constantine out of a desire to name a city after himself and in accordance with a divine oracle. The story is then told of how the emperor had first tried to establish his city at Sardica, then in Sigaeum in the Troad, but eagles seized the ropes of the builders and dropped them on the site of Byzantium on more than one occasion (XIII,3,3–4). On the strategic significance of the city of old Byzantium and the strength of its walls, Zonaras is able to rely on information from the Roman senatorial historian Dio Cassius who might have visited it during Septimius Severus' war with Niger – a source which Zonaras has done more than any other Byzantine chronicler to preserve for posterity (XIII,3,13–21). Unlike Zosimus who criticised the emperor for poor city-planning which led to overcrowding in some private quarters, Zonaras praised him for enlarging the size of the city manifold, for the lavishness of the public buildings and ornaments, especially the pillar of himself on the column of porphyry (i.e. the famous 'Burnt Column') which survived intact until 5 April (either 1100 or 1101) during the reign of Alexius Comnena when it was severely damaged by high winds (XIII,3,22–28, cf. Anna Comnena, *Alexiados*, XII,4,5. Cf. Di Maio, 1977: 209–10. See also below, p. **128**). Constantine also instituted a separate patriarchate of Constantinople, as its church there had been administered from Heraclea since the time of Severus. In so doing he preserved the prerogatives of old Rome but acknowledged the fact that the capital had moved to the shores of the Bosporus (XIII,3,29). This, of course, is an anachronism as the special ecclesiastical position of Constantinople was not formalised until the councils of Constantinople in 381 (canon 3) and of Chalcedon in 451 (canon 28). Zonaras' statement shows familiarity with these canons but the anachronism is an understandable one given the supreme status of the See of Constantinople in the Byzantine period, which must have been generally assumed to have been instituted by Constantine. Zonaras continues the excursus on the early history of the Byzantine patriarchate with details concerning the genealogy of Metrophanes the first bishop of Constantinople. He was said to have been a descendant of a brother of the emperor Probus called Domitius who left Rome for Constantinople and became patriarch (!). He was succeeded by his son (!) Probus who was in turn succeeded by Metrophanes (XIII,3,30–31). This of course is complete legend aimed at providing a link between Constantinople and old Rome and this bogus genealogy is significantly not found in the popular joint *vitae* of Alexander (of Alexandria) and Metrophanes in which the latter appears only as an aged bishop at the time of the Council of Nicaea. (Phot., *Bibl.*, cod. 256, 471b, 16, Henry.)

The Arian controversy, the one issue which dominated Constantine's last years and features prominently in his *vita* by Eusebius and in the works of the Church historians, is completely and probably deliberately ignored by pagan historians who steadfastly refused to show any interest in the internal affairs of the Church. Though manifestly writing a secular history, Zonaras cannot deny it coverage because of the influential role Constantine played in the theological deliberations. On the other hand, Zonaras clearly wanted to avoid the complex theological issues which would necessitate the citation of lengthy documents of faith or imperial writings. In any case he had already published lengthy commentaries on the canons of all the ecumenical councils. (Cf. Di Maio, 1977: 234.) The account of the Arian controversy in Zonaras' epitome is cursory and begins with a completely unjustifed attack on the Arian leanings of Eusebius the Church historian, citing as evidence quasi-theological statements taken from the first book of his *Ecclesiastical History* which was completed in 311, almost a decade before the outbreak of the controversy. (Cf. XIII,4,8–17.) Little is said about the Christological issues debated so heatedly at the Council of Nicaea (325). Zonaras comments instead on parts of the Creed of Nicaea; using, however, not the version promulgated at the end of the council but the version redefined more than half a century later at Constantinople, which shows his dependence on the Church tradition rather than the original documents of the councils although he certainly knew the latter from his commentaries on them. (Cf. Di Maio, 1977: 237–38.) Constantine's personal efforts to maintain harmony among the gathered bishops received considerable coverage. He kissed the wounds of those who had suffered persecution and when handed accusations (*libelli*) against certain bishops he burnt them in front of everyone, saying that even if he himself were to be an eyewitness to a bishop going astray, he would still clothe him in purple (XIII,4,20–21). Zonaras mentions in passing the death of Helena and her burial (4,24) and then turns to the final chapter of Constantine's life. In 327, Constantine, dissatisfied with his son Constantius' handling of the affairs of the East, decided to launch an expedition against the Persians. He crossed over to Soteropolis in a trireme but became ill and took the medicinal waters there (Pythiae Thermae). When his condition failed to improve, he drank some poisonous draught produced by his half-brothers and later died near Nicomedia with Constantius by his side (4,24–28). (See below, p. 227.) No mention of course is made by Zonaras of his baptism by the Arian bishop Eusebius of Nicomedia.

In his attempt to combine the secular and ecclesiastical sources to produce a broader, though not necessarily more balanced, account of the reign, Zonaras exudes an air of modernity. He rounds off the narrative of the reign by defending the character of Constantine, whom he regards as the equal of an Apostle, against the accusation of Julian, who in his satire on the Caesars implied that Constantine was a spendthrift and his inhumane indictions caused widespread misery (XIII,4,30, cf. Jul., *Caes.* 335B). Such awareness of criticisms of the emperor underscores the continuing popularity enjoyed by many Greek pagan writers throughout Byzantium and their indispensability to historians like Zonaras for the reconstruction of the secular events of the reign. (Cf. Bleckmann, 1991: 345.) An example of derivation from pagan sources, even for the miracles surrounding Constantine's conversion, is Zonaras' account of three visions which Constantine was said to have seen in battles against Maxentius and/ or Licinius which helped confirm in his mind that God was the author of his good fortunes. In the first he saw one of his horsemen bearing the sign of the cross instead of a standard. He rode at the head of the army and scattered the enemy ahead of him. At Hadrianople he saw two young men destroying the legions facing them, and at the siege of Byzantium he saw a light flashing all around the camp of his army (Zon. XIII,1,27–29). Though the first of the three visions reminds one of the second book of the Maccabees which tells us that a young man, dressed in white garments and carrying golden armour, appeared to Judas Maccabeus and led the Jewish forces to victory (cf. Di Maio, 1977: 173), the others are more typical of pagan visions. In Nazarius' panegyric on Constantine's victory over Maxentius, two young men of remarkable beauty on horseback performed such acts of gallantry that the emperor ordered them to be sought out and rewarded (*Pan. Lat.* X(4),15,4–7). The two young men were of course the Dioscuri who also appeared at the Battle of Lake Regillus in 396 B.C. to aid the Romans. The third appears to be unattested but the fact that it took place in Byzantium suggests that it was associated with the second war against Licinius, the events of which were particularly well attested in pagan sources. It is highly possible that all three visions were transmitted originally in pagan sources and later Christianised by Byzantine writers. The combination of pagan and ecclesiastical sources on the reign of Constantine is also apparent in the surviving fragments of the sixth-century historian John of Antioch, as some of the fragments for this period are derived from Eunapius and one from the church historian Socrates. (Cf. Bleckmann, 1992: 151.)

The modern study of the reign and personality of Constantine stands at the crossroads of three historiographical traditions: (pagan) classical, ecclesiastical and Byzantine. All three contribute much to our knowledge of the reign as well as the attitudes of the times of composition. Contemporary sources like panegyrics, laws and inscriptions too constitute a major part of the historical evidence. However, the sheer volume and contemporaneity of the ecclesiastical sources (see Appendix) and their general availability to scholars in English translation have allowed the reign to be over-studied from the angle of Church history. Until the publication of the major monograph by Barnes (1981) on Eusebius and Constantine, there is little in English-speaking scholarship save for the article by Baynes in the *Cambridge Ancient History* which attempts to study the reign as a continuum of traditional Roman history, applying the same technique of source collection, criticism and analysis standard in the study of earlier periods of Roman history. Now that the entire *Historia nova* of Zosimus (cf. Ridley, 1982) and the Neo-Flavian sections of the *Epitome* of Zonaras (cf. Di Maio, 1977: 5–60) can both be studied in translation, the balance can begin to be redressed even at the undergraduate level. The aim of our present collection is to redress this balance further by bringing together a selection of further representative pagan and Byzantine writings which can be used by both students and researchers. The ultimate aim of course is a corpus of sources – historiographical, hagiographical, literary, legal, epigraphical and papyrological. And, in this age of electronic editions and data-gathering, such a goal may no longer be unattainable.

APPENDIX: CHRISTIAN HISTORIOGRAPHY ON THE REIGN OF CONSTANTINE

The reign of Constantine witnessed the first major flowering of

Christian historical writing. Although the study of these better known sources lies outside the boundaries of this survey, it is nevertheless important to introduce readers to the principal exponents of this genre. The events of the early part of the reign became the main subject of a polemical history of Church and State relations by the Christian writer Firminianus Lactantius. A pupil of Arnobius of Sicca in North Africa, Lactantius was appointed to the chair of rhetoric at the imperial city of Nicomedia by Diocletian and had to forfeit it in 303, and at some subsequent date became involved, probably in Gaul, with the family of Constantine to which he was appointed as tutor to Crispus, the eldest son of Constantine and his first wife Minervina. (Cf. Barnes, 1986: 46–47.) His *De mortibus persecutorum* (*On the Deaths of Persecutors*) written after his return to Nicomedia in 313 is primarily an account of divine retribution on persecuting emperors and begins with emperors of the second century. The coverage of the events of his age, however, is much more detailed and is without doubt the most important contemporary literary source on the history of the Tetrarchy, the civil wars (to the end of Maximinus Daia) and the rise of Constantine. It was completed before 314 and hence its treatment of Licinius is entirely sympathetic.

The *Ecclesiastical History* of Eusebius of Caesarea, generally regarded as the father of Church history, was first issued *c.* 313 and then reissued sometime after Constantine's break with Licinius, as diatribe was crudely interpolated into passages concerning the latter (e.g. *H. e.* IX,9,12). Though more sober in style than Lactantius, Eusebius was also keen to stress divine justice and the special favour shown to Constantine by the Christian God. The work was originally finished before the end of the third century and comprised seven books. (Cf. Barnes, 1981: 128.) It was intended to be the first major history of the Christians as a self-identifying but peace-loving people or nation within the *imperium Romanum*. However, the outbreak of the Great Persecution under Diocletian and Galerius in 303 and the subsequent restoration of the religious peace by Constantine impelled him to extend the work further as well as producing a more detailed monograph on the suffering of the Christians in Palestine. The narrative of the second edition of the *Ecclesiastical History* (publ. *c.* 325/6) ends with the defeat and death of Licinius in 324 but the account of the events is hurried and schematic. It is clear that he was collecting material for a possible extension of the work when Constantine died in 337, and some of the material collected found its way into his panegyrical *Life of Constantine* (publ. 339, see below, pp. 97–99), which in parts reads distinctly like a Church history and also contains extensive verbatim borrowings from the last two books of the *Ecclesiastical History*.

Eusebius' *History* was translated (with certain omissions) into Latin by Rufinus of Aquileia who also added two extra books, taking the narrative down to the death of Theodosius in 395. Recent research has shown that much of the material for the additional books was translated directly from a now lost work in Greek of Gelasius who succeeded Eusebius as bishop of Caesarea. Rufinus' stature was such that Gelasius, together with Eusebius' uncle, Cyril of Jerusalem, were later said to have translated Rufinus' continuation from Latin into Greek. (Cf. Photius, *Bibl.*, cod. 89.) The extended version which also circulated in Greek came to be known as the work of Rufinus. In fact the joint authorship of 'Rufinus or rather Gelasius (of Caesarea)' is acknowledged in the *Syntagma* (I,8) of Gelasius of Cyzicus (see below). (Cf. Winkelmann, 1966: 23.) The work of Gelasius of Caesarea is cited by the anonymous author of the *Vita Metrophani* (*BHG* 1279) and by the Byzantine chronicler George Monachus (see above, p. 25).

A staunch supporter of the Nicene definition on Christology, Gelasius' (-Rufinus') work established the main anti-Arian narrative framework followed by other historians of a similar persuasion. As a continuator of Eusebius, however, the efforts of Gelasius were largely eclipsed by those of Socrates Scholasticus, who was generally considered to be the first major Church historian who continued the work of Eusebius. A native of Constantinople, Socrates practised at the bar (hence his appellation of *scholasticus*) after training in grammar and rhetoric. His work (publ. in 439), was a history of the Church from 309 to 439. In his youth he had known a certain Auxanon, a Novatianist priest who knew Constantine personally, and was therefore able to include snippets of personal detail such as what Constantine said to the Novatianist Acesius at the Council of Nicaea. (Soc., *H. e.* I,10,2; cf. Geppert, 1898: 59–65 and Barnes, 1993: 7.) He claims at the introduction to the second book of his *History*, that he had to rewrite the first two books because he had earlier relied too heavily on Rufinus and had not read for himself the writings of Athanasius (*H. e.* II,1,1–2). As a trained lawyer, Socrates would have certainly managed to consult Rufinus in Latin but critical research has shown that all the documents cited by Socrates are in fact derived from the Greek version of Rufinus-Gelasius. (Cf. Winkelmann,

1966: 22–27.) Socrates wrote in a simple and unaffected style and followed very closely the format of Eusebius' *History* in that he eschews almost all political events unless they actually affected the Church. Writing at a time when Christianity was already firmly established as the State religion, Socrates saw no need to repeat the events of the heroic age of the martyrs which preceded the reign of Constantine. There was also no necessity to reproduce the documents granting freedom of worship and special privileges to Christianity, and the restoration of Church property, which feature so prominently in both Eusebius' *History* and *Life of Constantine*. They are glossed over as the narrative moves swiftly from the standard account of Constantine's conversion based on Eusebius' writings to the history of the Arian controversy in the Greek East. The pagan restoration of Julian and the suffering of the Christians provided a major interlude to what was essentially a history of the internal politics of the Church. For the reign of Julian, Socrates had excellent sources and preserved an otherwise unattested letter of Julian to the citizens of Alexandria on the destruction of the temple of Serapis.

Wider in outlook, though following the same polemical stand against the Arians, is the *Ecclesiastical History* of Sozomen. A native of Bethelea near Gaza who settled in Constantinople after 425, he was also a lawyer and might have known Socrates personally. He was unhappy with the decision of Socrates to compose his *History* in a plain style which he believed to be inappropriate to the genre, and endeavoured to improve it. His account also begins with the conversion of Constantine and finishes with events *c.* 425. Sozomen's *History* is more than just a stylistic reworking of Socrates. He had, for instance, inserted documents granting privileges to the Christian Church overlooked by Socrates but which are clearly of great historical significance (Soz., *H. e.* I,8). He also read the highly inflammatory account of the reign of Constantine by the pagan Eunapius and sought to refute it. (See above, pp. **9–13**.) He devoted considerable space to the ascetical movement in Egypt – a topic which was almost totally ignored by Socrates. He was also deeply aware of the part played by the persecution of the Church in the Persian empire by Shapur II in Romano-Persian relations and provided one of the earliest versions in Greek of some of the stories of martyrdom from the Syriac *Acts of Persian Martyrs*.

To this Golden Age of Church historians belongs Theodoret, a native of Antioch (b. *c.* 393) who later became the bishop of Cyr in Syria. Unlike Socrates and Sozomen who, as far as we know, led

uncontroversial lives as laymen, Theodoret was a cleric who was
deeply involved in the Nestorian controversy, the second of the
major Trinitarian disputes to divide the Church. A personal friend
of Nestorius, he defended the Antiochene position of belief in the
duality of Christ and would only accept Mary as 'Mother of God'
in a figurative sense. He was deposed from his see by the so-called
'Robber Council' in 449 and was condemned to exile. He was later
summoned by the emperor Marcian to the Council of Chalcedon
(451) where he was forced to condemn Nestorius. He was then
allowed to spend his last years in peace as bishop once more of Cyr
(d. *c.* 466). Though he completed his history *c.* 448, he chose almost
the same time-span as his predecessors in order to avoid writing
about contemporary persons and events. The origin of the Arian
controversy rather than the conversion of Constantine was his
starting point but his work includes much material which cannot be
found in the histories of Socrates and Sozomen, especially on the
political and even military affairs as well as the ecclesiastical events
of the Syriac-speaking parts of the empire to which he had access
through being himself a Syriac speaker. (Cf. Gerland, 1937: 39–40
and Barnes, 1993: 8.) The account of the reign of Constantine,
however, is very much a 'scissors and paste' job and consists mainly
of documents which can be found in works of his predecessors.

The works of Eusebius, Rufinus, Socrates, Sozomen and Theodoret
soon became semi-canonical. The documents they contain on the
Arian controversy, especially on the Council of Nicaea, were excerpted and reproduced in a *syntagma* ('compilation') by Gelasius of
Cyzicus (*fl.* 475). Other Church historians of the period include
Philippus of Side, whose work was written between 434 and 439
(*CPG* 6026 and Winkelmann, 1966: 57–58 and *idem* 1990: 207), and
Hesychius of Jerusalem (d. after 451, *CPG* 6582, cf. Winkelmann,
1990: 207), but their works have not survived. The works of the main
continuators (i.e. Socrates, Sozomen and Theodoret) were translated
into Latin by Epiphanius and later compiled into a single work by
his friend Cassiodorus (*c.* 485–*c.* 580). The so-called 'Historia
Tripartita', despite its many imperfections, was a major source on
Church history throughout the Middle Ages.

The successors of Eusebius in the Greek East were all subscribers
to the Nicene formula and much of their work is devoted to
castigating the beliefs and deeds of the heretical Arians who had now
replaced pagan persecutors as the arch-enemies of the Church.
However, in Philostorgius, the Arian party possessed a historian of

their own whose importance has been increasingly recognised by modern scholars, especially for the material the work furnishes on the reign of Constantine. Philostorgius was born *c.* 368 in Borissos, a village in Cappadocia, to a father who was a follower of the Arian teacher Eunomius and who won his wife Eulampios over to Arianism from the 'consubstantiality' of the Nicene faith. This devotion to the cause of an extreme form of Arianism would be faithfully followed by their son Philostorgius. An exact contemporary of Socrates and Sozomen, he too received his higher education in Constantinople and also used it as a base for his wide travels throughout the Roman East. (Cf. Emmett Nobbs, 1990: 257.) His *Ecclesiastical History* begins with Constantine (*c.* 300) and ends with events *c.* 425. His work was completed probably before 433. One of his main sources for the period down to Valens which is now lost to us was an Arian, more precisely Homoaean, historical work which was completed in the late 360s which would have made him one of the earliest historians of the Church post-Eusebius. (Cf. Brennecke, 1988: 93–94 and 158–59, n. 3.) The stigma of heresy, however, certainly did not help the book to survive. In his summary of the work, the patriarch Photius, writing *c.* 835, was particularly dismissive of its unorthodox standpoint and the tendency of the author to polemise:

> I have read the so-called *Ecclesiastical History* by Philostorgius the Arian, the spirit of which is different from that of nearly all the orthodox. He extols all the Arianists and showers the orthodox with insults, so that his work is not so much a history as a panegyric of the heretics, and nothing but a bare-faced attack upon the orthodox. . . . He starts from the devotion of Arius to the heresy and its first beginnings, and ends with the recall of the most impious Aetius. This Aetius was removed from his office by his brother heretics, since he outdid them in impiety, as Philostorgius himself unwillingly confesses. He was recalled and welcomed by the impious Julian. The history, in one book and six volumes, goes down to this period. The author is a liar and the narrative often fictitious. He chiefly extols Aetius and Eunomius in his work, and presents them as having alone cleansed the doctrines of faith overlaid by time. For his accomplishments and his life he also praises Eusebius of Nicomedia (whom he calls the Great), Theophilus the Indian and several others. He severely attacks Acacius, bishop of Caesarea in Palestine, for his extreme severity and invincible craftiness, in which, he declares, Acacius surpassed all his

fellow heretics, however filled they were with hatred of one another, as well as those who held different religious opinions.

This was the extent of my reading. Soon afterwards, six other books of his were found in another volume, so that his whole work appears to have filled twelve books. The initial letters of each book are so arranged that they form the name of the author Philostorgius. The work goes down to the time of Theodosius the Younger, and stops at the time when, after the death of Honorius, Theodosius handed over the throne of Rome to his cousin Valentinian the Younger, the son of Constantius and Placidia.

(Photius, Bibl., cod. 40)

Despite the apparent misgivings, Photius made an extensive summary of the work, probably for the purpose of writing a series of series of sermons on Arianism from its inception to 381. (Cf. Emmett Nobbs, 1990: 253.) The extracts are very extensive and show that Philostorgius was in many ways more a tradition-bound historian than his contemporaries like Socrates and Sozomen. Like Herodotus, he showed wide interest in geography, ethnography and even palaeontology, although his sources are not always accurate. The reign of Constantine is the main theme for the first two books. Though the main focus is on the Arian controversy, the excerpts contain some unique information and interesting comments on the secular events of the reign. Philostorgius was highly laudatory in his depiction of Constantine as the latter had, by the time of his baptism and death, moved much closer to the Arian rather than the Nicene position on Trinitarian matters. Photius was not the only Byzantine author to have found Philostorgius a valuable source on Constantine. The anonymous authors of both a life of Constantine (*BHG* 365) and the *passio* of Artemius (see below, pp. **218–19**) made extensive use of him as a source for the political events of the reign and those of his sons.

1

THE ORIGIN OF CONSTANTINE

The *Anonymus Valesianus pars prior* (*Origo Constantini*)

INTRODUCTION

Sam Lieu

In 1636, Henricus de Valois (1603–76), the famous classical scholar on whom Cardinal Mazarin bestowed the title of 'Historiographe du Roi de France', published together with his *editio princeps* of the *Res Gestae* of Ammianus Marcellinus, a Latin work which has come to be known after its editor, the *Anonymus Valesianus* (more correctly the *Excerpta Valesiani*). It consists of two distinctive historical works: (1) excerpts from a history or political biography of Constantine written in a clear classicising style and (2) a brief history of the events in Italy in the last days of the Western empire (474–526) focusing mainly on Theodoric, the king of the Ostrogoths, written in a distinctive vulgar style. (Cf. Adams, 1976: 2.) The first part, commonly known as the *Origo Constantini*, gives the impression of being a biography of Constantine from his birth at Naissus to his death near Nicomedia. However, the narrative contained in the excerpts concentrates almost exclusively on political and military events of his early career (305–24). The last seven years of the reign receive the most cursory of treatments. Now generally acknowledged as 'a sober and accurate source' (Syme, 1974: 237 [63]) on the events which it covers, the work nevertheless remains an enigma although the famous pessimistic remark of Momigliano (1963: 87), 'all is in doubt about the first part of the *Anonymus Valesianus*', can now be safely consigned to history in the light of intensive research on the work in the intervening decades.

Authorship and date

The author of the anonymous work was almost certainly a pagan as evidenced by his predominant interest in the political and military history of the reign. The few sections devoted to Christianity are almost all *verbatim* quotations from the work of a Christian author, the *Historia contra paganos* of Paulus Orosius, which was composed *c.* 417. There is little doubt that the parallel passages are taken from Orosius' work by a later redactor to give what was a pagan work the much needed Christian garb, probably in the reign of Constantius III (417–421) at a time when there was much anti-pagan polemic. (Cf. Zecchini, 1993: 32–33.) A date close to the death of Constantine in 337 has often been suggested for the composition of the original work and this suggestion remains the most likely in view of the precise and valuable information it contains and, as Barnes (1989b: 161) has well pointed out, the avoidance of errors which became standard in later sources. These include presenting Theodora, the wife of Constantius Chlorus, as the daughter and not the step-daughter of Maximianus Herculius (I(1), cf. *Pan. Lat.* X(2),11,4, a contemporary work of 310) and the accurate chronology of Constantine's flight from the court of Galerius which took place in the summer of 305 when his father was preparing for a campaign against the Picts in Britain (II(4), confirmed by *Pan. Lat.* VII(6),7) and was not occasioned by news of his father's last illness in July 306, as implied in most sources. (Cf. Lact., *Mort. pers.* 24,8, Eus., *V. C.* I,21,1 etc.)

Content and sources

Despite its extreme brevity, the *Origo Constantini* has long been accepted by modern scholars as a major source on the reign of Constantine because of the precise and unique material it provides on some aspects of Constantine's early life, which is otherwise more poorly documented, and on the political and military events of his reign. The anonymous author gives the duration of the reign of each emperor after the account of his death. As the work begins with the duration of the co-emperorship of Diocletian and Maximianus Herculius, there is a distinct possibility that it once contained an account of the reign of these two emperors. (Cf. König, 1987: 6.) Particularly important is the information it gives on the *cursus honorum* of Constantius Chlorus, the father of Constantine, and on the birthplace of Constantine. Little, however, is said about the reign and administration of Constantius Chlorus (a favourite among Christian historians) and the narrative soon focuses on the early career of Constantine, especially on his exploits at the court of Galerius and his daring escape. The biographical elements may have been derived from a now lost 'biography' of Constantine (Praxagoras perhaps), which was also used by Byzantine historians like Zonaras. (See above, pp. **25–26**.) It is one of only two sources (the other being *Pan. Lat*. VII(6)) which disproves decisively that the reason for Constantine's desertion was the fatal illness of his father, as the campaign against the Picts (in which both father and son took part) must have taken place before the death of Constantius and not afterwards as Eusebius would have us believe (*V. C.* I,25,2).

The complex events following the abdication of Diocletian and Maximianus Herculius in 315 constitute much of the surviving portions of the work. From the abdication of Diocletian to the fall of Maxentius (5–12), the *Origo* shares many common themes with the *De mortibus persecutorum* of Lactantius (completed 314/15) but verbal similarities are rare and direct acquaintance cannot be proved. Thematic parallels with the *De Caesaribus* of Aurelius Victor, the *Epitome* of Eutropius and the *Epitome de Caesaribus* are numerous and presuppose a common source. The latter may well have been the so-called lost *'Kaisergeschichte'* postulated by Enmann – an epitome which may well have been utilised by Eunapius. (See above, pp. **11–12**.) The existence of such a source is deduced from the similarities as well as shared errors which exist in the three epitomators for the period from Diocletian to the death of Constantine and it has even been suggested that the *Origo* may well be our sole surviving *exemplum* of this chronicle. (Cf. Zecchini, 1993: 37–38.) However, exact verbal parallels between the *Origo* and the three main Latin epitomes are in fact rare, and on most common themes the *Origo* provides distinctive and, with few exceptions, the more accurate or more detailed information.

The civil war between Constantine and Licinius in two phases is recounted in considerable detail in the *Origo* and the latter is our only source which gives the names of the protagonists involved in the breakdown of the settlement between Constantine and Licinius, namely Constantine's brother-in-law Bassianus and his brother Senecio (§13). It is also the only source to give the troop strength of both contestants at the Battle of Cibalae (§16) and the name of the site of the second battle (Ardiensis, §17) of that campaign.

The causes of the second conflict between the two emperors are partly obscured in the *Origo* by an intrusive excerpt from Orosius (*Adv. pag.* VII,28,18) aimed at giving a religious (i.e. anti-pagan) flavour to the affair. Nevertheless it gives as the *casus belli* Constantine's victory over the Goths in the Balkans, which is seen as unacceptable interference in Licinius' allotted sphere of influence. Although the account of the actual conflict is much more extensive in Zosimus, that of the *Origo* contains much detail which cannot be found elsewhere such as the inspired leadership of Caesar Crispus, the son of Constantine by his first wife Minervina.

On the founding of Constantinople, the author of the *Origo* does not betray any knowledge of the pagan polemical version which links it to the execution of Crispus and the murder of Fausta, which helps to reinforce a pre-Eunapius dating to the work. (See above, pp. 16–17.) The figure of Crispus is cast in a heroic mode in the *Origo* and there is nothing to suggest that he would later be implicated in a domestic scandal.

Once the civil wars are over and the new capital founded, the narrative in the *Origo* peters out rather rapidly. The main events of the reign from the final defeat of Licinius onwards were ecclesiastical, punctuated by sporadic wars against the Sarmatians, and therefore of little interest to a pagan historian. The importance of the *Origo* to the modern historian remains in the unique information which it provides on Constantine's rise to power, and for this we owe a debt to the 'Redactor' whose crude attempts to Christianise the text also enabled its survival.

Editions etc.

The principal manuscript, now in the Staatsbibliothek in Berlin, was written in Verona in the 9th century (MS. Phillipps 1885, foll. 30v.–36v.) The standard and most often cited modern edition is that of Th. Mommsen in MGH (Auct. Ant.) IX (Berlin, 1892) 1–11. The first modern commentary by Westerhuis (1906) is in Latin and the Budé edition by J. Moreau revised by V. Velkov (Paris, 1968) remains little known to undergraduates and research students in the English-speaking world who mostly prefer the more widely accessible but vastly inferior edition with English translation by J. C. Rolfe which is appended to his Loeb edition of Ammianus Marcellinus (London and Cambridge, Mass., 1923) iii, 508–69. The more recent edition (with translation and extensive commentary) by König (1987) is an improvement on the text of Moreau and it is on this text that our present translation is based with the permission of Prof. König. On the various editions of the *Origo* see the valuable survey by Barnes (1989b).

THE ORIGIN OF CONSTANTINE
translated by Jane Stevenson

I(1) Diocletian ruled for twenty years with Herculius Maximianus. Constantius, a grand-nephew of the divine Claudius (Gothicus),[1] best of princes, through his brother, first became protector, then tribune, and afterwards governor of the Dalmatias. Then he was made Caesar by Diocletian, along with Galerius.[2] Having left Helena, his previous wife, he took to wife Theodora,[3] daughter of Maximianus, by whom he subsequently had six children, the brothers of Constantine. But by Helena,[4] his previous wife,[5] he already had a son, Constantine, who later became the most mighty of princes.

II(2) This Constantine, therefore, was born of a very humble mother,[6] Helena, in the town of Naissus[7] and brought up there (he later adorned this town most splendidly).[8] Having been scantily instructed in letters, he became a hostage with Diocletian and Galerius,[9] and fought bravely under them in Asia.[10] After Diocletian and Herculius had laid down their power, Constantius asked for Constantine back from Galerius: but Galerius threw him into the path of many dangers. (3) For when he was a young man fighting in the cavalry against the Sarmatians,[11] having seized a fierce barbarian by his hair, he captured him and brought him to the feet of the emperor Galerius.[12] Then, having been sent by Galerius into a swamp, he entered it on horseback and made a way for the rest of the army to the Sarmatians, and brought victory to Galerius, having killed many of them.[13] (4) Then Galerius sent him back to his father.[14] And Constantine, so that he might avoid Severus as he was passing through Italy, crossed the Alps with the greatest possible speed, having killed the post-horses behind him,[15] and came to his father at Bononia [Boulogne-sur-mer], which the Gauls previously called Gesoriacum. After his victory over the Picts,[16] his father Constantius died at York and Constantine, by the will of all the soldiers,[17] was made Caesar.[18]

III(5) Meanwhile, two Caesars had been created, Severus[19] and

Maximinus [i.e. Maximinus Daia].[20] Maximinus was given rule over Oriens,[21] and Galerius kept for himself Illyricum, Thrace and Bithynia.[22] Severus took Italy, and whatever Herculius [i.e. Maximianus] had previously gained. (6) After Constantius had died in Britain and Constantine his son had succeeded him, suddenly the Praetorian Guard in the city of Rome created Maxentius, the son of Herculius,[23] emperor.[24] But at the order of Galerius, Severus took an army against Maxentius, but he was suddenly deserted by all his men and fled to Ravenna.[25] After that, Galerius went to Rome with a vast force, threatening the destruction of the city, and encamped at the fort Interamna [Terni] on the Tiber. (7) Then he sent Licinius[26] and Probus[27] to the city as ambassadors, asking, in negotiation, that the son-in-law [Maxentius] should seek to obtain what he wanted from his father-in-law Galerius[28] by requesting it rather than by making war. This was spurned, and he learned that on account of Maxentius' promises, [many] men had deserted his side. Disturbed by this, he turned back, and so that he could give his army some kind of booty, he told them to steal things along the Via Flaminia.[29] (8) Maximinus himself fled to Constantine. Then Galerius made Licinius Caesar[30] in Illyricum.[31] Next, leaving him behind in Pannonia, he himself retired to Serdica, having been attacked by a fearsome disease, and he so melted away that he died with his entrails exposed and rotting, in punishment for the most dreadful persecution, a most just penalty returning on the author of a wicked edict.[32] He had ruled for eighteen years.

IV(9) Severus Caesar was ignoble both in his way of life and his birth, and an alcoholic[33] and thus a friend of Galerius. It was for this reason that Galerius made him and Maximinus Caesars, with Constantine knowing nothing of the matter. To this Severus were given cities in Pannonia, Italy and Africa. It is for this reason that Maxentius was made emperor: because Severus, having been abandoned, fled from his own men to Ravenna. (10) Herculius came there on behalf of his son after being summoned,[34] and having deceived Severus with false promises, took him into custody and brought him into the city in the guise of a captive,[35] and had him kept in a house belonging to the state thirty [Roman] miles down the Via Appia from Rome.[36] Afterwards, when Galerius sought Italy, he was murdered[37] and then brought to a place eight miles from Rome and put in the monument of Gallienus.[38]

(11) Galerius was such an alcoholic that when he was drunk he

would issue orders which ought not to be obeyed, and on the warning of his prefect he directed that none of his orders issued after dinner should be implemented.[39]

(12) Meanwhile Constantine, having defeated the generals of the tyrant [Maxentius] at Verona,[40] sought out Rome. When Constantine was coming to the city, Maxentius, coming out of the city, chose a plain above the Tiber as the place where they would fight.[41] There he was defeated and, fleeing with all his men, perished, trapped in the crowd of people and thrown down by his horse into the river. On the following day, his body was taken up from the river, and his head was cut off and brought into the city.[42] His mother, when she was questioned about his origins, confessed that he had been begotten by a certain Syrian.[43] He ruled for six years.

V(13) Licinius too was a man of humble birth from New Dacia,[44] who had been made emperor by Galerius so that he would fight against Maxentius. But after Maxentius had been suppressed, and Constantine had re-taken Italy, he bound Licinius into alliance with him,[45] provided that Licinius would take his sister Constantia as his wife[46] in Milan. Once the marriage had been celebrated,[47] Constantine went to Gaul, and Licinius returned to Illyricum. (14) Some time later, Constantine sent Constantius to Licinius, suggesting that he should make Bassianus (who had married Constantine's other sister Anastasia)[48] a Caesar, so that Bassianus could hold Italy as a buffer between Constantine and Licinius, following the example set by Diocletian and Maximianus.[49] (15) But Licinius spoiled this arrangement, and through the influence of Senicio, Bassianus' brother, who was loyal to Licinius, Bassianus took up arms against Constantine. He was seized while still preparing himself, and at Constantine's order, was convicted and executed. When Senicio, as the person responsible for the plot, was demanded for punishment, Licinius refused to hand him over, and the peace between them was broken.[50] There was an additional reason besides, because Licinius had destroyed images and statues of Constantine at Emona.[51] Open war was declared between the two of them.[52]

(16) Both their armies were taken to the plain of Cibalae.[53] Licinius had 35,000 men, infantry and cavalry; Constantine commanded 20,000 infantry and cavalry. After an indecisive battle, in which 20,000 of Licinius' infantry and part of his armoured cavalry were killed, Licinius escaped to Sirmium[54] with the greater part of his horse-troops under cover of night. (17) From there, having picked

up his wife and son and treasure, he went to Dacia. He made Valens, commander of the frontier, a Caesar.[55] Then, a huge force having been assembled by means of Valens at Hadrianopolis (a city in Thrace),[56] he sent ambassadors to Constantine, who had settled himself at Philippopolis,[57] to talk of peace. The ambassadors returned, baffled, and having taken to war again, they fought together on the plain of Ardia. After a lengthy and indecisive battle, Licinius' men gave way and fled under cover of night. (18) Licinius and Valens turned away and went into the region of Beroea, believing (which was actually true) that Constantine in order to pursue them would be heading further towards Byzantium. Then as Constantine was eagerly hurrying ahead, he learned that Licinius remained at his back. Just then, when his soldiers were weary with battle and route-marching, Mestrianus[58] was sent to him as an ambassador to ask for peace, at the request of Licinius, who promised that he would henceforth do as he was told. Valens was commanded to return to his private rank as he had been before,[59] and, when this was done, peace was confirmed between the two emperors, and Licinius held Oriens, Asia, Thrace, Lesser Moesia and Scythia.[60]

(19) Then, returning to Serdica, Constantine decided in Licinius' absence that Constantine's sons Crispus[61] and Constantine and Licinius' son Licinius[62] should be made Caesars, and thus rule should be carried on harmoniously, as from both of them.[63] Therefore, Constantine and Licinius were made consuls simultaneously.[64] (20) In the region of Oriens, during Licinius' and Constantine's consulship, Licinius, seized by sudden insanity, ordered that all the Christians should be expelled from the palace. Soon after that, war broke out again between Licinius and Constantine.[65]

(21) Again, while Constantine was at Thessalonica, the Goths broke through the neglected frontiers, devastated Thrace and Moesia, and began to take spoils. Then, in fear of Constantine, after their onset had been checked, they returned prisoners to him and peace was granted them.[66] But Licinius complained that this was a breach of trust, since an area belonging to him had been relieved by someone else.[67] (22) Then, since he alternated between wheedling and haughty orders, he justifiably roused the wrath of Constantine. During the time when civil war was not yet actually being waged but was being prepared for, Licinius wallowed in the crimes of avarice, cruelty and lust, murdering many wealthy men and seducing their wives.[68]

(23) Then the peace was broken with the consent of both sides. Constantine sent the Caesar Crispus with a huge fleet to take Asia,

and Amandus,[69] acting for Licinius, opposed him with a similarly large naval force.[70] (24) Licinius himself filled the slopes of a high mountain near Hadrianopolis with a great army. Constantine turned thither, with his entire force.[71] While the war was going on by both land and sea, Constantine was victorious, due to his troops' discipline in battle (though they had difficulty with the heights), and his luck, and the army of Licinius was thrown into confusion and disorganised while Constantine was slightly wounded in the thigh. (25) Licinius, fleeing from there, sought Byzantium; and while his scattered forces tried to reach him, Licinius, having closed Byzantium, prepared for a siege on the landward side, feeling secure to seaward. But Constantine put together a fleet out of Thrace. Then, with his usual foolishness, Licinius made Martinianus Caesar.[72] (26) But Crispus,[73] with Constantine's fleet, reached Callipolis,[74] and there he conquered Amandus in a sea battle so comprehensively that the latter was scarcely able to escape alive with the help of those who had stayed on shore. Licinius' fleet was either destroyed or captured.[75] (27) Licinius, abandoning hope of the sea, by which he saw that he would be blockaded, fled to Chalcedon[76] with his treasure. Constantine, having met up with Crispus and heard of his sea victory, invaded Byzantium. Then Licinius staged a battle at Chrysopolis,[77] greatly aided by the Goths whom their ruler Alica[78] had brought: Constantine's force was victorious, and destroyed 25,000 armed men of the other side, while the rest took to flight. (28) Then, when they saw Constantine's legions coming in troop-ships, they threw down their weapons and gave themselves up. On the following day Constantia, sister of Constantine and wife of Licinius, came to her brother's camp and begged for her husband's life, which he granted. Then Licinius was made a private citizen, and entertained at a feast by Constantine, and Martinianus' life was conceded to him.

(29) Licinius was sent to Thessalonica: but Constantine was influenced by the example of his father-in-law Herculius Maximianus; and lest he should assume again the purple he had laid down, to the danger of the State, he ordered Licinius to be killed,[79] as the soldiers of Thessalonica hotly demanded, and likewise Martinianus in Cappadocia. Licinius had ruled for nineteen years, and left a wife and son behind him. Although all the participants in the dreadful persecution were already dead, this man was also clearly asking for punishment, who had been a persecutor as far as he was able to.[80]

VI(30) Constantine, in memory of his famous victory, called

Byzantium Constantinople, after himself. As if it were his native city,[81] he enriched it with great assiduity, and wanted it to become the equal of Rome.[82] He sought out citizens for it from everywhere, and lavished so much wealth on it that he almost exhausted the resources of the imperial treasury. There he founded a Senate of the second rank; the members were called *clari*.[83]

(31) Then he took up arms against the Goths,[84] and gave assistance to the Sarmatians, who had begged for it. Thus, through Constantine Caesar,[85] nearly 100,000 died of starvation and cold. Then he accepted hostages, among whom was Ariaric,[86] son of the king. (32) Thus, when peace had been confirmed, he turned against the Sarmatians,[87] who had proved to be of doubtful loyalty. But all the slaves of the Sarmatians rebelled against their masters, and when the latter had been expelled, Constantine willingly accepted them, and distributed more than 300,000 people of all ages and both sexes throughout Thrace, Scythia, Macedonia and Italy.[88]

(33) This Constantine was the first Christian emperor except for Philip (the Arab) who, as it seems to me, became Christian simply in order that the thousandth year of Rome might be said to belong to Christ rather than to idols. From Constantine up to the present day all the emperors have been Christians, with the exception of Julian, whose impious life left him in the middle of what he is said to have been plotting.[89]

(34) Constantine made the change with due order and care. He issued an edict that the temples of the pagans should be closed without any loss of life.[90]

Soon after, he destroyed that most powerful and numerous race, the Goths, in the very bosom of barbarian territory – that is, in the land of the Sarmatians.[91]

(35) He destroyed a certain Calocaerus, who aspired to a revolution in Cyprus.[92]

He made Dalmatius, son of his brother Dalmatius, a Caesar. He gave Dalmatius' brother Hannibalianus to his daughter Constantia, and made him King of Kings and ruler of the peoples of Pontica.[93] Then he ordained that Constantine the younger should rule the Gauls, Constantius Caesar the Oriens, Constans should rule Illyricum and Italy,[94] and that Dalmatius should protect the Gothic shore.[95]

While Constantine was preparing to make war on Persia,[96] he ended his days in an imperial villa on the outskirts of Constantinople, near Nicomedia, handing on a well-organised state to his sons. He had ruled for thirty-one years, and was buried in Constantinople.

NOTES
Sam Lieu

1 On the legend of Constantine's Claudian descent, see below, pp. 68–70.
2 Constantius Chlorus was summoned to the court of Maximianus Herculius and was proclaimed Caesar on 27 Feb. 302. Cf. *ILS* 642 and Eutr. IX,22,1.
3 Theodora was commonly said to have been the step-daughter of Maximianus. Her mother is said to have been Eutropia but her father was probably Afranius Hannibalianus. Cf. *PLRE*, i, 895 (Theodora 1). This has been challenged by Barnes (1982: 33) who believes that the sources which make this claim all drew their material from an unreliable and now lost source written c. 337 (i.e. Enmann's *KG* for which see above, p. 41) whereas two reliable sources, the *Origo* and Philostorgius (*H. e.* II,16) both claim that she was a full daughter of Maximianus. She bore Constantius three sons: Fl. Delmatius, Iulius Constantius (the father of Julian the Apostate) and Hannibalianus, and three daughters: Constantia, Eutropia and Anastasia.
4 Flavia Julia Helena, as later tradition asserts, was born in Drepanum in Bithynia – a city later to be renamed Helenopolis and famous as the resting place of the remains of Lucian – a martyr whose cult Helena helped to establish. Where she first met Constantius remains an intriguing question. One suggestion is that Constantius, while serving as *protector* in the army of Aurelian, would have been active in Asia Minor in the emperor's campaign against Zenobia. Cf. Barnes (1982: 36, n. 37) who draws attention to the epitaph of a protector Aureliani Augusti at Nicomedia (*ILS* 2775) which may imply that emperor's presence in Bithynia shortly after 270. See below, pp. 142–43.
5 Constantius and Helena were probably what we would now regard as common-law husband and wife. Their cohabitation was *de facto* though perhaps not *de jure* recognised as a form of marital relationship. (Cf. Drijvers, 1992: 17–19.) Their separation appears to have been forced upon them by the need to cement political bonds within the Tetrarchic system. It is difficult to imagine that a scion of a Dalmatian noble house would formally marry an inn-keeper. On the other hand, if they were indeed legally married, her background would have almost certainly given rise to the insinuation that she was his concubine or that the union was not fully legitimate (e.g. Eutr. X,2,2). The uncertainty of their marital status led Jerome to claim that Constantius and Galerius were both compelled to divorce their 'wives' after they had been appointed Caesars, and to refer to Constantine later in the same work as the son of a 'concubine' (Hieron., *Chron.*, s. a. 292, p. 226,4 and s. a. 306, p. 228,23/4). The view that the two were officially married has been defended by Barnes (1982: 36) on the grounds that the sources (including epigraphical evidence) which claim Helena was Constantius' 'wife' are more reliable.
6 The low status of Helena is widely acknowledged in the sources, the most common version being that she was an 'inn-keeper' (*stabularia*). (Ambros., *De obitu Theod.* 42,1, *PL* 16.1463A etc.) See sources discussed in Drijvers, 1992: 9–19.

7 Modern Nish in Serbia, former Yugoslavia. It was an important and well-defended military base (Amm. XXI,12,1) situated on the highway which linked Aquilea and Byzantium. Cf. Syme, 1974: 273 [1983: 67]. It is likely to have been the place at which Constantius pursued his earlier military career, and was later much visited by Constantine. Cf. Barnes 1982: 74, 79 and König, 1987: 66. It was also conveniently near the site of a famous victory of Claudius 'Gothicus' (Zos. I,45,1). Naissus is given as Constantine's birthplace by a near contemporary source, the *Mathesis* of Firmicus Maternus (p. 38,2–3, ed. Kroll-Skutsch-Ziegler) – a work composed in the 330s before he was converted to Christianity and became the polemicist against paganism under Constantius II. Despite the popular belief in Byzantium that Constantine was born and brought up in Drepanum, Naissus was known to Byzantine antiquarians like Stephanus (*Ethnika* p. 467,3–4, ed. Meinecke) and administrators (e.g. the source for Constantine Porphyrogenitus, *De thematibus occidentis*, Thema IX, Dyrrhachium, *PG* 113.128) as Constantine's birthplace. On the *ortus* of Constantine see especially material collected in Callu, 1992: 255–56.

8 According to Stephanus (*op. cit.*, p. 467,3) the city was (re-)founded by Constantine.

9 The taking of the offspring of important personages as a pledge of loyalty was certainly practised in this period. See e.g. Zos. II,12,2. This suggests that Constantine was regarded as a legitimate son of Constantius and, as the son of an Augustus, Constantine was an automatic candidate for future appointment as emperor and resided in the royal court as heir presumptive. His career under Diocletian and Galerius suggests he was prepared for rulership as implied by Praxagoras (*FGrH* 219,2, p. 948,17, trans. above, p. 7). Cf. Barnes, 1981: 3. For other reasons why Constantine was sent to serve under Diocletian and Galerius, see below, pp. 110–11. During his sojourn at the imperial court he was betrothed to Flavia Maxima Fausta, the daughter of Maximinus and Eutropia who was then still a child. (They were married in March 307.) Constantine had earlier acquired a wife (or concubine), Minervina, who was the mother of his eldest son Crispus (born c. 305). Cf. *Epit.* 41,4, Zos. II,20,2 and Zon. XIII,2,37.

10 Eusebius (*V. C.* I,19) had seen him travelling through Palestine as Diocletian's adjutant. Constantine himself later claimed to have personally seen the ruins of Babylon and of Memphis (*or. ad s. coetum* 16,2) which implies that he had taken part in the successful campaign of Galerius against the Persian king Narses (298/9) and had visited Egypt in the retinue of Diocletian. Cf. Barnes, 1981: 18 and *idem*, 1982: 11–12 and esp. 41–42.

11 Originally a nomadic tribe related to the Scythians, the Sarmatians under the High Empire occupied a buffer zone between the Dacians and the province of Pannonia. Many were later resettled within the Roman empire by Constantine (see below, §32). The Limigantes of the Late Empire were formerly their subject people. Cf. Matthews, 1989: 304.

12 This episode of individual gallantry is surprisingly unattested in 4th-century sources on Constantine. It is found only in a late Byzantine

source (Zonaras XII,33, p. 623,11–15, CSHB) which says that a jealous Galerius sent Constantine to attack the leader of the Sarmatians who stood out because of his elaborate armour. He attacked and captured the barbarian and handed him over alive to Galerius. Zonaras and the *Origo* may have drawn material from the same biographical source on Constantine (perhaps the now lost history of Praxagoras).

13 The *Origo* seems to suggest a date of 305/6 for the campaign but it is possible that the incident was placed here to anticipate the emperor's journey to his father. Cf. Barnes, 1982: 41–42.

14 Lactantius (*Mort. pers.* 24,2) states that it was a seriously ill Constantius who requested the return of his son. Constantine's own ambition and unwillingness to accept the appointment of Severus and Maximinus Daia as Caesars (1 May 305) were clearly more cogent factors as Constantius was alive until 25 July 306. Cf. Aur. Vict., *Caes.* 40,1–2: 'Therefore, Constantius and Armentarius [i.e. Galerius] now succeeding Diocletian and Maximianus, the Caesars Severus and Maximus, natives of Illyria, allocate territories to themselves, the former Italy, the latter the lands over which Jovius had reigned. 2. Constantine could not accept such a situation, for his energetic and indomitable spirit had, since childhood, been motivated by a powerful desire to rule; also, according to the plan drawn up for his escape, he killed the post-horses in every place he had passed through in order to immobilise his pursuers, and reached Britain; because Galerius was detaining him as a hostage on a religious pretext', and Zos. II,8,1–2. The suggestion that he fled from plots instigated against him by Galerius (Eus., *V. C.* I,20) belongs probably to the realm of Constantinian propaganda.

15 The hamstringing of post-horses by Constantine to avoid pursuit is a well known *topos* in Constantinian biography. According to Lactantius (*Mort. pers.* 24,5–6) Galerius received a stream of requests from Constantius for the return of his son. Seeing that he was unable to refuse it any longer he gave Constantine his seal late in the day with the command that he should depart the next day – the delay was to enable him to send word to Severus to detain him (presumably to prevent him being acclaimed emperor by the army on the death of his father). Constantine however anticipated this and departed after supper when Galerius took his rest. Along the way he got rid of the horses of the public post. Thus the next day a fuming Galerius was unable to give chase. (See also the very similar account in Zos. II,8,3.) The story is clearly an early element of Constantinian myth-making. See next note.

16 Constantius crossed over to Britain from Bononia in 305 and the campaign was successfully concluded before July 306. The campaign is known to us otherwise from one other literary source, *Pan. Lat.* VII(6),7,1–4 (trans. see below, pp. 80–81) and was undertaken probably in search of military glory as there was no strong evidence to show that there had been an invasion of Caledonia by the Picts. Cf. Frere 1978: 332. Cf. Barnes, 1982: 61. While not denying the possibility that Constantius was ill when Constantine made his escape, though this seems unlikely as he was in the middle of preparing his campaign, the

THE ORIGIN OF CONSTANTINE

final illness of his father is most likely an early excuse for what amounted to desertion by a serving officer.

17 Eusebius (*V. C.* I,21) on the other hand claims it was purely a matter of primogeniture. Zosimus (II,9,1), however, gives as reasons for the choice of the soldiers Constantine's physical strength and his promise of large donatives.

18 He was actually proclaimed Augustus by the soldiers but later had to acquiesce with the title of Caesar which was allowed him by Galerius. Cf. *Pan. Lat.* VI(7),5,3. On this see Creed *comm. ad* Lact., *Mort. pers.* 24,9 (p. 105, n. 6).

19 Little is known about the career of Flavius Valerius Severus prior to his elevation to the rank of Caesar. He was probably the praetorian prefect of Galerius (or of Maxentius). Cf. Barnes, 1982: 38–39. Informative are the derogatory remarks of Diocletian on his suitability for the purple in Lact., *Mort. pers.* 18,12.

20 A former cattle-herd who rose through the ranks to tribune, Maximinus was formerly called Daia and was given the name of Maximinus by Galerius (Lact., *Mort. pers.* 19,6) who was his uncle (Zos. II,8,1).

21 Cf. Aur. Vict., *Caes.* 40,1, *Epit.* 40,1, Eutr. 10,2, Lact., *Mort. pers.* 19,6 and Zos. II,8,1, On the details of the 're-division' of the empire in 305–6 see Barnes, 1982: 197 and König, 1987: 79–82. In 306 Constantine ruled over Britain, Gaul and Spain.

22 Illyricum was a prefecture, Thrace a diocese and Bithynia a province. The confusion does not necessarily imply that the author of the *Origo* was unfamiliar with the East. It merely indicates his rash use of his sources. Cf. König, 1987: 80–81.

23 Zos. II,9,2–3 gives the most detailed account of Maxentius' revolt. He was apparently incensed by the laureated image of Constantine which the newly proclaimed emperor had sent to Rome. As the son of an emperor he was not prepared to stand idly by while someone whom he regarded as the son of a concubine declared himself emperor. He was assisted by three prefects (probably of the urban cohorts, cf. Barnes, 1981: 298–99, n. 7) and by the Praetorian Guards. Abellius the vicarius of the *praefectus urbi* who opposed the rebellion was killed (II,9,3). The people of Rome were in a turbulent mood because Severus extended the census to Italy which was traditionally exempt from fiscal assessment (Lact., *Mort. pers.* 26,2, cf. Jones, 1964: 64–65). Diocletian had earlier tried to reduce the political power of the Praetorian Guards by reducing the number of their cohorts as well as their unit strength (Aur. Vict., *Caes.* 39,47). The number of cohorts was still no less than ten according to a certificate issued on 7 Jan. 306 (*AE* 1961, inscr. no. 240: 60–61). But it is possible that since the imperial court was no longer in Rome, some units might have been re-deployed into the emperor's own army. With the creation of new units like the Ioviani and the Herculiani, the Praetorians were already a relic of the past. Cf. Barnes, 1981: 29 and König, 1987: 84–85.

24 The revolt took place on 28 Oct. 306 (Lact., *Mort. pers.* 44,4). In fact Maxentius at first avoided the titles of Augustus and Caesar and called himself princeps on his coins so as not to upset the Tetrarchic system of

two Augusti and two Caesars. Cf. Barnes, 1982: 13. Much interesting light on the relative positions of Constantine and Licinius has been shed by the so-called Čentur Hoard of folles found at Mali Čentur in Istria. Cf. Jeločnik and Kos, 1973: 134–38.

25 Cf. Aur. Vict., *Caes.* 40,6–7: 'Upon this news, Armentarius [i.e. Galerius] ordered Severus Caesar, who happened by chance to be near the city, to hasten there and confront the enemy. 7. But while he was camping outside the city, abandoned by his troops, whom Maxentius had won over to his side with the lure of rewards, he died, fugitive and besieged, in Ravenna.' See also Lact., *Mort. pers.*, 26,8. Zosimus (II,10,1) adds that even Anullinus (cf. Barnes, 1982: 117), his Praetorian Prefect, changed sides.

26 Valerius Licinianus Licinius, the future Augustus. Cf. *PLRE*, i, p. 509 (Licinius 3).

27 Pompeius Probus. He was consul posterior in 310 and was Praetorian Prefect (East) under Licinius. Cf. *PLRE*, i, p. 740 (Probus 6).

28 Maxentius was married to Galerius' daughter Valeria Maximilla (*ILS*, 677 and Lact., *Mort. pers.*, 18,9).

29 The famous highway built by C. Flaminius runs from Rome north-eastwards to Fanum Fortunae (modern Fano) where it runs along the Adriatic to Ariminum (Rimini) from where it is continued to Aquilea by the Via Popillia.

30 Licinius had long been a confidante of Galerius who, according to Lactantius (*Mort. pers.* 20,3), had originally planned to make him Augustus rather than Caesar.

31 The elevation was made on 11 Nov. 308 (Hydatius, *Chron.*, *s. a.* 308) at an important meeting at Carnuntum (near modern Pressburg) (*CP s. a.* 308, p. 519,6–7) at which Galerius unsuccessfully attempted to persuade Diocletian to come out of retirement (Lact., *Mort. pers.* 29,1, Zos. II,10,4 etc.); the latter declined, preferring the pleasures of the garden to the affairs of the State (*Epit.* 39,6).

32 Galerius was commonly regarded by Christian authors as the principal villain behind the anti-Christian edict of 303 which sparked off the so-called 'Great Persecution'. Cf. Lact., *Mort. pers.* 10,6–114 and Eus., *H. e.* VIII,16,2. The same authors also describe his death from an infected wound (to his genitals?) in gory detail: Lact., *Mort. pers.* 35,3 and Eus., *H. e.* VIII,16,4. The account in the *Origo* bears some resemblance to that of Orosius, *Adv. pag.*, VII,28,12–13 but the *Origo* is more moderate in tone. Cf. Den Boer, 1972: 102–3. Galerius died in May 311.

33 Cf. Lact., *Mort. pers.* 18,12. The same insinuation is made against Galerius (below, §11).

34 Faced with the threat of invasion, Maxentius appealed to his father, Maximianus Herculius, to come out of enforced retirement, as many soldiers were still loyal to him. Maximianus immediately tried to seize power from his son. Cf. Lact., *Mort. pers.* 28,1–2.

35 There are two main traditions on the capture and death of Severus. According to one (Cf. Lact., *Mort. pers.* 26,9–10, Eutr. X,2,3 and Aur. Vict., *Caes.* 40,5–7), upon entering Italy, the army of Severus refused to march against Rome. Maximianus who had resumed the purple then

appeared on the scene and won over many of Severus' soldiers as they had remained loyal to the old emperor. Severus fled to Ravenna where he later surrendered to Maximianus and chose an honourable death by cutting his veins (or was put to death by his captors, cf. Eutr. and Aur. Vict., *loc. cit.*). The *Origo* on the other hand follows a tradition (the lost work of Eunapius?) which is most fully preserved by Zosimus (II,10,1–2): 'When Maximinius Galerius got wind of this, he sent Severus Caesar to fight Maxentius; while Severus, having left Milan, was advancing with a body of Moorish troops, Maxentius, having neutralised most of the soldiers accompanying him, thanks to distributions of silver, then even won over Anullinus, the praetorian prefect, before winning an easy victory. Severus took refuge at Ravenna, a very secure and populous city in which were available sufficient quantities of rations for him and for the soldiers who were accompanying him. 2. When Maximianus Herculius heard of this he was perturbed, not without good reason, for the fate of his son Maxentius; he left Lucania where he was then living, and went to Ravenna. Having seen at first glance that it was impossible to make Severus leave against his will, given that the place was secure and provided with sufficient provisions, he persuaded him, by using false promises, to go to Rome; therefore, when he reached a place called Three Taverns, an ambush set up by Maxentius seized hold of him and killed him by strangulation with a noose', and in an extremely abridged form by the anonymous *Epitome de Caesaribus* (40,3). See also the next three notes.

36 Zosimus (*loc. cit.*, above) and the anonymous author of the *Epit.* (*loc. cit.*) names the place of his captivity as the Three Taverns (Τρία Καπηλεῖα, Tres Tabernae). If the place so named was on the Via Appia then it was situated to the south of Rome – an unlikely stopping place for a traveller from Ravenna – unless it had been confused with a Tres Tabernae which was known to have existed on the Via Flaminia to the north of Rome. Cf. Hanson, 1974: 67 and Schlumberger, 1974: 189–90.

37 Barnes (1982: 5, n. 13) has noted that Severus' name was still given as that of a reigning Augustus on 29 Sept. 307 in an Egyptian document (*P. Mil.* 55) which suggests that the *Origo* is correct (*contra* Lactantius) in stating that he did not meet his death until after Galerius had invaded Italy. However, such delay in the up-dating of the reigning emperor is not uncommon on papyri from Roman Egypt. The *Chron. an. 354* (p. 148,31) preserves the tradition that he was killed on 16 Sept. 307 but the news of his death might not have reached Egypt before the end of the month. The invasion clearly rendered Severus valueless as a hostage.

38 Cf. *Epit.*, *loc. cit.* The emperor Gallienus was killed outside Milan. Although he was deified, he was *persona non grata* in Rome and his exact place of burial is not otherwise known. Cf. Hanson, 1974: 66. A 19th-century British scholar (Burn, 1871: 436) who appears to be unaware of the literary evidence cited here, placed the tomb of Gallienus at the ninth milestone south of Rome. Cf. König, 1987: 103.

39 Maximinus Daia was also described by Eusebius (*H. e.* VIII,14,11) as a heavy drinker who when drunk would issue such orders as he would

repent the next day when he was sober – clearly a standard epithet for a ruler in decline. See above, note 33. See also Schlumberger, 1974: 192.

40 Cf. *Pan. Lat.* IX(12),7,1–8,2. Constantine crossed the Alps probably in the late spring of 312 and defeated an army of Maxentius which included heavy cavalry near Turin. Verona, which was well defended, held out and only surrendered after Constantine had defeated a large relief-force led by Maxentius' prefect Pompeianus. Cf. Barnes, 1981: 42.

41 Maxentius had originally prepared to withstand a long siege and presumably had all the bridges over the Tiber cut. However, the populace of Rome rioted and declared Constantine emperor, thereby forcing him to take the field against Constantine. A bridge of boats therefore had to be constructed to enable his army to advance to battle. The fullest accounts of the battle at the Milvian Bridge (28 Oct. 312) are to be found in Lact., *Mort. pers* 44,5–9 and Zos., II,16,2–4. See also the more rhetorical descriptions in *Pan. Lat.* IX (12),16,3–6 and Eus., *H. e.* IX,9,2–8. Aurelius Victor (*Caes.* 40,23, cf. Praxagoras, 4, p. 948,27, trans. above, p. 7) says that Maxentius advanced, unwillingly, as far as Saxa Rubra, about nine miles from Rome, where he was defeated and fell into a trap which he set for the enemy while crossing the Tiber. The bridge probably broke apart because of the weight of the fleeing army rather than its being 'booby-trapped' to break under the pursuers. Cf. Barnes, 1981: 42–43.

42 Cf. *Pan. Lat.* IX(12),18,3 and X(4),32,7 and Praxagoras, *loc. cit.*, line 25.

43 Maxentius was the illegitimate son of Eutropia. She treated him as her son in order to satisfy her husband Maximianus' desire for an heir. Cf. *Epit.* 40,13. See also Di Maio, 1977: 71 and Barnes, 1982: 34.

44 Nova Dacia was created by Aurelian in 271 south of the Danube after he had evacuated Trajan's Dacia. Cf. Syme, 1974: 239 [1983: 64].

45 After the death of Galerius, the territories in his possession were partitioned by Licinius and Maximinus Daia. Licinius obtained Pannonia which was already under his possession and also Moesia and Thrace. Cf. Lact., *Mort. pers.* 36,1. See also the Brigeto Tablet of 311 A.D. (= *FIRA* I, no. 93, pp. 455–58) trans. Lewis and Reinhold, 1990 (ii): 491–92. Cf. Barnes, 1981: 39–40 and Grünewald, 1990: 59.

46 The marriage alliance between Constantine and Licinius was already agreed in 311 with the intention of pre-empting a pact between Licinius and Maxentius, but was interpreted by Maximinus Daia as directed against him. Cf. Lact., *Mort. pers.* 43,2. Constantia was the daughter of Constantius Chlorus and Theodora.

47 The marriage took place in 313.

48 Her name 'which only occurs in Jewish and Christian surroundings' (cf. Vogt, 1963: 43) appears to suggest Christian influence on her parents. She may also have been the founder of the church in Rome which bore her name. Cf. Vogt, *op. cit.* 47. Some baths in Constantinople were named after her (Amm. XXVI,6,14). However, the possibility that she adopted a Christian name as a *signum* after her conversion cannot be entirely ruled out. In which case her original *nomen* is unknown to us. Cf. Grünewald, 1990: 81–82.

49 This does not necessarily imply the revival of the Diocletianic Tetrarchy.

More likely it was part of a scheme of Constantine to have ready his candidacy for Caesar (or Augustus) in the East while Licinius took to the field against Maximinus Daia. Constantine would not have been likely to create a situation which would prejudice the chances of his own son Crispus from becoming Caesar. Barnes' argument that Constantine was spurred on to appoint his brother-in-law as Caesar by the birth of a son to Licinius and Constantia in 316 (1981: 66) depends on a post-316 date for the outbreak of the war. See esp. König, 1987: 114–16 and next note. Whatever Constantine's motive, Licinius was bound to have interpreted the proposal as the nomination of a successor to him who was a family member of Constantine.

50 Eusebius (*H. e.* X,8,5 and *V. C.* I,50,1) gives as reasons Licinius' persecution of the Christians in the East and his plotting against Constantine, as the stereotyped *casus belli* between a just ruler and a tyrant. The *Origo* is the only source to give a more detailed account of the events leading to the outbreak of war. Zosimus (II,18,1) puts it down to Constantine's naked ambition: 'The empire thus being in the hands of Constantine and Licinius, differences arose between them in a very short time, though Licinius was not responsible for this. Since Constantine, as usual, was demonstrating his lack of faith in the arrangements which had been decided, and wishing to seize some of the provinces attributed to Licinius' empire, their rivalry had therefore become obvious; they each gathered their forces and met to fight it out.' The date of the outbreak of hostilities remains uncertain. Jerome (*Chron.*, p. 230,2) places it between 313 and 315 and this is confirmed by the *Origo* (below, §20) which says that after the settlement of this 'first' war between the Augusti, they celebrated a joint consulship; the last time both names appeared together on the Fasti was for the year 315. Cf. Grünewald, 1990: 109–10. A later date (316/7) has been argued for by Bruun (1953: 17–22 and 1961:10–22) on the grounds that Constantinian coinage from Arelate continued to bear the images of both emperors till 317, and by Barnes (1981: 66) who sees the birth of Constantinus II (7 Aug. 316) as the reason for Constantine's decision to challenge Licinius who had had a son (Licinianus Licinius) by Constantia (*c.* Aug. 315). The later dating, which is now widely accepted, implies an error on the part of the late Roman chronographers.

51 Modern Ljubljana in Slovenia, former Yugoslavia. It lay on the border of Constantine's territory and the disturbance caused by Senicio or Licinius there might have been intended to embarrass Constantine. Cf. König, 1987: 118.

52 The part played by Senicio in the conflict between Constantine and Licinius is not noted in our main sources. The closest parallel to it is made by the Byzantine historian Leo the Grammarian (pp. 84,21–85,3, CSHB): 'Constantine gave his sister's hand in marriage to Licinius and made him emperor. Some of Constantine's men took refuge with Licinius and when they were requested back by Constantine as deserters but were not returned, Constantine marched out against Licinius and drove him back to Pannonia.' Cf. Bleckmann, 1992: 158–59.

53 Modern Vincovci in Croatia, former Yugoslavia. The most detailed account of the battle is given by Zosimus (II,18,2–5): 'Now Licinius

assembled his army at Cibalis, a city in Pannonia situated on a hill; the road leading to the town is narrow; a deep marsh five stadia wide surrounds the major part of it, the rest of the terrain is mountainous, the hill on which the town is situated is also there; then there is a wide open plain, very broad and extending as far as the eye can see. It was here that Licinius set up his camp, deploying his battle lines lengthwise at the foot of the hill, in order to avoid the flanks being too weak. 3. For his part, Constantine had positioned his army near the mountain, with the cavalry in the front line; in fact this seemed to be more advantageous, to avoid the enemy falling upon the slower-moving infantry and preventing them from moving forward because of the difficult terrain. With this arrangement and having quickly gained the upper hand in the first skirmish and given the signals, he marched immediately upon the enemy and there took place a battle, practically the fiercest possible; once the two armies had used up all their missiles, they fought for a long time with their swords and lances. 4. The battle had begun at dawn and had lasted until the evening when the right flank, commanded by Constantine, gained victory, and the enemy were routed. When Licinius' battle lines saw him jump on to his horse, ready to flee, they no longer had the courage to hold their positions or take any nourishment. Abandoning the cattle, the pack animals and all the rest of their equipment, they only took enough provisions to prevent them from suffering from hunger during the coming night, and made all haste to Sirmium with Licinius. 5. Sirmium is a town in Pannonia which has on one side of it the river Sava, which flows into the Danube; he passed quickly by this town, cut the bridge which spans the river and continued his advance, intending to regroup his forces from the regions of Thrace.' See also Eutr. X,5, Aur. Vict., *Caes.* 41,6, and *Epit.* 41,5. The battle was fought on 8 October 314, according to the *Consularia Constantinopolitana* (p. 231).

54 Modern Mirovica in former Yugoslavia.

55 Aur(elius) Val(erius) Valens, as the text signifies, was *dux limitis* (in Dacia) at the time of his elevation. His coins depicted him as Augustus even though he was called Caesar in the literary sources. Cf. *PLRE*, i, p. 931 (Valens 13).

56 Formerly called Uscudama (Amm. XIV,11,5), Hadrianopolis (modern Edirne) was the capital of the post-Diocletianic province of Haemimontus in the diocese of Thrace. Cf. Barnes, 1982: 206.

57 Modern Plovdiv in former Yugoslavia.

58 Some important supplementary details of the embassy of Count (*comes*) Mestrianus showing that Constantine did not hold all the cards in the negotiations are given by one fragment of Petrus Patricius' history as found in a collection of sources on diplomatic history compiled under the aegis of the Byzantine emperor Constantine Porphyrogenitus (*r.* 911–59). Frag. 15 (*FHG* IV, p. 189 = *Excerpta de legationibus gentium*, ed. de Boor, p. 394,18–37): 'Licinius then sent Count Mestrianus as envoy to Constantine. When he arrived, Constantine delayed him for a long time. Only after he had considered the uncertain outcome of the war, especially that the forces of Licinius had captured his baggage together with his royal retinue by a sudden raid, did he receive him. But

he who was entrusted with negotiating peace between the two emperors said that the one who had triumphed should not be harsh to his fellow citizens. For whatever was lost, would remain lost for the victor, not for the defeated. But if he were to reject the peace unilaterally then he would be the cause of countless civil wars. The emperor made clear the extent of his rage by his facial expression and by the contortion of his body. Almost unable to speak, he said, 'We have not come to this present state of affairs, nor have we fought and triumphed from the ocean till where we have now arrived, just so that we should refuse to have our own brother-in-law as joint ruler because of his abominable behaviour, and so that we should deny his close kinship, but accept that vile slave [i.e. Valens] with him into the imperial college.' He therefore commanded Mestrianus, who was giving up on this aspect of the embassy, to say whatever else he would wish to ask and he resolved that Valens should be removed from rule.'

59 He was later executed by Licinius. Cf. *Epit.* 40,9.

60 According to Zosimus (II,20,1), Constantine should rule Illyricum and all the territories beyond (i.e. to the West) and Licinius should have Thrace, the East and all beyond that. Valens, who had been appointed Caesar by Licinius, should be removed from office. In short Constantine acquired virtually all the Danubian area, mainland Greece and most of the Aegean islands. Cf. Soz., *H. e.* I,2,2 and Eutr. X,5. For detailed discussion on the geo-political implications of the settlement see esp. Paschoud, 1971: 210–13 and Barnes, 1982: 198.

61 Son of Constantine and his 'concubine' Minervina. He was born before 300, probably as early as 292 or 293. Cf. Barnes, 1982: 44.

62 I.e. Valerius Licinianus Licinius. See above, note 50. The appointments of the Caesars took place on 1 March 317. Cf. Hieron., *chron., s. a.* 317, p. 230,8–11, Aur. Vict., *Caes.* 41,6 and Zos., II,20,2. For discussion of the epigraphical evidence of the appointments see Grünewald, 1990: 116–17.

63 The conference at Serdica took place before 2 June 315 when Constantine legislated at Sirmium (*CT* II,30,1). Cf. Grünewald, 1990: 111. See, however, Barnes, 1982: 72, n. 113.

64 The last time the two emperors were jointly listed in the consular Fasti was in 315. Cf. *Cons. Const.* p. 231 and *Chron. Pasch.* p. 522,20/1.

65 A near *verbatim* quotation from the Christian author Orosius (*Adv. pag.* VII,28,18) who gave it as the main cause for the *first* war between the two Augusti. See above, p. 40. Licinius appeared to have reduced the number of Christians in his entourage after his court had moved to Nicomedia but Eusebius of Caesarea appears to have retained a prominent position. Cf. Barnes, 1981: 68–70.

66 A more detailed account of the campaign is given by Zosimus (II,21): 'When Constantine learned that the Sarmatians living near Lake Maeotis had crossed the Danube by boat and pillaged the territory beneath his jurisdiction, he led his legions against them. The barbarians also rose up against him with their king Rausimodus, and the Sarmatians first stormed a town which had an effective garrison. The lower part of its ramparts, from ground level upwards, was built of stone, whereas the upper part

was wooden. 2. The Sarmatians, therefore, having thought that they would seize the town very easily by burning the part of the wall which was built of wood, brought torches and shot arrows at those who were on the wall. While those who were on the walls were massacring the barbarians by overcoming them with arrows and stones from the height of their dominant position, Constantine, having gone into the attack and come upon the barbarians from the rear, killed a large number of them and took even more of them prisoners, so that the remainder of them fled. 3. Having thus lost most of his forces, Rausimodus crossed the Danube by boat, intending immediately to pillage the Roman territory. When Constantine heard of this he set off in pursuit, and crossed the Danube himself; as the barbarians were fleeing towards a thickly-wooded hill he attacked them, killed a large number of them, among them Rausimodus himself, took a lot of prisoners, accepted the surrender of the multitude of those remaining and returned to his quarters with a crowd of prisoners.' Constantine was saluted 'Sarmaticus Maximus' in 323. Cf. Barnes, 1982: 258.

67 Constantine clearly had not fully respected the frontier with Licinius in his military operations against the Goths. Cf. Barnes, 1981: 76. Zosimus adds (II,22,1) that when Constantine had concluded his campaign, he used the opportunity of being in Thrace to build a new harbour in Thessalonica where he assembled a fleet and an army in preparation for war against Licinius.

68 Stereotyped vices of a tyrant. Cf. *Epit.* 41,8. On this see Barnes, 1981: 68.

69 Abantus *ap.* Zos. II,23,3. Cf. *PLRE*, i, p. 50 (Amandus 2)

70 The figures are given by Zosimus (II,22,2). The size of Constantine's forces – 200 triaconters and more than 2,000 transport together with a land force of 120,000 infantry and 5,000 cavalry – leaves little room for doubt that he was preparing for a final showdown with his rival.

71 The most detailed account of the battle, fought on 3 July 324, is again provided by Zosimus (II,22,3–7): 'Licinius had his camp at Hadrianople in Thrace; whereas Constantine sent for his ships from the Piraeus, as the majority of them came from Greece, and, having advanced with his infantry from Thessalonica as far as the bank of the River Hebrus which has Hadrianople to its left, he set up his camp. 4. Licinius himself arranged his forces in battle formation along a line 200 stades in length, from the mountain which overlooks the town as far as the place where the River Tonoseius flows into the Hebrus. The legions camped opposite each other for several days in succession; while Constantine, having noticed the place at which the river was narrowest, prepared the following strategy. 5. He ordered the troops to bring down wood from the mountain and to plait ropes as though he intended to throw a bridge across the river and thus enable his army to cross. Having deceived the enemy in this way and climbed up on to a hillside covered with woods thick enough to hide anyone present there, he positioned 5,000 bowmen on foot and 80 horsemen. 6. Then he took with him twelve horsemen, crossed the Hebrus with them at the narrowest point where the river

was most easily crossed, and fell upon the enemy unexpectedly, so much so that some of them were killed, many of them fled in disarray and the rest, terror-struck at this sudden turn of events, remained open-mouthed at his surprise crossing of the river. 7. When the rest of the horsemen had crossed the river in complete safety, followed by the whole army, there was a great massacre: there were about 34,000 dead; Constantine withdrew his legions just before sunset; and Licinius, having taken with him as many of his own troops as he could, departed through Thrace to rejoin his fleet.'

72 He was formerly Licinius' Master of Offices (*magister officiorum*) and was said to have been the first person to hold that office (Petr. Patr. *ap.* Ioh. Lyd., *De mag.* II,25, p. 120,20–23, ed. Bandy). Cf. Aur. Vict., *Caes.*, 41,9 and Zos. II,25,2. He was immediately sent to thwart the crossing of Constantine's army from Thrace to the Hellespont. Cf. Zos., *loc. cit.*

73 He had already earned his military spurs in Gaul in 320. Cf. allusion in *Pan. Lat.* X(4),17,2.

74 Modern Gallipoli (Gelibolu) in the Dardanelles.

75 Licinius' fleet was too large to have operated effectively in the straits. On the following day, Amandus (Abantus) ordered what remained of the fleet to hug the coast and avoid battle with Crispus' ships. But a storm blew up and wrecked many of his ships, leaving 5,000 men drowned. Cf. Zos. II,24,1–2.

76 Modern Kadiköy, north-east of Gallipoli.

77 Modern Skutari (Üsküdar) on the Bosporus. The battle was fought on 18 Sept. 324 (cf. Barnes, 1981: 77) and by then Licinius had rebuilt his army to 150,000 men (Zos. II,26,3). On the battle see esp. Zos. *loc. cit.*, and Soc., *H. e.* I,4,4.

78 Otherwise unknown. Cf. *PLRE*, i, p. 45. For variant forms of the name, see Westerhuis, 1906: 43.

79 So also Orosius, *Adv. pag.* VII,28,10 which may have again been the source for the *Origo*. Socrates Scholasticus (*H. e.* I,4,4) alleges that he was executed because he tried to plot against Constantine with the help of some barbarians – a reference perhaps to the earlier help he had received from Alica.

80 Another *verbatim* quotation from Orosius (*Adv. pag.* VII,28,21).

81 The phrase can also convey the meaning of the city being his patrimony. Cf. Dagron, 1974: 27 with reference to Eus., *V. C.* IV,51.

82 Constantinople was dedicated in 330 (Malalas, *Chron.* XIII, p. 319,21–2) and Zosimus, representing a pagan tradition, links the desire to found a new capital with the execution of Crispus and the murder of Fausta in 327 (II,30,2). For a full examination of the literary sources on the foundation of the New Rome see esp. Dagron, 1974: 29–47 and 1984: 61–97 and Mango, 1985: 16–18.

83 I.e. 'the eminent'. Senators were normally addressed as *clarissimi* (i.e. 'the most eminent'). This distinction may indicate that some members of the Senate in Constantinople, especially those who were formerly councillors of Byzantium, were regarded as of lower rank. See esp. Dagron, 1974: 123.

84 Cf. Iord., *Get.* 112. This was probably a reprisal attack for the Goths' earlier intervention on behalf of Licinius. Cf. Heather and Matthews, 1991: 19.

85 The future Constantine II. The decisive battle was fought on 20 April 332 (Hydatius, *Des. cons. s. a.* 332, *PL* 51.907). For this victory Constantine was saluted 'Gothicus Maximus'. Cf. Zon. XIII,2,42 and Barnes, 1982: 258.

86 Perhaps the father of the future Gothic leader Athanric for whom a statue was erected; *ILS* I, 840ff. Cf. Heather, 1991: 99 and esp. n. 50.

87 This campaign was conducted in 334, for which Constantine gained a second salutation of 'Sarmaticus Maximus'. Cf. Hieron., *Chron., s. a.* 334, p. 233,13–15. On Romano-Gothic relations under Constantine see esp. Heather, 1991: 109–14. On the 'revolt' of the Sarmatians cf. Eus., *V. C.* IV,6, Amm. XVII,12,18–19, XIX,11,1. See also Barceló, 1981: 115–16 and Barnes, *loc. cit.*

88 The resettling of conquered barbarians as colonists within the empire was a standard practice. See below, Lib., *Or.* 59,83 (trans. below, p. **183**). We know of at least one Sarmatian colony settled near Trier. Cf. Aus., *Mosella* V,9. The victory was the occasion for a gold medal for Constantine II. Cf. König, 1987: 176–77.

89 Another 'Christian' interpolation from Orosius (*Adv. pag.* VII,28,1–2).

90 Cf. Orosius, *op. cit.* VII,28,28. The edict referred to is probably the same as the one given by Eusebius (*V. C.* II,45,1) forbidding pagan sacrifice. This however may have only applied to sacrifices in private (*CT* XVI,10,1, p. 897). The edict to Orcistus (331, *FIRA* I, p. 95, trans. Jones, 1970 (ii): 251) restores to the Phrygian city the sum of money which it had formerly received for the maintenance of local cults. Though the building of new temples was probably not encouraged, there was no systematic campaign to close down existing temples during the reign of Constantine.

91 An 'over-run' of the same quotation from Orosius (*op. cit.* VII,28,29). The event has already been narrated in §§31–32. Cf. Klebs, 1889: 63–65.

92 The revolt, which took place c. 334 (Hieron., *Chron., s. a.* 334, p. 233,16), was suppressed by the *censor* (not the Caesar) Dalmatius (Thphn., *Chron.,* A. M. 5825, p. 29,28–31), and the captured rebel leader was burnt alive in Tarsus. Aurelius Victor (*Caes.* 41,11–12) is probably wrong in linking the insurrection to the death of Crispus in 327. For discussion of the extant evidence on this revolt, probably led by a local brigand, see esp. Barnes, 1982: 15–16. The material from the *Origo* appears to have been the source for Polemius Silvius, *Laterculus* 63, ed. Mommsen, MGH, A. A. IX, p. 522. Cf. Klebs, 1889: 69.

93 The term King of Kings is reminiscent of the Persian title Shahanshah, and Barnes (1985: 132) has suggested that Constantine intended to install him on the Persian throne as a Christian 'King of Kings'. However, 'King of Kings' had long been part of the titulature of the kings of Pontus and Armenia, and Constantine had a much more suitable candidate in the person of the exiled Persian prince Hormisdas. Cf. Dodgeon and Lieu, 1991: 382, n. 29.

94 Including Africa. See next note.
95 On the division of the empire in the last years of Constantine's reign see Barnes, 1982: 198 and also below, pp. **147–49.**
96 On the causes of the war against Persia see Barnes, 1985: and the sources collected in Dodgeon and Lieu, 1991: 150–63.

2

CONSTANTINE'S 'PAGAN VISION'

The anonymous panegyric on Constantine (310), *Pan. Lat.* VII(6)

INTRODUCTION

Sam Lieu

Historical background

When Diocletian abdicated before the army on 1 May 305 at Nicomedia, his imperial colleague Maximianus Herculius was forced to do the same at Milan (Mediolanum) under the collegial system which saw the empire governed by two Augusti and two Caesars who were also the formers' heirs-apparent. Diocletian and Maximianus were replaced as Augusti by their Caesars, Galerius in the East and Constantius Chlorus in the West. In their place Severus and Maximinus Daia were named as Caesars – much to the chagrin of Constantine and Maxentius, the son of Maximianus, both of whom had been groomed for leadership. According to a contemporary source many wondered if Constantine's name had been changed, but Maximianus pushed aside Constantine who was standing on a platform and introduced Maximinus Daia who had shed his private attire into the centre of the *contio militum* (Lact., *Mort. pers.* 19,4). Constantine and Maxentius were not the only aggrieved party at Nicomedia; Maximianus did not seem to share his senior colleague's delight in gardening (Aur. Vict., *Caes.* 39,48 and Oros. VII,25,4) and almost immediately after his enforced retirement plotted for a return to the centre of the political stage. While Constantine fled to rejoin his father's retinue at Boulogne, Maxentius took up residence in a villa outside Rome and waited for a suitable moment to realise his dynastic ambitions.

His chance came when Constantine was saluted emperor by his

father's troops upon the latter's death on 25 July 306. This was strictly an act of usurpation because Constantius' successor as Augustus under the Tetrarchic system should have been the Caesar Severus. Constantine immediately sent a laurelled image of himself to Galerius, the senior Augustus who at that time was facing unrest in the empire, especially in Italy, because of his decision to include the urban populations under the imperial tax system. To avoid outright military confrontation, Galerius presented Constantine with the purple but granted him only the title of Caesar. This Constantine was prepared to accept for the meantime. However, if one prince could be elevated to purple by the army in blatant violation of the Tetrarchic principle of elevation by merit (although merit was clearly not much in evidence over the promotion of Severus), another one could do the same, and Maxentius seized control of the city of Rome after having won over the support of several of her urban prefects (see above, pp. 52–53). Severus was prevailed upon by Galerius to depart from Milan and recover Rome from Maxentius. The latter, fearing that his troops were inadequate for a pitched battle against Severus, called his father Maximianus out of retirement and saluted him Augustus. Maximianus wasted no time in accepting the offer (Lact., *Mort. pers.* 26,5). 307 saw Constantine and Maximianus *de facto* Augusti, and the marriage of Constantine to Fausta was finally sealed. In the event, the troops of Severus, many of whom had once served under Maximianus, deserted in large numbers. Maximianus found himself negotiating between his son and the defeated Augustus who had sought refuge behind the seemingly impregnable fortifications of Ravenna (*Anon. Vales.* 3,6; 4,9). Severus was induced to surrender and was kept as a hostage and later executed under suspicious circumstances when Galerius invaded Italy in autumn 307 (Lact., *Mort. pers.* 26,9–10, *Anon. Vales.* 4,10, Zos. II,10,2). Maximianus, however, soon discovered that the loyalty of the troops in Rome was to his son, and after failing in a public *contio* to win them over to him left Italy for Gaul (Lact., *Mort. pers.* 28.1–4 and Zonaras XII,33).

Meanwhile, Constantine had his hands full asserting control over his father's territories. Since 306 he had resumed the struggle against the Franks on the Rhine, in particular against those who had taken advantage of the events in Britain to break the truce and cross the river. It was during this campaign that he accomplished an exploit which greatly impressed his contemporaries, in which he captured the two kings of the rebelling tribes, probably the Bructeri, Ascaric and Merogaise (*Pan. Lat.* VII(6),10, see below, pp. **82–83**). Immediately after these battles a punitive expedition brought devastation to the Bructeri's country to the north of the Rhine and the Lippe. After these expeditions, in 307 or 308, the prince decided to keep open a secure route towards a fearful enemy and began the construction of a bridge at Cologne – an enterprise which had the immediate benefit of bringing about the submission of the tribes living along the banks of the river before it was finished (*Pan. Lat.* VII(6),13, trans. below, p. **84**).

In 307–8 seven emperors had, or pretended to have, the title of Augustus: Maximianus, Galerius, Constantine, Maxentius, Maximinus Daia, Licinius and, in Africa, the usurper Domitius Alexander. At a conference in 308 at Carnuntum, in which Diocletian once more took part, a final attempt was made to restore the Tetrarchy. Diocletian absolutely refused to resume control of the affairs of the State – he preferred gardening to being an emperor (*Epit. de Caes.* 39,6). Maximianus was obliged to renounce his imperial title. Galerius was confirmed as Augustus, and to replace Severus, Galerius proposed Licinius, an army officer, who was duly proclaimed emperor on 11 Nov. 308, his realm consisting of Thrace, Illyricum and Pannonia.

Constantine and Maximinus Daia remained as Caesars. In reality, Constantine and Maxentius in Rome used the title of Augustus. Although the conference resulted in discord, it seems that in public, at least, there was a show of unity; Eusebius (*H. e.* VIII,13,5) notes that Licinius was made emperor by common assent of all the emperors. Additionally, the emperors restored the Mithraeum at Carnuntum: 'To Mithras the unconquered sun(god), the protector of their rule, the Iovii and the Herculii, Augustuses [i.e. Galerius and Licinius] and Caesars [i.e. Maximinus Daia and Constantine] have restored his shrine' (*CIL* III, 4413 = *ILS* 659).

Humiliated at Carnuntum, Maximianus turned to the court of Constantine in the hope of regaining his power. To allay any suspicion, he even declined to wear his royal vestments (Lact., *Mort. pers.* 29,3). When the Franks revolted, he persuaded his son-in-law to depart first with the greater part of the army. When he thought Constantine was well inside enemy territory, he declared himself emperor (*Pan. Lat.* VII(6),16,1). However, Constantine reacted swiftly and besieged his father-in-law in Massilia and his troops gained entry to the city by winning over those who had gone over to Maximianus. The latter was duly forced to commit suicide under suspicious circumstances. (see below, p. **95.**) In the course of the same year (310), Galerius' health gave way to the first symptoms of the dreadful illness which must have carried him off the following year, in May 311. The scene is now set for the major confrontation between Constantine and Maxentius for the sole sovereignty of the West. (Cf. Demandt, 1989: 64–65.)

The panegyric of 310 and Constantine's Claudian descent

The (enforced?) suicide of Maximianus, the senior Augustus and father-in-law of Constantine, created a new problem of imperial legitimacy for Constantine. The Tetrarchic system was based in theory on election by merit and sealed by mythical links between the members of the imperial college and the deities Jove and Hercules. Heredity alone was no seal of legitimate succession. Constantius was not born to the purple and Maximianus was the only original member of the First Tetrarchy from whom Constantine could satisfactorily derive his rule. (Cf. Lippold, 1981: 360–61.) A new principle of imperial genealogy was required and this was given one of its first public hearings in a panegyric delivered by an anonymous rhetor from Autun at Trier on the anniversary of the foundation of the city in the year 310. The speech is one of seven surviving panegyrics in the so-called 'Gallic corpus' which is devoted to the celebration of specific events featuring the family of Constantine. The *Panegyrici Latini*, as the collection is commonly known, is prefaced by Pliny the Younger's panegyric on the emperor Trajan (delivered in 100 A.D.) which the Gallic rhetors had obviously used as a model. The eleven subsequent panegyrics which form the main part of the collection are devoted mainly to the period of the Tetrarchy and the early reign of Constantine. Two exceptions are Mamertinus' speech on Julian (trans. Morgan *ap.* Lieu, 1989: 13–38) and Pacatus on Theodosius the Great (trans. Nixon, 1987: 18–54). Besides the panegyric of 310 (*Pan. Lat.* VII(6), Budé numbering in Roman numerals and traditional in brackets), the speeches delivered in the period between the end of the First Tetrarchy and the rise of Julian in chronological order are:

(1) *Pan. Lat.* IV(8): Anonymous speech, delivered on the *quinquennalia* of the Caesar Constantius Chlorus (? 297), in gratitude also for the return of more secure conditions to Gaul. (Cf. Gerland, 1937: 38–39, Seager, 1983: 137–39 and Portmann, 1988: 26–28.)

(2) *Pan. Lat.* V(9): Plea of Eumenius in ?298 to the provincial governor of Lugdunensis to restore the rhetorical school at Autun. (Cf. Seager, *op. cit.*: 139–42 and Portmann, *op. cit.*: 28–30.)

(3) *Pan. Lat.* VI(7): Anonymous panegyric of 31 March 307, celebrating the marriage of Constantine to Fausta, the daughter of Maximianus, and his elevation to emperor. (Cf. Seager, *op. cit.*: 142–44, Portmann, *op. cit.*: 30–33 and esp. Nixon, 1993: 231–34.)

(4) *Pan. Lat.* VIII(5): Speech by an anonymous rhetor of Autun celebrating the *quinquennalia* of Constantine (312 or 313) and expressing gratitude for his acts of kindness to the Aeduans. (Cf. Seager, *op. cit.*: 147–49 and Portmann, *op. cit.*: 34–36.)

(5) *Pan. Lat.* IX(12): Anonymous panegyric delivered at Trier celebrating Constantine's victory over Maxentius. (Cf. Seager, *op. cit.*: 149–51 and Portmann, *op. cit.*: 36–38.)

(6) *Pan. Lat.* X(4): Panegyric of Nazarius on the *quinquennalia* of the Caesars Crispus and Constantine (II). (Cf. Seager, *op. cit.*: 152–55 and Portmann, *op. cit.*: 39–41.)

To the panegyrics in the Gallic corpus one should add the Latin poems of the pagan senator Publilius Optatianus Porfyrius which were also highly laudatory of Constantine. Porfyrius was twice briefly Praefectus Urbi (*Chron. ad 354., s. a.* 329 and 333, p. 329) and had earlier been Praeses Provinciae Achaiae (*AE* 1931, 6). He wrote from exile a cycle of twenty poems for presentation to Constantine in 324. These poems bear the title of 'Panegyricus Constantini' in the manuscripts and contain a substantial number of allusions to contemporary political and military events, especially Constantine's campaigns over the Sarmatians in 322. (Cf. Barnes, 1975.)

The panegyrics of the Gallic corpus were preserved because of their literary value and had therefore not been 're-worked' to bring them into line in the light of subsequent political developments. For this reason they are extremely valuable as documents of their time, reflecting contemporary imperial propaganda and ideals, but being delivered by rhetors who were not themselves closely connected with the imperial administration. (Cf. Nixon, 1993: 231.) As Warmington rightly reminds us:

> It is easily forgotten that the panegyrics are not proclamations for empire-wide distribution but ephemeral formalities, occasions for which would arise several times every year. Our

collection contains only a few out of many; its core of five speeches seems to have been assembled at Augustodunum [Autun] in 312, partly to celebrate the efforts of Constantius and Constantine to restore the city to its former glory, partly to preserve examples of the talents of the speakers, four of whom appear to have been teachers of rhetoric there. These speeches, with those added later, were preserved because they provided models for students (or practitioners) of rhetoric in the schools of Late Roman Gaul, not because they were historically important documents.

(Warmington, 1974: 372)

The panegyrist of 310 might have startled some of his listeners at the beginning of his speech with his assertion that the rights of Constantius' father to the imperial throne had been transferred to him by the emperor Claudius Gothicus, whose victories over the empire's barbarian invaders he recalls, and whose premature death he greatly regrets (2,1–4). Such an assumed link with an earlier dynasty would hardly have entered Diocletian's mind when he founded the Tetrarchic system in 293, and there is no evidence that Constantius Chlorus made any reference to it during his reign (*contra* Lippold, 1981: 360–69). The rhetor himself had to admit this descendancy was not very well known to the masses and knowledge of it was limited to the closest friends and supporters of Constantine. The emperor, he claims, was joined by ancestral relationship to the divine Claudius, and he implies that Constantius was no less than a son of Claudius. Such a claim would have given Constantine an imperial ancestry far older and more distinguished than that of any of his rivals.

One simple way of interpreting this claim is that Constantius Chlorus was the son of a concubine of Claudius, and Constantine himself would later style himself as a 'grandson of the Divine Claudius' in one of his inscriptions (see below). However, such a solution seems to have appeared too simple to the next generation of Roman writers. Eutropius (IX,22,1) preferred to establish the link through a daughter of Claudius who was married to the father of Constantius. As we have already seen, the anonymous author of the *Origo Constantini* (I,1) makes Constantius Chlorus a grand-nephew of Claudius. The author of a fanciful *vita* of Claudius (who claims to have written it early in the reign of Constantine but who actually wrote in the last quarter of the fourth century), begins his work with the obloquy that he was writing with all due respect for the Caesar (*sic*) Constantius (*sc.* Chlorus) (*SHA, Claud.* 1,1, see also *Gall.* 7,1; 14,3). He went as far as providing us with parts of the missing genealogy with names redolent of the Constantinian family: Claudius had a brother called Crispus (Constantine's eldest son by Minervina had the same name) who in turn had a daughter called Claudia. She married a certain Eutropius, a Dardanian (*sic*) of noble birth, and Constantius was born of their union. (*SHA, Claud.* 13,2–3.)

This link with an imperial personage in the not too distant past appears however to have been totally unknown before its 'official' disclosure in 310. The speaker himself had to apologise for springing this fact – known only to Constantine's (and why not Constantius'?) closest friends – on his listeners. The silence on this matter of Lactantius and Eusebius, the two major contemporary pro-Constantinian sources, is certainly significant. Moreover, as Syme (1974: 245–46 [1983: 70–71]) has astutely observed, in the panegyric of 298, Eumenius the panegyrist from Autun mentions an urgent appeal from the city, then besieged by the Batavii, for help from the Roman 'princeps' (i.e. Constantius) (V(9),4,1) without any further elaboration – help apparently proved to be unforthcoming – whereas the anonymous panegyrist of 310 from the same city would make great play of Constantine's imperial links (2,5; 4,2). The claim (or fraud) of royal descent therefore must have been perpetrated in the intervening years. Claudius Gothicus was a convenient choice as the object of a genealogical fraud. His reign was brief and not much was known about it except for a major victory against the Goths won near Naissus, the birth-place of Constantine. (Cf. Syme, *loc. cit.*)

Despite the uncertainties over its authenticity and the apparent discrepancies in the details of the claim itself, the Claudian descent of Constantine through his father was generally accepted from 310 onwards. It was referred to by another panegyrist who lauded the emperor after his decisive victory at the Battle of Milvian Bridge (*Pan. Lat.* VIII(5),2,5), and even as staunch a critic of Constantine as his grand-nephew Julian the Apostate (whose full name was Flavius Claudius Julianus) praised the ancestral Claudius in his panegyrics on his cousin Constantius II (6d–7a and 51c; cf. Burch, 1927: 109). In his satire the *Caesares*, Julian also ranked Claudius among the 'good emperors' whose descendants would hold power for as long as possible because of the greatness of the ancestor's spirit (313d). Coins after 313 feature the deified Claudius on the reverse with a concentration of such issues for the years 317–18 (see e.g. *RIC* VII (1966) p. 180, nos 203 and 207, both from Trier, and p. 310–11, nos 106, 109, 112, 115, 116, 119, 122, all from Rome). Curiously the epithet 'divi Claudi nepos' is rarely attested in the abundant epigraphical remains of the reign (a rare example being *CIL* XI,9 = *ILS* 699 Ravenna, post 18 Sept. 324. Cf. Grünewald, 1990: 216, no. 233). Two inscriptions (*CIL* II,4844 = Dessau 730 and III,3705 = Dessau 732) make Constantius the grandson (*pronepos*) of the deified Claudius. As a propaganda motif, the Claudian descent was used by Constantine probably only against the *parvenu* Licinius after 316. (Cf. Grünewald, 1990: 50.)

To reinforce the notion that Constantine was a scion of a distinguished line of emperors, the panegyrist took pains to show that this incomparable heredity was favoured by the gods. At the end of the part of the panegyric devoted to the exploits of Constantius, which incidentally gives the lie to the belief that Constantine was recalled from Galerius because Constantius was nearing death, the orator dwells at length upon his last campaign in Britain and represents the dying ruler as haunted by the mystery of the after-life, and wishing to go to the far north of Scotland and look upon the days when the sun never sets; a prelude to the eternal light towards which the gods are calling him. This supernatural atmosphere pervades the last days of Constantius, who even before his death was accepted into the divine ranks, where, on Jupiter's request, he designated his own son as his successor, and where the heavenly throng accepted his choice. It is highly probable that Constantine won over the support of the troops while on campaign with his father – note the support given to him by the British (?) king. The lie of the Claudian descent was unchallenged by contemporaries because it probably echoed the sentiment of a whole section of public opinion.

The usurpation of Maximianus and its suppression

Maximianus Herculius was undoubtedly the *vilain de la pièce*, the foil against which the panegyrist of 310 sets the heroic achievements of Constantine to greater advantage. Driven out of Rome and Italy by his son, Maximianus was welcomed generously at Constantine's court (most probably at Trier), surrounded with marks of respect, then he took to the road, in all likelihood for a personal residence pre-arranged with Constantine. An agreement took place between the two men in which the twice deposed emperor undertook on oath not to cause trouble in his son-in-law's territory, precautions which were necessitated by his involvements with Maxentius. A residence, probably at Arles, was also assigned to Maximianus. For it was later towards this town that Constantine's expedition turned (§18,4). One learns from Eutropius (X,2) that on arriving there Maximianus left it for the large port which would have allowed him to escape by sea to be with his son. The panegyrist says nothing about these plans and the account gives the clear impression that when Maximianus came to seek hospitality in Gaul after his break with his son, he was no longer anything more than a private citizen. No mention is made by the panegyrist of his attempt to resume the imperial title in Italy or in Gaul. Instead his need to do everything through his imperial son-in-law is stressed and it was out of the kindness of the latter that Maximianus was granted the use of the imperial transport service.

The kindness was, however, repaid by perfidy (see above). On hearing of this *coup d'état*, Constantine hastily left the campaign which he was conducting on the Rhine and hastened first to Trier and then along the military high road to Chalon-sur-Saône, and embarked his troops in this town to descend the Saône and the Rhône as far as Arles. There it was learned that the usurper had decamped to Massilia (Marseilles). Thus the army made the journey from Arles to Massilia on foot and immediately laid siege to this town. The first attack gave them possession of the port, but the assault on the ramparts of the city itself failed, because, we are told, the ladders had been made too short for the height of the walls, and above all because the emperor wished to avoid spilling Maximianus' blood in the turmoil of taking the town, and to offer the rebels a chance to deserve his clemency. In his desire to flatter his hero, the orator claims that nobody in Constantine's army listened to the old man's suggestions for clemency and that in this his men showed the impartiality of true philosophers. Such remarks contradict Constantine's decision to capture Marseilles by force and the clemency which he showed to those who had surrendered whom he believed to have been led astray. The account finishes with the statement that a number of stubborn men refused to take advantage of the prince's generosity and that the gods avenged him nevertheless.

The panegyrist of 310 thus had the delicate task of publishing a father-in-law's crimes in front of his son-in-law, and one which he did not begin until he had sought the emperor's sign of approval (14,1). He was probably aware that it was only three years before that Maximianus was lauded as the senior statesman in a partnership

forged by the marriage between Constantine and his daughter
Fausta. Constantine then was depicted merely as a young ruler
emerging (*oriens imperator*) from the shadow of his father's military
achievements (*Pan. Lat.* VI(7),1, cf. Nixon, 1993: 238–39). The
second panegyrist did everything he could not to burden the memory
of the deceased with accusations, proffering the excuses of an age
which no longer had a very healthy outlook, and referring oppor-
tunely to the theory of the philosophers who saw an inescapable
destiny as the cause of human crimes. To make his blatantly feeble
arguments seem more convincing he unfolds before his audience
some scenes from that tragedy. In providing 'hot news' (cf. Nixon,
1983: 93) for his audience he also furnished the modern historian with
a major source for the period of Constantine's rise to power which
is otherwise inadequately treated in contemporary sources.

In military terms, this siege of Massilia was a failure; the author
partly concedes this – the ladders were apparently too short – while
attributing the greater share of it to imperial magnanimity. It is a pity,
however, given the scarcity of contemporary documents or their
contradiction, that the panegyrist did not shed more light on the
events from the point of view of Maximianus and particularly on the
events which led to his suicide. According to Lactantius (*Mort. pers.*
30,2–5), he attempted to involve his daughter Fausta in the plot,
asking her to see that Constantine's bed-chamber was left unguarded.
A eunuch was substituted in Constantine's bed-chamber and Maximianus was allowed to enter. The moment that Maximianus murdered
the eunuch, Constantine appeared and rebuked his father-in-law for
his action. Maximianus was duly forced to take his own life (probably
at Arles) before the end of July 310. The panegyrist of 310 has
undoubtedly played down Maximianus' multifarious activities, and
the only plot which he chose to remember must have taken place not
before but after Massilia was besieged and the pardon obtained.

The pagan vision (?) of Constantine

On his way either to or back from Massilia, Constantine received
news of the final collapse of the barbarian uprising on the Rhine. The
news was conveyed at the precise point of the journey at which there
was a road leading to a sanctuary of Apollo described by the
panegyrist as 'the most beautiful temple in the whole world'. It was
there, according to the panegyrist in the climactic part of his speech,
that the god himself appeared to the emperor, accompanied by

Victory, and both held out crowns of laurel to him, each of which brought him an omen of thirty years. The panegyrist was categorical that Constantine personally 'saw' (*vidisti*) the pair of gods and the account of the vision was not simply pure adulation or an oratorical fantasy designed to boost the reputation of the sanctuary. This first recorded and purely pagan religious experience of Constantine has been seen by some modern scholars as 'the only authentic vision of Constantine, the legend of the vision of 312 being nothing but a Christian distortion'. (See esp. Grégoire, 1930/31: 256–57 and Piganiol, 1932: 51.) The pagan vision also implies an element of self-admission on the part of the emperor in the same manner as the account of the 'Christian' vision was confided to Eusebius by Constantine, but long after the event itself:

Constantine also considered the fact that he would need more powerful aid than military might could give him, since the tyrant [i.e. Maxentius] was making great efforts to obtain evil arts and deceitful magic spells. He sought a god to be his helper and depended on the soldiers and size of the army only in second place. For he thought that that was of no use anyway without the help of a god. He considered divine aid to be invincible and unconquerable. So now he thought seriously about which god he should enlist as helper, and it crossed his mind that most previous rulers had put their hopes in several gods when they came to power and had worshipped them with offerings of wine, sacrifices and votive offerings. Having been initially deceived by positive prophecies and oracles that promised good auspices, they did not, however, come to an auspicious end. Not one of the gods had stood by them to protect them from the ruin which was destined by heaven. Only his father had taken the opposite way, had rejected their error and all his life had worshipped that God, who is enthroned over all, and had found Him to be saviour and protector of the kingdom and giver of all good things. He thought about this to himself and fully considered that they had put their trust in a great number of gods and thus had come to great disaster, so that nothing was left either of their generation or their family, not a root, nor a name nor a memory among men. But his father's God had given his father very many clear signs of His might. He went on to reflect that those who had already waged war against the tyrant and had dared to go into battle trusting in their many gods had come to a shameful end. For example, one of them had withdrawn from the encounter in disgrace without achieving his aim, the other was killed in the midst of his soldiers and so became death's subject. After he had thought about all this, he would have considered it stupid to waste time on gods which do not exist, and to be seduced by error even after such obvious proof. He believed rather, that he must worship only his father's God.

So in prayer he called upon this God, asking and pleading with Him that He might reveal who He was and offer him His right hand in his forthcoming undertaking. While the emperor prayed thus, pleading fervently, a quite incredible divine sign appeared to him, which perhaps would not be easy to believe, if anyone else had told of it. But since I [Eusebius], who have produced this writing, heard it from the victorious emperor himself a long time ago, when I was honoured with his acquaintance and his company, and he swore on his word with oaths, who would have second thoughts about believing the account? And more particularly so since the following time provided confirmation of his word. About midday, when the day was already on the wane, he said he saw with his very eyes the victorious sign of the cross composed of light situated above the sun and linked to it the writing: 'By this conquer!' Upon this vision, I am told, astonishment seized both him and the whole army, which was marching with him to somewhere and saw the miracle.

(Eusebius, *V.C.* I,27–28)

Both visions are associated with military victory, the former in the guise of divine congratulation for the emperor's achievements to date and an oracle of greater ones to come, and the second a promise of victory which promises not only the triumph of a just rule over tyranny but also that of true religion over false oracles and divinations. While accounts of the Christian vision based on that of Eusebius are found in many later sources (e.g. Soc., *H. e.* I,2,4–5; Soz., *H. e.* I,3–4 (closely based on Eus., *V. C.* I,27–30); *AP* 45, below pp. **241–42**, Ruf., *H. e.* IX,9,1–3 (= Aufhauser 1911, no. 4); Philost., *H. e.* I,6, p. 7, 3–7; *Chron. Pasch.*, *s. a.* 311, p. 520,18–21; Thphn., *Chron.* A.M. 5802, p. 14,1–8; Zon. XIII,1,10; Niceph., *H. e.* VIII,3, *PG* 146.16B, etc.), the panegyric of 310 is the only extant account of this incident which features in no other source whether pagan, Christian or Byzantine. Constantine never referred to the incident in his orations or letters as recorded by Eusebius and it would of course have been inappropriate for an emperor who devoted so much of his energy to ecclesiastical affairs to invoke Apollo and Victoria as his guardian deities. As the panegyric of 310 was clearly the most propagandistic of the extant panegyrics on Constantine, questions are inevitably asked about the purpose of the inclusion of this pagan epiphany.

The most often adduced reason for the panegyrist's apparent desire to forge a link between Constantine and Apollo was the putative need for a new patron deity for the new Claudian dynasty now that the cult of Hercules, the eponymous god of the Herculian dynasty, had been dragged into disrepute by the murky events leading to the death of Maximianus Herculius. Claudius II it was who had the sun represented on the obverse of his coins, and Constantius and his son both favoured a kind of solar monotheism. From 310 onwards the figure of Hercules disappeared from Constantinian coinage and gave way to the radiant bust of Sol Invictus. While offerings and honours with which Constantine filled the sanctuary of Apollo are evidence of Constantine's own pagan belief, one is inevitably tempted to speculate that in this search for a new tutelary monotheism are the signs of certain anxieties which will one day lead the emperor to Christianity.

The identification of the Roman emperor with the Sun has a long history. Caligula and Nero were both proclaimed Neos Helios. Nero also erected outside his Golden House a colossal statue of Sol Apollo with a radiant crown. The emperor Aurelian was a devotee of the Syrian cult of Sol Invictus, which was also embraced by a number of philosophers who used the sun as the bridge to the transcendant. A magnificent temple was erected to Sol on the Agrippae and its dedication day (*natalis*) was 25 December. Apollo was also similarly honoured in Rome, as Ammianus mentions (XXIII,3,3) a temple dedicated to him on the Palatine which was consumed by the fire of 363 that nearly destroyed the Sibylline Books kept in the pedestal of the statue. In the third century the dedicatory inscriptions to Sol, Apollo and Mithras were sometimes interchangeable but it was Sol and never Apollo who appeared as the divine protector of Constantine. In any case the need for changing from Hercules to Apollo as the dynastic god was hardly pressing as epigraphical and numismatic evidence shows that Constantine did not appear to have embraced the divine protector of his father-in-law as his own. Apollo as distinct from Sol Invictus also did not feature on Constantine's coins as his divine *comes*. Moreover, the question which temple of

Apollo Constantine visited matters in our speculation. The location by most modern scholars is Grand (Vosges) on the border between Belgica and Germania Superior. The worship of Apollo-Grannus, which had flourished along the Rhine since the High Empire, was the Romanised version of the healing cult of Grannus which was centred round medicinal springs – hence the reference in the panegyric of 310 to 'steaming fountain springs' (§22). Patients practised incubation and, as is common with many of the healing cults in antiquity, visions of the deity's epiphany played an important role in the healing process. There is therefore a strong likelihood that Constantine visited the Apollo sanctuary for no other reason than to enjoy a 'Kur', as do many modern Europeans. If the visit took place before the siege of Massilia, then it would have been entirely appropriate for Constantine to stop at the sanctuary to pray for victory and be reassured of it by what he witnessed there while deep in prayer. The laudatory motifs in the account of the vision echo Vergil's equation of Augustus with Apollo in his Fourth *Eclogue* (see below, p. **95**) and are intended to mark the beginning of a new golden age with Constantine as a 'young emperor, blessed, our saviour and a most handsome one' (*imperator iuvenis et laetus et salutifer et pulcherrimus*) replacing the gerontocrats of the Tetrarchy. It might have been purely a gesture to the Gallic aristocracy and to local pride. Constantine took it as no more than the panegyrical embroidery of his fascination with or admiration of the temple of Apollo-Grannus, and probably promptly forgot all about it as he appears to have mentioned the incident to no one else. (Cf. Kraft, 1955: 10–14, n. 1, Barnes, 1981: 36, Grünewald, 1990: 50–54, Rodgers, 1980: *passim*, Müller-Rettig, 1990: 330–50 and Warmington, 1974: 377–78.)

Authorship and editions

The author is anonymous but we can infer from the panegyric that he was not a young man as he was already the father of five sons and one of them was in the upper echelons of the imperial civil service (§23,1–3). He was a native of Autun (§22), the venue of an important school of rhetoric in late Antiquity.

The edition of the *XII Panegyrici Latini* used for this translation is the Edition Budé of E. Galletier, *Panégyriques Latins* II (VI-X) (Paris, 1952) 54–74. The editions of V. Paladini and P. Fedeli (*Scriptores Graeci et Latini consilio Academiae Lynceorum editi*,

Rome, 1976) and Sir R. Mynors (Oxford, 1964) have been consulted with profit and some of the principal divergences are noted in the commentary. The excellent German translation with comprehensive commentary of the panegyric by Müller-Rettig (1990) has been a constant source of help and guidance especially on topographical matters and on bibliography. I am privileged to have been given access to the still unpublished major work of C. E. V. Nixon and B. S. Rodgers which contains a translation of eleven of the twelve Latin panegyrics, and I have benefited much from its extensive commentary.

THE ANONYMOUS PANEGYRIC ON CONSTANTINE (310), *PAN. LAT.* VII(6)
translated by Mark Vermes

1 I would act, most saintly Emperor,[1] as a while ago many people urged me to, since your majesty had given me in my mediocrity this day the most solemn in this city[2] to make my speech, and base my speech's introduction on that very fact, were it not that a two-fold reason dissuaded me from doing so, when I reflect that a man in middle age ought not to display a sudden oratorical ability, and that nothing not written at length and often revised should be brought before the hearing of such a divine presence. 2. Anyone who improvises a speech before the emperor of the Roman people does not realise how great the empire is. 3. Added to this is the fact that plenty of people think I will speak for too long, and they make this judgement, I suppose, not because of my intellect which is limited, but because of the copious supply of your laudable qualities. I shall fail to meet their expectations, albeit unwillingly, with the brevity of my speech. Indeed I had planned a longer speech, but I prefer my speech to be short than to be rejected through tedium. 4. So first I shall make this abridgement because, although I look upon all of you, invincible rulers whose majesty is harmonious and unified, with the veneration that is due to you, yet I shall devote this little speech only to your divinity, Constantine. 5. For just as with the immortal gods themselves, though we worship them all in our hearts, sometimes we venerate them individually in their own temple and home, so too I think it is right for me to remember all leaders in pious respect, but to adorn with my praises the one who is present.

2 I shall begin with the first deity in your ancestry, which most people are perhaps still ignorant of, though those who love you know very

well. 2. For you are joined by ancestral relationship to that divine Claudius[3] who was the first to restore the lax and ruinous discipline of the Roman empire,[4] and who destroyed on land and sea[5] the vast hordes of Goths[6] who had burst through the straits of the Black Sea and the mouth of the Danube.[7] Would that he had stayed longer to revitalise mankind than passed too soon to join the gods! 3. Although that most happy day which we have recently commemorated is counted as the anniversary of your emperorship, since it first saw you decorated with that honour, yet it was from Claudius the founder of your family that the destiny of empire descended upon you. 4. Moreover that ancient prerogative of the imperial family elevated your own father, so that you too would stand in the highest rank above human necessities, as the third emperor following two others in your family. 5. Among all the factors which contribute to your sovereignty, Constantine, I avow, is especially the fact that you were born an emperor, and such is the nobility of your ancestry that the emperorship added no honour to you, nor could fortune attribute to your divinity that which is yours already, without the need for canvassing or electioneering.

3 It was no accidental agreement among men nor any sudden wind of favour that made you emperor, but you deserved the emperorship by your birth.[8] 2. Indeed it seems to me to be the first and greatest gift from the immortal gods, to enter upon life blessed from the start, and to accept as a family heirloom those things which others scarcely achieve by a lifetime of hard work. 3. Certainly a considerable felicity, worthy of admiration, is shown by those who serve out appointments in succession, and step up the ranks of the military and reach the top rung of command, and depending only on the supports of virtue have the strength to reach the very height of power. Indeed you too followed this path, as soon as you were old enough,[9] and although fortune had placed you beyond all obstacles to the acquisition of glory, you chose to advance through military service, and by facing the dangers of war and joining battle with the enemy even in single combat,[10] you made yourself more notable to all peoples, though you could not have been more noble. It is, as I say, a great achievement to set out relying on oneself and attain the heights of power. 4. But it is one thing to struggle up the steep slopes and reach the mountain ridges from the plain, and quite a different thing to find the peak of fortune resting on the very eminence of one's birth and to own, rather than yearn for, the position at the top.

4 You entered that sacred palace not as a candidate for the emperor-ship, but as emperor-elect, and straightaway your father's Lares saw you as the legitimate successor. 2. For without doubt the inheritance belonged to the first son that the fates had given to the emperor. For it was you that the great emperor on earth, and god in the sky, had fathered in the first flower of his manhood, while he was still at the height of his physical powers and possessed of that dynamism and valour which so many wars witnessed, especially on the fields of Vindonissa.[11] 3. That is why such a physical resemblance passed from him to you that it seems impressed on your features by nature's own mark. 4. For it is the same countenance that we venerate a second time in you, the same dignity on your brow, the same tranquillity in your eyes and voice. In the same way your complexion is a sign of your reserve, and your conversation evidence of your integrity. 5. Accept, Emperor, this ambivalent avowal of our sensibilities: we are sorry that Constantius has left us but, so long as we see you, we cannot believe that he has left us. 6. And yet why do I say that 'he has left', when his immortal achievements live on and are com-memorated on the lips and in the eyes of all mankind?

5 Who is there that – I won't say doesn't remember – but doesn't still see in some way the achievements with which Constantius enlarged and embellished the empire? 2. When he was granted his first command, by his very arrival he barred access to the Ocean which was seething with an enormous enemy fleet.[12] That army which had occupied the coast of Boulogne he hemmed in both by land and sea at the same time, after obstructing the ebb and flow of the tides by placing dams among the waves, with the result that where previously the water had washed against their gates, they now had lost access to the sea which they neighboured.[13] 3. He captured that army by his valour and spared it through his mercy, while prepara-tions were made for the reconquest of Britain by building fleets.[14] He purged of every enemy the land of Batavia which was occupied by various Frankish tribes under a former inhabitant. Not content to have defeated them, he transported the very tribes into Roman territory so that they would be obliged to lay down not only their arms but also their savagery. 4. What can I say about the recovery of Britain? He sailed there with such a calm sea[15] that it seemed the Channel, amazed at such a traveller, had lost its power to move. And his journey was such that Victory did not accompany him, but awaited him there.[16]

6 What am I to say of the clemency whereby he spared the vanquished? Or of the justice whereby he restored what they had lost to the plundered? Or of the foresight with which he acted as judge among the allies on his side, so that those who had suffered subjection were cheered by the recovery of liberty, while those with a guilty conscience were brought to repentance by their pardon? 2. What need is there to mention again those tribes deep in Frankish territory which were torn, not now from the areas once invaded by the Romans, but from their own original locations, from the furthest shores of the barbarian world, and established in empty regions of Gaul, so as to contribute to the peace of the Roman empire by their agriculture and to provide recruits for the army? 3. Why should I recall the victory at Lingonica[17] which was made famous by the wound received by the emperor himself? 4. Or the fields of Vindonissa filled with slaughtered enemies and to this day strewn with bones?[18] Why recall that huge multitude of different peoples of Germany? The frozen Rhine had enticed them to dare to cross to an island, surrounded by a fork in the river, with a force of infantry. Suddenly the river melted and shut them off. At once boats were despatched and they were blockaded and forced to surrender, and, all the more awkwardly, by a lottery which involved them all to choose whom they would hand over to captivity. So they would return with their remaining troops and the ignominy of betrayal of their own people.

7 The day would finish before my speech did, if I were to enumerate all the achievements of your father even as briefly as so far. That final expedition of his was not in search of mere trophies from Britain, as was commonly believed; but now that the gods were summoning him to them, he advanced to the furthest outpost of the earth. 2. After so many magnificent achievements he did not deign to conquer the woods and marshes[19] of the Caledonians and other Picts,[20] I am sure, nor yet Hibernia close at hand, nor distant Iceland[21] nor even the Isles of the Blest, if indeed they exist. But, though he would admit it to nobody, as he was now about to go to the gods, he intended to look upon that father of the gods who rekindles the fiery stars of heaven: the Ocean. As he was about to enjoy the everlasting light above, he intended now to see on earth the almost never-ending daylight. 3. Truly, the temples of the gods opened for him and he was admitted into the assembly of the immortals, as Jupiter himself offered a welcoming hand. Moreover straightaway when asked his opinion as to whom he would declare emperor, he spoke as befitted Constantius the Pious. 4. Most clearly you were elected by the declaration of your father, O Emperor. Truth bids us state this, while it is also most appropriate to your own filial piety, I consider. But why pay homage only to your personal attachments, when that was the declaration of all the gods, who had long since signified their authority, even though only now was it confirmed by their full council? 5. For you were first summoned by divine decree to save the empire, at the time when your father was sailing for Britain, and as the fleet was setting sail, your sudden arrival gave them splendour. It seemed you had not travelled by public means of transport, but had flown in on some chariot of the gods.

8 No Persian or Cretan arrow has ever reached its target with so sure an aim as your timely arrival to join your father when he was about to depart this earth. By the assurance of your presence you soothed all the anxieties which quietly troubled his watchful intellect. 2. Ye gods, what happiness you granted Constantius the Pious even at his hour of departure! The emperor, ready to make his journey to Heaven,[22] saw the heir he was leaving behind. For, the moment he was released from earthly life, the whole army gave its approval to you, the minds and eyes of all marked you out, and even though you had consulted the senior authorities as to their decision about the leadership, everyone else's enthusiasm anticipated the subsequent considered approval of those authorities. 3. The first time your presence gave an opportunity, the soldiers threw the imperial purple upon you, despite your tears, ministering to public interest rather than your own feelings. For it was not right to weep any longer for an emperor who had been consecrated as a god. 4. It is reported, invincible Emperor, that you tried to escape that enthusiasm of the army which claimed you, by spurring onwards your horse. This was, to tell you the truth, an error of youth.[23] 5. No Centaur or Pegasus could have rescued you whom empire was attending. That sovereignty, I say again, which was granted by the will of Jupiter, and not entrusted to Iris the messenger goddess but to the wings of Victory, descended on you as easily as the messages from Heaven swiftly reach the earth. 6. And so your modesty and piety were demonstrated by your attempt to postpone the emperorship, but overwhelmed by the good fortune of the State.

9 How happy is Britain, and more blessed now than all other countries, that first saw Constantine as Caesar! 2. Deservedly did

Nature bestow on you all the advantages of climate and soil. There is neither excessive chill in winter nor heat in summer. The crops are fertile enough to supply the two-fold gifts of Ceres and Bacchus. There are no monstrous beasts in the forests, or deadly snakes on the ground, but on the contrary an immense profusion of tame animals with udders full of milk, or loaded with fleeces. 3. The main reason why life is loved is that the days are very long and no nights are without a little light, as the level extremity of those shores does not throw up shadows, and a view of the sky and its stars overcomes the limit of the night, so that whereas the sun itself seems to us to set, over there it appears to pass along the horizon. 4. Gods above, why is it that always from some furthermost boundary of the earth come new manifestations of the gods to be venerated by the whole world? Thus did Mercury from the river Nile, whose source is not known, and thus did Bacchus from India, practically the place where the sun rises, present themselves as powerful gods to mortals. 5. Assuredly, places neighbouring the sky are more sacrosanct than areas in the middle of the lands, and from there, closer to the gods, where the earth ends, was sent our emperor.

10 So then, as son of an emperor, and such a great emperor, and you yourself having attained the emperorship so felicitously, how did you set about defending the State? A band of barbarians had despicably, in my opinion, made trial of the first stages of your rise to power by a sudden attack and unexpected banditry, and you imposed on them the penalty for their audacity. 2. The actual kings in Frankish territory had taken advantage of the absence of your father to violate the peace, but you did not hesitate to punish them with the severest penalties, dreading neither the everlasting hatred nor the inexpiable wrath of that nation. 3. For why should an emperor worry about any offence caused by a warranted severity, when he can maintain his actions? 4. It is folly[24] to show clemency by sparing one's enemies and considering one's own position rather than showing genuine pardon. Whereas the enemy may hate you, Constantine, as much as they want, provided they tremble. True valour is to ensure that those who do not like you are peaceful. Perhaps it is more circumspect to keep one's enemies chained by pardoning them, but it is braver to trample them down when they are vexed. 5. You restored, Emperor, that former loyalty to the Roman empire established by exacting the death penalty from captive enemy leaders. 6. For in former times captive kings attended

to embellish the processions of generals in triumph all the way from the gates to the Forum, but as soon as the general had turned his carriage towards the Capitol, the captives were taken off to prison and executed. 7. Only ever one man, Perseus, when Paullus himself who had accepted his surrender vouchsafed for him, avoided that severe law.[25] All others were enchained and executed, and gave other kings a lesson to prefer to cultivate friendship with Rome than to provoke her justice. Inflicting the proper penalty on one's enemies also brings the advantage that not only do one's foes never dare to rebel, but also one's friends show more serious respect.

11 So that is the source, Emperor, of the peace which we now enjoy. No longer are we protected by the currents of the Rhine, but by the terror inspired by your name. Whether the Rhine dries up in the heat of summer, or solidifies with ice, in neither case will the enemy dare to make use of the crossing. 2. In fact there is no insuperable barrier erected by nature that cannot be scaled by audacity, if someone hopes still to achieve something by the attempt. But an insurmountable wall is built by a reputation for valour. 3. The Franks know they can cross the Rhine, and you would gladly let them come to their destruction, but they can hope for neither victory nor clemency. They can gauge the fate awaiting them from the penalties inflicted on their kings, and so far from planning a crossing of that river, they are instead full of despair because of the bridge that has been started. 4. Where now is that ferocity? Where is your constantly treacherous inconstancy? Now you dare not dwell even at a distance from the Rhine, and hardly feel safe when you drink the waters of the rivers within your territory. 5. Whereas on our side the forts placed at intervals serve more to adorn than to protect the frontier. That once fearsome bank is ploughed by weaponless farmers, and our cattle bathe in all the 'two-pronged river'. Thanks to the punishment of Ascaricus and Merogaisus this victory of yours, Constantine, lasts for today and all time, and takes pride of place before all earlier military successes. A single victory is won by battle, but an example lasts for ever. 6. Most people take no notice of their own defeat, however many people die, so the shortest route to subdue the enemy once and for all is to do away with their leaders.

12 You carried devastation into the land of the Bructeri,[26] and so brought it about that the savagery of the barbarians would be shattered in every way, and that the enemy would lament not only

the punishment of their own kings. 2. Invincible Emperor, the first purpose in this plan of yours was to convey the army across suddenly and attack them unawares, not because you lacked confidence in open warfare (since you would have preferred a pitched battle), but so that this tribe, which often avoided fighting by taking refuge in woods and marshes, would lose the opportunity for flight. 3. And so countless enemy were slaughtered, and very many captured. All their cattle were seized or butchered, all their villages burnt. The adult men who fell into your hands, because their treachery made them unfitted for military service, and their ferocity made them unsuited to subservience, were made to pay the penalty in a public show, and exhausted by their very numbers the bloodthirsty wild beasts. This is what it means, Emperor, to rely on one's valour and fortune, this means not purchasing peace by clemency, but seeking victory by endeavour.

13 Furthermore by building the bridge at Agrippinensis,[27] you defy the remnants of that defeated tribe, and compel them never to abandon their fears, but to be in constant terror, and to keep outstretched their hands in submission. However, you are doing this more for the glory of your empire and to embellish the frontier, than to create an opportunity to cross into enemy territory whenever you wish. For the whole of the Rhine is equipped with warships[28] and all its banks as far as the North Sea are garrisoned by troops ready to strike. 2. Yet it seems to you a splendid idea – and indeed it is most splendid – that this Rhine not only in its higher reaches, where it is either fordable by its width or narrow because of its proximity to its source, but also at the place where it is at its fullest, should be straddled by a new bridge. Here it has absorbed many tributaries brought in by the great river on our side and by the Neckar and the Main on the barbarian's side, and surging along with its vast current and unable to contain itself within one channel, it bursts irrepressibly into its two branches. 3. To be sure, Constantine, nature herself serves to enhance your divine purpose, since in that depth of water foundations of such size must be laid that they will have a reliable and secure stability. 4. Perhaps the all-powerful king of Persia did once link the straits of the Hellespont by stringing his fleet across; but that crossing was temporary.[29] With a similar chain of ships the second Caesar after Augustus traversed the bay of Baiae; but that crossing was a mere whim of a decadent emperor. Whereas this structure is both difficult to build and will be used for all time to

come. 5. Certainly it brought you at its inception the submission of the enemy, who came in supplication for peace and offered well-born hostages. So no one can doubt what they will do when the bridge is complete, if they are so servile when it is only just started.

14 While you were involved in these operations to benefit and enhance the empire, your attention was distracted by the rebellious manoeuvres of a man who above all should have regarded your successful achievements with favour.[30] I am still not at all sure how to speak about this man, and I am awaiting advice by a gesture from your divinity. 2. For however much he is deservedly convicted on charges of neglecting his duty towards you, yet the voice of an individual should exercise restraint, especially since even though he is a man who has remained ungrateful to you after such great kindnesses and such favourable treatment by your family, nevertheless consideration for you compels us to respect him, however angry we may be. 3. What can I do then to handle delicately such deep wounds? Forsooth I shall make use of that familiar vindication of all crimes which is generally accepted even by the philosophers, that no man sins except by destiny, and that the very misdeeds of mortals are acts of fate, while on the other hand their virtues are gifts of the gods. 4. Give thanks, Constantine, to nature and to your own character that you were sired by Constantius the Pious, and fashioned by the will of the stars, so as not to have it in your power to be cruel. 5. Whereas he, I can scarcely believe, when he was about to come to being and faced the choice of life that he would lead, fell upon a lot that he should have shunned and which would bring wrongful death to many men, and at the last his own death, self-willed upon himself. 6. For, to pass over the other points, wasn't it inevitable fate that brought it about that he owed this obligation to your sense of duty, when, expelled from Rome, exiled from Italy and banished from Illyricum, you had sheltered him in your provinces, among your troops and in your palace?

15 What did he want, I ask you? What did he hope for? To obtain something greater than what he had acquired from you? You had given him the greatest and most contrasting gifts: the leisure of a private citizen and the wealth of a king. When he went out he had mules and carriages from the court, and you had instructed us to service his requirements even more urgently than your own. You had determined to obey all his orders so much so that the accoutrements of empire were with you, while he had the real power. 2. So what was that enormity – not a passion for power, for what power did he not have while you were emperor? – but an aberration of advancing senility, which inspired him at such a great age to undertake the most troublesome burden of a civil war? 3. The truth is that no bene-factions of fortune satisfy men whose lusts are not limited by reason, and their good fortune flows by without appreciation, so they remain always full of hope but bereft of pleasures, and miss the present while anticipating the future. 4. Whereas that divine individual,[31] who was the first both to share and to lay aside the emperorship, does not regret either his decision or his deed, and does not consider he has lost that which he voluntarily transferred. He is happy and truly blessed in that your respects and those of great leaders attend him even now he is retired. 5. He relies on an empire with many supports and is happy to be protected by your aegis, when he knows you have grown from his stock, and he rightfully claims your glories for himself. 6. The other one who had been accepted as a brother by him, did not see fit to imitate him, but regretted having sworn the oath to him in the temple of Capitoline Jupiter. I am not surprised that he also forswore his son-in-law.

16 So much for his word, and so much for his oath sworn in the sanctuary of the sacred Palatine. He completed his journey slowly and tentatively, already no doubt with those plans of war in mind, and emptying the supplies of the staging posts so that no army could follow him. Then suddenly he established himself within four walls, clothed in imperial purple, and for a third time took up the emperorship that he had twice laid aside. He sent letters to allure the armies, and tried to undermine the soldiers' loyalty by a display of bribes – no doubt he thought he would have safe use of an army that he had taught corruption! 2. In fact the only thing demonstrated by his aberration, Emperor, was the strength of your soldiers' affection towards you. They preferred you to all the gifts that he had promised, and all his proffered honours. 3. That rare virtue of restraint has been preserved with difficulty, but at times, by a few practitioners of philosophy; but because of you, Constantine, it has become a common virtue among all men. Not only men mellowed by their reason, their education or their quiet life, but even valiant military hearts have scorned gain through their respect for you.[32] 4. Maybe there have been other armies comparable to yours in mobility and strength, but only you have been privileged to have an army of wise men. 5. Perhaps in the past many degenerate leaders with inferior armies have competed by means of bribery, but their popularity was brief and fleeting, and any imitator easily vanquished them. 6. The strong and lasting guardian of the State is the one whom the soldiers love on his own account, and who enjoys not a feigned or purchased adulation, but a straightforward and genuine devotion. 7. Your gifts, Constantine, are manifestly welcome to the soldiers, but all the more welcome because they are yours. 8. Anything offered by your hand becomes more acceptable. No one can hope to compete with you in popularity! It is an unbeatable type of largesse, when the emperor himself is the soldier's reward. 9. And so you award your armies more than they desire, but what gives you greater approval is your name, your authority which derives from your father's memory, the appeal of your age, and above all your captivating appearance.

17 For it is a splendid and heaven-sent miracle, by the gods, to have a young emperor whose valour is at its height but is still increasing, and whose brilliant gaze and majestic appearance, equally admirable and attractive, both dazzle and draw everyone's attention. 2. I imagine that great king was like that, and the Thessalian hero,[33] whose supreme valour is renowned to have matched their beauty. 3. For scholars are right to claim that nature herself allots to great souls bodies worthy to accommodate them, and that from a man's appearance and physical attractiveness one can assess the type of divine spirit that has entered to dwell there. And so as soon as the soldiers see you approaching, they admire you and love you, they follow you with their eyes, keep you in their minds, and think they are obeying a god whose presence is as fine as his divinity is assured.

18 So the moment they had heard about that dreadful crime, of their own accord they asked you for the signal to depart. While you were giving them their provisions, they said that it was causing them delay, and that they already had more than enough from your generosity. 2. Then they seized their arms and made for the gates, and completed a journey of so many days from the Rhine all the way to the Saône without any rest: their bodies tireless, their hearts aflame, their passion for vengeance growing each day the closer they approached.[34] 3. Next, your concern, Emperor, in providing boats from the harbour at Chalon to replenish their strength, almost failed to please them in their haste. That sluggish and loitering river seemed never to have been slower; as their vessels glided silently along and the banks

receded slowly, they shouted that they were standing still, not moving. 4. Then they began to use their hands instead of feet and fell upon the oars, and by their effort overcame the nature of the river. 4. When at last they had surmounted the delays of the Saône, they were hardly happy with the Rhône itself: it seemed to them to be flowing with little urgency and to be advancing towards Arles with less haste than usual. 5. Well, to be brief, I must confess, Emperor, that for all your bodily vigour and all your mental energy you struggled at times to keep up with the army that you were supposed to be leading. 6. For they were all carried along with such momentum that, when they found out that he had left Arles and gone off to Marseilles, they immediately flew out of the ships and in headlong haste outstripped no longer the currents of the Rhône, but even the very blasts of the wind. 7. Such an affection for your divinity had inflamed them that although they knew they had to assault a very well-fortified city, they thought it was enough to arrive there.

19 For Marseilles, so I gather, juts out into a deep sea, and is equipped with a well-fortified harbour, where the sea to the south flows in by a narrow passage. It is joined to the land by an isthmus of only 1,500 yards,[35] which is protected by a very solid wall with many towers. 2. Indeed the Greeks and Italians, who were the original settlers there,[36] despite their technological and intellectual prowess, were taught by the place itself how to arrange more profitably in the part which was accessible the requirements for defence, since nature had spared them the expense of fortifications in the other places. 3. And so at the time when the city, to its detriment, closed its gates to Caesar on behalf of the elder leader, siege engines were brought up by land and sea, earthworks were constructed,[37] and it was attacked in frequent naval engagements without any alarm being caused; barely did an inordinately long siege force the city to open its gates, after a few Greek officials had repulsed both Caesar himself and then his generals and their forces, not so much by their own strength as by their walls. 4. But on this occasion at your first approach, Emperor, and at the first attack of your army, neither the height of the walls of this self-same Marseilles, nor its serried towers, nor yet the character of the place caused you any delay in capturing both the harbour and the city straight away after, if you wanted. 5. In fact the soldiers had attacked all along the wall with such confidence that they would beyond doubt have immediately climbed it, if while preparing the ladders to bring up to it they had not guessed the wrong height

when observing it. 6. But even so, many of them, though deceived by the inadequate height of their ladders, tried to cover the remaining distance to climb by stretching out their bodies, and by stepping on the shoulders of the men behind them they had just reached the gaps in the battlements with grasping hands. In carrying out their plan of vengeance they feared no danger, with the result that they thought they were not climbing a wall, but fighting on level ground.

20 What extraordinary probity you showed, Constantine, by observing the proprieties even in the thick of battle. By giving the signal for withdrawal you deferred your victory so that you would have the opportunity to pardon them all, and so that no soldier would commit in anger an atrocity out of keeping with your natural clemency. 2. Although by doing so you showed the concern of an excellent emperor, that soldiers who had been led astray should obtain a period of contrition and voluntarily sue for pardon, yet we who observe your gentler sensibilities – and there is nothing more manifest than the virtue in your heart – we realise that you spared that man, whom, if the first offensive had reached him, no one could have saved from the sword. 3. And so, as far as your own piety is concerned, Emperor, you preserved both him and all his band of followers. 4. It was his own fault if anyone refused to take advantage of your kindness and deemed himself unworthy to live, when you had given him permission to live.[38] For your part, which satisfies your conscience, you spared even those who were undeserving. But, please pardon my phrase, you cannot do everything: the gods avenge you despite yourself.[39]

21 Indeed we must always hope that you will meet with successes even beyond your own prayers. For we place all our hope in the bosom of your sovereignty and we seek everywhere your presence, as if it could be granted. 2. For example, during the short period of your absence from the frontier, what alarms were spread abroad by the treachery of the barbarians! No doubt they were asking themselves: 'When will he get there? When will he win? When will he bring back his weary army?' But when they heard of your sudden return, they subsided as if shocked, so that anxiety did not disturb your devotion to the State for longer than one night. 3. For, the day after you had heard that news and doubled the daily route-march, you learnt that all the waves of rebellion had calmed, and all the tranquillity you had left there had returned. Fortune herself so

ordered this that the felicity of your situation reminded you to bring what you had vowed to the immortal gods, in the very place where you had already made a detour to the most beautiful temple in the whole world, or rather to the god who was manifest there, when you saw him. 4. For you did I believe, Constantine, see your patron Apollo,[40] and Victory accompanying him, offering you crowns of laurel, each of which represents a foretelling of thirty years.[41] That is of course the length of human generations, which are certainly due to take you beyond the old age of Nestor.[42] 5. And yet why do I say 'I believe'? You did see him,[43] and you recognised yourself in the image of the one to whom the sacred poems of bards prophesied that the kingdoms of the whole world were due by right. 6. That has now I think at last come to pass, seeing that you are, Emperor, like him, young, blessed, our saviour and a most handsome one! So quite rightly did you adorn those most venerable temples with such offerings that they no longer miss their former ones, and now all temples seem to be calling you to them – and especially our Apollo, in whose boiling waters are punished perjurers, whom you above all have good cause to hate.

22 Ye immortal gods, when will you grant the day that this most benevolent deity shall have established peace everywhere and may visit those groves of Apollo as well, and the sacred temple and steaming fountain springs? Their bubbling waters, warm and gently gushing, seem eager to smile upon your eyes, Constantine, and to flow into your lips. 2. To be sure, you will marvel too at the shrine of your patron god there, and the waters heated without any indication of the ground boiling. There is no bitterness in their taste or appearance, but a clarity of flavour and aroma like that of cool springs. 3. There too you will make donations, establish privileges, in short restore my own home country by worshipping that very place. 4. That ancient noble city[44] which once prided itself in its fraternal relations with Rome, is awaiting the assistance of your sovereignty, so that there too public buildings and splendid temples may be repaired by your generosity. In such a way I observe this happy city,[45] whose foundation day is being commemorated by your gracious visit, reviving so much in every quarter that it may even yet rejoice to have once collapsed, since it has grown greater through your benevolence. 5. I see a Circus Maximus to rival the one in Rome, I warrant, and I see basilicas and a forum, royal edifices and a court-house rising to such heights that they promise to be worthy neighbours of the stars in heaven. 6. Without doubt these are all benefactions due to your presence. For all the places that your divine presence most frequently dignifies expand in population, settlements and munificence. Indeed new flowers spring forth from the ground where Jupiter and Juno have lain[46] no more quickly than cities and temples arise around your footprints, Constantine. And so my prayers are only that your piety may inspire you to visit my home city, because it will be restored the moment you do so. But it is a question whether someone of my age is entitled to such happy fortune.

23 In the meantime, through your favour I have achieved the highest of my prayers, to devote to your hearing this poor voice of mine, practised in various private and official duties. So I give your divinity my heartfelt thanks. It remains for me to commend to you my children, and especially the one who is now engaged in the highest offices of the imperial treasury. My devotion has made me completely dependent on him, and if you ever notice him, his happy service will most accord with your requirements.[47] 2. In fact, as I have spoken about all my children, my ambition is far-reaching, Emperor. For besides my five sons I count also as my own those that I have nurtured to the guardianship of the forum, and to official duties. Many distinguished tributaries, as it were, flow from me, and many of my former charges are even administrators of your provinces. I rejoice at their successes, and count all their honour as my own; and if perhaps today I have spoken below what was expected of me, I trust that I have given satisfaction at least through them. 3. But if your gracious divinity may also grant that from this speech I may win a reputation, not for my eloquence, which would be too much, but for a little common sense and a devotion to you, then let all trivial concerns with private matters cease: the everlasting subject of my speech shall be, if he grants me his approval, my emperor.

NOTES
Sam Lieu

1 The Latin word translated here is 'imperator', not 'Augustus'. Constantine was not Augustus until after his defeat of Maxentius.
2 I.e. the anniversary of the foundation of Trier. See Introduction (above, p. 66).
3 On Constantine's Claudian descent see Introduction (above, pp. 66–70).
4 Claudius' achievements in his short reign were mainly military.

5 Reference to his victory near Naissus and the subsequent defeat of the Goths at sea in the eastern Mediterranean.

6 Since the mid-century, the empire had been beset by the invasion of a number of different 'barbarian' tribes, the most prominent of which were the Goths, the Heruli and the Germans. Cf. Millar, 1969: 12–29, Müller-Rettig, 1990: 54, Potter, 1990: 7–64. The numbers of the Goths were given in the fictional *SHA Claud*. 6,4 as 320,000 warriors and 2,000 ships. The number is even larger in Zos. I,42,1. Both sources probably derive ultimately from a now lost part of Dexippus' *Chron*. and *Scythica*.

7 According to Zos. *loc. cit.*, the Goths were assembled at the mouth of the river Tyra (Dneister) which flows into the Black Sea. Under Claudius, the Goths were defeated at Anchialus and Nicopolis (*SHA Claud*. 12,4) and also at Tomi and Marcianopolis (Zos. I,42,1). It was the fleet of Claudius which relieved the siege of Athens (Dexippus, *Scythica* F 28,4, p. 472,33–473,2) but the main naval reverse suffered by the Goths was the result of bad weather and poor seamanship (Zos. I,42,2). Cf. Millar, 1969: 26–29.

8 This reminder of Constantine's royal lineage (viz. the son of an emperor) clearly diverts the audience from any suggestion of his being a usurper.

9 Constantine served as a *tribunus primi ordinis* under Diocletian (Lact., *De mort*. 18,10) in Asia (*Origo* II,2) and in Palestine (Eus., *V. C.* I,19) and was a cavalry officer in Galerius' campaign against the Sarmatians (*Origo* II,3, see above, p. 43) and against the Persians (Constantinus, *or. ad sanct*. 16,2; cf. Dodgeon and Lieu, 1991: 134, §5.4.4).

10 See also n. 12 on *Origo* II,3, above, p. 43.

11 On Constantius' victory at Vindonissa see n. 18 below. The ms. is corrupt and *Vindonii* is the suggested reconstruction of Galletier. Barnes (1982: 37) draws attention to the fact that two medieval manuscripts read *videre Sydonii* – a reminder undoubtedly of his service under Aurelian against Zenobia. However, as Barnes himself is aware, no major battle was fought against the Palmyrenes in the vicinity of Sidon. See sources collected in Dodgeon and Lieu, 1991: 92–95, §4.8.2.

12 Allectus, formerly the *rationalis summae rei* of the usurper Carausius (Aug. in Britain since 286, cf. Aur. Vict., *Caes.*, 39,41), seized power in 293 and declared himself Augustus. Cf. Frere, 1978: 380–81.

13 Bonnonia (earlier Gesioracum, cf. *Pan. Lat.* IV(8),14,4, modern Boulogne), one of the two main ports of the *classis Britannica*, was Carausius' main base on the continent. It was recovered by Constantius in 296 after the construction of a mole had prevented the garrison from being resupplied. Cf. Frere, *op. cit.*: 378.

14 Two separate forces were involved in the expedition: one under Constantius sailed from Bonnonia while the other, under the command of his Praetorian Prefect Asclepiodotus ventured from the mouth of the Seine (*Pan. Lat.* IV(8),14,4, Aur. Vict., *Caes.*, 39,42 and Zon. XII,31).

15 The force under Asclepiodotus, however, appears to have encountered adverse weather in the channel-crossing. Cf. *Pan. Lat.* IV(8),14,4.

16 The crossing was unopposed because Allectus had concentrated his fleet in the vicinity of the Vecta Insula (i.e. the Isle of Wight) in the hope of ambushing Constantius. This Constantius managed to bypass, and his

forces set fire to the enemy fleet in the ports. Uncertain of the loyalty of his regular troops, Allectus had to rely on his barbarian mercenaries. He was defeated near Silchester and killed trying to escape. *Pan. Lat.* IV(8),13–19 (trans. Ireland, 1986: 133–35) gives the most detailed account of this, Constantius' first campaign in Britain.

17 Langres. Eutropius (9,23) is our only other source of information on the victory of 301 – achieved only after Constantius was initially taken by surprise: 'At the same time, a battle was fought in Gaul, in the land of the Lingons, by Constantius Caesar; he experienced failure and success in a single day. In fact, forced by a sudden invasion of barbarians to take refuge within this city, he found the gates closed to him in his urgent need, and had himself hauled up the wall by ropes; but, thanks to the arrival of his army scarcely five hours later, he cut nearly 60,000 Alamans to pieces.'

18 This second, and also otherwise unattested, decisive victory was presumably achieved in the same year.

19 The description of the hardships of the campaign caused by the terrain finds numerous echoes in that of Dio Cassius on the campaign of Septimius Severus which was the last major campaign in Scotland by a Roman emperor. Salway (1981: 319) rightly remarks: 'Indeed, one begins to be sure that even if the fourth-century writer is not simply drawing on conventional material about such campaigns he is at least expecting his well-read public to draw the parallels and to credit Constantius with doing as well as, if not better than, the great generals of the past.'

20 There is no clear motive for the second British campaign (305) other than showing the flag. The commonly held view that under Allectus the Picts took advantage of the absence of the Wall-garrison to invade is unattested in the sources and cannot be proved from archaeological evidence. Cf. Frere, *op. cit.*: 382, 387.

21 *Thylen ultimam.* Cf. Tacitus *Agr.* 10.4. There is much dispute as to the location of Thyle/Thule. Pytheas, an explorer from Marseilles contemporary with Aristotle, had first named Thule; and it seems he did mean Iceland. Tacitus transferred the name to one of the Shetlands (mainland, or possibly Foula). However our present author is making a rhetorical rather than a geographical point, so 'Iceland' seems more appropriate a translation.

22 See above, pp. **51–52**.

23 The panegyrist is alone among contemporary writers in his description of a reluctant Constantine. According to Eusebius (*V. C.* I,22,1) Constantine was already wearing the purple when he led the funeral procession: 'But the empire did not remain without an emperor; already wearing his father's purple, Constantine came out of his father's palace and to all he seemed to be the very image of his father, as if the latter had come to life again and now ruled in his son.' [Aur. Vict.], *Epit.* 41,3 mentions especially the support given by a Gallic chieftain called Crocus who had accompanied Constantine as head of an auxiliary force.

24 Reading 'Stul*t*a clementia est' (Galletier, following Acidalius). The reading 'Tu<t>a clementia est' (Mynors and Paladini-Fedeli, following Livineus) gives an inferior alternative meaning: 'It is safe to show

clemency by sparing etc.' For *stulta clementia* cf. Juvenal *Sat* I 17–18.

25　Perseus, son of Philip V and the last king of Macedon, was defeated by L. Aemilius Paullus at Pydna on 22 June 168 B.C. For the latter's intercession see Livy XLV,42,4. This was not a unique instance of clemency to a defeated sovereign. See e.g. Livy XLV,42,5 (Bithys), 43,9 (Genthios), Plut., *Pomp.* 45,5 and Josephus, *Ant. Jud.* 14,92 (Aristobulos) (cf. Müller-Rettig, 1990: 160–61) and *SHA, Tyr. trig.* 30,27 (Zenobia) (cf. Dodgeon and Lieu, 1991: 108–9).

26　The Bructeri were a powerful west Germanic tribe who inhabited the territories between the Ems and the Lippe and were southern neighbours of the Frisii and the Chauki. They allied with the Cherusci (Tac., *Ann.* I,51,4 and 60,4) against the Romans in the first century A.D. After 58 A.D. they spread into the district left vacant by the migration of Usipi southwards. According to the Peutinger Tables they occupied the areas on the right bank of the Rhine between Cologne and Koblenz in the Late Empire. Constantine's victory over them was achieved in late 308–early 309, for which he was acclaimed 'Germanicus' for the second time. Cf. *CIL* III 5565 = Dessau 664, cf. Grünewald, 1990, 237 insc. no. 375.

27　The bridge, *c.* 420 m long and 10 m wide and built of timber with two spans, linked the city of Colonia Claudia Ara Agrippinensium (modern Cologne) with the military outpost/bridgehead at Divitia (Cologne-Deutz) on the eastern bank of the Rhine. See the engraving 'Das römische Kastell Deutz um 319 n. Chr.' reproduced in Whittaker, 1994: 164. An inscription of *c.* 315 found at Deutz by the abbot Rupert of Deutz in 1128 (*CIL* XIII, 8592 = Dessau 8937, cf. Grünewald, 1990: 183, insc. no. 15) and celebrating the subjugation of the Franks by the emperor Constantine, marks probably the completion of the bridge. Cf. Petri-kovitz, 1960: 77–79 (with diagram) and on Constantine's frontier policy on the Rhine see *idem*: 1978: 221–22 and Demandt, 1989: 64.

28　The *classis Germanica* was based at Xanten and later at Cologne. Its primary task was to keep the main waterways of northern Europe under Roman control.

29　Hdt. VII,33. The bridge was built by Xerxes from Abydus to Sestus to facilitate his campaign on land against the Greeks.

30　I.e. the 'conspiracy' of Maximianus Herculius. He resumed the title of Augustus in the autumn of 309 at Arles. It is important to note that the entire incident, which is recounted in some detail by Lactantius (*Mort. pers.* 29,3–30,6), is entirely omitted from both the *H. e.* and *V. C.* of Eusebius.

31　I.e. Diocletian, who would not agree to come out of retirement at the conference at Carnuntum.

32　The ensuing remarks on the loyalty of Constantine's troops are a deliberate contrast to Maximianus' need to seize the treasury to pay his usual large donative (*donat ut solet large*) to win over the loyalty of the troops (Lact., *Mort. pers.* 29,5).

33　Alexander the Great; and Achilles (or perhaps Agamemnon).

34　On hearing of the coup, Constantine hastily left Cologne and route-marched his troops along the military high road from Trier (colonia Treverorum) (?) to Chalon-sur-Saône (Cabillonum), and embarked his troops in this town to descend the Saône and the Rhône as far as Arles, from where it was learned that the centre of the rebellion had moved to Marseilles (Massilia). After another exhausting march from Arles the soldiers loyal to Constantine immediately laid siege to this town.

35 The panegyrist has grossly misrepresented the distance between the Lakydon and the Anse which was about 800 m, i.e. more like 500 *passus* than 1,500.

36 Massilia was a former Phocaean colony and a well-known centre of trade and of higher education under the Romans; among its alumni was Agricola.

37 Massilia was besieged by Julius Caesar after failing to maintain its neutrality in his war with Pompey in 49 B.C. Cf. *Bell. civ.* I,34ff.

38 The relevant part of Zosimus (II,11) is brief and confuses the coup with the assassination attempt: 'Maximianus Herculius . . . also tried to plot against Constantine with the latter's soldiers; meanwhile, Fausta discovered the venture and told Constantine of it; filled with embarrassment following the failure of all these intrigues, Herculius died of an illness at Tarsus.' (Tarsus was where Maximinus Daia committed suicide after his defeat by Licinius.) The works of the other pagan historians are equally vague. Eutropius (X,2) seemed unaware of the military *coup d'état* and only explains the punishment inflicted on the culprit who had taken refuge in Massilia in terms of an assassination attempt against Constantine. Aurelius, while aware of accusations of conspiracy, put the blame, like the panegyrist of 310, entirely on the character of Maximianus (40,21–22, cf. Zon. XII,33): 'For Herculius, by nature totally lacking in moderation and fearing his son's inertia, had rashly seized power again. And while he was hatching plots against his son-in-law Constantine on the pretext of serving him, and attacking him bitterly, he finished by meeting a well-deserved death.' The *Epit.*, which uses a different source from Aurelius for this period, makes a brief mention of the incident immediately after the death of Galerius (40,5): 'Maximianus Herculius was besieged by Constantine at Massilia, was then captured and finally paid the ultimate penalty by strangulation.'

39 A reference to the death of Maximianus, described earlier as 'voluntarium exitium' (§14,5).

40 Echo of Vergil's vision of a golden age under Augustus in *Eclogue* IV,10: 'Your own Apollo now is king! (*tuus iam regnat Apollo*).'

41 These are probably signs which were visible in the crowns of the pagan deities and are most likely to be those which served to express the *Vota publica* on sculpted monuments and coins, and were represented in the form XXX. Cf. Piganiol, 1932: 51.

42 The offer implies that Constantine, who was then nearing forty (born 272 or 273), would outlast even the longevity of Nestor, who alone had seen three generations of men. These are the ways in which the minds of our official orators usually work, and their methods of flattery. The presence of Victory and the laurel crowns was an omen to the prince of the success which awaited him during the course of this unusual reign.

43 Rodgers, 1980: 270 translates: '. . . and you recognized yourself in the figure of that [famous] person to whom was owed the rule of the entire

world, as the divine songs of the poets prophesied'. The [famous] person was, according to Rodgers (272), Augustus. The panegyrist had earlier (§9,1–2) already compared Constantine favourably with Caesar. Warmington (1974: 376), on the other hand remarks: 'Taken by itself this sentence would presumably be taken as referring to Jupiter; such are the pitfalls of the religious language of the panegyrists.'

44 I.e. Autun.
45 I.e. Trier, where the speech is being delivered.
46 An evocation of the copulation of the Olympian deities Zeus (Jupiter) and Hera (Juno) on Mt Ida (*Iliad* 14.346–49). While they lay asleep enveloped in a golden cloud, the 'divine earth' made fresh grass, hyacinths and crocuses to grow. Cf. Müller-Rettig, 1990: 303.
47 *aetati* literally 'your age', suggesting the son referred to is a contemporary of Constantine.

3

CONSTANTINE BYZANTINUS

The anonymous *Life of Constantine* (*BHG* 364)

INTRODUCTION

Sam Lieu

The *Vita Constantini* of Eusebius of Caesarea and its reception

The life of Constantine was the subject of a major literary and historical work completed shortly after his death in May 337. The original goal of its author, Eusebius of Caesarea, was to compose a panegyric in the classical tradition of a *basilikos logos* (see below, pp. **159–61**), or more precisely an *epitaphios logos* as the hero was dead, which lays stress on the personal virtues and political achievements, especially in war, of the imperial person being praised. (Cf. Barnes, 1994: 3.) However, for a Christian panegyrist Constantine was no ordinary emperor. He was the first emperor to grant Christianity the status of *religio licita* in the Roman Empire and his achievement in the religious field (especially on behalf of the Christian Church) was unprecedented; Eusebius had no literary model which could do justice to his subject matter. A Christian *Cyropaedia* would in any case not have been an easy task for Eusebius whose knowledge of Constantine's personal history was not very deep. He had certainly conversed with Constantine on several occasions during the latter's lifetime but he was anything but the emperor's confidant and religious advisor as has sometimes been alleged. Besides these conversations which formed the basis of the accounts of two miraculous events in his hero's life (viz. the famous dream and vision before the Battle of Milvian Bridge and the anecdote on the salvific standard of the cross in battle against Licinius), Eusebius had to resort to imperial propaganda as his main source for the historical events.

97

The first of the four books of his *Life of Constantine* (hereafter *V. C.*) follows fairly closely the guidelines of rhetorical handbooks for such encomiastic compositions. It passes over Constantine's place of birth and his low-born mother, despite the fact that she is praised for her works of piety later in the work (III,42–46). The influence of classical models on rhetoric is evident in the story of his father Constantius preferring voluntary contribution to higher indiction from his subjects to fill his treasury (I,14) which is paralleled in Xenophon's *Cyropaedia* (8.2.15–22, cf. Barnes, 1989a: 104). The biographical framework was followed up to the end of the conflict between Constantine and Maxentius, and Eusebius did not hesitate to lift substantial passages from his earlier work, the *Ecclesiastical History,* on the events of the conflict (see esp. *V. C.* I,33–35 and *H. e.* VIII,14 etc. See the references to *H. e.* in Winkelmann's edition of the *V. C.* See also additions in Hall, 1993: *passim*). Once the civil conflicts were settled and Constantine became sole ruler, the *V. C.* became more of a continuation of the *Ecclesiastical History* (originally completed before Constantine's break with Licinius in 316/17 and subsequently revised) than an encomiastic obituary. Constantine's religious policy, especially his legislation favouring the Christians, and ecclesiastical matters, especially those relating to the Arian controversy and the Council of Nicaea, came to dominate the narrative of the second part of the work so much that well-known secular events such as the foundation of Constantinople, or important biographical data such as the execution of his son Crispus and the death in suspicious circumstances of his wife Fausta, were hardly touched upon. The complex negotiations between Shapur II and Constantine in the years prior to the renewal of hostilities between the two empires which features so prominently in Libanius' *Basilikos Logos* on the sons of Constantine (trans. below, pp. **179–80**) were completely glossed over, and the only evidence of contact between the two hostile powers was a letter of Constantine to Shapur, imploring the latter to end persecution of Christians within the Eranshahr (IV,9–13, cf. Dodgeon and Lieu, 1991: 155–63 and Barnes, 1985: 130–32). Like the *Ecclesiastical History*, the *V. C.* is suffused with documents, especially legislation and imperial letters. Their intrusion into the narrative further reduces the *bios*-element of the work.

The apparent shortcomings of the *V. C.* as a biography or encomiastic obituary can be accounted for by the fact that Eusebius was not in a position to know a great deal of the political happenings of the reign as distinct from ecclesiastical politics in which he was a key player, and that the *V. C.* as we have it is a merger of two drafts, one an *epitaphios logos* of the dead emperor and the other a 'documentary history of a hagiographical nature' (Barnes, 1989a: 110) of the reign. This hybrid of a literary work was nothing short of a publishing disaster. It was read perhaps by the sophist Libanius (see below, p. 206) and certainly used by the Church historian Socrates whose *Historia Ecclesiastica* covers the reign of Constantine and devotes much space to the Arian controversy. The other major Church historians of the fifth century, Sozomen, Theodoret and Gelasius, show only vague awareness of its contents. Some documents were reproduced but little verbal similarity was preserved in the narrative parts. (Cf. Winkelmann, 1962: 71–88.) Despite its hagiographical tone, the work was considered suspect by many Church leaders in the Greek East – with the exception of Palestine-Syria – due to the uncertainty over its author's loyalty to the Christian faith during the Diocletianic persecutions (Epiph., *Haer.* LXVIII,8,4; iii, 149,2–7, *GCS*) and the equivocal role he played in the Arian controversy. (Cf. Winkelmann, 1964: 108–12.) That the *V. C.* was little read from the late fourth century onwards explains John Chrysostom's lament that by his time the greater part of the emperor's deeds were already forgotten (*PG* 49.216), and Chrysostom's evidence is supported by other sources testifying to an early confusion between the various members of the Constantinian dynasty with similar sounding names. It would later be used by Church historians and hagiographers in Byzantium when Arianism was no longer a major threat to ecclesiastical unity. Nevertheless, the difficult style of the *V. C.*, which still limits us to only one English translation executed in the last century, certainly did not help the diffusion of the work in Byzantium, and in the Latin West there is no known Latin translation of it prior to the Renaissance.

The Byzantine lives of Constantine

In Byzantium, Constantine was not merely a Christian emperor or even the first Christian emperor. He was celebrated as a saint and 'isapostolos' i.e. the thirteenth Apostle. The importance given to the cult of the saints by the Byzantine Church demanded that the saints' ascetical achievements be celebrated in hagiography and summarised in menologions – these are collections of saints' or martyrs' lives arranged according to the date of their festival. The *V. C.* with its cumbersome archive of documents and scanty narrative is hardly an ideal source for the hagiographer or the menologist. Moreover, the *V. C.* did not provide information on a number of major landmarks in the life of Constantine which were regarded as essential for commemoration, namely the foundation of the city of Constantinople and the discovery of the True Cross by his mother Helena. Nor does it attempt to disguise the awkward fact that Constantine became a baptised Christian on his death-bed (IV,57–58) and many could infer from the lateness of the event that he was baptised by an Arianising bishop (Eusebius of Nicomedia).

Once the main contemporary source on the life of Constantine was put to one side, the Byzantine hagiographer or menologist had precious little to draw from in terms of contemporary material on the life of the first Christian emperor. The *De mortibus persecutorum* of Lactantius, though contemporary, was usually regarded as too close to the events, and in any case was completed before Constantine's final break with Licinius and therefore provides no information on Constantine's sole rule. In any case, few monks in Byzantium were likely to have had access to a work in Latin. The pagan epitomes in Latin would have been similarly inaccessible save for that of Eutropius which was translated into Greek by Paenius and used by at least one Byzantine hagiographer – the author of *BHG* 369 (cf. Winkelmann, 1973: 273). The Greek pagan historians could only be used for information on political and military events because of their bias against Constantine (see above, pp. **7–23**) although their negative verdicts were known to Byzantine authors who had the task to refute them. The works of Praxagoras and Bemarchius (see above, pp. **7–9**) on Constantine were known only to highly educated men like Photius or the anonymous compiler of the *Suda* (Lexicon) but were little read by monks who were the main compilers of saints' lives in Byzantium. The lack of a main source meant that for the life of Constantine and the pious exploits of his mother whose joint feast-day with her son was and still is celebrated on 21 May, the Byzantine menologist had to turn for information to later sources, especially lives of saints who flourished or were believed to have flourished during the reign of Constantine such as Alexander and Metrophanes and some like Artemius (see below, pp. **224–56**) and Eusignius who perished as martyrs under Julian. Whether a *Vorvita* for the Byzantine lives of Constantine dating back to the fifth or sixth century had existed is no longer a matter of scholarly speculation as the only group of *vitae* which can be shown to be dependent on a literary antecedent is that which is represented by *BHG* 364. On the other hand, it is clear that the extant lives show parallels with and/or borrowings from saints' lives (and lost *vitae?*) which were used by Byzantine chroniclers. (Cf. Kazhdan, 1987: 211–30.) The treatise by Alexander the Monk on the discovery of the True Cross (*De inventione sanctae crucis*, *PG* 87.4016–76) deserves mentioning in this context as it was probably completed as early as the sixth century. Because of its early date, the hagiographical elements on the life of Constantine it contains could be used profitably as signposts to the developing legend.

Innumerable lives of Constantine composed in the Byzantine period are extant in hagiographical collections and menologions, and had long been noticed by scholars of Byzantine manuscripts. However, the study of this legendary material by historians did not begin until their systematic publication at the end of the last century. Of the *vitae* available for general study, the following are the most important and they are listed in the chronological order of their generally accepted date of original compilation:

(1) *BHG* 365z, 366 and 366a (compiled text in Winkelmann, 1987: 632–38). This epitome of a *vita* (ἐν συντόμῳ) is found in slightly variant forms in two partial and one full menologions (8th–9th century A.D.). It contains already a number of features found in later and longer *vitae* such as the discovery of the True Cross by Helena and of Constantine consecrating his eponymous city with the bishops who attended the Council of Nicaea during the patriarchate of Metrophanes. The lack of any mention in the three versions of the (legendary) baptism of Constantine at Rome by Pope Sylvester which occurs in nearly all later *vitae* gives a pre-sixth-century date to the proto-*vita*. It is clearly a source for a later Byzantine *vita* (see next item) of Constantine, judging from the innumerable verbal parallels apparent between the two texts.

(2) The 'Guidi-Vita' = *BHG* 364 (text in Guidi, 1907: 306–40 and 637–60, trans. below, pp. 106–42). With more than forty extant manuscripts of its two versions (one earlier, namely 11th century and one later, 12th century), this is by far the most popular of the 'Pre-Metaphrastes' Byzantine lives of Constantine compiled before the monumental hagiographical endeavours of Symeon Metaphrastes (see below). Internal evidence and its apparent use of the *Chronicle* of Theophanes

(completed *c.* 820) suggest a mid-to late ninth-century date (cf. Heseler, 1935: 322–28) but it is possible that the long excursus on the building work of Helena in Palestine was a tenth- or even eleventh-century addition. (Cf. Schneider, 1934: 46–47, 1941b: *passim*, Winkelmann, 1973: 268 and Kazhdan, 1987: 201.) The work is of substantial length and contains a number of features which are commonly found in later Byzantine lives of Constantine:

(a) Visit of Constantius Chlorus to Drepanum, his meeting with Helena at an inn and the conception of Constantine under unusual auspices.

(b) Recognition of the young Constantine by courtiers by a special 'gift' and his physical resemblance to his father. His subsequent reunification with Constantius and his assignment to the court of Diocletian for grooming as a future emperor.

(c) Baptism of Constantine by Pope Sylvester in Rome after the emperor's refusal to cure his leprosy through bathing in the blood of innocent children.

(d) Constantine's Persian campaign, his capture and escape.

(e) Foundation of Constantinople and the earlier history of Byzantium.

(f) Arian controversy and miraculous happenings at the Council of Nicaea.

(g) The discovery of the True Cross by Helena and her building programme in Palestine.

(h) Victories for Constantine in various battles through the presence of the symbol of the Cross.

These became so standard in Constantinian hagiography that they soon passed from legend into history in Byzantium. Substantial parts of the 'Guidi-Vita' are reproduced in the sections on the reign of Constantine in the massive *Ecclesiastical History* of Nicephorus Callistus (compiled *c.* 1320, *PG* 145, the relevant sections span cols 1241–1325) The borrowings are particularly numerous on Constantine's origins and youth (VII,18–19 = *BHG* 364, p. 307,14–316,2 + Eus., *H. e.* VIII, 13,2ff.; VII,20 = 319,20–320,15 + Eus., *H. e.* VIII,13) and in the section on Helena (VIII,27–32 = Thdt., *H. e.* I,15–17 + Soc., *H. e.* I,17, Soz., *H. e.* II,2 and *BHG* 364, 649,18–652,17 and 653,2–14) (cf. Gentz, 1966: 73 and 84 and Winkelmann, 1978: 181). A distinctive feature of this *vita* is the detailed account of the foundation of churches on holy sites in Palestine by Helena. (Cf. Schneider, 1934: 45–47.) It also repeatedly stresses the important role played by the True Cross, either in its heavenly manifestation or in its earthly reproduction, in Constantine's military victories (see below, §§13, 14, 17, 20, 22, 23, 24, 25 of our translation) as well as the devotion lavished upon it by Helena (§§31–33). These features are not found in the 'Vorvita' (i.e. *BHG* 365z etc.) and are likely to have developed during the Iconoclast controversy when there was an increase in the veneration of the Cross as a replacement for images. (Cf. Kazhdan, 1987: 242f. and Bleckmann, 1992: 152.)

A high point in Byzantine hagiography was reached towards the end of the tenth century with the compilation by Symeon Logothetes ('Metaphrastes') of a menologion apparently at the bidding of the reigning emperor. Most of the lives were copied from earlier collections or self-standing *vitae* but worked over (metaphrased) to make them acceptable in style and theology to the readers of his time. A good example of this reworking is the version given of the life of Artemius (*PG* 115.1159–212) which was in the main a *verbatim* reproduction with addition of some later information of an earlier and longer work by a certain John the Monk. The menologion of Symeon surpassed all other such collections both in importance and in popularity and was frequently added to in later times. A curious omission under 21 May is the combined *vitae* of Constantine and Helena. This was made good in many later collections (especially those that originated from Constantinople) from a variety of sources, giving the modern scholar a bewildering choice of hagiographical material on these imperial saints. The main post-Metaphrastes versions which are readily available to modern scholars are:

3) The 'Opitz-Vita' = *BHG* 365. This was first edited by Franchi de' Cavalieri (1896/97) from Codex Angelicus gr. 22 (10th/11th century) foll. 1–54 in the Vatican, and re-edited with a more detailed historical commentary by Opitz (1934, 545–90). The text is acephalous and begins with Constantine's activities in Rome after his victory over Maxentius. Additional sections from its lost beginning which are likely to have been derived from the lost Arian Church historian Philostorgius have been supplied by Bidez from Codex Sabbaiticus gr. 366 (13th century) foll. 9–22. (Cf. Bidez, 1935: 421–26 and reprinted in the

revised edition of his *GCS* edition of Philostorgius, pp. 377–81.)
Further fragments from the lost beginning were supplied from
the same Palestinian manuscript by Halkin (1960: 6–8 and
11–15) together with the principal variants between the two
manuscripts (15–17). The work is dated to between the end of
the 9th and the 11th century Though its purpose was pietistic
commemoration like other Byzantine *vitae* of Constantine, the
work is characterised by its extraordinary familiarity with
earlier sources such as Eusebius, Socrates Scholasticus,
Theodoret, Philostorgius, Georgius Monachus and even the
pagan historian Zosimus (on the Battle of Milvian Bridge and
the deaths of Fausta and Crispus). A feature not found in earlier
vitae is the role played by a legendary figure, the chamberlain
Euphratas, in the conversion of Constantine. A fuller edition of
this important text combining material from the two main
manuscripts is eagerly awaited.

(4)   The 'Halkin (or Patmos)-Vita' = *BHG* 365n, edited by Halkin
(1959a: 73–105 and 1959b: 371–72) from Cod. Patm. gr. 179
(12th/13th century) foll. 4b–25b, is the product of a monk from
Berroea in the neighbourhood of Thessalonica and contains a
number of fascinating local details as well as some geographical
howlers such as Britain and Gaul being separated by the
Danube. Though the work repeats many familiar themes and
shows strong similarity with the *Passio Eusignii* (*BHG* 639), it
nevertheless displays much material not found in other lives.
The trials of the young Constantine at the court of Galerius, for
instance, were graphically depicted as the labours of a new
Hercules or Jason. Instead of facing the normal opposition of a
bear and a lion without claws or thirty men armed with dry
sponges, Galerius sent him against a normal bear and lion as well
as thirty men armed with rocks. The *vita* also contains a detailed
account of the achievements of Euphratas in the foundation of
Constantinople. (Cf. Winkelmann, 1973: 271.)

(5)   The 'Gedeon-Vita' = *BHG* 363. This was edited by Gedeon
from Cod. Kultumus. 23 (Lambros. 3092) (11th–12th century)
foll. 286b–299b. (Cf. Gedeon, 1900: 253–54, 262–63, 279–80,
303–4.) It is the oldest example of a group of texts known as the
'Imperial Menologion B' containing *vitae* which are not independent new works but are 'metaphrased' versions of older
works. (Cf. Ehrhard 1939: 341.) This is a highly mechanical

compilation of material from earlier sources (esp. *BHG* 364) and from the *Vita Constantini* of Eusebius. (Cf. Winkelmann, 1962: 102–3.) The purpose of the work is to produce an ideal Constantine totally shorn of controversy and complication. Its panegyrical section on Helena was equally wholesome and omits any mention of her low origin or her 'affair' with Constantius Chlorus. (Cf. Winklemann, 1978: 190.) The rarity of the original publication by Gedeon makes the work inaccessible to many modern scholars.

(6) Life of Constantine by bishop Ignatius of Selymbria (John Chortasmenos) = *BHG* 362. The first of the main Byzantine lives of Constantine to be made available to modern scholars is also one of the last Byzantine *vitae* of Constantine to be compiled, and the manuscript Cod. Ottob. gr. 441 – a miscellaneous manuscript but containing no other hagiographical work – can be dated to 1481. (Cf. Ioannes, 1884: 164–229.) It can be shown from another manuscript in the British Museum (Cod. Brit. Mus. Add. 31919) that its author flourished *c.* 1430s. Ignatius' real name was John Chortasmenos, a man of letters and theologian who was born *c.* 1370 and held the office of notary in the patriarchal chancery until *c.* 1415. At an unknown date he became the monk (and then hieromonk) Ignatius and by 1431 metropolitan of Selymbria, a town in Thrace. (Cf. Hunger, 1969: 18.) A highly polished literary effort, it depicts Constantine as a man of letters and, unlike most other Byzantine *vitae*, contains detailed summaries of Constantine's legislation (e.g. p. 186). The author is surprisingly well read in pagan literature of the fourth century and mentions the *Caesares* of Julian and Libanius' *Funeral Oration* (i.e. *Or.* XVIII) on the same emperor (p. 174).

Such was the popularity of these legendary accounts that they exerted very considerable influence on accounts of the reign of Constantine by Byzantine historians from the ninth century onwards. By that date fact had become so intermingled with fiction in the popular perception of the history of the reign in Byzantium that her historians would not have hesitated to cite *in extenso* from the *Actus Sylvestri* on the baptism of Constantine, or to indulge in the tales surrounding Constantine's fictional victorious campaign against the Persians, or to praise the achievements of Constantine's Christian vizier Euphratas. On the other hand the Byzantine chroniclers also had access to excellent sources now lost to us and familiarity with the legendary material is therefore an essential requirement in our utilisation of their works.

Edition etc.

The text of *BHG* 364 published by Guidi is based primarily on Cod. Paris gr. 1453 (11th century) foll. 68–91b and constituted part of a four-month menologion which has been dated to the second half of the 9th century Guidi used in the apparatus Cod. Messin. 26 (12th century). Variant readings from Vat. gr. 974 (11th/12th century) and Vat. gr. 1079 (14th/15th century) are given in the appendix. The following translation, the first into any modern language, is based entirely on the text as presented by Guidi with occasional changes of punctuation. Brackets [] indicate the manuscript folio pages; {} indicate pages in the Guidi text. The commentary takes into account that, as with so many Byzantine *vitae*, history and legend are inseparably mixed, and therefore does not attempt consistent correction of historical errors.

THE ANONYMOUS *LIFE OF CONSTANTINE* (*BHG* 364)
translated by Frank Beetham; revised by Dominic Montserrat and Sam Lieu

[68r]

Life and ways of the holy, glorious and reverent great rulers Constantine and Helena, and the revelation of the precious and life-giving holy Cross of our Lord and God and saviour Jesus Christ. Bless him, O Father.

Life and ways of the devout (in blessed sense), most faithful, great and first ruler of us Christians, Constantine, and Helena his mother. Bless [them], O Father.

1. I wish to set out clearly and in detail for your reverence, O attentive and learned congregation and readily-obedient audience with the appellation called by Christ's name, the life of the great emperor Constantine, most blessed and holy and first of the Christian religion, faithful by the grace of God, and the exalted and virtuous ways of his parents, both of his father Constans[1] and of his holy mother Helena as truly having surpassed the ways of the multitude and almost, through good works and the most pure conduct, having approached the practice of the holy angels; nay, I beseech you, extend

to me your most unsullied sense of hearing with a view to paying attention to and listening to the things that are being said. For I should not have reckoned it just nor holy to allow the virtue, displayed in their works and in their faith, of such wonderful great emperors, famous in song and story, and especially of Constantine, who is among the saints, to be drowned in the depth of oblivion and lost to view in the silence of ages, but rather to attempt to tell it in the manner of the gospel under the illumination of description so that, when his praiseworthy way of life {p.307} has been made manifest, both the Trinity which is consubstantial, the one deity and kingdom, may be glorified as befits God, and there may be proclaimed clearly from the teaching about God according to the gospels, the word of God which says: 'let your light shine before men, so that they may see your [68v] good works and glorify your father in heaven', and much profit from his soul-saving and beloved virtue may be stored up for the more serious kind of people, who are the friends of virtue. So let us justly and fittingly come to the present story, having as our leaders and precursors the saints Constantine and Helena themselves, by whose prayers even now we are fortified; the words themselves have the power to speak freely.

2. At the exact time when Diocletian, having killed Carinus the son of Carus, had made himself emperor instead in the older, great Rome, he also enlisted Maximianus Herculius; and when these emperors had rekindled an implacable war against the Christians, at once through their actions all kinds of God-driven chastisements had befallen the land of the Romans. For the Persians and the Parthians[2] and the Sarmatians with their king Varachthes,[3] and the rest of the multitude of barbarians began to plunder the territory of the Romans and, realising this, those who held the imperial sceptre, I mean Diocletian and Maximianus Herculius, decided together to send to their priests Theonas and Hymenaeus, from the western parts of the empire to the East, a report ordering a meeting through them with the Parthian king Varachthes with a view to a reconciliation so that the Parthians should never make expeditions against the Romans but offer them all the benefits of peace, and the Romans should pay tribute to the Parthians; and this was achieved after Constans, also known as the Most Eminent and Chlorus, had been sent by the emperors Diocletian and Maximianus from Rome to Persia, obviously for this purpose.

3. For Constans was the cousin of Claudius[4] who had been emperor before Aurelian and Diocletian and had married in Rome Theodora, the daughter of Maximianus Herculius and the sister of Maxentius who was killed in Rome, about whom {p.308} I shall give an account later. This Constans, the father of the holy emperor [69r] Constantine the Great, was kind in his manner and brave physically, a great hearted man if ever there was one, and invincible in war. Having been invested with the rank of tribune[5] by the emperors, he went from old Rome with certain other eminent men, themselves also enrolled in various grades of appointment, and began to make his way to Persia for the purpose of the delegation;[6] and when, with the men, he had reached the end of the cities and territories of the Romans, it happened that in completing their journey the soldiers and Constans himself came to the place called Drepanum[7] which later was also called Helenopolis, and arrived in an inn which was clearly marked as such. So, since they were all pleased with the condition of the place, having fixed their quarters there, as they were weary from travelling, they rested awhile; and while these men were making their camp in that place, it happened that Constans suddenly longed for a bed of love (or, at any rate, union, sexual intercourse); and when he announced his desire for intemperate pleasure to the guide, he, having observed his imperial bearing, since he had his young daughter Helena with him, a girl who was uninitiated about the male sex, was glad to offer her to the gentleman to enjoy himself; and Constans, having noticed that the young lady was good looking and was just at the height of her beauty, received her with altogether the greatest pleasure. So Constans took the girl and, having made love with her, he gave her an embroidered mantle dyed in purple as an expression of his gratitude, in return for her admitting him to her bed; and while he was entwined in her embraces, and night enfolded the whole affair, a wonderful vision was revealed just for that night; for the sun that shines by day, having, contrary to nature, run backwards out of its bed which is beside Oceanus in the west, was unexpectedly directing its four-fold rays on the house where Constans was sleeping with the girl. So Constans, amazed at the sight, because he was a religious person, that is to say, an ardent devotee of his own faith, [69v] thinking that Apollo {p. 309} was with them to preside over some great political change, remained dumbstruck and spent, as if afraid to leave the nuptial embrace, and could not think what the unnatural vision might be, suspecting that it might be some sign of wrath of the gods of those days, and stayed the whole

time till morning light, so that he might escape the trouble there; and it was a double punishment for him that the night was made longer. As soon as the sun was up, being under the constraint of great terror, he sent for the girl's father and after sweetening him with many presents he gave him his daughter back, with a solemn recommendation to keep her undefiled and unblemished for him as a very great treasure; and Constans, who was awaiting the miracle that would result from the nocturnal vision, said that if, in the fullness of time, she should have a baby, he should guard the infant that would be born as if it were the apple of his eye. After resuming his journey to the Parthians and conducting the delegation to the king of the Persians and receiving an answer, and after establishing peace with the Romans, Constans completed his journey to the west by another route; and after presenting the peace treaty to the emperor Diocletian he received the requisite honours and presents. And when the time came round, it happened by divine providence that Constans was proclaimed Caesar together with the younger Maximianus, who is also called Galerius by name, by the emperor Diocletian; and after some time, intending to leave Rome and go to Nicomedia, Diocletian left Maximianus, also known as Herculius, behind in Rome; and it was on that occasion that both Constans, the father of the holy and mighty emperor Constantine, and Maximianus Galerius who had formerly been Caesars, were proclaimed Augusti. And as time went on, again it became necessary to send a delegation to the Persians {p. 310} and Constans, having picked the distinguished members of his court, sent them away into Persia; [70r] and it happened that those ambassadors went through those places where the holy Helena was living bringing up the child, that is, the wonderful Constantine, that she had had by Constans. And while the men were being accommodated there, it happened that the lad was teased by the gentlemen who were staying at that time, and was upset; and when the men were taken aback at this and were beginning to act in an ill-tempered way, the boy's mother retorted and made it clear to them whose child he was, saying that he was the emperor's son; when they heard that, the imperial officers laughed at her and said, 'Madam, are you making fun or telling the truth?' But she said, 'By the gods, gentlemen, I am not cheating you; what I told you was true.' When they heard what she said they could not believe it, and began to question her rather officiously; they said to the girl, 'How and when did this happen? Satisfy us.' She then said, 'Constans, who is now emperor, when he was tribune, stopped with me on his way from the Sarmatian war, and after I had become pregnant by him, I had this child; and if you want to know the exact truth, I shall also show you the price he paid for going to bed with me.' Then she brought out the purple-dyed mantle and showed it to them, and when they had seen it and been convinced that the matter was true, they began to beg her pardon for their presumption and ignorance, and after they had smothered the child with embraces and flattery, they soothed him by putting silver coins into his hand.[8]

4. And so they set out from there and went away into Persia; and after being admitted to the presence of the king of the Parthians and delivering their message to him and receiving his response, they returned by another route {p. 311} to the West, where the emperor Constans was living. And after he had welcomed them gladly, he asked them what strange and foreign things they had seen in the East; and they all described different things, but the most eminent of them explained to the emperor about Helena and the boy, [70v] and said the distinguishing mark of royalty was evident on the face of the boy who had been born of her and was being brought up in Drepanum: 'Truly, he is the very image of you, my lord,' he said. When he heard this, Constans sent the others away; then he began to question this man closely, because he wanted to learn all about Helena and the boy. After the man had given a clearer account, Constans himself remembered on what day he had slept with Helena, and how the darkness of the night had been lit up by the sparkling of the sun; he also saw that the result of his vision had been fulfilled, and so after rewarding his informant appropriately with honours and also giving him many presents, he instructed him to go to Drepanum with many warrants and a large imperial bodyguard and fetch Helena and the child as quickly as possible. They did as he commanded; having seated her with her son in an imperial carriage, they brought her to Constans. And when he saw them, Constans rejoiced exceedingly; he embraced them and led them inside his palace. Moreover, he made a practice of instructing the child about imperial rescripts; so from childhood he had all the qualities of an emperor: prudence, character, bearing, {p. 312} reverence, courage and, in sum, all the finest qualities in word that he later came to fulfil in his deeds.

5. Moreover, as this incredible affair concerning Helena and her son was becoming common talk, it came to the ears of Theodora, the legitimate daughter of Herculius, who was Constans' wife, by whom

he had also three male children and one daughter; the sons were called Constantius and Hannibalianus and Dalmatius, and the daughter, Constantia, was espoused to Licinius, but none of them was considered worthy to inherit their father's imperial office. However Constans, fearing that the young lady and her child might be murdered for jealousy, after some consideration sent the boy with a letter [71r] to the emperor Diocletian and to Maximianus his relation by marriage, who was staying then at the city of Nicomedia in Bithynia; so the boy left and was received in the imperial court and was given an appointment on the staff of imperial officials as he was a hostage of imperial rank, that is to say, a guarantee that Constans would observe peace; so he circulated at court, Constans having made arrangements also to thwart any plot by his older wife Theodora against Helena, as we have already explained. But as the boy Constantine was growing to manhood and being educated in the wisdom of the Greeks, the demon that is a hater of the good aroused envy against him. For the retinue of Diocletian and Herculius, who passed their lives in superstition and foretelling the future by the observation of birds and the inspection of livers, suddenly realised that he was destined {p.313} to attain supreme power, and moreover that he would be a God-fearing emperor who would destroy and abolish the superstition of the Greeks and would be a very great proponent of the divine kingdom of Christ, and for this reason they began to prepare manifold traps of all kinds so as to do away with him; they resorted to this in their guiltiness and wickedness.

6. However God, who always reveals that the souls of the saints are mightier than those who try to wrong them, delivered the pious child from the murderous attempts of the tyrants, by endowing the youthful Constantine with a swift perception of the plot against him. Once he had learned of this, and of the secret treachery and the hidden war, with the guidance of God, by discretion and sound judgement he thwarted their vain folly; for on the following night, having persuaded certain men, on his assurance, to aid him, he formed a notion of escape, so beating off their wicked design, and immediately mounting a horse and leaving Nicomedia with all the speed he could, he came unexpectedly upon his father who was in Britain, suffering from a dreadful illness and facing death, just as he was both making his will and surrounded by all his sons but only looking for Constantine, again and again calling his name, that had been so long missing. [71v] And while his father was still uttering

this and crying aloud, and was invoking Christ (for indeed the great man was most gentle and peaceable in all respects and exceedingly disgusted with idols and welcoming to Christians) all at once Constantine was there, and disclosed to his father in detail everything that had happened to him after he had reached Maximianus, his own bravery in war, affairs in Egypt and Palestine, his manly deeds and prowess in battle, and how he always fought at the head of the phalanx, both in an entrenched camp and in the front line and prevailed over all his foes, mostly in {p. 314} hand to hand combat.[9] Then after he had related the treachery of Maximianus' disposition and jealousy occasioned by suspicion, the narrow escape from death, the plot, his realisation of it and his escape which had been the answer to prayer, he said, 'Not only did Maximianus plan to murder me, but the abominable Diocletian also, with his subordinate generals, considered forming a secret plot against me, and if I had not, by divine providence, discovered the treachery that was being rehearsed against me and contrived my own safety by escaping, I should by now have been killed.' Constans, for his part, had been yearning for his son for a long time; but although he was being overcome by the law of nature, it was as if his son's unexpected escape and coming to him after a long absence had made him forget his own illness. He confirmed with warm tears the love he felt for Constantine. He directed his gaze at him, and declared the young man to be worthy of the empire which was the gift of God; so after his illness had become still worse, constrained by his love for Constantine the Great and passing over the rest of his children, his father transferred everything to Constantine: his sceptre, his purple and his imperial power. Moreover, he said, in so many words, to the Senate and to his whole army, 'Now death is becoming more pleasant than life; now I die as I would wish, receiving as my greatest memorial your principate, O my son; for to leave behind upon the earth an emperor [72r] able to wipe away the tears of the Christians who have suffered in the time of the abominable Maximianus is giving me a foretaste of my place in blessedness.'[10] After speaking these words to his son Constantine and seating him on the imperial throne, {p. 315} and after calling together the whole Senate and Praetorian Guard, and the multitudes of Christians besides and all the local people, and those who had taken refuge in his empire from the territories of the other emperors (for Constans was the only one willing to strengthen Christianity, while his fellow emperors filled the whole inhabited world with murder, civil war and abomination, and the cities ruled by him were enjoying peace, so that all those who took refuge with him were also in safety), Constans, looking back alike at the multitudes of assembled Christians, said, 'Take courage, all you who do not deny God; for henceforth, with Constantine, Christ will take up arms on your behalf; he will fight on our side.' With these words, having addressed them all in prayer and given them his greeting, he grasped his son and both robed him in the purple and placed the crown upon him and, imitating in his actions David, king of the Hebrews, he displayed the faithful heir of his power and empire, having in person made himself herald of the boy in front of the others. So then this is the manner in which Constantine, the reverent Augustus, was proclaimed monarch of the Roman empire in the first year of the 200th Olympiad, whose life had been saved contrary to expectation and whose succession to the principate had also been quite remarkable;[11] and when his father Constans had died in Britain and had, by a blessed transference, departed from life here, he had reigned thirteen years; and he was fifty-six {p. 316} years old when he left the principate to Constantine, his son by Helena.

7. But Constantine, the Christ-loving Augustus, after a brief interval taken up by the death of his most blessed [72v] father, and his funeral as ordained by law, and after paying him every other honour, having heard about the war with the Persians who had made an expedition against the cities of the Roman empire and were overrunning and enslaving them, having chosen about 20,000 men of skill and strength who were experienced in warfare, to their delight, departed with them to fight the Persians. And before an engagement had taken place between the two sides the Persians, like treacherous villains, at night having overcome by treason the Roman guard, or at any rate the sentries, and having slain them, suddenly charged the trenches and made an entry through the middle, and both cut down many of the Romans and surprised the emperor Constantine and overpowered him; they appropriated the imperial pavilion and all its staff, and removed some of the generals and prefects of cohorts by the sword, and pursued others as far as the boundaries of Roman territory; but all those who, having swift horses, were able to escape the abominable hands of the Persians hid on a tree-covered mountain in Persia. The thrice-wretched and thrice-accursed Persians, flushed with their victory in the war, took the emperor Constantine and bound him securely with fetters and made an agreement to celebrate the day of the birthday feast of their abominable gods and at the feast,

inside the temple, to slay him with the sword; yet how {p. 317} great is your endurance, O my Christ! See how the weeping that had settled over us in the evening was turned to rejoicing in the morning! Some of the Romans who had escaped to the mountains belonging to the Persians observed that some of the slaves of the Persians had come out to those mountains to cut wood. So they leapt out from behind the trees at full speed, surrounded them, encircled them and overpowered them; the slaves, for their part, had become half dead through fear of the Romans, who began to question [73r] them precisely about what had happened to the emperor, the blessed Constantine. The slaves fell on their faces before the Roman soldiers and began to beg for their lives, saying that they had never committed any offence against the Roman army, 'For', they said, 'we are slaves of the Persians; so act humanely towards us.' So the soldiers agreed not to kill them if they would tell them the truth without more ado; and they said, 'Listen to us, gentlemen of Rome; our king and our rulers have appointed a day to celebrate the birthday of the gods, and they have determined to sacrifice the emperor Constantine upon the altar tomorrow; but there is a wall encircling the altar, and there is only one entrance leading to the altar; now then, the Persians do not usually wear weapons when they worship the gods, and so they leave all their weapons behind outside the wall while they themselves go in unarmed, and whenever they dance and sing to their own gods, that is when they offer sacrifices. Tomorrow is the appointed time of the sacrifice; if you keep us safe, we shall keep a careful lookout, and we shall tell you when the Persians begin the dancing; {p. 318} so then your part will be to come in secretly and seize the weapons that are lying outside, and once you have got inside, begin to cut them down and slay them; in this way you will save your emperor without risk.' And this method of betraying the Persians found favour with the Romans who said, 'Depart unharmed, in the name of Christ and our God.' Furthermore, they appeased them with words of peace and took them as confederates in the plot to betray the Persians. And lo! the day came to a close, and the next day they brought the emperor Constantine in, like some sacrifice, to the altar, with his hands and feet tied; and as the Persians were finishing dancing thrice in a ring round the altar, the Romans received a signal from the slaves in the entrance [73v] and rose up and seized the Persians' weapons that were lying outside the wall; and after they had come in and reached the altar they began to cut the Persians down and made a mighty onslaught on them which they never withstood, and having run up to the emperor Constantine they undid his chains and called upon God, praising him and saying: 'Great are you, O Jesus Christ who were crucified under Pontius Pilate for our sake and alone perform great miracles.' Then the king of the {p. 319} Persians and those with him fell down before the feet of the emperor Constantine the Great. He requested that peace should be made for a specified time and that he should be granted his life as a favour, which the most peace-loving and all-holy emperor Constantine did; moreover, the king of the Persians handed over to the emperor of the Romans a thousand Persian guards,[12] who received from Constantine, who is truly one of the saints, the title of Long-haired Persians.[13] And so, having returned with joy from Persia, Constantine who is among the saints and his army reached the parts of Gaul, which are in the neighbourhood of Britain.

8. The saintly Constantine was indeed a man distinguished in every way for the courage of his spirit, the keenness of his intelligence, the erudition of his discourse, the uprightness of his sense of justice, the readiness of his benevolence, the propriety of his appearance and the bravery and fortitude he showed in war; he was of great reputation among barbarians and unequalled among those of his own race, firm and unshaken in honesty. Furthermore, in looks and in elegance of beauty he was both the most seemly and the most handsome, with a pleasing expression, the height of his body being of good stature, that is to say, neither tall nor short; he was rather broad across the shoulders and his neck was thick, and his complexion was ruddy; the hair of his head was not bushy, and he kept his chin quite bare, and he was inclined not to allow hair to grow on many parts of his face; his nose was hooked and his countenance was keen-eyed almost like a lion's; his hair was naturally tawny; against all his enemies, it was by prayer that he brought victory within his grasp.

9. It was almost at the middle of that sequence of events [74r] when suddenly by agreement both Diocletian and Maximianus Herculius abdicated, according to Eusebius of Caesarea because Diocletian had become deranged, and after resigning from the principate with Herculius adopted the life of a private citizen. Now Herculius ended his life by hanging himself, but Diocletian, after taking revenge on Saint Photius and Anicetus, was subjected to ordeal by wrath sent from God; his body swelled and burst out in many places and wasted away; his blasphemous tongue rotted in his windpipe and seethed in

a multitude of worms; and this is how after loud bellowing he snapped the thread of his utterly evil life. {p. 320} But according to Gelasius, the bishop of the same Caesarea, they changed their minds and wanted to be emperors again, and were killed by a resolution of the Senate applying to both of them. Therefore after these things had happened and the Christian-minded Constans, as we said, had departed to God, or rather was said to have departed, two men controlled the Roman empire, the saintly Constantine and Maximianus, also known as Galerius. He based his administration in the city of Nicomedia in the East, while the most godly and Christian Constantine was ruling reverently in the provinces of Gaul and Britain. At that time, Saborias held the sceptre of Persia, and the holy high priest Sylvester, who is numbered among the saints, was bishop of the Church of the Romans. So the following four men were emperors at the same time with Constantine: Maximianus known as Galerius with two Caesars, Severus and Maximianus the son of Galerius, and Maxentius the son of Herculius who was proclaimed emperor in Rome by the soldiers. These strove to outdo each other in the war against the Christians, for this is the right name for their persecution. Maxentius the tyrant, who was not merely the son of Maximianus Herculius but also the brother of Theodora, the wife of Constans, the father of Constantine the Great, [74v] and so the uncle of Dalmatius and Hannibalianus, was more wicked than any of his predecessors; he had set up his administration in Rome, and in the course of his lawless reign there committed utterly terrible deeds, robbery, extortion and every other crime of that kind; indeed, he sent many of the leaders of the Senate to execution without trial on the grounds that they were Christians, and when he lusted after the free-born wives of strangers, in some cases he used to make a mockery of his impure and foul action through flattery and {p. 321} deceit as he corrupted them; but in others he used to resort to force, like a tyrant.

10. The blessed and holy emperor Constantine heard of this and very much besides, and when he also received delegations from the Romans about these very matters, asking him not to overlook it when Rome, the mother of cities, was being destroyed by a rough tyrant with the manners of a wild animal, he became angry and exceedingly wrathful; for in the case of virtuous and God-fearing men, injustice committed in other people's affairs causes personal grief; he often sent letters to Maxentius warning him to abstain from evil-doing, and when he was not heeded the only course open to him seemed to be

to take up arms to aid the Romans who were suffering such things, for to rescue those people was as much as to say that he was rescuing the whole human race. But Maxentius, a most irreligious man, did not refrain from evil-doing even when he heard that, and further east Maximianus, known as Galerius, was committing even worse crimes. It was while two evil potentates had been allotted East and West and were fanning war against the Christians that the Senate of the Romans voted Licinius as Caesar, and proclaimed that as emperor he should have all authority, thereby gratifying the holy Constantine because he was his brother-in-law through Constantia, his sister, and especially because he was pretending to our religion (though falsely). Accordingly, when Severus had met his end (he had obviously died at the hands of the army), the time came that the most godly and saintly emperor Constantine, hearing that Rome was labouring under the crimes of Maxentius and that the East was suffering under the tyranny of Maximianus known as Galerius, concluded that the peace of the Roman empire [75r] would have to be sacrificed in order to achieve the downfall of the tyrants. But when he had learned that Constantine, the lover of Christ, {p. 322} was setting foot in Italy, using much speed the impious Maxentius led his army forth from Rome and, having bridged with boats the river that flows past the city, on which also the Milvian bridge stands, he drew his forces up against Constantine the Great.

11. But the great and holy emperor Constantine had already become alarmed about the deceitful sorcery of Maxentius, for the wretch used to cut new-born babes up for the purpose of obtaining oracles and do, on the pretext of seeking portents, many unspeakable deeds and commit many works of impiety; naturally, for this reason, the noble-minded and great-hearted Constantine began to seek the aid of the God worshipped by his father, beseeching him and calling upon him to let Constantine see who he was, and to lend his right hand for the tasks facing Constantine; and this actually happened. For while Constantine was in earnest prayer and entreaty, on a certain plain with his army, he experienced a miracle about the middle hour of the day; for a shooting of rays shining out above the sun in the sky was changed into the form of a cross with an impression in stars, in Latin letters, declaring to the emperor Constantine, 'in this conquer'. Of course, the emperor was puzzled at this and asked those with him if they had seen anything, and when they all admitted to having seen the same vision, the emperor was utterly astonished; however, when

117

also night had overtaken him, Christ, along with the sign that had been revealed in the sky, appeared to the emperor where he slept and said, 'Have a reproduction made of this heavenly vision that you have seen, and decree that it shall go before your front line, and not only will you keep those who oppose you now in subjection, [75v] but all your enemies, both earthly and supernatural, will tremble at you.' At once, it was day; the emperor's heart was strengthened, and he was full of courage and ardour; he got up and told his friends the secret; then he summoned goldsmiths, demonstrated the appearance of the cross-like sign, and commanded them to imitate it in gold and precious stones.

12. {p. 323} And it was constructed in a shape like this: a lofty pole fashioned in gold had an oblique arm made in the shape of a cross; and above, near the tip of the whole device, was a crown drawing its middle in to form a letter rho crossed with a chi, declaring the name of Christ through its first element; and from the cross arm, which was pierced at the pole, a cloth made of gold hung, bearing the likeness of the God-loving emperor himself made in gold down as far as his breast, and of his children. And Constantine the Great used this saving sign, that had been revealed from heaven and created in the works of the most skilful gold beaters, which has continued to exist to the present day and is guarded as a great gift in the imperial store rooms, as it is a bulwark against any opposing or hostile force; he commanded forthwith that it should be set on a very high pole and should go at the head of his army.[14] And when the armies were joined in combat in the war, what happened? Those on Maxentius' side were defeated, and the foe was crushed by the power of the cross and mostly perished by the sword. Maxentius for his part left the field and fled with a few followers; when, therefore, the saintly Constantine began to pursue him, in his flight he fell in a device of his own contriving; for by the power of God the bridge broke completely and the worthless Maxentius was drowned in the river, together with his guards and his retinue, as Pharaoh was drowned of old with all his army; and the river and the bridge which is called the Milvian bridge was filled with horses and riders; both were drowned; we may pronounce over him the sentence in the prophets [76r]: {p. 324} *he dug a pit and excavated it, and he shall fall into the hole which is his own work*.[15]

13. Such was the end of the tyrant Maxentius; but the citizens of

Rome, since it was they who had asked Constantine to arouse himself and rescue them, and since they had been ransomed from the tyranny of the wicked Maxentius, decorated the city with garlands and welcomed the great emperor Constantine with great joy and acclamation, calling upon both the cross, which had bestowed the victory, and him as saviour and benefactor; and in this way the war against the Christians ceased.

14. The first action of the God-promoted emperor after gaining control of Rome was to order the remains of the holy martyrs to be collected and given consecrated burial; then he commanded that all prosecutions of Christians should be annulled and those in exile should be recalled, those in prison should be released, and those whose property had been confiscated should have it restored, and the churches of God should be rebuilt with much zeal and costly offerings; he also commanded that the shrines of idols should be pulled down and destroyed with fire, and that their revenues should be paid to the holy churches of God; and all these actions proceeded quickly, so as to keep pace with his words, and everything was done in order, as an emperor should, and with due authority. When the Romans saw these things, they rejoiced and were very glad, and observed a festival for seven days to thank God for the victory; and they began to worship the venerable Cross of the Lord and bow down to it and salute it, and they extolled Constantine as a conqueror famed in song and story. So passed the seventh year of Constantine's reign.

15. But because up to this time the blessed Constantine happened to be {p. 325} uninitiated in holy baptism, what fearful vision came before his eyes? He was smitten and fell into a leprosy resembling elephantiasis all over his body, and was so terribly afflicted that he was in a state of despair. At this, many treatments were offered to him by sorcerers and enchanters, [76v] and experts in the healing arts were even fetched from Persia, but far from being able to give him relief, they tended to do him harm, and actually made him worse; and the Greeks, those workers of wickedness, wise only in their own magical arts, who are called the devil's most genuine armour bearers, came within an ace of deceiving the saint in their utter wickedness. What did those wretches say? That a bathing pool ought to be made on the Capitol at Rome and that it should be filled with the blood of innocent young children, and that after the emperor had bathed

in it while the blood was still living and, as it were, steaming, he would be able both to be cleansed from the troublesome illness and subsequently to benefit from unimpaired health. What folly on the part of the Greeks, or rather, what inhumanity and depravity! You were fools and madmen, to advertise that as the result of such treatment one man should be cured through the slaughter of many infants, thus advising and persuading the emperor Constantine to become a slayer of children. Away with your wicked and disgusting counsel! But the evil and deranged Greeks caught the emperor's attention with their promise of health and made haste to prepare the devil's food for him by their own deceitfulness. For when the emperor heard this he became very cheerful at the prospect of recovering his own health and in haste despatched soldiers up and down every province to bring together a great multitude of children; and these they mustered with speed, and fixed a day for {p. 326} slaughtering them. Now as the emperor was leaving to ascend the Capitol, and the men who were to slaughter the children were ready, he was confronted by the children's mothers tearing their hair, howling and lamenting and bursting out in screams of hysterical laughter, so that the air was filled with their wailing. And when the emperor enquired what might be the reason that compelled such a great crowd of women to approach him with cries of woe, and when he understood that they were the mothers of the children who were going to be killed, and when he had been overcome by the sheer excess of their hatred, [77r] he groaned with heartfelt emotion and began to weep and say in a loud voice: 'The fountainhead and root of the reputation of the Roman empire is respect for religion; therefore, so that I may reveal it to all in its proper light, I judge the safety of the children to be more important than my own health; this cruel and inhumane decree arising from the blood of infants shall be overthrown; it is Roman respect for religion that shall restore these dear children to their mothers. For it is better for me to die for the sake of the lives of these innocent children than by their death to renew my brief and transitory life. Indeed, let the dear children be restored to their mothers so that the delight of having their sons back may sweeten the bitterness of the mothers' tears.' With these words he returned to the Palatine Hill and he not only restored the children to their female parents, but also commanded that as the mothers went home they should be offered money for their subsistence allowance and expenses; the result was that though they had arrived in Rome with tears of grief, they regained their own homes in gladness, jumping for joy.

16. In the course of this night the emperor saw a vision in which the holy Apostles appeared to him and said, 'We are Peter {p. 327} and Paul, and we have been sent from beside almighty God to give you a token of salvation, so that you may send to Sylvester the bishop and fetch him to you; he has a pool of reverence to show you, in which you have hitherto had no share; once you have bathed in that, you will soap away all the filthiness of your sores and once you have become well you will be judged worthy of eternal life, in the same way as you yourself granted it to the innocent children.'

17. While these words were being spoken, the noble and godly emperor Constantine woke up and noticed the usual doctor standing beside him, the one who regularly put the dressings on his sores. Constantine said to the doctor, 'Human aid shall no longer be applied to me, but the hand of almighty [77v] God shall be my helper. Go away from me for ever.' And with these words he sent away at once to the blessed Sylvester and arranged for him to receive every mark of respect when he arrived; and as Sylvester came in, the emperor rose and greeted him first, saying: 'As we welcome you, we are glad that you are well.' Saint Sylvester replied and said: 'May peace and victory be granted to you from heaven.' Then the most worthy emperor Constantine told him about the vision and said: 'In a dream two men called Peter and Paul appeared to me and told me everything about you, and lo, you have arrived! So I request to be baptised by you in the name of Christ and our God; but I also have this request to make to your reverence; if you have any portraits of the saints whom I have seen, show them to me so that I may recognise their features, if these really are the saints who said that they had been sent from beside God.' Of course, the chief bishop handed the portraits to the emperor at once, and made him even more joyful; and when the emperor saw them and recognised that they were those who had appeared to him while he was asleep during the course of the night, he began to shout and say: 'Really, nothing is more true than these portraits; for these {p. 328} are those whom I saw saying to me "Send for bishop Sylvester and he will come and show you a pool of reverence, and when you have bathed in it you will find healing from your sores."' And the blessed and holy Sylvester commanded the emperor to fast for seven days and blessed him, and after making him

a catechumen he departed from him; and on the sabbath during the evening of which the prescribed fasting was completed, having already prepared his usual train of acolytes, the holy Sylvester said to the blessed emperor, 'O Emperor, this water which you see, because it receives divine power through the invocation of the holy and life-giving Trinity, not only cleanses the exterior of bodies from every blemish, but also cleanses [78r] souls from every sin and every stain and makes them brighter than the sun; therefore enter it now in this precious and holy bath of baptism and you shall be cleansed both in your body and of all the faults that you have committed.' After saying this, and more besides, the saint blessed the water, and once the emperor had been anointed with the holy chrism of olive oil and had entered the sacred pool, what a great miracle then occurred! For in the very act of him being baptised by Saint Sylvester in the name of the utterly holy and life-giving Trinity, suddenly a light of immeasurable brilliance shone forth and there was a sound like a cymbal being struck, and the great emperor Constantine emerged from the pool entirely cured, leaving behind him the water of baptism full of what looked like fish scales, and said to Saint Sylvester, 'O servant of God, as I was standing there, at the time of my holy baptism, I felt a hand grasping my whole body and cleansing my disease.' {p.329} His eldest son Crispus was also baptised with him, both being clad in white robes. Furthermore, this is said in corroboration of his sacred baptism, and we have heard it from reverent men, that in Old Rome to this very day they preserve the baptistery as evidence that Constantine the Great was baptised in Rome by our saintly father Sylvester whose authority as a teacher is recognised all over the world, and also in corroboration that the holy and all-sacred Cross appeared in heaven and that its power was made manifest in the utter extermination and destruction of Maxentius, who had been such a tyrannical emperor. And let no one be surprised that it was before his baptism that Constantine, who is altogether to be praised, obtained such grace as both to hear a voice from heaven and see an image of the precious cross and behold Christ's [78v] holy Apostles Peter and Paul clearly visible. In point of fact, he was recognised earlier as Christian in his ways, and besides, miracles have been revealed to many unbelievers; how much more are they likely to be revealed to those who believe so greatly? Moreover, he was worthy to see them by reason of his actions, for indeed he was prudent, compassionate, humble, merciful and endowed with every other virtue.

18. But those who dwell in the East, Arian-minded persons holding false beliefs, say that it was in Nicomedia, where he actually ended his life, that he was baptised near the time of his death by Eusebius of Nicomedia, the Arian. For they say that he was prone to defer his baptism because he hoped to be baptised in the river Jordan. But remove {p. 330} the object of their frivolity from their vain and diabolical imaginings! This is not how the truth is, ye mad and senseless people! Nay, to me the notion of his having been baptised by the blessed Sylvester in the older Rome[16] seems nearer the truth, and it does indeed cling fast to the truth, and I accept it and unhesitatingly believe it as something safer and secure, and I testify this to everyone, that the regulations which are attributed to Miltiades are inventions found in the writings of the Arians who are eager to claim some credit for themselves from them, who also want to slander the all-reverent emperor Constantine by showing him as an unbaptised person, which indeed is unworthy of belief and untrue; for if he had not been baptised, then he could not have taken part in the holy sacraments at the Council of Nicaea, nor could he have joined the meeting with the holy fathers, which it is as absurd to think as to say.

19. Assuredly it was frivolous of the Arians and the Greeks to invent this; let us leave them to their nonsense and direct our tale once more to the great emperor Constantine and his mighty deeds.

20. So during this time the great and Christ-loving emperor Constantine was ruling in Rome, praising God for all the deeds which he performed so magnificently in his case; [79r] however, Maximinus the son of Galerius at that time made an assault upon the empire, but in Cilicia he too brought his life to a dishonourable end;[17] indeed, both Maximinus and his father Galerius had heard that Maxentius the son of Herculius, after wreaking his vengeance on the holy Panteleemon, had been overwhelmed by Constantine the Great through the power of the glorious and life-giving Cross; Maximinus was so frightened that he broke off his persecution of the Christians. But the account of the sufferings {p. 331} of Christ's servants at the hands of the tyrant in Nicomedia stung Constantine, that great and godly emperor, to the heart, as he was a saint who had detested wickedness ever since his childhood; accordingly, under the guidance of God, he set out from Rome with the Caesar Licinius and made an expedition against Maximinus the son of Galerius by land and sea.[18]

And Maximinus for his part had prepared an expedition against them and joined battle with them, supported by a numberless host, in the district of Astacus, relying on the oracles of demons and the treacherous artifices of wizards. When the life-giving Cross led the vanguard for Constantine the Great, Maximinus commanded all his archers to take careful aim and direct their shots at the glorious cross; so when the enemy attacked *en masse* the one who bore that victorious piece of armour was suddenly afraid, for he was inclined to paganism and made haste to hand it on to another; but one of the orthodox Christians, who was proud to call himself the son of a martyr, tore off his breastplate and helmet and leaped forward, clad only in his tunic, and seized the glorious Cross. By now there were arrows flying all round, and the man who had excused himself from the victorious piece of armour received a fatal blow, and was seen at once to fall dead, whereas the man who had taken on the glorious Cross remained unwounded, though many men were shooting at him; for by some miraculous divine power, many arrows that were aimed at that symbolic emblem stuck in it, but they all flew away from the man who was carrying it, even though he was in the midst of danger. [79v] Moreover, it is said that no other man carrying this piece of armour has ever met with misfortune or been wounded or taken prisoner.[19] So when, as has been said, battle had commenced and the glorious Cross had been displayed, the tyrant, who was relying on demonic sorcery, was routed at the first assault and would have been slain along with his host, {p. 332} but he fled, discarding even his imperial robes, and having clad himself in the manner of a common soldier he made his escape with a few of his most faithful supporters and departed from village to village, and after calling all the priests of idols and seers together, and those who were proclaimed as prophets because of their magical arts, slew them as frauds.[20] Indeed, the most holy emperor Constantine was on the point of overpowering this Maximinus the son of Galerius when the wrath of God intervened and caught him; for as it were a flame was lit from the middle of his entrails and the marrow of his bones and laid him prone on the ground with unendurable pain, so as to cause both his eyes to leap out of their sockets and leave the impious man blind; and his flesh became altogether putrid and began to fall off his bones with immeasurable burning; and in this manner he rotted away altogether and ended the life that he had spent fighting against God.[21] Moreover, the godly emperor Constantine, as one ruling in Christ, allotted to Licinius, his comrade in arms, who was craftily feigning

Christianity, a separate portion of Roman territory opposite the all-blessed city of Nicomedia and the city of Heracleia in Thrace, since Licinius happened to be his brother-in-law through marriage to his sister Constantia. He had previously proclaimed Licinius emperor and had demanded in return a treaty from him not to commit any evil deed against the Christians and to administer the eastern part of the empire well and in a God-fearing manner.

21. Henceforth, by the grace of Christ directed towards us, the war against the tyrants ceased and so Constantine the Great, having become sole ruler of the whole Roman empire [80r] diverted all his attention to the affairs of God, encouraging churches and enriching them from his own treasury. He was the first emperor to promulgate, as his foremost statute, a decree that the shrines of idols should be restored to those who had been consecrated to Christ; furthermore, his son Crispus joined him in making this legislation. {p.333} Constantine's second enactment was that only Christians should serve in the army and be held worthy of imperial rank, while those who persisted in the worship of idols and attempted to bring Christ into discredit should suffer capital punishment; his third was that for our holy and salvific feast of Easter, in which Christ saved us by fulfilling all his ministry, two weeks should become holidays, both that before the resurrection and that after; the first because of our Lord's suffering and the Cross, the second because of the resurrection.[22]

22. This is how the great-minded and holy Constantine, having enjoyed such generous benefits from God and having strengthened the faith, was rendering grateful thanks and praise to Christ his benefactor for every instance; profound peace had been unfolded over creation, and tranquillity had taken possession of the creatures, the faithful were making merry and rejoicing over the complete transformation, and daily all the nations were joining the faith of Christ and being baptised, and crushing their ancestral idols to pieces; but all the time Licinius went on secretly holding his pagan opinions. He hated the Christians, and though, for fear of the emperor Constantine, he refrained from stirring up open persecution against them, he used to make much mischief against Constantine without being detected; and as time went on, he actually began to stir up open persecution in his own territory. At first this opponent of God persecuted the Christians at his own court, forgetting the

downfall of the tyrants before him and his own treaties with Constantine the Great [80v]; but he became so addicted to woman-ising, committing injustice and murder that there were many ex-amples of martyrs for Christ in various ways at different places. When the godly Constantine sent him rescripts ordering him to desist from {p. 334} his folly, it was of no avail; then Constantine the Great, seeing that Licinius was conducting the persecution more frenziedly and was meditating a plot against his benefactor, took arms against him by land and sea; the clash of war that would affect the whole State was heard throughout Bithynia; Licinius was beaten and fled, and was making his escape to Chalcedon when he was caught just after he had reached Chrysopolis, and the wretch was handed over, alive, to the authority of Constantine the Great. But Constantine exercised his customary clemency and did not kill him but granted him his life and banished him as a prisoner to Thessalonica. However, it was not long before the wretched Licinius gathered a force of barbarians and having hired them as mercenaries was contemplating a revolution, if the most godly Constantine, having foreseen this, had not condemned him to execution by the sword, and had his abominable head cut off.[23] In this way henceforth the Christian State enjoyed perfect tranquillity, since the tyrants and Christ-hating emperors had been got rid of with the help of Christ and the power of his glorious and life-giving Cross. Constantine the Great, since he had become the sole ruler of the whole Roman empire, proclaimed his own sons as Caesars and so henceforth Christianity prevailed and the cities of the Romans passed their time in profound peace.

23. Byzantium was a small city founded in the days of Manasseh, king of Judaea, by Byzas who called it by his own name.[24] {p. 335} It was inhabited by barbarian people not subject to Roman rule who displayed much independence and discourtesy towards the Romans; accordingly, after slaying Licinius, Constantine the Great marched against them from Nicomedia. [81r] However, the Byzantines were unwilling to accept Constantine as emperor and to bow their necks to his yoke and pay tribute to him, and so war broke out between them.[25] What is more, on the first day of their encounter, 6,000 Romans fell; nevertheless, Constantine the Great had pitched his tent and fixed his quarters where the forum now is, though he was sorely distressed over the loss of the 6,000 men. So for a second time battle was joined, and again likewise 3,000 of the Romans fell; furthermore,

the Byzantines drew their forces up to join battle for yet one more day, hoping to take the Romans prisoner and put them in chains; for Constantine the Great had brought only a few soldiers with him on that occasion because the bulk of his army had been sent back to Rome on garrison duty by reason of an invasion by the Persians.[26] Overtaken by night, therefore, and reduced to despair, the great emperor raised his eyes to heaven, and he saw, just as he had also formerly seen in the war against the tyrant Maxentius, writing in stars which said to him: 'Call on me in the day of your distress and I shall rescue you and you will glorify me.' Amazed at the miraculous vision, he looked again and saw a cross made out of stars fixed in the sky and the following written message: 'In this sign you will conquer all your foes.' At once he was reminded that the {p. 336} sign had come to him again, just as it had when he had slain the villainous Maxentius through the agency of the power of the glorious cross beside the Milvian bridge over the river at Rome, and without delay he drew his dirk and made the emblem of the Cross out of a piece of wood, and began to take the initiative in the war. So when both the Byzantines and the Romans joined battle on the next day the Romans both won a mighty victory over the Byzantines and captured Byzantium. [81v] Constantine, the truly great, became emperor in Old Rome in the year 5718 after the foundation of the world, which is the year 318 after the incarnation of our Lord Jesus Christ the son of God; he was the thirty-second to become emperor in the Roman empire counting from the reign of Augustus.[27]

24. Indeed, this thrice blessed Constantine the Great, who is numbered among the saints, being moved by the command of God, wanted to found a city called after his own name in the plain in front of Ilion, over Ajax' tomb where, according to tradition, the Greeks who were on the expedition against Troy had kept their ships beached, but God commanded him in a dream to build it at Byzantium, which he actually did. He first took possession of the place that had been indicated to him and both inspected it all round and surveyed the lie of the land, noting that the climate and weather were good; then he purified the sacred groves from their defilement and as far as possible levelled the elevated parts among the more hollow places; then, having smoothed out the land to suitably gentle gradients, he made and established according to the vision that had been revealed to him that same God-protected city to which he gave the title Constantinople, bestowing his own name on it; and in the

part that faces the rising sun he constructed a most delightful palace filled with works of art and bordering the sea, and built a racecourse and two very large porticoes onto it, and if it were desired to form an accurate impression of the skilfulness of their layout, one would say {p.337} that these buildings were not inferior to the works of Pheidias. Moreover, having endowed this city munificently, he transferred to it as settlers eminent persons of importance from Rome, and having selected a different location for each single one, he granted them large mansions which he bestowed upon them according to their family, and in this way caused the city to be inhabited. Accordingly he decreed that Constantinople should be styled New Rome [82r] and commanded that it should have a Senate;[28] he also caused a column carved from a single block of porphyry to be erected in the place known as the forum surmounted by a statue of himself in bronze.[29] In his hand was an orb, and onto the orb he had the glorious cross affixed, engraved with the words 'To you, O Christ my God, I dedicate this city'.[30] When Constantine the Great had decorated the city with such fine buildings, and columns also, he brought into it all the finest works of art and statues of bronze or marble from every city and province. Indeed, it is said that inside the stonework under the column of porphyry that stands in the forum, in two vaults near the base of the pillar, are stored the very loaves distributed to the 5,000 in the presence of Christ and his disciples, as is written in the gospel, that is to say, what was left over, and the twelve baskets and the seven creels, and the axe which Noah used when he made the joinery for the ark, and it is said that Constantine the Great put them inside the column with his own hands and sealed them there.[31]

25. This same Constantine the Great also crossed the river called Danube, that is, the Ister, built a stone bridge over it, and subdued the Scythians, after the all-revered cross had appeared in the sky there also and had fought on his side, as before. Moreover, he nominated his son Constans for appointment as Caesar and despatched him to the Gallic {p. 338} provinces. In Rome, on the other hand, the all-praiseworthy emperor with his own hands demolished the building which is called in Latin the Lateran, that is, 'the palace', and after making a design, constructed a church in the name of our Lord Jesus Christ. Likewise also in Nicomedia, in a high place called Tracheia he built their shrine for the 3,618 holy martyrs[32] of Christ who had contended there in the time of Maximinus the son of Herculius;[33] in

the same way, he was personally responsible for building the eight-sided church of the Lord [82v] in the city of Antioch. Indeed, he also founded a city at Drepanum to the honour of the martyr Lucian and called it Helenopolis, after his mother's name.[34] What is more, in his devotion to Christ, the emperor also built the colossal shrine named after Holy Wisdom, not the one visible now, but a much smaller one, and the shrines of the holy Peace and of the holy and renowned Apostles, and of Saint Mocius,[35] and of the holy martyr Agathonicus, and of Saint Menas, and the shrine at Sosthenium, on the lower mouth of the Bosporus, of the holy and most glorious archangel Michael. The cause of building the shrine of the archangel at Sosthenium was as follows: when the famous Argonauts in the time of the Greeks were sailing up the Bosporus to its mouth with the intention of plundering that same country also, and when Amycus, the king of the place, made war on them, in fear of his might they took refuge in a bay surrounded by woods in a remote, wild district, and they saw approaching them a miraculous vision of a fearsome man with wings like an eagle's on his shoulders, who actually made a heavenly proclamation to them that they would be victorious over Amycus; they were encouraged and interpreted the vision to such effect that they conquered and killed Amycus. Afterwards, in gratitude for what had been revealed to them, they set up a temple in the very same place where they had seen it {p. 339} and put up a representation of the miraculous apparition and called the place, or rather the temple, the Sosthenium, because they had been saved when they had fled there. So when, after he had become ruler of Byzantium, the emperor Constantine, that co-worker of God, saw the representation, he said to his great men, 'This is the representation of an angel who is honoured according to the teaching of the Christians.' For their part, they were all amazed at seeing not only the beauty of the temple but also the likeness of the representation. Well, after the emperor had said a prayer and had prevailed upon God, who oversees all things, to reveal to him what miracle [83r] was represented, he went to bed in that place and heard, as in a vision, a loud voice saying to him: 'I am Michael, the commander-in-chief of the powers of the lord of Sabaoth, the one who stands in the front rank of the Christians and protects them with his shield, the one who has helped you against impious tyrants and every unbelieving and barbarous nation invisibly, as you are the faithful servant of my master, Christ.' At once the most holy emperor Constantine arose with great joy and gave thanks to the God of heaven and earth; he embellished the place and the temple worthily, building an altar facing the east, and named it the shrine of Michael in the holy place Sosthenium. And this great emperor built many other churches of the holy martyrs of Christ in various places and countries, both decorating them gloriously and endowing them from his imperial resources; the glorious and holy emperor Constantine, by the grace of Christ, also decreed peace for the churches.

26. However, at Alexandria, Arius, after whom the madness is called, had revealed his heresy to the Church and, with the aid of the wicked one, who cannot endure to behold the Church at peace, had succeeded in causing schism; {p. 340} for being possessed by the spirit of wickedness, Arius senselessly and discordantly used to say and lay down as doctrine 'there was a time when He was not', and that it was later when Christ became our true God; in addition to this, he prated that the one who is immutable and unalterable, the one who is independent of time, both infinite and impalpable according to the word of divinity, was created and subject to suffering and death, and was fallen, limited and bounded by time.

27. {p. 637} Constantine, the triumphant and great emperor, learned all these matters from a letter sent by Alexander, that true saint, who was archbishop of Alexandria. The unexpected report stung his mind like a goad, and being greatly distressed he immediately made use of imperial directives to command [83v] all those in authority and all the bishops who were strong in Christian belief to go to Nicaea, the capital of Bithynia, not only for a scrutiny of the news that was reaching him but for a declaration of the true and unimpeachable faith and the excision and utter removal of the dangerous and devilish heresy of those whose beliefs were not orthodox. It was the twelfth indiction of the cyclical calculation of the times, and the thirteenth year of the removal of the holy and blessed Constantine from Rome to Byzantium.[36] As these matters had proceeded in this way according to the will of God, certain bishops were found who had been preserved at that precise moment in time in the knowledge of the all-holy and life-giving Spirit. Each of them rose up from his own church and made his way to the stronghold of Nicaea. Accordingly, the holy and worldwide {p. 638} Council of the saints, consisting of 318 holy fathers inspired by God,[37] convened on the twentieth of May, and it marked the culmination of three and a half years. And so, when these holy fathers had met, the majority were miracle-workers and equal

to angels, because they bore the stigmata of Christ from their earlier persecutions. Among them was Paphnutius of Egypt, a holy man and a worker of miracles, and Spiridon likewise, and he who was greatest in miracles, Nicolaus of the unguents, Paul the bishop of Neo-Caesarea in Euphratesia, Gregorius the bishop of Greater Armenia, Leontius the bishop of Caesarea in Cappadocia and James of Nisibis, both miracle workers who had not only raised people from the dead but had performed many other marvels. So when this holy Council had come about in Nicaea in Bithynia, in the presence of the emperor Constantine the Great, most victorious in Christ, with the aid of the holy Trinity which is consubstantial, life-giving and indivisible, the godly and holy fathers who were adherents of the true faith [84r] overthrew Arius and his supporters; and when they had cast him out and anathematised him and defined him as being outside the true faith and the holy Catholic Church, the 318 composed the holy formula of the faith unanimously and proclaimed the Son of God to be co-eternal and consubstantial and indivisible from the Father and the Holy Spirit, having signed the decree together with the emperor Constantine, who is worthy of veneration.[38] After the Council was over, though almost all signed, 316 actually, there were two who had been omitted before the signing; for it had befallen them to die a common death. And the story concerning them also will reveal, for the glory of Father, Son and Holy Spirit and for the edification of those whose opinions are grounded in our unimpeachable faith, how God takes thought for those who are orthodox both in their lives and in their understanding, {p. 639} and how the one who has brought the whole universe into existence from non-existence performs miracles in every individual case; and we have judged the miracle that occurred then to be worthy of record for our own glory and to inspire shame and respect among unbelievers. For when two of the holy bishops, Chrysanthus and Musonius, had not yet put their signatures to the decree, it befell by divine providence that they should depart from this life and go out to God; therefore the holy and inspired fathers were not at all distressed, but upon discovering that they had fallen asleep in death, came with confidence and pronounced the following memorial over them: 'O glorious fathers Chrysanthus and Musonius, you have fought the good fight along with us, you have completed the race, you have proclaimed the faith; if you have judged what has taken place to be dear to God, for now you meditate upon the uncreated and blessed Trinity in greater purity, let there be nothing to prevent you also from signing the decree.' Not only did they say this together, but they sealed the papyrus roll and placed it inside the glorious tomb of the holy [84v] fathers, and passed the whole of that night in prayer without sleeping. And so, on the next day, when they came to the tomb, where the seals that had been placed upon the sacred document were intact, on unrolling it they found inserted in it the signatures, still fresh, of the holy bishops Chrysanthus and Musonius who had already departed to the Lord, with the following declaration: 'We, Chrysanthus and Musonius, who took part with all the fathers who were unanimous at the holy, first, worldwide Council in Nicaea, even though we have departed in the body, nevertheless with our own hands have appended our signatures.' What a wonderful and extraordinary miracle, or rather fact and report, that in some way though their bodies were cold, being corpses lying in the tomb, {p.640} nevertheless the dead listened to the deliberations of the living and signed with their own hands and so caused that holy and glorious choir of saintly fathers to be complete! How fearsome are your works, O Lord! Who is able to speak of your might or make all your praises heard? Indeed, I extol you, O Lord, and I proclaim your glory, O God, lover of mankind, to the man who never turns aside or who does not hearken to those who put their trust in you.

28. But let the narration of the story of the blessed and saintly Constantine be taken up again. For after the ecclesiastical disputes and after both the publication of the sacred canons and the divine and orthodox decree of the holy fathers had been made and put in order, and after the emperor Constantine the Great had been acclaimed and the Council had broken up, the most holy lord Constantine rose from his imperial throne and standing in the middle of the assembly he said to the Council, 'I am calling upon you, holy fathers; if you really love me like a legitimate son, I ask you for one favour. Just grant it.' And they, with one accord, said to him, 'O most reverend emperor, command whatever may seem good to you.' And he said, 'Do not hesitate, after so long a time, to indulge me for a few days, and to come into the [85r] city with me, and consecrate the city that has been founded by me in my name and bless the city walls and fortifications that have been set up there.' And the 318 holy fathers in Nicaea obeyed him very readily and came into that prestigious city in the eleventh day of the month of May and blessed the walls that had been built by the emperor Constantine the Great, and offered a bloodless sacrifice of prayer to God.[39] This was during the

time that the saintly Metrophanes was Patriarch of Constantinople. After this, {p. 641} when the prayer had been concluded, the emperor Constantine urged all the holy fathers to come to a banquet,[40] and he was glad and rejoiced greatly to see them there. And he actually kissed the sockets from which the eyes of Paphnutius and his fellow confessors had been gouged out, and their limbs that had been mutilated during the persecution, obtaining sanctification from them.[41] And he spent time exhorting all the bishops to preserve peace and refrain from abusing their neighbours and consigned to the flames accusations which [certain gentlemen, quarrelsome among themselves] had published against their own bishops, affirming with an oath that if he saw a bishop committing adultery, in his own words, 'I would eagerly choose to cover him with my purple robe to prevent the spectacle of what was being done from harming those who were looking.' And after granting many favours to all the churches and exhorting the rulers of the pagans to honour the clergy, he was glad to send them all away rejoicing.

29. However, when the Christ-loving emperor Constantine was criticised by certain learned Greek persons in Byzantium on the grounds that in making innovations in religion he acted wrongly and against the custom of Roman emperors, after giving audience the emperor decided to send one of the philosophers to the most holy Alexander in order to debate with him; he was a Greek, and an altogether most skilful philosopher, while the blessed Alexander, though a holy man, was unskilled in dialectic. The philosopher who was [85v] skilled in dialectic talked until his tongue ached, but Alexander said, 'I command you in the name of Jesus Christ our true God to be silent and cease utterance.' As soon as he said that word the philosopher of the Greek religion was muzzled and became speechless; so that all of a sudden having come under the influence of speechlessness, the philosopher approached the choir of saints in fear and trembling and requested not only release from this restriction but also the gift of holy baptism. In this way did the Lord of signs and wonders call the philosopher with his whole household to salvation, {p. 642} and revealed him who had, the previous day, been a critic of the orthodox faith, on the day after to be an advocate of the truth.[42] Furthermore, at that time, the emperor, during the Council, had commanded Macarius, the current archbishop of the holy Church in Jerusalem on his return to search out the place of the holy resurrection of Christ our God and Golgotha, the place of the

skull, and the life-bestowing piece of wood, that is to say, the glorious and holy Cross of our Lord Jesus Christ, which he endured for the sake of the salvation of the human race when he redeemed it from error.[43]

30. Meanwhile, as his affairs were prospering, he crowned his devout and most holy mother Helena and assigned coinage to her as an empress;[44] she had seen a vision bidding her to journey to Jerusalem and bring to light the holy places and the sacred crosses that had been buried by the impious Jews. Moreover, she begged her son Constantine to fulfil the command that had been sent to her from God, which he did by despatching her with much money to Jerusalem for the purpose of discovering the life-giving and salvific and glorious Cross of Christ, our Lord and God and saviour. And the blessed and holy Helena departed for Jerusalem, and the holy Macarius, the archbishop of Jerusalem, met her with the deference due to an empress, and conducted with her the search for that life-bearing wood; and they fasted and prayed without ceasing.[45] But [86r] the Lord, who loves mankind, swiftly revealed the place of his holy tomb by informing Macarius in a vision. It was where also the shrine and statue of the unclean spirit Aphrodite were erected. And the holy Helena used her {p.643} imperial authority and swiftly demolished it with an army of workmen, digging it up from the foundations and hurling the mound of earth aside; for it had been built with care and great expense long before, by Hadrian the son of Aelius.[46] The holy tomb and the place of the skull were revealed at once, and nearby, to the east of them, three crosses covered with a heap of soil. After continuing their search, they found also the holy nails with which Christ, our God, had been nailed. But while they were all at a loss to discover which was the Lord's Cross, the holy and kingly one, and the blessed Helena was greatly distressed, Macarius, the well-named bishop, solved the riddle through his faith; there was a certain lady of an illustrious and famous family whose life had been despaired of, and who was almost dead; he brought the crosses near to her and discerned which belonged to the Lord, for when only its shadow had come near the sick woman, though she had ceased to breathe or move, by a divine miracle she was made well and leaped up in good health, praising God in a loud voice. The all-reverent and all-blessed Helena picked the life-giving wood of the glorious Cross up with fear and great joy; part of it, with the sacred and precious nails, she took and kept by her, being anxious to take them to her

son, the Christ-loving Constantine, in Byzantium, which in fact she did; she had the rest placed in a silver casket and gave it to the godly Macarius, the archbishop of the holy Church of God in Jerusalem, for the salvation of future generations.

31. Then this blessed [86v] and truly holy lady, the empress Helena, ordered churches to be founded in places where our Lord had walked on account of our salvation and performed his wonderful miracles; to begin with, she dedicated a church in the name of her son, Saint Constantine, in Jerusalem, {p. 644} where was found the life-giving wood of the Cross that is altogether to be revered; likewise she also erected churches in the sacred tomb where the sacred resurrection of Christ our God took place and at the place of the skull, and built a flight of marble steps towards the east of the holy city leading down to holy Gethsemane; and since in this place is the tomb of the holy mother of God, she also first made a very beautiful church on the actual tomb itself in the name of the mother of God who is altogether holy, and then around her tomb that is altogether sacred she built a wall within the sanctuary of the church; indeed, it is said by many, as we have heard, that the same place, which slopes down steeply, is called the vale of weeping and the torrent of the cedars and the valley of Jehosaphat. But the garden in which Christ our God was betrayed is also there, as is the place in which the Lord prayed on the night he was betrayed. When she had left there, the wonderful Helena ascended the Mount of Olives to the east, where Christ our God was taken up, and having with faith established there a church dedicated to Christ our God and saviour, she went down to Bethany, which is two miles from the city, to the tomb of the blessed and holy Lazarus, and after kneeling on the ground and worshipping almighty God and besprinkling the tomb of the righteous Lazarus with her warm tears and giving orders for a church in the name of holy Lazarus to be built over his tomb, she reached the river Jordan in which Christ our God was baptised for the sake of our salvation; and after crossing the Jordan she also found the cave in which the Forerunner used to dwell, and made a church in the name of John the Baptist. Right opposite the cave is a higher place, in which holy Elijah [87r] was taken up into the heavens; having commanded that an altogether venerable shrine should be established there in the name of the prophet Elijah, she departed for the city of Tiberias, {p. 645} which is four days' journey from the holy city. The following places are round about Tiberias: the place called Twelve Thrones, where Christ our God

used to sit and teach, where also he multiplied the seven loaves and fed the four thousand;[47] also Capernaum, a place where Christ our God made his dwelling, where also is the house of John the Theologian, where the divine dinner attended by our Lord with the disciples took place; so that is where also the miracle of the centurion took place; this also is where they lowered the bed of the paralytic man from the roof, and in all these places the blessed and holy Helena commanded holy churches, worthy of veneration, to be built to the glory of Christ and the holy places. And after that she crossed back over the river that runs past, accompanied by her imperial escort and by eminent men whom she had brought from Constantinople, and having found a rock bearing the mark of the Cross, upon which Christ healed the woman with an issue of blood, she erected a church there in the name of the glorious and life-giving holy Cross, and set out again from there and having come to a fort called 'Seven Fountains' near to the aforementioned Cross in which there is a large spring, where Christ our God performed the miracle of the five loaves and the two fish, she raised a most wonderful church and from there went back to the sea of Tiberias and found the place in which our Lord Jesus Christ appeared to the holy Apostles after the resurrection when they were fishing, on the occasion when there was the charcoal fire and the baked fish laid on top with the loaf of bread, [87v] where also he took some of it and ate it with them, and where he caught the 153 fish, and there she built a church in the name of the holy and wholly blessed Apostles. Then leaving there with the same eagerness she went two miles farther exulting and rejoicing and found the house of Mary Magdalene, and erected a church there, {p. 646} and after the blessed Helena had visited all the holy places round about Tiberias and had erected churches in each, she entered Tiberias, taking with her such devout men as she had to hand, and when she had discovered in the middle of it the house of the mother-in-law of Peter the Apostle, the woman who had been healed from the fever by the touch of the Master's hand, she put up an altogether beautiful church, St Peter, since he was the leader of the Apostles. Setting out from Tiberias, she travelled twelve miles and ascended Mount Tabor, where Melchisedek blessed Abraham, and after seeking the place where Christ our God was transfigured and finding it, there too she erected a church in the name of the saviour and the holy Apostles Peter, James and John and established a body of saintly and devout men to sing psalms there and endowed them with a great deal of money.

32. Then having come down the mountain in this way towards the east she made her way to Nazareth and sought the house in which the mother of God, who is worthy of all praise, received the greeting of the archangel Gabriel, and there she caused to be completed a wonderful church of the altogether holy [88r] mother of God; and from the city of Nazareth she went to the place called Cana in Galilee and sought the place in which the wedding of Simon the Canaanite occurred, where also Christ our God made the water into wine, and raised a very holy church. She left there for Bethlehem which is six miles from the holy city, where she built in the name of {p. 647} Christ our God a large cruciform church of the kind called 'dromic' and enclosed beneath the great altar both the manger and the holy grotto; she went out of Bethlehem and looked for the place where the holy infants were killed that were slain by Herod, and having honoured the grotto in a worthy manner she built a church in the name of the holy infants and went down to the holy sheepfold, and found the place in which the angels proclaimed the birth of our Lord to the shepherds and said: 'Glory among the highest to God and peace upon earth.' After she had built a church which is held in very great honour to the glory of Mary the mother of God and Joseph her suitor, her course took her back to holy Zion. This is on the highest projection of the holy city facing south. Here, the blessed and holy Helena, the spouse of Constans, the mother of the emperor Constantine the Great, built a 'dromic' church large both in length and breadth, and roofed it with lead instead of tiles; she enclosed within the rear of the church on the right hand side the building where the holy disciples had been hidden for fear of the Jews [88v] and where Christ had appeared to them although the doors were closed, and on the left the column of porphyry to which Christ our God had been bound and flogged by the Jews. Moreover, the holy washing of the disciples' feet is depicted near the right hand side of the altar, and also the descent of the Holy Spirit at holy Pentecost; and at the left hand side of the sanctuary, which contains the tomb of the prophet David, this same blessed and holy Helena built the receptacle for the oblation, and she also converted the courtyard of Caiaphas into a church of Saint Peter, the leader of the Apostles, who is praised by all; and the distance from the place of the holy resurrection to holy Zion is a mile. {p. 648} And the holy empress Helena, who was also the first empress among Christians, built many other Christian churches in those holy places, both at the pit of the prophet Jeremiah and at the pool of Siloam and at the potter's field

which is where beggars are buried, and at the oak of Mambre where the Saviour appeared to Abraham, and the church of Saints Cyrus and John at the sacred stone pavement. After she had commanded that these precious and holy churches, dedicated to our God, should be built, the generous and truly Christ-loving Helena, the blessed mother of the blessed and holy emperor Constantine the Great, having also faithfully uttered the praises of God, who in so short a time made his presence known among those places, and after she had placed the churches in Jerusalem in the authority of the most holy patriarch, the holy Macarius, taking with her the portion than she had kept of the Cross that is worshipped by all and the precious and holy nails, returned to Byzantium, to her son the emperor Constantine who is praised by all. He welcomed her with joy and both placed the portion of the life-giving Cross in a golden casket and handed it over to the most holy bishop [89r] Alexander to keep, for the blessed Metrophanes had died, and as far as the quantity of nails was concerned, some he had welded into his crown, and others melted down and used in the bit of his horse, so that the saying of the prophet might be fulfilled: 'In that day what is on the king's bit shall be sacred to the Lord Almighty.' Moreover, the emperor Constantine the Great, whom all praise, used continually to send senior officials to Macarius in holy Jerusalem {p. 649} to urge on with much haste the construction of those churches of the blessed and holy Helena which had not yet been completed; he also sent supervisors of the work with much money with orders to bestow on all the holy churches which the holy Helena, his mother, had ordered, such trouble that there should not be comparable beauty in the whole of the inhabited world. He also wrote to the governors of the provinces to support the work zealously, and to meet whatever expenditure was necessary from the public purse.

33. Moreover, it was the custom of the emperor to celebrate the festivals with joy and give thanks to God who had done such good things during his lifetime; but since he used greatly to glorify and honour the power of the glorious and life-giving Cross, for he had been converted by reason of the miracles that had occurred for him on each occasion through it, both how he had put the wicked Maxentius to flight and overthrown him, and how he had utterly routed his enemies, the pagan Byzantines, by its power, and how he had subdued the Scythians, the most pious Constantine, being carried away by divine zeal after his mother's return from Jerusalem,

made three great crosses, one for each occasion on which it had appeared to him in time of war, the first in Rome, when he had caused Maxentius to be drowned, the second in Byzantium, the third when he built the bridge over the [89v] river Danube in Scythia. Accordingly he made three crosses out of pure bronze, after the pattern of the three visions, and gave them the following altogether sacred names: Jesus, Christus, Conquer! The precious cross called Jesus he adorned by having it dipped in gold and erected it facing east over the vault, in the place where the forum is now, displaying to all the warmth {p. 650} both of his faith and the reverence he felt because through its power he had overthrown the arrogance of the Greeks. The cross called Christus, holy and to be revered by all, he fixed on top of a pillar of Roman marble in the Philadelphium, and it still stands today in the same place. The other life-giving cross, teeming with miracles and named by the emperor Constantine the Great 'Victory', was renamed 'Invincible' by the most faithful and Christ-loving emperor Heraclius, and from that day to this has been called the 'Life-Giving, Precious Cross of Our Lord, Holy Invincible' by all the faithful who bear the name of Christ, since the power of Christ is also invincible; this cross Constantine the Great suspended upon the top of a very high column of composite marble which he set up in the bread market, an altogether delightful location. And to this day Christ our God, who was nailed to the precious Cross of life-giving wood, displays to us in his precious and holy cross, Sacred Invincible, many miracles by getting rid of all kinds of illness, relief for those suffering from shivering and ague and both health and recovery of sight for those with ophthalmia and cataracts. Let no one disbelieve what I intend to say; on the contrary, let everyone Christian believe it; for it is said by many people, as I have heard, concerning this awesome and divine cross, for there is a slave market on the very spot, that an angel comes down at dead of night three times a year, like [90r] a flash of {p. 651} lightning from heaven, on the first occasion on the seventh of May, when also the precious and life-giving cross appeared through stars in heaven, and on the day of its holy elevation through the faithful priests, the fourteenth of September, and in the middle week of Lent, when also a glorious service of worship is held for it; on these three festivals of the precious and holy cross an angel of God, as they say, flies round this all-glorious and all-holy cross of Christ, Holy Invincible, and burns incense around it, and with a shrill sound through a slender trumpet makes a signal about it, which seems to me to convey a hint of the last trumpet which the mighty angel is going to sound and awaken all the nations to the fearsome judgement at which there will be no respect of persons, and then, after playing a sublime tune with its thrice holy sound, departs to the place whence he came. And many, who have been deemed worthy to see it, on account of purity of mind and the habits of a blameless life, have proclaimed the miracle that is performed by God on account of our salvation at the precious and life-giving Cross, and let no one disbelieve or dispute the tale; for where God wills, even rocks, though by nature silent, are overcome and give utterance. Therefore, as regards this precious and holy cross belonging to the Lord, the one I call Sacred Invincible, which the emperor Constantine the Great suspended upon a lofty pillar as I have related, in the days of the Christ-loving rulers Mauricius and Constantina, in the eighteenth year of their reign, when a great earthquake occurred in Constantinople through our sins and {p. 652} lasted for seven days and nights, and many houses and pillars collapsed, and the western part of the great dome of the cross crashed to the ground, and even the column of the wife of the emperor [90v] Theodosius the Great whose name was Placilla collapsed and was shattered even though it stood on the crest of a dry hill, and many other houses and columns had crashed and been rendered useless by the fearsome rumbling of that earthquake, it happened that, arising from the violence of the wrath of God that occurred throughout seven days and nights through our sins, the precious and holy cross Invincible, revered by all, was loosened from the place where it was set on top of the column [or at any rate from its foundation] and rocked and was within an ace of falling down, except that by divine providence the emperor Heraclius the Great, warned by certain magicians, had ordered men who were expert stonemasons to go up, and had fixed it again and made it thoroughly firm with lead and the use of iron clamps, having inscribed on the base of the cross: 'Heracles made firm the work, pleasing to God, of the great emperor', and these words are preserved until the present day. But though the Christ-loving emperor Constantine the Great had called this all-powerful, life-giving, holy cross belonging to the Lord 'Victory', because in its power he had conquered all his enemies, the emperor Heraclius, himself a lover of Christ, entitled it 'Invincible', as I have explained above.

34. Enough has been said about the precious, life-giving Cross and the extraordinary miracles that it performed upon the sick; the

blessed and holy Helena who had come piously to the end of her life, had acquired a precise belief in the holy Trinity which is consubstantial and indivisible, and had extended the faith of the Christians, {p. 653} moved to Rome and there welcomed her blessed departure from this life, radiant in beauty and wisdom and every other virtue; she had lived to the age of eighty, and was buried outside the city of Rome in a circular chapel with a vault, in a porphyry coffin; but two years after she had fallen asleep she was brought back with her porphyry coffin to Constantinople and laid to rest in the church of the holy Apostles which the most Christian [91r] emperor Constantine, her son, had founded in honour of the holy Apostles who are praised by all, and for the purpose of the burial of Christian emperors there at such time as they should die. The blessed and holy Helena was the first to be buried there, honoured with memorial services and joyous vigils. The holy virgins in Jerusalem also, whom the holy Helena had established and served personally like a handmaid, used to hold an unbroken and continuous series of services to her blessed memory.

35. After this, and after the blessed Constantine, famous in song and story, had placed the whole administration of the empire on a sound footing, had become the protector and helper of orphans and the poor, and had piously managed the supreme authority of the Roman empire, which is the greatest on earth, for thirty-one years and a few months,[48] the Persians were clearly seeking war against the Romans. He went up to the city of Nicomedia and drew his army up in battle order against the Persians, and experienced a few days' illness at a royal palace in the suburbs, and realising that he was going to die, left his three sons, Constantinus, Constantius and Constans the Younger, as heirs of his empire; for his first son, Crispus, had died.[49] The emperor Constantine the Great, famed in song and story, had these four sons and one daughter named Helena who became the wife of Julian the Transgressor, by Fausta the daughter of Herculius. {p. 654} He departed this life on 21 May, having lived with peace and sanctity all the sixty-five years of his life, and having been emperor for thirty-two. Some say that the emperor Constantine the Great died by treachery at the hands of Dalmatius,[50] the brother of Hannibalianus, whose mother was Theodora, the daughter of Herculius, and that he had given Constantine a harmful drug in order to make himself master of the empire, [91v] but the godless fellow was deceived in his hopes and did not obtain his desire.

36. After the emperor Constantine the Great, crowned by God, had died, the generals and consuls and all the rest of the multitude placed his precious and holy remains in a gold coffin and conveyed it to Constantinople, all going before and behind and lamenting bitterly for his loss, for they were weeping because they had all found him like a kind and gentle father.[51] To write of the amount of honours accorded to his corpse and the time it remained in the imperial palace while the magistrates awaited the return of his sons from Rome, I consider superfluous, for others have written about this, and it is easy for those who wish to find and learn about it from the chroniclers of the common people. But if anyone should disbelieve them, let him observe the respect that is still felt for the tomb of Constantine, and how many cures it effects, and let him come to believe in what has been written and let him glorify the Lord God who glorifies His own servants; {p. 655} for He has said 'I shall glorify those who glorify Me and I shall bring to naught those who set Me at naught.' But, O God, you who have performed great miracles, who have glorified your holy servants Constantine and Helena on account of their precious and very great goodness and their absolute belief in you, deem also our orthodox rulers who govern the Roman empire according to succession worthy to emulate their goodness up to perfection, so that your people, passing their lives in peace, cheerfulness and every kind of joy because of them, may send a prayer of gratitude up to you the Lord of creation, to your glory, Father, Son and Holy Spirit now and always and for ever and ever. Amen.[52]

NOTES
Sam Lieu

1   I. e. Constantius Chlorus.
2   The Parthians had ceased to be the main oriental enemy of the Romans since 226 when their dynasty was overthrown by the House of Sasan. However, Parthian and Persian were often confused in late Roman sources, even by as seasoned a campaigner on the eastern frontier as Ammianus (XXV,4,23).
3   Varachthes suggests the Persian name Vahram which was transliterated as Varranes (Agathias IV,24). A succession of three Shahanshahs with the name of Vahram ruled from 271 to 294.
4   See above, pp. 68–70.
5   Cf. *Anon. Vales.* I(1) (see above, p. 43).
6   Constantius Chlorus served in the East under Aurelian and Constantine himself took part in the successful campaign of Galerius against Narses in 298 and may even have been part of the embassy led by Sicorius which

finalised the peace terms. (Pet. Patric., frags 13 and 14, cf. Dodgeon and Lieu, 1991: 131–34.) The legend of the embassy might therefore reflect memory of historical details.

7 By placing the venue of the meeting between Constantius and Helena at Drepanum, the legend simplifies one of the more complex issues regarding the origins of Constantine. Drepanum was the place of residence of Helena for most of the time when Constantius was Augustus in the West and she would remain during the reign of her son. Her long association with the city, especially her devotion to the cult of the martyr Lucian whose remains were said to be carried there from Nicomedia after his martyrdom by a dolphin, led to it being made a *civitas* named Helenopolis. (Hieron., *Chron., s. a.* 327, p. 231, 21–24 and Philost., *H. e.* II, 12–13, p. 24,23–28. Cf. Drijvers, 1992: 11–12.) In popular thinking in the East, Drepanum inevitably was the birthplace of Helena, and the question of how a girl from Asia would have married an officer from Dalmatia and later given birth to a son at the garrison town of Naissus was in part answered by the tale of a romantic liaison which took place in Drepanum.

8 The story of Constantine's birth and early youth at Drepanum and later discovery by officials is found also in *BHG* 365, Cod. Sab. 366, fol. 9f. pp. 11–12, Halkin (incomplete) and *BHG* 365n, 2, pp. 74–75, Halkin. The relish with which the hagiographers recounted Helena's murky role may point to an attempt by the Iconoclasts to parallel Helena with the empress Irene. Cf. Kazhdan, 1987: 248.

9 Closely paralleled by *V. Metroph.* (*BHG* 1279) 1.20ff., p. 150, Winkelmann.

10 Cf. *ibid.* 2.12–25, p. 151.

11 Cf. *ibid.* 2.28–3.22, pp. 151–52.

12 These 'Persocomites' are also mentioned in *Pass. Eusign.* (p. 219,10 and 221,14–15) which says that 'a thousand Persokomitai guard the frontier between the Persians and the Rhomaioi'. Kazhdan (1987: 204) suggests that 'this institution was on the Arab frontier rather than on the Persian, and this allows the hypothesis that this Vita (i.e. *Pass. Eusign.*) was written in a later period, when Caesarea really became the base of military operations in the east'.

13 The episode of the capture of Constantine by Persians and his subsequent rescue which is entirely legendary is paralleled in *BHG* 365n, 9 and *Pass. Eusign.* 11, pp. 225–26, Devos. The incident was regarded as historical by the time of Cedrenus (p. 496,15–16). The version of the story in *BHG* 365n results in the massacre of the Persians in the temple – an action which brought about a revenge expedition by the Persians (§ 11, pp. 87–88, Halkin). The geographical impossibility of a Persian war being conducted from the West is corrected in *BHG* 369 which places the event after Constantine's victory over Maxentius.

14 The account of the vision parallels Eus., *V. C.* I,30–31,3, pp. 30,15–31,16. However the similarities are not close enough to suggest that the author of *BHG* 364 has first-hand knowledge of the *V. C.* Cf. Winkelmann, 1962: 96–99.

15 Cited also in Eus., *V. C.* I,38,3, p. 35,7–9.

16 The pope at the time of the death of Constantine was also called Eusebius and it would not have taken long for those who wish to deny that Constantine was baptised by an Arian bishop mentally to replace the future bishop of New Rome with his namesake who was the bishop of Old Rome. Once the association had been made, an earlier pontiff had to be found in order for the baptism to take place before the final victory of Licinius allowed Constantine to conduct his affairs mainly from his new capital. Cf. Dölger, 1913: 420 and Fowden, 1994: 158–60. In later tradition Sylvester was credited with the interpretation of the emperor's vision which led to the foundation of New Rome on the Bosporus. See e.g. Aldhelm, *De virginitate* 25, MGH Auct. Ant. 15, p. 258,21–259,2.

17 Maximinus Daia took his own life in Tarsus. Cf. Lact., *Mort. pers.* 49,1 and Philost., *H. e.* VIII,1.

18 Constantine never took part in an expedition against Maximinus Daia. The latter fell victim to Licinius. Cf. Lact., *Mort. pers.* 47–49 and Eus., *H. e.* IX,11.

19 This much repeated episode first appears in Eus., *V. C.* II,9 where it is found in the context of the war between Constantine and Licinius. The version here, however, is derived from Soz., *H. e.* I,4, 3–4, pp. 12,20–13,8. Cf. Winkelmann, 1962: 99.

20 Echoes of Lact., *Mort. pers.* 47,4.

21 According to Lactantius (*Mort. pers.* 49,4), the horrible manner of Maximinus Daia's death was caused by his attempting to take his own life with poison which did not kill him instantly but wrought havoc on his body, especially on his digestive system.

22 Similar summaries of Constantine's laws against paganism are found in other Byzantine *vitae*. See e.g. *BHG* 362, p. 186f. and *BHG* 365, 10, p. 553,2–5 Opitz. They reflect the spirit of the measures outlined in Eus., *V. C.* III,54–56. For a study of the actual laws of Constantine in relation to paganism in chronological order see Huttmann, 1914: 59–103. See also Winkelmann, 1962: 234–36, Errington, 1988: *passim* and Barnes, 1984: *passim*. On the laws of Constantine in medieval *vitae* see the helpful remarks of Linder, 1988: 499–507.

23 See above, p. 60, n. 79. The charge of Licinius' attempt to stage a revolt with the help of barbarian mercenaries would have provided Constantine with the perfect excuse to remove his last rival and would also absolve Constantine from the accusation of perjury.

24 Numerous Byzantine legends surround Byzas, the eponymous founder of Byzantium. According to *BHG* 365 (38–42, pp. 568–71, Opitz), which contains a very full version of the legend taken from the pagan mythographer Hesychius of Miletus (d. after 518, 5–12, ed. Preger), he was the leader of the Megarian colonists. He was challenged to a hunting contest by Melias the king of the Thracians. Upon his victory, Byzas sacrificed a bull but an eagle snatched the heart of the victim and flew away and perched near the farthest point of the headland of the Bosporus opposite Chrysopolis. It was here that Byzas marked out the city of Byzantium and built the walls with the help of both Poseidon and Apollo. He made them more mighty than any description, for he harmonised the seven towers so that they would re-echo and resound

to each other. 'For if ever a trumpet call or a shout should strike one of the towers, one tower used to pass the echo on to the next, until it reached the tower lying at the far end.' He also completed the parapets and built many temples. Byzas later defeated Haemus, the despot of the Thracians, while his wife Phidalia defended the city against the Scythians by hurling live snakes as missiles at the enemy. Cf. Dagron, 1984: 62–78.

25 After his defeat on the Hebrus, Licinius withdrew to Byzantium where Constantine besieged him by land and sea. The city was later abandoned by Licinius after a fierce contest. Cf. Zos. II,23–25. There is no record of further resistance by the citizens of the city, and the account of the battle between Constantine and the Byzantines does not feature in the better historically informed *BHG* 365.

26 An example of the many geographical impossibilities found in the Byzantine *vitae* of Constantine. Another example is found in *BHG* 365n (4, p. 78, Halkin) where the barbarians crossed the Danube to destroy the land of the Britons!

27 *Verbatim* from *BHG* 365z etc. 1.34–37 (p. 633).

28 Cf. *BHG* 365, 48, pp. 574–76.

29 *Verbatim* from *BHG* 365z etc. 3.46–49 (p. 634).

30 On the famous 'Burnt Column' constructed around 328 see esp. Fowden, 1991: 122–25. See also above, p. 29.

31 Cf. Georg. Mon., *Chron*. ii, p. 500,13–15, which includes the relics of the True Cross among the list. The Byzantine *vitae* of Constantine show remarkably little interest in the veneration of icons and relics. Cf. Kazhdan, 1987: 233.

32 As the first city to suffer the full onslaught of the Great Persecution, Nicomedia already boasted of a long list of martyrs during the reign of Constantine. Cf. Eus., *H. e.* VIII,5–6.

33 I.e. Maximinus Daia, son of Galerius.

34 The *passio* of the saint was clearly closely associated with Byzantine legends of Constantine; see especially the detailed account of the martyrdom at Nicomedia and the miraculous transportation of his body by a dolphin to a place where later Helenopolis was founded by Helena in *BHG* 365, 52–63, pp. 579–85, Opitz.

35 Mocius was the patron martyr of Constantinople whose memory was celebrated on 11 May, the date of the foundation of Constantinople. He was said to have been martyred under Diocletian and decapitated at the decision of the curia of Constantinople. A church was dedicated to his memory by the beginning of the fifth century as Dioscurus, bishop of Hermopolis and one of the enemies of the patriarch Theophilus, was buried there (Soz., *H. e.* VIII,17,5). Cf. Janin, 1969: 354–58 and Cameron and Herrin, 1984: 167–68.

36 Cf. *BHG* 365z etc. 5.64–65 (p. 635).

37 *Verbatim* from *BHG* 365z etc. 5.66 (p. 635).

38 *Verbatim* from *BHG* 365z etc. 5.68 (p. 635)

39 Near *verbatim* from *BHG* 365z etc. 6.75–79 (p. 635). The blessing of the new capital by the prelates which is found in Zon. XIII,4,22 and in other later sources is unlikely to be historical. Cf. Di Maio 1977: 241. The

emphasis on 'bloodless sacrifice' is clearly aimed to stress the Christian, or at least non-pagan, character of the dedication ceremony.

40 Near *verbatim* from *BHG* 365z etc. 6.79 (p. 635). The feast is detailed in Eus., *V. C.* III,15,1. The occasion was his Vicennalia.

41 Cf. Thdt., *H. e.* I,11,2.

42 The debate which is not found in the other main versions of Byzantine Constantine-*vitae* may be a prototype of the debate between pope Sylvester and the Jewish rabbis. For references see above, p. **27–28**.

43 On the controversy surrounding the date of the discovery of the relics of the True Cross and of Helena's role in the discovery see esp. Drijvers, 1992: 81–93.

44 On coinage to Helena Augusta, see Drijvers, 1992: 39–42 and 73.

45 The emphasis on the role of Macarius in the identifying of the sites of the Passion in Jerusalem (and later of the relics of the True Cross) in a *vita* of Constantine is interesting as he was not mentioned in the relevant sections of the *V. C.* (i.e. III,25–30) except as recipient of an imperial letter (III,30,1), perhaps because of the long-standing rivalry between the sees of Jerusalem and Caesarea. See, however, Soc., *H. e.* I,17,5. Cf. Rubin, 1982: 87–88.

46 Eus., *V. C.* III,26,3. See esp. Drijvers, 1992: 88.

47 According to the *Liber de locis sanctis* of Peter the Deacon (completed in 1137 but compiled from earlier sources), the site of Heptapegon (i.e. 'Seven Fountains', modern Et Tabgah) was noted for the four steps on which the Lord stood and an altar marked the place where the Lord multiplied the five loaves and two fishes (V,2–3, p. 99) The present excavated remains of the Church of the Multiplication of the Loaves are mainly fifth century or later in date. The church was destroyed by earthquake in the seventh century. It is possible that the original altar (now under the fifth-century altar) originally marked the spot of the resurrection appearance of Jesus which was the first event commemorated at Et Tabgah. Cf. Schneider, 1934: 14–15 and 49 and Wilkinson, 1971: 196–200.

48 *Verbatim* from *BHG* 365z etc. 7.83–86 (p. 636).

49 Near *verbatim* from *BHG* 365z etc. 7.83–90 (p. 636).

50 I.e. Flavius Dalmatius (cos. 333), father of the Caesars Dalmatius and Hannibalianus. On the alleged poisoning of Constantine by his relatives see below, p. **227**.

51 The sentence, especially the version in Red. A, is taken nearly *verbatim* from *BHG* 365z etc. 8 (p. 626) 93–98.

52 *Verbatim* from *BHG* 365z etc. 10.108–115 (pp. 637–38) .

4

THE SONS OF CONSTANTINE

Libanius, *Oratio* LIX
(Royal Discourse upon Constantius and Constans)

INTRODUCTION

Sam Lieu and Dominic Montserrat

The 'promiscuous massacre' of 337 and the re-division of the Empire

Two years before his death in 337, Constantine had divided the empire among his three sons, Constantine II (b. 316), Constantius (b. 317) and Constans (b. *c.* 320), and his nephews Dalmatius the Younger and Hanniballianus the Younger. Upon Constantine's death this unwieldy arrangement was upset by the imperial armies who declared that they would have nobody but the sons of Constantine to rule over them. (Eus., *V. C.* IV,51 and 58, Greg. Naz., *Or.* IV,21). Egged on by the rumour that Constantine was poisoned by his 'half-brothers', the soldiers carried out a massacre of the surviving male members of Constantius Chlorus' family together with their male offspring. The army, or a faction of it, clearly feared that Constantine's final arrangement of a five-fold division of the empire was a sure recipe for civil war. (Cf. Bowen, 1982: Di Maio and Arnold, 1992: 158–75.)

Constantius, who was the only one of the three sons of Constantine to reach Constantinople in time for the funeral, and thus present at the new capital when the massacre took place, was universally blamed for instigating what Gibbon (rev. Bury, ii, 1909: 236) terms the 'promiscuous massacre' of 337. He was then in charge of defending the eastern frontier against an impending attack by

147

Shapur II and would have only just arrived at the new capital. Unsure of the rival forces, both political and ecclesiastical, Constantius probably knew of the plot but did nothing to prevent it. Later tradition would place the blame squarely on him; this was indeed the view of Julian (*Ep. ad Ath.* 270C (3.5–8, p. 215, Bidez)), who blamed his cousin's childlessness on his murder of his paternal relatives, and the view of historians who supported Julian as this provided them with justification of Julian's later rebellion against his imperial cousin. The remorse which Constantius was said to have shown for the massacre was probably caused more by his sense of guilt in not preventing the murder rather than actually instigating it. It was rumoured that the emperor had left a will which was entrusted to Eusebius, the Arian bishop of Nicomedia, when he feared he was being poisoned by his half-brothers, and that the will ordered their execution. If such a will had existed, it would have served to exonerate Constantius. Flavius Dalmatius (cos. 333), the half-brother of Constantine, was probably the first victim. He was followed by his sons among whom were Caesar Dalmatius (the Younger) whose appointment to Caesar was deeply unpopular with the soldiers (Aur. Vict., *Caes.* 41,22 and Eutr., X,9,1) and his brother Hannibalianus (the Younger) – the recently appointed King of Kings to the Pontic regions (Zos. II,40,3). (See above, pp. **61–62**.) Prominent among the other victims was Julius Constantius, the half-brother of Constantine, who perished together with an elder son whose name is lost to us. His other two sons were spared because the soldiers thought that Gallus appeared too sickly to live for long and Julian's extreme youth (he was in fact about eight years old) aroused the soldiers' pity (Jul., *loc. cit.* and Soc., *H. e.* III,1,8, Soz., *H. e.* V,2,7–9 etc.). Nepotianus the son of Constantine's sister Eutropia was another one spared and would attempt to usurp the throne thirteen years later. The Praetorian Prefect Ablabius who was probably instrumental in Constantine's policy of involving his nephews in government and to whose daughter Constans was betrothed (Amm. XX,11,3 and Athan., *hist. Ar.* 69), was later (early 338?) executed in cold blood at the entrance to his house. (Cf. Eunap., *Vit. soph.* 464 and Zos. II,40,3.)

With the demise of the Caesars Dalmatius and Hannibalianus, a new division of authority was now urgently required and Constantius met his brothers Constantine II and Constans at Viminacium in Pannonia in September 337. Constantius remained in charge of the East and to his former sphere of government was now added Thrace, part of Dalmatius' original territory. Constantine II obtained Gaul,

Britain and Spain, to which was probably added Mauretania. To Constans was allocated Italy, Illyricum and Africa. However, this arrangement lasted for less than two years. Constantine II was said to have attempted to increase his allotted territory by demanding Africa or Italy from Constans. The latter's apparent disregard of his brother's request for a fairer division opened the way for rivalry and intrigue between the two courts (cf. the role of the tribune Amphilocius in Amm. XXI,6,2). Constantine II waited until Constans was in a province which was loyal to himself and then sent in an army under the pretext of their being *en passage* to the eastern front. Constans, then in Dacia (Jan.–Feb. 340), was apprised of the real intention of his brother and sent a vanguard to oppose the invasion to be followed by the main force. His generals made a feigned attack on Constantine's forces near Aquilea and then withdrew, leading the enemy forces into a series of well-laid ambushes. Cut off from behind, Constantine was killed along with a large number of his forces (March 340). (Cf. Aur. Vict., *Caes.* 41,21, Eutr., 10,9,2, Ruf., *H. e.* X,16, p. 982,10–12, Soz., *H. e.* III,2,10, Zos. II,41, Zon. XIII,5,7–16.) His territories were now incorporated into those of Constans with approval of Constantius (Jul., *Or.* II, 94C–D). He was declared a public enemy (Cf. *CT* XI,12,1) and his memory partially condemned (*CIL* V, 8030, VIII, 12272, *AE* 1935, 4 etc.).

The Persian wars and ecclesiastical conflicts

Constantius meanwhile was fully occupied by the events in the East. In the last years of Constantine's reign, Shapur II, the Persian Shahanshah, appeared to have either instigated a coup in the now increasingly Christianised kingdom of Armenia or taken advantage of political unrest to intervene. A number of Armenian nobles may have fled to Roman territory and set up a rival government probably in what would later become the pro-Roman half of the kingdom after the division of Armenia under Theodosius. Shapur also demanded from Constantine the return of the frontier provinces lost to the Romans through the victory of Galerius in 298. When this was refused, Constantine embarked on his last major campaign which he did not live to accomplish. (Cf. Baynes, 1910 [1955]: 187–89 and Dodgeon and Lieu, 1991: 380–81, n. 22.) Shapur then launched the Persian army, which was in a high state of alert, together with some Armenian allies, against the frontier city of Nisibis in an attempt to gain a major foothold in Roman Mesopotamia. He was thwarted by the bravery of its defenders among whom were civilians and clerics. The defeat plus the very presence of Constantius on the frontier with a major force compelled the Persians to withdraw, and Constantius was able to settle the affairs in Armenia to Rome's advantage. Arsak (Arsaces), the king of Armenia, was allowed to return to his kingdom together with a number of hostages/exiles (Jul., *Or.* I,20A–21A, cf. Dodgeon and Lieu, *op. cit.*, 384, n. 11). When Constantius reached the frontier with the relief force, the main Persian army had withdrawn (Lib., *Or.* LIX,81, trans. below). However, instead of continuing with Constantine's plans of a full-scale invasion of the Persian empire, Constantius was content to reconnoitre in force and captured a Persian city across the Tigris. The Persian response was swift and overwhelming. Shapur fitted out a large army with new levies, crossed the Tigris and set up base near Singara with the clear intention of drawing the Roman army into an open battle on ground which would give the superior Persian armoured cavalry maximum advantage. The battle fought in the summer of 334 (see below) was to be the last major pitched battle between the two empires until Julian's invasion of 363, and was an indecisive affair. (Cf. Barnes, 1993: 312, n. 19.) The Romans drove the Persians back to their camps after a hard-fought contest in the exhausting afternoon heat and even managed to kill the Persian crown prince in the melée. However, once the Romans had gained entry to the fortified camp, discipline evaporated as the tired and thirsty soldiers searched for water in the falling dusk, their torches making them easy targets for the retreating Persian archers. Both sides claimed victory but in reality the losses were so heavy that neither belligerent was eager to seek a decisive battle in the open again. The battle would remain as an unsatisfactory high-water mark in Shapur's achievements before his full-scale invasion of 359, and more importantly would act as the psychological barrier against open battle against the Romans. (Cf. Amm. XVIII,5,7.)

Constans now controlled two-thirds of the empire. Constantius' only territory in mainland Europe was the diocese of Thrace. However, faced with the Persian threat and the fear of an attack from the West in the event of any major disagreement between him and his brother, Constantius had no alternative but to accept the *fait accompli*, although he would continue to regard himself the senior of the two emperors. Constans now possessed military capabilities which were more than equal to those available to Constantius, and could therefore afford to be arrogant towards his brother, and this was shown particularly in his handling of ecclesiastical matters – the one major barrier to a harmonious relationship between the two emperors.

The years following the Council of Nicaea saw the strengthening of the position of the Arian party who found a vocal and influential champion in Eusebius of Nicomedia, and it was he who baptised Constantine on his death-bed, thereby causing a major embarrassment to hagiographers and panegyrists of the emperor who were not of the Arian persuasion. Of the three sons of Constantine, Constantine and Constans sympathised with the orthodox (i.e. Nicene) party (Athan., *Apol. c. Ar.* 87, p. 102 and *idem, Apol. ad Const.* 2, p. 131) while Constantius, who like his father was baptised on his death-bed, was in strong sympathy with the Arians and was reviled as a heretic or worse as an apostate by champions of orthodoxy like Lucifer of Cagliari or Athanasius of Alexandria. (Cf. Athan., *De synod.* 30–31, pp. 203–4, ed. Bright.) In the years after the Council of Nicaea, Eusebius of Nicomedia strove to have Arius re-admitted to the communion of his bishop and to procure the downfall of his principal opponents: Eustathius of Antioch, Marcellus of Ancyra and Athanasius of Alexandria. A group of Arian bishops led by Eusebius of Nicomedia came together at Antioch and convened a sort of synod *c.* 330. In it they accused Eustathius of Sabellianism and also produced a woman carrying a child whom they alleged to be the mistress and offspring of Eustathius. This revelation was effective and Eustathius was duly exiled to Thrace where he died (Soc., *H. e.* I,24, II,44 and III,6, Soz., *H. e.* II,19, IV,28 and V,13 and Thdt., *H. e.* I,21,3–9, II,31,1–13 and III,4,3–5,4). Marcellus paved the way for his own exile when he refused to subscribe to the decisions of the Councils of Jerusalem and Tyre in 335 which re-admitted Arius to communion and declared his views orthodox. When he was forced to forfeit his see unless he communicated with Arius, Marcellus composed a tract of some 10,000 lines attacking both Arius and his supporters such as Asterius as heretics and presented it to Constantine. This was quite clearly the last straw and at the Council of Constantinople (336), when he refused to burn his tract forthwith, he was immediately deposed and sentenced to exile.

Athanasius, the third of the trio, had been exiled by Constantine in 336 to Trier, then the court of Constantine II, after he threatened to use his influence to disrupt the corn supply from Egypt to Constantinople shortly after the Council of Nicaea. He returned to his see, Alexandria, on the death of Constantine in 337, but Eusebius had now also gained ascendancy over Constantius. A number of bishops, including Athanasius who had returned from exile, were declared deposed by the Council of Antioch in 339 where the Eusebian party ordained Gregory of Cappadocia as archbishop of Alexandria in place of Athanasius. Constantius was soon actively intervening on behalf of the Arians. The secular arm was much in evidence when Gregory was forcibly introduced into the see of Alexandria (Athan., *Ep. encycl.* 2, pp. 3–4, Bright). In 339, Eusebius of Nicomedia was translated to Constantinople, thereby completing a series of Arian victories. The patriarch Alexander had died in August 335. Of the candidates, Paulus – a Nicaean – was said to be spiritually qualified and his principal opponent, Macedonius – an Arian – had political influence. After a series of riots, Paulus was duly elected but he was exiled, probably at the same time as Marcellus of Ancyra, having been accused of having engineered the riots – charges which were later confirmed by Constantine. (Cf. Soz., *H. e.* III,3,1, Thdt., *H. e.* II,5,1, *Synax. Cpol.* p. 197 and Photius, *Bibl.* cod. 257.474a–b). Upon the emperor's death, Paulus returned from his Pontic exile to his see but was soon replaced by Eusebius of Nicomedia at the insistence of Constantius (Soc., *H. e.* II,7,2, and Soz., *H. e.* III,4,2–3). However, Eusebius' tenure of office only lasted to 341 and the populace brought Paulus back into his church. The next year, Constantius sent his *magister equitum* Hermogenes to drive Paulus from his see but Hermogenes was killed in the resultant riots when the house in which he was residing was burnt down by the mobs (Soc., *H. e.* II,13,1–4 and Soz., *H. e.* III,7,3). Constantius had to visit Constantinople in person and exiled Paulus to Singara. Constantius did not confirm Macedonius, the Arian rival, claimant to the throne but left him as *de facto* patriarch (Athan., *Hist. Ar.* 7,1–2 and Zon. XIII,11,23).

In the meantime Athanasius was received with great honour at the court of Constans, for whose use he had prepared some books of Holy Scripture (Athan., *Apol. ad Const.* 4, p. 133, Bright). Constans was determined to convoke another ecumenical council, and obtained his brother's concurrence. The place fixed upon was Serdica, on the frontier of the Eastern and Western empires, where about 170 bishops met in 343. Then occurred the first great open rupture between the bishops of the East and the West, with the minority consisting of Western bishops siding with Athanasius, while the Eastern or Eusebian faction seceded to Philippopolis across the border. After the dissolution of the council, Constans still attempted to enforce the decrees of Serdica, by requiring of his brother the restoration of Athanasius and Paulus (Athan., *Hist. Ar.* 20,2). When this request was not immediately complied with, he sent a second letter stating his case bluntly: either restore the bishops and punish their enemies or else risk military intervention (Soc., *H. e.* II,22, Soz., *H. e.* III,20). A plot hatched by Stephanus, the Arian bishop of Antioch, to introduce a naked prostitute at night into the quarters of bishop Euphrates, one of the bearers of the threatening message to Constantius, backfired completely and led to the deposition of the perpetrator (Athan., *loc. cit.* and Thdt., *H. e.* II,9–10. Cf. Klein, 1977: 45–52). The pressure of the war with Persia no doubt inclined Constantius to avoid anything like a civil war, and he therefore put a stop to some of the Arian persecutions. Ten months later, after the death of the intruder Gregory, he invited Athanasius to return to his see, which Athanasius did in 346, after a curious interview with the emperor at Antioch (see the letters in Soc., *H. e.* II,23 from Athan., *Apol. c. Ar.*, 54f.).

The Praetorian Prefect Philippus and the rhetor Libanius

Among the exiled bishops whom the Eastern bishops at Serdica wished to reinstate was Paulus of Constantinople, but Constantius was reluctant to reinstate bishops who had taken refuge in the West. Paulus took matters into his own hands and returned to Constantinople, and late in 344 Constantius sent his new Praetorian Prefect Philippus to expel him. The son of a sausage manufacturer, Philippus became a close adviser of Constantius and, in spite of his low-born social status, he would later be elected consul (348) and would resume his office as prefect till his death in late summer 351. His election to consulship in the historic year of 348 – the 1,100th anniversary of Rome – inevitably led to questions being asked as to whether he was chosen deliberately because he was the namesake of Philip the Arab, the only emperor before Constantine who was generally reputed to have had Christian leanings (Aur. Vict., *Caes.* 28,2). Philippus was all too aware of the likely public reaction to any attempt to remove Paulus by force. He therefore kept the order secret and requested Paulus to present himself at the baths of Zeuxippus as if to do him honour. But when Paulus presented himself, Philippus had ordered all the entrances but one to be locked and produced the emperor's order. The bishop was duly bundled onto a ship and deposited at Thessalonica, the nearest port within the jurisdiction of Constans. (Cf. Soc., *H. e.* II,16 and Barnes, 1992: 254–55 and 1993: 213–14.)

After expelling Paulus from Constantinople, Philippus passed through Nicomedia on the Sea of Marmara. Formerly the seat of one of the two senior emperors under the Tetrarchy and hailed as 'Queen of the Cities', Nicomedia had now been considerably eclipsed in importance by the nascent Constantinople. Nevertheless, it was still a metropolis and it was there that Philippus was informed of the forensic triumphs of a young orator from Antioch who had chosen to restart his career after being forced to leave the new capital under a cloud in 343.

The rhetor Libanius was born in 314 in Antioch, the metropolis of Syria, two years after the Battle of Milvian Bridge. His life is exceptionally well documented because he left us with an autobiographical oration (*Or.* 1, 'On His Fortune') which he composed when he was already an established figure of his own city, as well as a voluminous correspondence (1,544 letters!). Both his parents belonged to leading families of Antioch but his father died when he was young; his maternal uncles, who were leading figures in the Council of the city, assisted his widowed mother in the upbringing of Libanius and his two brothers.

In his fifteenth year, he says in his 'autobiography', he was seized by a consuming passion for study (*Or.* I,5). But fifteen was already a relatively late age for a young man in Antiquity to take up the serious study of the Classics. Libanius had to work feverishly hard to make up for lost ground, and he was fortunate in being able to find a tutor who had a prodigious memory of the Classics. He attached himself so wholeheartedly, he said, that he would not leave him even after class had been dismissed, but would trail after him, book in hand, even through the city square, until he had to give Libanius some instruction even reluctantly. A most unfortunate incident took place in the course of his studies in his twentieth year, and one which would have lasting effects. One day while he was standing beside his teacher's chair reading the *Acharnians* of Aristophanes, he was struck by lightning. Although it did not lead to a permanent loss of sight, he would be plagued by severe attacks of migraine until the end of his life (*Or.* I,8–10).

For a Hellene with any serious ambition for a career in rhetoric, a place in the famous schools of Athens would have been his ultimate goal. At the age of twenty, Libanius left Antioch for the first time in his life to pursue this aim. His high expectations of Athens as the foremost seat of learning, however, were quickly dispelled once he arrived to take up his studies there. The teachers of Athens were vying with each other for students like the admissions officers of modern-day universities were a few years ago. To avoid a perpetual state of war between the various schools in Athens for students, the sophists had come to an agreement sometime before Libanius' arrival to allot themselves special recruiting areas, and special arrangements had already been made with ship-owners to whisk newly arrived students to particular teachers. Thus to Diophantus was awarded the monopoly of students from Arabia and to Prohaeresius students from Asia Minor. As a native of Antioch, Libanius expected himself to become the pupil of Epiphanius, a teacher who enjoyed the highest reputation. However he fell into a trap set for him by the students of Diophantus, the teacher for students from Arabia, as soon as he landed. Registration for this school took the form of his being locked up in a cell about the size of a barrel from which he was not allowed out until he had taken the oath to become a student of Diophantus.

As Libanius was considerably older than his fellow students in Athens, it did not take him long to realize that the applause which his contemporaries accorded to their teacher was a reflection of how easily they could be impressed and moulded by older men. He found Athens nothing out of the ordinary, 'for the guidance of the students had been monopolised by people who were little better than the students themselves'. Naturally he was held by the others to be guilty of not respecting his professors. He could hardly be blamed for doing so because we know from other sources that Diophantus, the person to whom he was compulsorily assigned, was a lousy teacher. He posed as the arch-rival of Prohaeresius, arguably the most distinguished of the teachers in Athens at that time. The comparison between the two, as Eunapius puts it, was like opposing Homer to Callimachus. Eunapius knew Diophantus personally and often heard him declaim in public. But he did not think it fit to quote any of his speeches or what he remembered of them. 'For this document', he says of his *The Lives of the Sophists* (§494) 'is a record of noteworthy men; it is not a satire'.

Realising that he was not going to receive much help from his teachers, Libanius devoted his time to working on his own to improve his already very strong grasp of basic skills in rhetoric. As Eunapius says, Libanius literally rubbed shoulders with the ancients and modelled his composition on those ancient authors who were best known for their style. He benefited from having a bad teacher, as Eunapius points out, because he did not run the risk of being obscured, partly by a great crowd of students, partly by the celebrity of his teacher.

155

As he gained confidence in his studies, the thought of leaving Athens began to cross his mind. He found himself in the awkward situation of being asked by the proconsul to become the head of the school to which he felt such strong loyalties due to the fact that he did not take part in the riots. Although the proconsul later changed his mind, the request did not endear him to the other students. He was therefore glad to take the opportunity to spend a year in Heraclea in Pontus with a companion who was returning there as the public orator of the city and needed the support of a friend. They went via Constantinople and were given a warm reception by the many men of letters who had recently flocked there to establish their careers in the *salon culture* of the imperial court. Many aristocrats and rich men had now taken up residence in the new capital and there was a drastic shortage of good schools and well-qualified teachers for their children (Lib., *Or.* I,26–30). Thus when Libanius found himself in Constantinople again after his travels in Asia Minor, he was asked by one of the teachers there to stay. 'That is not the tack for you (going back to Athens),' said his friend, 'Stay with us here my dear fellow and be master of the sons of our many wealthy citizens'. He added, 'When you can be in charge yourself, why sail off to be under someone else?' (*ibid.* 31). He promised he could marshal a viable group of students within a day. Libanius was then mentally and emotionally unprepared for leaving Athens and he stepped into the ferry; but within a year he was back in the capital by fast carriage. He witnessed, however, on his return to the new capital, the installation by the city council of a sophist from Cappadocia to the post of public rhetorship, appointed on the strength of one speech. Libanius was accordingly obliged to turn to public competitions in order to establish a name for himself as a private teacher, and in a short time he obtained so large a number of pupils that the classes of the other professors on public pay were completely deserted (*ibid.* 33–37). Eunapius attributes Libanius' success to his unrivalled skill in rhetoric and also his ability to understand his students.

For he knew at first sight every man's character for what it was, and understood the propensities of his soul, whether to vice or virtue. And indeed he was so clever in adapting and assimilating himself to all sorts of men that he made the very polypus look foolish; and everyone who talked with him thought to behold in him a second self. At any rate those who had had this experience used to declare that he was a sort of picture or wax

impression of all the manifold and various characters of mankind. So multiform was he that he was all things to all men.

(Eunap., *Vit. soph*. §495, trans. Wright)

Success brought with it the jealousy and envy of his fellow teachers
who were also his rivals. They began to cluster round Bemarchius –
a flatterer of Constantius and those around him, as well as the author
of a now lost panegyrical history of Constantine. In return for this
fawning he drew a large public salary. His favourite topic of oration,
and an unusual one for a pagan orator, was the architecture of the
Great Church in Antioch which was begun by Constantine in 327
and completed by Constantius in January 341. Bemarchius had just
returned proudly from a highly remunerative single-lecture tour
which had taken him as far as Egypt. He was appalled to discover
that his students had, during his absence, gone over to Libanius and
showed no desire to return to him. He was further humiliated in a
rhetorical competition on a theme of Libanius' choice and a rendition
of his standard lecture full of descriptions of 'pillars, trellised courts
and intercrossing paths' cut no ice with the audience. He then
attempted to prevent Libanius from delivering further orations and,
failing that, to dissuade Alexander, the proconsul of Constantinople,
from attending. This only had the effect of making Libanius even
more popular with the citizens of the capital. He now had to try a
different tack. He lodged a charge of being worsted by magic against
Libanius with the latter's Cretan copyist as chief witness. At a time
when religious change was creating a general sense of uncertainty,
such a charge against an exceptionally successful rival for winning by
underhand means was easy enough to make and one which could
incur severe penalties. (Cf. Brown, 1970 [1972]: 127–28.) However,
even the application of torture on the chief witness yielded nothing
incriminating.

Then in 343 occurred the riots associated with the attempted
expulsion of Paulus of Constantinople by Hermogenes the *magister
equitum* (see above). Alexander, the proconsul from whom Libanius
had hoped for a favourable judgement in his case, was wounded
trying to quell the riots and control of the city passed over to
Limenius. Bemarchius immediately formed a cabal with other sophists and took over the case. Eunapius mentions that a charge of
pederasty was raised against Libanius but was dropped (*Vit. Soph*.
§495). Libanius was forced to leave the capital and went to Nicomedia
in Bithynia via Nicaea where he was warmly welcomed by the

populace. Afterwards he would describe his five years at Nicomedia as the happiest of his life (Lib., *Or.* I,51). Here Julian, one of the two surviving younger princes of the House of Constantine, made the acquaintance of Libanius' writings. He was not allowed to attend the lectures of the pagan sophist in person but he managed to obtain copies of his orations, which he admired greatly and later used as models of his own (Lib., *Or.* XVIII,13–14).

Professional jealousy once more dogged Libanius. The former orator of the city who had lost his post to Libanius because of bad temper and poor memory, now accused him of causing his wife's death through magic. He made such a poor case of the charge that he faced punishment for perjury. The governor took pity on him and released him to the ridicule of the populace. He then took his case to Philagrius, the governor of Bithynia and Cappadocia, who had studied with him at Athens, and despite the more urgent calls for the preparations for the Persian war, he sent for Libanius to come before him under an armed guard. He was about to charge Libanius with murder when news was announced of Philippus' tour of inspection and he realised that the time for favours was over and the law had to be maintained. He tried to placate Libanius by agreeing to attend one of his declamations at Nicomedia despite the summons to see the prefect. At the appointed time, Libanius' rival arrived with his advocate and demanded that the governor should allow him to declaim first, but then his memory failed him and he was unable to perform, and the governor had to ask that his script be read by Libanius (*ibid.* 62–71).(Cf. Sievers, 1868: 55–56.)

The news of Libanius' public humiliation of his rival might have prompted Philippus to ask him to deliver a panegyric on the reigning emperors Constantius and Constans (trans. below). This 'masterpiece of equivocation' (Norman, 1965: vii), delivered in late summer of 344, undoubtedly further enhanced Libanius' already well-established reputation. Philippus later restored him with the help of imperial summons to an official appointment with an imperial salary at Constantinople (*c.* 348). Although he was reasonably successful at Constantinople and honoured with gifts from Constantius, he was not truly happy. In the summer of 353 he managed to obtain leave to pay a visit to Antioch – the first in seventeen years. The visit so kindled his desire to return to his native city that he returned in 359 without imperial permission to intrigue for succession to the Chair of Rhetoric in the city, which he eventually obtained, and was granted permission to stay after many pleas to the emperor on grounds of ill health.

As a staunch pagan, Libanius was greatly excited by the decision of Julian to winter in Antioch in 362 and showed great approval of his attempts to revitalise paganism. He gave the speech in honour of the emperor becoming consul on 1 Jan. 363 (i.e. *Or.* XII). The two also renewed their personal friendship and entered into a regular correspondence. It was to Libanius that Julian addressed one of his last surviving letters (*ELF* 98) and after his tragic early death it fell upon Libanius to deliver the official funeral oration (i.e. *Or.* XVIII) Under the Christian emperors, Libanius continued to enjoy considerable influence as a local celebrity and was even granted the honorary title of Praetorian Prefect by Theodosius despite his being a pagan and an advocate for social justice. He did not have a legal wife but lived with a concubine who gave him a son. Much effort was needed to secure his legitimisation as heir to his property. This was granted only after a great deal of string pulling in 385. Then tragedy struck: while on a visit to Constantinople, his son Cimon broke a leg and was brought home to die in Antioch. Soon afterwards his mother also died. The last years of Libanius were plagued by recurrent attacks of gout which explains the preoccupation with his health and faith-healing in the second half of his autobiography. He died around 393, leaving his autobiography unfinished. His students incorporated into the text some biographical notes and unfinished parts of the speech.

Libanius, *Oratio* LIX and the *basilikos logos* genre

The imperial oration, or *basilikos logos*, is the name of a particular type of royal encomium. Composed by professional orators and delivered on important festal occasions, such as royal jubilees, these speeches were an integral part of the court rhetoric about the emperor and also had an important role in publicising and reinforcing dynastic ideology. The clearest ancient discussion of the genre is given by Menander Rhetor of Laodicea (*fl.* late third century A.D.) in his treatise on epideictic oratory (§368–377.30, ed. Russell and Wilson) which became an important exemplar for Byzantine authors. (Cf. Previale, 1949: *passim.*) The structures and conventional elements of *basilikos logos* as laid down by Menander are well exemplified by Eusebius in his panegyric of Constantine I, and even more closely by Libanius' *Oratio* LIX to Constantius and Constans, translated into English here for the first time. Libanius' work is a magnificent, if sometimes impenetrable, rhetorical tour-de-force, the result of a lifetime spent studying oratory, and thick with scholarly allusions to mythology, history and the ancient authorial canon. Because of its great length and its enormous wealth of detail (over 20,000 words), *Oratio* LIX can seem diffuse; in fact, it is very carefully modelled on Menander's rules, which becomes clear if the structure of both texts is looked at closely.

Basilikoi logoi typically begin with an acknowledgement that a portrayal of an ideal emperor is being given, rather than an historical account. Menander (§368) states that the encomium should 'embrace a generally agreed amplification of the good qualities of an emperor, but should not permit anything ambiguous or dubious about him, because of the extraordinary glory of the subject' (trans. Montserrat). Libanius develops this idea by making the praise of the emperor in the *basilikos logos* into something that the emperors are owed by their subjects, in accordance with Menander's dictum that 'having, as we do, so many blessings from the emperors, it is absurd not to return to them our due and proper offering'. In Menander's model, these *proemia* lead on to discussions of origin, birth, education and the imperial qualities shown in youth, all substantiated with examples to show that the emperor is indeed a perfect subject for such an oration (§369.17–372.12). *Oratio* LIX §10–42 closely follows this paradigm: Libanius takes Menander's advice by glossing over the undistinguished origins of Constantine and stressing the miraculous portents surrounding the births of Constantius and Constans and the fact that they were born to the purple. As Menander suggests (§372.13–373.6), all of these should be backed up with exempla from history, and followed by a discussion of actual achievements. The main body of *Oratio* LIX (§43–120) is just such a recounting of *praxeis* or glorious deeds, with accomplishments made in war taking precedence over those made in peace, and the glory of the subjects hyperbolised by Libanius' choice of historical authority, with Alexander the Great, Darius and Cyrus all being unfavourably compared to the youthful emperors. The next section (§121–25) discusses the other qualities of the emperor, divided up, as Menander suggests (§375.6–376.23) in accordance with the order of the four cardinal virtues of courage, justice, self-control and wisdom. Towards the end of the speech, Libanius diverges slightly from Menander's model. After a brief digression in imitation of Thucydides (§126), he paints a detailed picture of his subjects as successful pacifiers of the entire empire (§127–67) and finishes with a final summation (§168–73), where the youth of the emperors is stressed to make their achievements seem all the more remarkable. Menander suggests that the paradigmatic *basilikos logos* should conclude with a discussion of the subject's *tyche* or fortune, a final comparison with some great figure from the past, an epilogue and last of all a prayer. Libanius' divergences from Menander are interesting: the passage on *tyche* and the concluding prayer are presumably omitted because they would have been problematic for a writer with pagan sympathies, like Libanius, to compose for Christian emperors. It is probably for the same reason that Libanius makes no mention of the emperors' piety, an important *topos* of later Byzantine encomia, though another factor to consider is Constans' opposition to Arianism and support of Athanasius. Given all this, it is unsurprising that Libanius is discreetly non-sectarian and steers clear of religious matters in defiance of Menander's model. It is less easy to see, however, why there is no final historical comparison. Again, it might have been that finding a comparison suitable for two individuals was problematic: the obvious parallel to Constantius and Constans, Romulus and Remus (see §30), contains some unfortunate elements. Also unlike Menander is the general tone of Libanius' oration. Whereas Menander seems to have a rather cynical view of how to manipulate fact, fiction and rhetoric to present the optimum picture of the subject, Libanius is much more earnest, despite his somewhat self-conscious erudition.

Date, content and significance of Libanius, *Oratio* LIX

The speech is one of a number of extant *basilikoi logoi* delivered in honour of Constantius which touched upon the events of the early part of his reign – the others being that of Julian (*Or.* 1, delivered *c.* 355) who composed two orations in honour of his cousin prior to his usurpation in 360, and those of the famous orator Themistius (*Orr.* 1 and 2) which were delivered before the emperor in Ancyra sometime between 347 and 349. Of the various speeches, those of Libanius and of Julian contain the most historical information. The oration of Libanius was also the earliest. It was delivered in 344 when the events of the Battle of Singara were still topical. Some scholars prefer a date after 348 following Jerome who dated the battle to 348 in his *Chronicle* (*s. a.* 348, pp.236,3–237,2). However, the date of 344 is fairly secure. It was the date given by Julian who in his oration (26a) says that the battle took place about six years before the revolt of Magnentius (350). Moreover, the movements of Constantius in 344 as adduced from where his laws were issued suggest major activites in the Eastern frontier. (Cf. Barnes, 1993: 220 and esp. 312–13, n. 19.) The speech covers political events from the last years of Constantine to the early 340s in considerable detail while nothing of note between 344 and 348 is included. (Cf. Portmann, 1989: 7–10.) It was not delivered before Constantius on the occasion of a royal visit. Instead Libanius was clearly coerced into giving it, probably at the personal insistence of Philippus. Libanius' disclaimer that no one compelled him to deliver the oration (§1) is clearly transparent and later in the speech he praised Constantius for regularly changing his prefects (§164). Philippus had recently (July 344) replaced Domitius Leontius who had been prefect since 341 or 342 (Barnes, 1992: 253–54). The recent major but indecisive battle at Singara required immediate propaganda for it to be perceived generally as a Roman victory which would help public opinion in view of the high Roman casualty figures. Moreover, a speech in praise of both emperors, Constans and Contantius, which laid stress on their harmony, could help to ameliorate any public fears of a diplomatic rupture and subsequent armed intervention by Constans on behalf of the exiled bishops.

Oratio LIX of Libanius and *Oratio* I of Julian cover so many of the same events down to 344 that they need to be studied in juxtaposition. The later date of the oration of Julian means that it covers events down to the usurpation and defeat of Magnentius. As Constans fell victim to the usurpation, Julian did not have to labour on the harmony between the two royal brothers as Libanius was impelled to do at some length. Both orators followed the guidelines laid down for such speeches in the handbook of Menander Rhetor. They both include an eulogy on Constantine which is significant from the point of view of traditional rhetoric in that neither mentioned the emperor's patronage of Christianity or interest in religious affairs in general. Where the same events were described in both speeches, such as Constantius' activities on the Eastern frontier, there was so little verbal agreement that it is clear that Julian did not have access to a copy of Libanius' work. The two did not begin to correspond with each other till after Julian had been elevated to Caesarship and given command over Gaul in 355. The synopsis of the parallels between the two speeches drawn up by Gladis (1909: 20–31) shows few genuine borrowings by Julian from Libanius and the closest similarities are found mainly in the sections on the reign of Constantine. For the historical events like the Battle of Singara, Julian clearly used sources other than Libanius. There might have been officers whom Julian had met in Greece or later in Gaul who were veterans of the battle.

The earlier date of Libanius' speech compared to that of Julian and those of Themistius gives the work added significance. Not only is it a major source on the early years of the reign of Constantius, it also preserves a unique record of the Romano-Persian negotiations in the last years of the reign of Constantine. The account has gaps – the absence of any mention of the events in Armenia is a case in point. It also passes over the heroism of the defenders of Nisibis – a topic which would find a special place in Julian's two orations (I,27B–28D and II,62B–67A) both of which were delivered after the third and probably the most severely contested of the three sieges in 350. Libanius may have followed strictly the guidelines for the *basilikos logos* in extolling the emperor only for those deeds of valour in which he was personally engaged. Moreover, successful defences do not lend themselves to encomium as readily as victory in open battle. Libanius' oration also provides information on Constans' military activities in the West, especially his invasion of Britain, which cannot easily be found elsewhere.

The Church historian Socrates, in his refutation of Libanius' funeral oration on Julian (i.e. *Or.* XVIII), reminds his readers that Libanius composed panegyrics on Constantius while he was alive, but after his death he heaped insults, rich in accusations, on his memory. The same is true of Julian who would later present his cousin's achievements in the most disparaging fashion. However, as the main surviving Church histories of this period were written from a pro-Nicaean point of view, their authors were not overly en- thusiastic to enhance the posthumous reputation of the Arian Constantius save for occasionally defending this Christian emperor from undue vilification by his pagan critics. In his better known Julianic orations, Libanius made no mention of the regular raids across the frontier by Constantius which he undertook in the early part of his reign, nor the Battle of Singara which features so prominently in *Oratio* LIX. His preoccupation with the merits of an offensive strategy undertaken by the emperor in person versus defence in depth conducted by his commanders – a policy pursued by Constantius after 350 – precluded him from eulogising the tenacity and success with which the frontier cities withstood repeated onslaughts by the Persians between 337 and 350. This attitude was also shared by the pagan historian Eutropius who characterised Constantius as a victor in civil wars but a failure in foreign wars especially against the Persians, save for the Battle of Singara (X,10,1). In terms of depth of penetration into Persian-held territory and the number of cities captured, Constantius' achievements in the earlier part of his reign were insignificant compared with the initial gains of Julian's campaign, but the latter's ill-planned expedition and his death in battle led to the permanent loss to Persia of two major Roman frontier cities (Singara and Nisibis) at the conference-table, which was far more serious diplomatically and strategically than any suffered under Constantius, even the temporary loss of Amida and the permanent loss of Bezabde.

Editions etc.

The following translation is based on the acclaimed critical edition of R. Foerster (*Libanii opera*, iv, 1907, pp. 208–96). The Latin translation of F. Morellus, *Libanii Βασιλικός seu Panegyricus Constanti et Constantino impp. dictus* (Paris, 1614) pp. 2–93 and the notes in the edition of J. J. Reiske (*Libanii sophistae orationes et declamationes*, iv, pp. 272–332) have been consulted with profit. The present translation was initiated by Dodgeon in 1982 and has since then been extensively revised by Vermes and Lieu. The latter is also grateful to Dr Christopher Lightfoot for allowing him to consult his unpublished translation of the first twenty-nine sections of the oration. There is no known published translation of the oration into a modern language.

LIBANIUS, *ORATIO* LIX (ROYAL DISCOURSE UPON CONSTANTIUS AND CONSTANS)
translated by M. H. Dodgeon; revised by Mark Vermes and Sam Lieu

Preface. It is especially worth observing that although there are two personalities[1] under discussion the speech commences from one opening and progresses to a certain point through shared encomiums. However, it is divided to deal with their exploits in war and certain other subjects worthy of praise, but is joined together again and comes to a shared ending, so that in essence it would seem to be unified and not a two-fold speech. The style does not become obscure by attempting sublimity nor in giving precedence to clarity does it decline into mediocrity.

1. Of my own accord and prompted by nobody I already had it in

mind, I think, to embark on this speech because I myself was roused to a panegyric by the merits of the case. In the first place it would have been most inappropriate, since emperors do not hesitate to risk their lives to win our security, that we should not dedicate to them even a share of those speeches which we compile in safety,[2] but shall fall so far short of propriety that we shall not even compose a speech which is a small fraction of what should rightly be made first of all. 2. Secondly I considered it most disgraceful that whereas those who work the fields offer the first fruits of their crops to the emperors, those who pass their lives in philosophy should abandon the public contribution that is their duty, although they are assumed to have chosen a life that is better and more worthy of respect than that of farmers. 3. But apart from this, if men do not contribute their own praises towards the most noble of exploits, they both do an injustice to the authors of the deeds and at the same time they bring a charge against themselves, depriving them of the praise they should rightly enjoy and revealing their own nature as not understanding how to marvel at achievements. 4. For these and even more reasons I was urging myself towards my subject without waiting for the signal to be raised by others. When as I was still contemplating the matter the injunction confronted me and my intention and the request concurred, I no longer thought there was place for deliberation, but that the time was at hand for bringing my ready zeal to the task. Alternatively, I would have been the most remiss of all men if I had forgone so marvellous an occasion and looked for a formula not for action but for silence, especially when three very important advantages result. For not only shall we preserve for the emperors as much as is possible of their achievement, but we shall ourselves also gain, perhaps, a better reputation and we shall give the proposer of the speech the opportunity to be honoured. For just as in gymnastic competitions some of the glory from the winners' crowns comes to the trainers, in a similar way the sponsor of the speech shares in the glorification from it.

5. Now it is the custom of those embarking on a speech of praise to criticise their own powers as being greatly deficient in describing the achievements, and to express wonder at the extravagant nature of those achievements as far surpassing mere words.[3] But even if this had not been said by anyone in the past, I am utterly convinced that the present necessity would have provided the theme. 6. For if it had been possible to divide up the enterprise and to refer in turn to each

man, and now to settle in full the debt to the older, and a little later to return to the other contribution, even so we would not have been a match for their merits and in truth being so overwhelmed we would perhaps have retired. But the proposer of the contest showed equal love for both men and did not consider our powers rather than how on the one occasion both emperors might be included, and in short was not able to separate fairly for eulogy those who were united both by natural disposition and by temperament and virtues. How can we avoid falling as far short of the measure of praise, as we would if we tried to measure earth and sea in a single day?[4] 7. But yet even if exactly this were to occur, we shall feel very grateful to those who are celebrating the victory. For since words make known deeds, and the brave achievements of rulers are to the advantage of their subjects, those who are not even able to say how much has happened to them are clearly in everyone's sight enjoying good fortune that surpasses every description. The result is, even if it is a paradox to say it, that in this respect alone defeat is more profitable than victory.

8. In many ways it seems to me difficult to match a eulogy with the virtues of the emperors. For there are those who have been judged worthy of the imperial palace and march away with the emperors on campaign and are well acquainted with what is done in peace day by day; these men experience the one difficulty of seeking what they should say that is worthy of what they know; whereas for the rest of us even if we have knowledge of many of the facts, yet we are ignorant of more things than we know. 9. So the double danger besets us, if we shall not only fail to do justice to what we do know, but shall also be silent upon more of the issues. So you must not demand everything in sequence nor what is more than the sum total, but when you hear our speech be indulgent of what we pass over, even if we shall not attain the limit even of those facts that we know.

10. From what point then is it right to make a beginning? Indeed clearly with the cause which brought these emperors to perfection.[5] Let the saying of Plato be quoted of them (and it is more appropriate for them than for those of whom it was said), namely that 'they were born good because they were sprung from good stock'. For as in the case of fruit crops, if someone has sown selected seed of high quality, in the passage of the seasons he reaps produce that is free of defect and pure and excellent. But if someone is remiss over his sowing and scatters upon the same earth seed chosen at random, he preserves the

second rate nature of the seed in the crops. In similar fashion in the case of human nature the virtue of progenitors normally passes to descendants, whenever malignity is unable to overpower good fortune. 11. It seems to me that the present time has very clearly produced this effect. For nobody could show that the birth of emperors has proceeded from a better stock nor an offspring that was a better match to the stock.

12. Now in every case when the lot of justice is present in a man, it completes and guarantees its possession and accompanies him with the sweetest hope for all time. And emperorship wishes more than others to possess a just government, the more that it attracts envy through its status and surfeit of fortune and desires to proceed on a more secure foundation. 13. In these circumstances it is more fitting to wonder at the justice of the present government than its prominence. For they did not enter authority by expelling the holders to a foreign province, nor again did they flatter the populace and purchase the office like something from the wares in the marketplace, but just as men who individually inherit their fathers' and grandfathers' property are entitled to this by law, so also the emperorship belongs to these men from the third generation into the past.[6]

14. If then we were to refer to the forefather[7] of the family and examine the manner in which he conducted government, it would not be difficult to discover some aspect bearing upon his distinction, but rather to find the time for the wealth of description. So after mentioning the one quality which he uniquely among our former rulers displayed, I shall pass on to his son, the father of these emperors. 15. For all the others who held power at that time regarded it as a punishment upon themselves that their subjects should live in plenty, and transferred their prosperity to the treasury, judging that their good fortune was at an end if their treasure houses were straitened for ready money. The result was that those who were robbed lived in tears and penury, but the wealth lay stored without profit to the takers. Whereas that emperor, excellent in every respect, was in full agreement with Demosthenes, and taking his law from that source he considered that the households of private owners were safe treasuries, for he thought that wealth would nowhere be kept more honourably. But when the urgent necessity of expenditure overtook him, it sufficed for him to advertise his need and all the coffers were filled with money as men willingly contributed to their

fellows.[8] In this way the volunteer gains distinction, whereas the man who is under compulsion is not naturally inclined to obey with a good grace. 16. And indeed by taking this attitude he neither suffered the same fate as the others nor did he inflict it. He did not take advantage for a short period of the misfortunes of his subjects for his own pleasure only to be slain later by those he trusted, but for the rest of his reign he was under the protection of the good will of his subjects. At the end of his life he was privileged to hand over his emperorship to his son. Such a foundation to his divinely favoured government and a structure set firm with justice would least of all be shaken by moments of crisis.

17. Eager though I am to press on it appears to me unrighteous, so to speak, to disregard a matter which holds me in check and, if unmentioned, does not have an excuse. For although he had a number of sons, he knew the one who would be the more meticulous guardian of his emperorship. The others he instructed to be inactive, but this one whom he knew to be more suitable he summoned to join his government, considering that his foresight was more important than that his sons be placed on an equal footing before him. 18. So he took over the administration with his father's favour and with the approval of heaven. Among everyone to whom he gave counsel he fulfilled the prayer of Homer as he executed his tasks while running at his father's side. And the greatest accomplishment was that the more victories he won, the more was the respect he gained for his father, for the victory of the son became the proof of the father's judgement. He did not think he should relax and luxuriate, but showed himself to be active right from the start, and he did not dissipate his father's labours to further his own convenience. He considered that he would do an injustice if he should not appear the inheritor also of his labours, and if someone did not come to him he did not judge it a gain that his leisure was free of trouble; but if a man did not bring down those who were ruling with injustice, he supposed that he was an accomplice in their injustices. 19. Such were the thoughts that he addressed to himself as he reinforced his natural sense of daring with such reflections. He saw that the capital city was in theory being governed but in fact was being ruined by its ruler. He did not tolerate that same autocrat as his enemy, and he did not find it endurable that while he himself was alive and looked upon the sun he should overlook the capital of the world being devastated by a despot's violence.[9] But immediately without further ado he put on

his arms and was the first to undertake war on behalf of the capital of all. By personal risks he dispersed the misfortunes of others. 20. So he advanced to the walls and confronted the tyrant against his will and obliged him to come forth though he was hiding in cowardly fashion. That tyrant did not dare to engage in combat but pursued his struggle with guile, by his technique in bridging the river, when the contrivance did no harm to those against whom it was devised, but sufficed for the destruction of its creator, and as the proverb goes, he was surrounded and caught in his own schemes. All these feats and even more have long ago been adequately celebrated both by speech-writers and poets, and even if we had a very strong desire to recount them, the time on the present occasion would not allow it. 21. He freed the great city from the cloud that beset it and allowed it to breathe once more and changed its misfortunes to easy contentment. Starting from so excellent an achievement he visited every area of the empire, cleansing land and sea. He drove away all outrage and introduced instead salvation everywhere, and made war on the barbarians, but showed no envy towards his fellow Roman emperor for what belonged to him. Hence he exhibited a proof of his double virtue. For he neither desired to wage war when it was possible to conduct peace, nor when war was necessary did he hold back. But he was so punctilious towards peace and courageous in respect of war that while the one emperor promoted agreements, the other brought the full force of war.

22. And let no one assume that I am being carried beyond the critical point and have made a fruitless discourse on their father. For it should have become clear to all that the sons were not short of the best examples. For if men are born of inferior fathers and either outstrip their progenitors or appear no worse in any respect, there is nothing that one should admire them for, as there is no need of assiduity in such a rivalry. But we must express extreme admiration at men who have noble precedents from their fathers, if they come near to them, because they have applied their attention to imitation of the best.

23. Now that I am about to proceed to the blessed birth of the emperors, I consider a notion from certain poets and those who record unusual events in their histories; and when I investigate I find that those who were celebrated in former times had their characters embroidered with stories and wondrous events, but that nevertheless

the wealth of stories would fall short of the truth for these present characters. 24. So for instance those who exalt Cyrus say that Astyages had a vision in his sleep, that a vine would sprout forth from Mandane the future mother of Cyrus and would encompass all Asia.[10] And those who feel it a disgrace for Alexander the Great, that he should be considered the son of Philip, make a snake bed down with Olympias and fabricate the union for the utter amazement of young boys. 25. Whereas the birth of our emperors does not require stories or dreams for its embellishment, but just as the fairest of bodies obtain their bright sparkle from within and do not carry their lustre from an outside source, so the generation of these surpasses every strange tale and has required only itself to provide its dignity.

26. But if anyone thinks it a great thing to be born with favourable signs and if any admirers of this element are seated here, and would attach great value to being privileged to hear the auguries with which their birth coincided, we shall not dismiss these men still searching for what they desire rather than having fulfilled their wish. I shall refer to nothing merely for purposes of romance by diverting my account to the obscure, but I shall state what everyone knows. 27. But there will be present in the well-known some element also of brilliancy. For the most godlike father of these princes was always engaged in his tasks both in practice and through reasoning. And neither by light of day nor when night came on could anyone say that he ceased either from both or indeed from either one of them. In fact one cannot contradict the view that whatever he did or resolved on entirely fulfilled to its last degree the requirements of royal virtue. 28. If therefore it is worthwhile to consider such things, we would not truly be putting it exactly, to say that at the times which brought forth the appearance of these princes a more favourable bird of omen preceded the labours; but it is possible to state simply that when they were born it could not happen that favourable signs should not be manifested, if the entire period thereafter was full of good portents. 29. Thus I say confidently that when the most noble travail of childbirth[11] was coming to a close, both the earlier one and the one after that, either the army was going forth to victory or the army was returning from victory, or a nation of the Scythians was falling in battle, or a tribe of the Sarmatians was surrendering, or some other barbarian race was offering gifts, or the great emperor was putting up a trophy with his own hand, or he was disbursing a mass of money from the treasury upon his subjects, or a long-stay

offender in the prisons was being set free by the mercy of the ruler. To put it concisely, either a reasoning surpassing all human nature was coming to his mind or the deliberation was being put into practice. Are not these things better than a vine flourishing in dreams, are they not surer signs than the flight of birds? Are they not more credible than a phenomenon of snakes?[12]

30. So after they were born and came forth into the light, worthy of their father's nature and worthy of our common expectation, let no one expect to hear tales of peaks of Pelion and the Centaur's double-natured body and a half-human tutor and brutalised rearing, which poetry fabricated and assigns to the child of Thetis since it cannot portray his upbringing admirably in the company of Peleus. Instead they were raised where they were born, in the palace whose very entrance on one's approach does not cause one to think of Chiron's cave; and they did not suck the breast of a she-wolf[13] (as some authors have ventured to celebrate of other heroes), but one that was fitting to be brought to imperial lips, so that civilised nourishment would follow their civilised birth. 31. Their father carried them, whenever he turned his heart towards them, not upon the hide of a wild animal but upon his blessed purple robe. Perhaps more factors of a more sacred nature contributed to their imperial upbringing, of which the majority are unaware, while those who know are not allowed to tell, as it were, something secret.

32. Therefore I think it is the right moment to proceed to their education, with the end result that all can know that it was not through the impulse of a random fate that they turned out perfect in virtue, but that they marched along the road to which their training had directed them from early on.

33. A double form of education shaped the personalities of the emperors. For by the one they were educated for the administration of the great business of empire, and by the other they were moulded for shrewdness in argument and the vigour of rhetoric. For whoever has one of these skills but lacks possession of the other, this man's excellence must be defective in whichever one of them he is lacking. For if a man has knowledge of administration but is deprived of the knowledge of how to express himself, he appears a somewhat boorish emperor; he does not lack the capacity to direct his government but holds it without graciousness. Equally if a man is conversant with

oratory to the highest degree, but has not gained an understanding of more important matters, such a man appears a babbler and reduces the august aspect of emperorship to vulgar smart talk, and is very far removed from the sublimity appropriate to that emperorship. 34. But both our emperors are clever in the skill of words that befit Romans after acquiring the best guides of their generation, while they did not have to search for a teacher of imperial knowledge; they had close at hand their father himself, who did not intend to conceal out of envy the timely opportunities for knowledge – for he was by nature superior to such a vice – nor was he going to harm his wards for lack of exposure; for no one advanced further into experience of empire.[14]

35. Now the majority of people consider that the measure of education amounts to this: mounting a horse, drawing a bow and hitting the target with the arrow, striking with a sword and raising a right hand strong enough to throw a spear, tolerating the frost and never complaining about the extremes of heat.[15] Such things make a considerable contribution towards the teaching of emperors; but for them this was not the limit of their education. 36. While these elements were present in their everyday exercises, there was also another consideration much more valuable than these. For whenever they ceased their exertions in these things, their father would train their minds with practical exercises and introduce them to justice, leaving no room for injustice. He drew a distinction between the right time for anger and for mildness, explaining what is absolute rule and showing what is emperorship, and how the man who seeks the former has lost the latter. No one could match the sense of discrimination with which he equipped his sons during every day. 37. But I shall tell you what I especially find to admire in that education. When he embarked them upon the prelude to emperorship at a very young age, and transferred them from their station as private citizens, he trained them in imperial government as follows. For he knew that greatness of mind is the quality most appropriate to the pursuit of action and that without this the greater part of brilliancy is lost. From men's habits, whatever they might be, is implanted in them their spirit of resolution. 38. He wished indeed that by passing their life from their youth in more stately dress and habits they should remain ignorant of pettiness, so that they would pay attention to nothing that was paltry or humble, but that whatever they planned should look towards greatness. Because, I think, whatever learning you inculcate in the minds of the young when they are still quite tender,

is easily established and after its first attachment remains unchanged. Neither does the man accustomed to greater status, if he falls into difficulties, lose his resolution in shock at his time of trouble, nor can the man who is brought up in meanness, when called to greater things, make his judgement equal to the tasks, but he remains within the limits of his old character, like a man who refuses greatness, and is unable to bear it. 39. When he had examined these matters carefully and had understood fully the power of nurture and education, wishing his sons to grasp their greater obligations not among more ordinary folk but to learn of the nobler qualities in a better fashion, he dressed them in clothing which was a token of emperorship.[16] He made a proclamation to the soldiers and cities, that by his approval they had advanced to the government, and that reverence must be given to them also. 40. After giving these preliminary instructions he provided for them camps, attendants and 'ears' and 'eyes', in every way relating the copy to the original model. He gave them a form of address superior to their earlier one but second to his own. This represents, so you might say, a more precise ranking of emperorship. 41. And he did this probably for the following reasons. He did not leave them to remain among private citizens nor did he immediately advance them to the summit of power, fearing the meanness of the former and the excess of the latter. For if he had allowed them to belong to the ordinary citizens and attempted to educate them thus, they would have been less enthusiastic to receive their instruction without the accompanying status, whereas if right from the start he had brought them to the zenith of authority, they would have been more indifferently disposed towards their studies when they had already obtained everything. 42. But he delineated for them the appropriate measure which was going to instil along with thought a love for diligence, and he included an additional more important element. For he did not immediately send them abroad with authority outside his own supervision, giving them straight away their responsibilities, but he held them back and thought it right to keep a watch on their actions. In the same way clever teachers of the helmsman's art place at the rudder those who are just now acquiring the skill and keep watch at the prow, so that if the pupils steer the vessel according to the right principle, they may rejoice with them, but if something untoward happens they may be near to help.

43. So when they seemed to have had the benefit of his company for the time being, just as an eagle trains its nestlings for flight, so he now

handed over their powers and despatched them, one to guard the East[17] and the other to guard the West.[18] 44. And he did this for three very important reasons. Firstly he wished the barbarians dwelling on both borders forcibly to be restrained through fear of those set against them. He thought in fact that he would provide safety for everybody if he could secure the borders of the empire. Secondly he did not consider it right that his sons should pass their time in complete security and remain oblivious of the concern of war, but that they should have some cause for anxious thought. 45. Thirdly – and this is the most important reason – he knew that he could conduct a more exacting examination of them at a distance. For everything that was done during the time they spent with him he considered did not prove the judgement of men acting with discretion so much as result from the necessity of sharing his company. If, however, when they were on their own, and had gained the freedom of their separation, they maintained an equal guard upon their rank, he thought this would likely show their discretion to be natural, and that they would appear superior to the proverb according to which decency is restricted to what can be seen.

46. He despatched them for such considerations, while they desired to remain through longing for their father; but as they dared not offer resistance they hastened on to where they had to go. When they reached their given stations, they proved in the event to surpass every prayer when they appeared in the place of their forefathers before the nations that received them, but in every way they displayed the greater majesty of the one who had sent them. Some requirements they already knew and had secured through their exercises, others they had to master and gain by their experiences. In terms of age they were still classed as youths, but in the greater sharpness of their sagacity they rivalled the older generation. They discovered that action is better than anything, but they carried out no decision before communicating with their father; they made him a judge of their own resolutions and revealed themselves as servants of his decrees. They were possessed of great authority but made very little use of their powers. They defeated pleasures with their self-control while strengthening their bodies with physical exercises. They provided their father opportunity to boast over themselves rather than over trophies of victory, and even when separated from their father by a wide continent they considered he was with them in all that they did. 47. Although if one takes a superficial view of these things, only the

honour of those who make accomplishments is established, yet in truth a good repute is generated to be shared between the accomplishers and the one who has made the selection. For while they are honoured in the revelation of their deeds, for the man who has made a suitable choice the glory of a correct judgement endures. So it works out that both sides are highly esteemed because of each other: they because they receive the approval of the greatest emperor, and he because his selection is confirmed by the virtue of those who were chosen.

48. For my part I have always thought that the steering of the present empire lies under the hand of the Almighty, and many facts accumulating from many sources have provided the proof of this, and I am sure that, even if there was nothing else which promoted this notion, as I am about to describe, I would nevertheless have come to this opinion. For when, as seemed right to the Almighty, the father of these princes, after directing the inhabited world, departed to join again the One who had sent him down here, despite such momentous change the mainstays of the empire were not shaken, nor did any of the events affect the heirs of the government, but it remained on an even keel. However it remained not without a degree of trouble nor without the successors having to make use of their hands for firmly retaining what was granted to them. 49. I especially rejoice with the emperors for these two reasons: that they received the government from their father and that they proved superior to the ensuing disorder. In this instance, more than anywhere, were united the quality of justice and that of courage. For if they had not received approval from him but had obtained the empire through their own devices, their possession of it might have shown a proof of their gallantry, but the portion of justice would not have been present in the events; and if when he gave it no difficulty had been attached, but it had been possible for them to enjoy in perfect ease what had been given, the justice of their rule might have been accepted, but the glory of bravery would not have coexisted with the considerations of justice. But in fact it is a mark of justice that they received the empire from him according to his wish, and it is a sign of the utmost valour that they proved superior to the crisis.

50. Anyone who wishes may examine whether I am attributing God's solicitude to small benefits or whether the excess of their achievements persuades me to this view. Who then could demonstrate an

empire better than this one obtained by their forefathers, increased by their father and strengthened by the present possessors? Who, in trying to set beside these princes the best men in recorded history, would not appear to be ignorant of the nature and boundaries of their successes? 51. Let us pass over Xerxes, if we agree, who suffered the greatest misfortunes through his folly, and Cambyses who plunged headlong into madness. But let us compare Darius, if anyone wants, and the famous Cyrus whose wonder practically overwhelmed everyone, and let us evaluate them. Immediately upon Cyrus' birth he was condemned to death and that at the hands of his family, and if the chance intervention of a herdswoman had not preserved the infant, Cyrus would never have existed. 52. When he came of age and set the Persians against the Medes, he attacked and destroyed his grandfather; in so doing he betrayed a degree of self-seeking and he did not fall far short of impiety. For it was self-interest to seize a government that did not belong to him, and it was not an act of piety that afflicted a murder on his own family. Whereas in Darius' case it was the skill of a groom, a love-sick horse and a contrived whinnying that gave him his kingdom. But our emperors from the very day they were born were nurtured under the shared prayers of everyone, and after being invited they took the empire, and they did not seize it by force after being excluded.

53. I expect then that some people will desire to see in my speech Alexander proving inferior to the emperors. But it is not difficult to effect this victory. First of all they have outstripped Alexander through the rank of their forefathers. For how could Amyntas, a man subject to tribute, or Philip the stealer of cities, be compared with or even approach the virtues of fathers that touch the heavenly orb? 54. Furthermore Alexander, having inherited nothing with which he could justifiably be content, attempted a greater enterprise, and by effecting an addition to his existing territories he also effected an amazing admission of having had nothing from the beginning, so it follows there was a time when Alexander was not famous. Whereas our emperors began from greatness in their origin and have maintained their greatness to maturity. Apart from this, when Alexander was increasing in power there were from the beginning those who said an injustice was being done, because he grew more powerful by taking away the possessions of others; but these emperors are both the most powerful of all and do not plunder the territories of others.

For from the start they have held all the territory due to them and they need no addition.

55. When therefore Alexander, Darius and Cyrus are demonstrated to fall short of their reputation when set in comparison with these princes, where shall we place in order the remaining list of kings, when we consider these?

56. It appears that our discourse as it makes gradual progress is proceeding now to the very deeds which were accomplished in hazard. In fact I see a greater hazard besetting those who speak than beset the very men who were drawn up in battle. Thus it is no more trivial matter to say something about the most important of events, than it is to accomplish them. It is right to say this much by way of introduction. For it is our present intention not to compose a history which embraces everything, nor to prolong a bare account that leaves out anything of external interest, but to dedicate a panegyric to the saviours of the world. 57. It is the duty of the composer of a history to go through all the accomplishments in sequence, but of the man trying to deliver an encomium to omit no form of eulogy, rather than to recount each detail throughout. And so the technique we adopted with regard to their nurture and education which we mentioned for each one of them, without dealing with everything they each did, is the form we must employ also for their deeds in the wars. 58. If then it were possible to have one's prayer granted, I would have requested that I had been given ten mouths as Homer did, but above all I would have wished for two tongues to be provided by the Almighty so that, as in other respects my speech of eulogy proceeded in conjunction, likewise in their deeds of war I could have preserved equilibrium. But since it is easy to pray for this but not possible to receive it, let my speech follow the sequence of the age of our emperors and when it has honoured as well as it can the Persian campaigns of the elder brother, let it transfer from there to the West to light upon deeds both diverse and very important.

59. It is necessary for me to speak briefly first about their most divine father, but I think this section will contribute no less than all the rest to the eulogy that is my theme. For Constantine is acknowledged to have outrun all his predecessors in all respects relating to virtue; since this is so clear and does not admit a variant opinion, he is also admitted to have as far outstripped himself in courage in war as he

did the rest in everything else. For when many wars, I believe, had beset him, some of them against fellow Romans and some against the barbarians, there is no war which he did not finally settle according to his plan, nor to which he regretted turning his attention nor which sent him away without spoils, but as if he had made a covenant with Fortune for eternal victory, with such confidence did he bear arms and win a result that accorded with his hopes. 60. However, the Persian nation raised its arm against Constantine, excellent as he was in all respects and accustomed to victory and experienced in the art of war.[19] Should any knowledgeable person examine the dates, he will find that the beginning of the war preceded Constantine's death, so that, although the war was commenced against him, the labour of the war fell on his son. 61. So why do I mention this and to make what point did I introduce the subject? It is because if they had remained at peace while he was alive, but when he quit his life, they had rushed into arms, they would not have seemed to be showing confidence in themselves rather than despising whoever succeeded Constantine; for if they had made his life the limit of their peace, they would have demonstrated this to everyone. But since they realised that they were venturing to oppose Constantine in person, it is clear that they began the war with confidence in their resources, but not thinking that the object of their fear had been removed.

62. Accordingly, I wish to relate what induced the Persians to run such a great risk. Indeed it does not seem reasonable to anyone at first impression that those who were content in earlier times, provided nobody troubled them, should have wished to go to war when it was possible to live in peace. Therefore I wish to say this quite concisely, so as to make it clear to all, that they did not come to war with a trifling intent. 63. The condition of the Persians was not peace but a postponement of war, and they did not desire peace so as to avoid fighting a war, but they cultivated peace to enable them to fight properly.[20] They did not avoid absolutely running a risk, but, in being prepared for a host of dangers they combined after a fashion peace with war. They presented a peaceful appearance but had the disposition of men at war. For when in earlier times they had been caught unprepared and heavily defeated, they did not blame their own courage but they attributed responsibility to their deficiency of preparation. They agreed to peace for purposes of preparation for war, and continued from that time onwards to adhere to the treaty by means of embassies and gifts, but arranged everything towards

their ulterior purpose. 64. They equipped their own forces and brought their preparation to perfection in every form: cavalry, infantry, archers and slingers. They trained to a consummate degree in the methods that had been their practice from the beginning, and they introduced from elsewhere methods with which they were unfamiliar. They did not give up their native techniques, but added to their resources a more remarkable capability. 65. Hearing that his forefathers Darius and Xerxes had extended for ten years their preparation against the Greeks, he despised their attempt as inadequate; Shapur[21] himself resolved to prolong the period to four decades. During the length of this time a mass of money was gathered, a multitude of men was collected and a stockpile of arms was forged. And now he assembled a supply of elephants, not just for empty show, but to meet the needs of the future. Everyone was instructed to dismiss all other pursuits and practise warfare; the old not to lay down their arms and the youngest to be enrolled in the levy; to hand the care of the fields to their women and to spend their time under arms.

66. Something that I almost omitted but that is quite significant is worth bringing into the open. The king of the Persians praised one aspect of his own land, but found fault with another. With regard to the production of manpower he considered it second to none, but he criticised the country because it did not equip its armed forces by supplying a domestic source of iron.[22] In short he realised that he commanded men but that his power was defective as a result of the shortage of equipment. 67. When, therefore, he had sat and considered this and fretted over it very greatly, he came to the decision to enter upon a deceitful and servile path, and sent an embassy and ingratiated himself, as was his practice. He made obeisance through his envoys and requested a great supply of iron, under the pretext that it was for use against another nation of neighbouring barbarians, but in truth with the intention to use the gift against the donors.[23] Constantine was well aware of the real motive, for the nature of the recipient caused suspicion. But despite knowing exactly to what end the benefits of the technology were leading, though it was possible to resist, he gave it with eagerness. He saw in his calculations all that would happen as if it had already occurred, but he felt it would be shameful to leave his son enemies who were unarmed. He wanted every excuse the Persians might have to be removed in advance, and he restricted his opponents carefully, so that although they flourished

in all respects they would be brought low. For the splendour of the vanquished contributes to the glory of their conquerors. 68. Constantine then with such magnanimity and hopes granted the request readily, as if wishing to make plain that even if they exhausted the mines of the Chalybes, they would not appear to surpass in this respect men to whom they were rated as inferior. Thereupon the equipment of the Persian king was complete, both in terms of native resources and in external supplies, the former existing in abundance while the latter had been added to satisfy requirements. 69. Arrows, scimitars, spears, swords and every implement of war were forged with the abundance of material. By examining every possibility and omitting nothing from investigation, he aimed to make his cavalry practically invulnerable. For he did not limit their armour to helmet, breastplate and greaves in the ancient manner, nor to placing bronze plates before the head and chest of the horse; but he caused the rider to be covered in protective armour from his head to his toes, and the horse from its crown to the tips of its hooves, with a space left open only for their eyes to see what was happening, and for breathing holes to avoid asphyxiation. 70. You would have said that the name of 'bronze men' was more appropriate to these than to the soldiers in Herodotus. These men had to ride a horse which was obedient to their voice instead of a bridle, and they carried a lance which needed both hands; their only consideration in action was to fall upon their enemies without hesitation, and they had entrusted their body to the protection of iron mail. 71. When everything had been made ready and his force had been equipped in every way, he could no longer restrain himself. He saw the multitude of his army and he saw the unbreakable nature of their armour, and he reckoned up the length of their preparation and the period of training; envisaging the hope of a successful fortune he sent an embassy to dispute about the borders so that, should we retire from our territory, he might win it without effort, but if we in no way conceded, he might allege this as a pretext for war.

72. But when the great emperor heard about this, he loathed the Persian for his arrogance and said that he wished to give him his answer in person. And deeds followed upon words. When he arose, everything was immediately put into action. He had just embarked on the journey, when he came into this city, and the Almighty considered that Constantine was inscribed upon many trophies but that of his two sons the one who had been appointed against the

Persians should gain distinction by victories over the barbarians. Having made such a decision He called up the old emperor to Himself, but brought the task and delivered it to the son.

73. So it is easy to conjecture how what had happened excited the Persians to audacity and how they considered they already possessed the cities, but in fact a guardian had been left for the cities that was 'far greater', to quote Homer, and was really second to none. However, at that critical time two very important necessities coincided. For on the one side his father's burial drew his attention, and on the other the din of the Persian assault. He was obliged either to meet the enemy and neglect the funeral rites or to observe the rites and lay the empire open to the enemy. 74. So what did he do? He did not consider advantage more highly than the rites, but rather both duties were successfully combined and the secondary purpose of the journey was more honourable than any deed. For he himself hastened energetically to the burial,[24] while fear held the Persians back in their own land.[25] Whether they received their fright from heaven and were restrained or whether it was through not knowing anything of his withdrawal but thinking they would encounter the emperor's right hand, either explanation is equally sufficient for a eulogy. For the one holds proof of God's favour, and the other holds evidence of the efficiency in his government, if indeed the facts of his absence eluded the enemy. 75. After accomplishing his other duties he met with his brother[26] who is in every way deserving of our admiration. Hearing that his adversaries as though smitten by God had quit the river bank, he did not suffer that which had long been common talk, nor did he expect that his wishes would be fulfilled automatically and devote the remainder of his time to leisure; but considering that such times of crisis required action, not hope, he ran back to complete the homeward course, as if in all truth he was running up and down continually in a stadium rather than traversing the greater part of the world.

76. His swift journey was followed by another march under arms and he stood upon the borders of Persia eager to stain his right hand with blood. But there was no one to meet his anger.[27] For those who had initiated the war deferred the war by flight, not as men who succumbed to fear after encountering the enemy but as men who did not await the encounter because of their fear.[28] Their rout was not the result of hand-to-hand fighting, but reputation sufficed to cause

181

the reversal. 77. What took place deserves special admiration. For the emperor had resolved to undertake neither a blockade nor a permanent withdrawal, but occupied as winter quarters the greatest of the cities in that region; and when the fighting season began he blazed forth, attacking as much Persian territory as calculation permitted. While he considered it irksome to be entirely involved in events there, he nevertheless considered it an act of passivity not to go for an all-out offensive. 78. For that reason he divided his time between campaigning and planning. The chief aim of his planning was not how he must defeat the Persians when they appeared but how he had to persuade them to put in an appearance. He had so completely confounded their expectations that what they hoped to inflict on others when they started the war was what they were suffering when enveloped by our counter-attacks. 79. Previously it was their usual practice to launch an invasion and a necessity for us to abandon our own territory when they advanced, with the result that you would have found that the cities bordering them were the oldest in date but the most recent in the building of their foundations. For the inhabitants had to return and rebuild the cities after the Persians had burnt them down and departed. But now the situation has been so much reversed that the majority of the Syrians do not hesitate to live in unwalled cities, whereas it seems almost a sign of victory for the Persians if their concealment escapes detection.

80. Let no one think that I am either ignorant of the surprise raids which they now employed, or unaware that they were able to push forward some force unexpectedly, or that they invented a treaty for the cessation of hostilities and employed our lack of defence resulting from the oaths to further their advantage; or further that they had clear understanding of this and willingly transgressed the terms. Far from being embarrassed at these facts, I think I would have reasonable cause for embarrassment if none of them had occurred. For he who has nothing that is worth recording to say of the defeated has also precluded the praise due to the victors. It is just as in the athletic contests, whenever the draw sets a man who is greatly inferior to fight against the best, victory belongs to the better man but applause from the spectators does not accompany the victory crown. So also in warfare the inferiority of the defeated detracts from the value of the victors' glory. 81. I agree that the Persians are experts in robbery and deceit, and they do not desist very quickly and would very easily make many depredations through perjury. Nevertheless those who

had discovered so many paths to war could not bear to gaze steadily upon the emperor's helmet. The surest proof of both of these statements is that if they heard he was approaching, they would vanish into thin air; but when they received notice of his absence, they would attack those arrayed against them. In the first instance they admitted their fear, and in the second they demonstrated their stealth. It such a way they had acquired their military experience, but when the emperor made his appearance they were so frightened that they lost all memory of that experience. That it was not unreasonable to use their opportunities in this way, but perfectly sensible, was demonstrated by events. When they were not able to hide their true nature, no sooner had they made their appearance in front of the emperor than, being caught in the net, they immediately transferred their allegiance to us. It was not that there were some who surrendered and others who were taken captive in the course of battle, but absolutely all of them crouched down in the same manner and extended their hands in supplication.

83. At his word the entire population of a very important city among the Persians, as if caught in a net, was transferred with all its households.[29] They cursed those who had sown the seed of war, and lamented the desolation of their native land, but had not altogether despaired of better hopes because of the mild disposition of their conqueror. And they were not deceived. I mean by this that in my judgement his policy after the capture was much more admirable than the capture itself. For when he captured them, he did not kill them as the Corcyraeans slew the Corinthian settlers from Epidamnus, nor did he sell them as prizes of war, as Philip did with the prisoners of the Olynthians. Instead he had the notion to make use of the captives in the place of a victory monument and trophy. He transported them to Thrace and settled them there to act as reminders to later generations of their misfortune.[30] 84. And these facts cannot be disbelieved. For we are not recounting an action which has vanished in the mists of time, as Antiquity contends to create falsehood, but I think that everyone can still recall before his eyes the procession of prisoners that took place yesterday and the day before. 85. It was this that I mean is finer and more statesmanlike than the winning of a victory. Many men, to be sure, on many occasions, have brought cities to terms, but it has not been the achievement of many to arrange the results of the capture to fit in with necessary policy. Let us consider how much he combined in

this one deed. Firstly, he civilised a very considerable wild region of Thrace by providing colonists to bring it under cultivation. Secondly he transmitted the memory of his achievements for all time to successive generations, and did not allow forgetfulness to prevail over his accomplishments. Thirdly he exhibited the very ideals of kindliness and generosity by being moved to pity at their tears and by discarding his anger upon their change of fortune. 86. Furthermore, he did not leave us who were dwelling further away from the enemy's land to feast only on the report of what had happened, but he made us eye-witnesses of everything and filled us with much joy and good hope. We rejoiced at his successes and judged the future from his achievements. 87. But if I must speak about what particularly gratified me, after so long he had wrought justice for those Greeks carried off from Euboea, by taking these prisoners away from their native land in return for the Eretrian families.

88. So then this would have been a measure sufficing both requirements and no element of distinction would have been lacking, even though it was possible to add nothing to the achievement of the older emperor. For he left no requirement of the funeral rites undone but despite being so far removed from control of affairs, he managed not to lose anything; he inspired fear among his opponents, whenever his approach was announced, and raised their morale again when the time for retreat was at hand. He relocated some cities and founded others. How could anyone fail to say that altogether he met the call of his duty? Certainly one cannot be short of subject matter, but actually the most important points have been left out, namely the final battle, and certain other things that provide a touchstone for his ultimate wisdom. We can see it in some respect in what follows.

89. We are all well aware that this section of the empire is enclosed by the two greatest nations of the barbarians; on the one side beyond the Danube are the dense throngs of the Scythians, and on the other is the vexatious multitude of the Persians. Of these the former despite their confidence take no action, while the latter are not even restless to start with. Who then is so carefree or indolent that he would not examine with the greatest pleasure the nature of such an incredible situation? What on earth is it which persuaded the Scythians, the most murderous of men and devoted to Ares, and who judge inactivity as a misfortune, to love peace, to lay down their arms and to treat our emperor as equal to their own leaders even when he is

far removed from the Danube and marshalling his forces against others? 90. What is the reason for so important a development? It is that the emperor, being possessed of courage and intelligence in equal measure, has mastered the one front by his soundness of judgement while he pursues the other out of necessity. You would see this if you were to compare with our present lack of fear of the Scythians their former raids, which we could not bear to look upon, and from which the granting of one prayer alone could save us. This prayer was that the ice on the Danube should not be frozen solid, to be sufficient for their crossing. And who would still be amazed at the security of the peace when he hears of their enthusiasm for an alliance? 91. Thus there is no achievement which does not contribute some new sense of wonder, but the earlier feeling is always obscured by the subsequent one. There is something very pleasant to hear of but never yet achieved in any deed before now, which some people have not even contemplated, and has been considered impossible by others, and you will find nothing to compare with it in all the acts of everyone else. This is what was both planned and without any hesitation has long since been brought to fulfilment. 92. A Scythian army went out to contribute to the strength of the Romans and to oppose the power of the Persians; ready to guard unshaken the empire of the Romans and to help in undoing the Persians' domination. What is even more significant, they did not make their expedition in order to fulfil their obligations, and they were not seen to be doing wrong out of necessity. Nor when they as barbarians saw other barbarians approaching did they lose their resolution upon the sight and immediately change their allegiance, as once before the Thessalians did, but as though they were fighting for their own land they showed no lesser enthusiasm for their tasks than those who had summoned them. 93. And the cause of this behaviour should be attributed not to their nature but to the emperor's wisdom, because he made them loyal instead of untrustworthy, obedient instead of undisciplined, reliable instead of unstable, allies in place of enemies, and in a single strategy both gained an auxiliary force against the Persians and emptied a considerable part of Scythia, and through his schemes involved in war those who were united by the name of barbarian. Consequently it is not easy for me to decide whether he is worthy of admiration more for his courage or for the wisdom of his policy.

94. The following provides confirmation of the same view. For while

this great war was being prosecuted through to its end, sedition broke out unexpectedly from within against the emperor, and a very considerable disturbance seized the greatest of the cities in this part of the world, second only to the greatest of them all.[31] Yet the man who looks simply upon this will consider it a misfortune, whereas the man who can adequately reflect upon it, will view what happened as the summit of good fortune. For just as extreme cases of illnesses profit the best doctors by providing the opportunity to demonstrate their skill, so for rulers the difficulties of crises bring advantage, if they are destined to be resolved for the better through the rulers' wise planning. Nothing would have prevented even Aeacus from losing the greatest proof of his justice, if the unruliness of the winds had not brought the Greeks to need his help and allowed him to show who he was. 95. I congratulate the emperor on this remedial policy, that it allowed him to imitate skilful helmsmen, who when the vessel is buffeted by many winds from many directions hold out through everything and prove their skill is superior to the squall. Likewise the emperor standing in the midst of war and sedition, and encircled by a multitude of problems, did not lose his composure in the waves, but was as adequate for both challenges as if he were fully at leisure from either of them. 96. So now what must I say first or last? Or what must I record and what leave out? How he departed from Persia without taking account of the Persians on the grounds that they would nowhere put in an appearance, or the speed of his march in which he outran the Spartans, or the excesses of the winter weather or the snowstorms or the continuous rain? He laughed at all of these as if he was a man of iron. 97. Or rather how he extinguished the madness of the rebels before he appeared? How he sailed across the strait as if concealed in a divine mist? How he treated those under accusation? How he separated out those who were blameless? How he executed no one but chastened the malefactors? How when he had provided the opportunity for discussion within the Senate he won most of it over with his speech? But is it right to omit all this and recall the exchange of dialogue, in which he swiftly overthrew the cleverest part of the Senate? How no sooner had he settled their affairs than he again stood facing the enemy even before resting from his march? 98. Thus, as I said, we can debate whether the possession of courage or intelligence is better, but whichever one may be judged to be superior, it is in the control of the emperor. Yet when we know that even the foremost among the heroes came to the rescue in the early days with only one of these qualities, which of those heroes can we possibly put in the same category as the emperor who possesses both qualities in superabundance?

99. Well then, let us also mention the final battle.[32] We can call the same battle both the final and the great one, and much more deserving of the title of great than the celebrated battle at Corinth.[33] I promise to demonstrate how the emperor defeated in this battle the Persians together with their allied forces. And let no one distrust the hyperbole before hearing the account, but let him await the arguments and then express judgement. I want to begin a little earlier on. For thus the observation of the whole story may be more accurate.

100. When the Persians grew tired of the emperor's inroads[34] and were distressed by the length of the war, they treated the necessity of their situation as an inspiration to take risks; for death is not oppressive to men who take no enjoyment from life. They were willing in fact to suffer through their actions, and they raised their levies amongst the men from youth upwards and did not grant immunity from military service to the very young. They conscripted their womenfolk to act as sutlers in the army. There were various nations of barbarians on their borders, some of whom they persuaded by entreaty to share their dangers, while others they compelled by force to serve in the hour of need. To others they offered a quantity of gold, a hoard preserved since ancient times and now for the first time expended in payment to mercenary soldiers. 101. When they had scoured all the land in this region, they left the cities empty and herded the whole populace together in a crowd on foot. They practised their training on the march and set off towards the river. The emperor got to know of what was afoot. How could so massive a cloud of dust have gone unnoticed, rising up as it did to fill the sky? Not to mention that the confused din of horses, men and arms, made it impossible even for those very far away to snatch any sleep, and that our scouts who personally watched the manoeuvre brought back news which was based on observation and not on guesswork using other sources. 102. When an accurate report of this reached the emperor, he did not grow pale like a man whose heart is struck with terror, but he sought a strategy that was suitable to meet the present emergency. His orders to those maintaining the garrisons along the frontiers were to retreat with utmost speed, and neither to harass them when they bridged the river, nor to prevent their landing nor to hinder their fortification of a camp; but to allow them to dig

trenches, if they wished, to put up a palisade, to fence themselves in, to lay in a supply of water and to occupy the most favourable terrain. For he was not concerned if they crossed over and encamped, but that if they were beaten off from the start, they would seize an excuse for flight. The strategy required that the enemy be beguiled by the ease of their landing.

103. When these apparent concessions had been made and no one from our side opposed them, they bridged the river at three points and began crossing over in large numbers at each point.[35] At first, without stopping by night and day they ceaselessly poured across the river. Afterwards, when it became necesssary to fortify their position, they raised a circuit wall in one day more quickly than the Greeks at Troy. By now the entire area was full of those who had crossed over the river banks, the breadth of the plains and the mountain peaks. Every type of military contingent furnished their army: archers, mounted archers, slingers, heavy infantry, cavalry and armed men from every quarter. While they were still deliberating as to where they should muster, their king made his appearance, surpassing any Homeric image in his brilliance, and wearing his armour he supervised the whole operation. 104. Then the Persians developed a strategy along the following lines. They drew up their archers and javelin-throwers on the peaks and on the fortified wall, and placed their heavily armoured troops in front of the wall. The remaining soldiers took up their arms and advanced against the enemy to provoke them. When they saw that the Romans were moving into action, they immediately gave way and turned to flight, enticing their pursuers within missile range so that they could be shot at from above. 105. And so the pursuit continued for some time and indeed for the greater part of the day, until those who had fled had retreated within the wall. This was the opportune moment for the archers and those in front of the wall who had not been engaged. At this juncture the emperor won a victory not in the style of the usual victories nor like those that have occurred frequently both in the present age and in the past. Nor was it a victory whose result depended on skill at arms and military equipment, nor one for which there was need of association with others, that could not otherwise have been accomplished. But it was a victory which we are permitted to class as rightly belonging to the victor. 106. What is meant by this? He alone discovered the intention behind what was happening, he alone was not deceived by the purpose of the battle formation and

he alone shouted out the order to our troops not to pursue nor to be forced into obvious danger. Now indeed I admire all the more the concept of the poet who says that a plan that has its share of wisdom is more effective than the work of many hands. By following this maxim, the emperor immediately grasped the entire situation and could see the future just as well as he saw present circumstances as they unfolded. 107. This was most natural. For between the camps there was a distance of 150 stades,[36] and they began the pursuit in the forenoon and were already drawing near the wall by late afternoon. In fact, considering the entire position, the burden of their weapons, the length of the pursuit, the burning heat of the sun, their critical state of thirst, the onset of night and the archers on the hilltops, he thought it right to disregard the Persians and to yield to the needs of the situation. 108. If the Roman troops had been receptive to reasoning and their ardour had not overborne his advice, nothing would have prevented both the enemy from being defeated as they are at present and the victors from winning safely through. But as it was, the more one finds fault with them, the more one increases the emperor's reputation. For as they blundered by not obeying orders they have enhanced the counsel of their adviser. 109. I do invoke those victories of the emperors which they achieve in partnership, but I consider much more honourable those where it is not possible to name more than one participant. As a result, even if one should strive very hard that one's verdict should not go wholly against the soldiers, nothing would have prevented them from completely restoring the position, and the emperor from winning total victory, first and foremost over the very men whose judgement he surpassed.

110. It is appropriate to examine the merits of those who fought and to make clear to all from what disadvantages they started out and the qualities they emerged with. First of all when they clashed with the heavily-armed cavalry in front of the wall, they invented a tactic superior to their armour. For when the horse charged forward the infantry soldier stepped out of its way and rendered the attack useless, while he struck the rider on the temple with his club as he rode by and knocked him off, and finished off the rest of the business quite easily. Secondly no sooner had they laid hands on the wall, than it was totally demolished from the battlements to its lowest foundation, without anyone to stop them. 111. I would have considered it valuable also to relate who was the first to break through the encircling wall and to digress on their act of courage – for perhaps

this would be no less pleasing to hear than about the fire which spread over the ship of the Thessalians. But since time does not allow, I think one should not be side-tracked anywhere. 112. The encircling wall therefore was totally flattened, and they poured in, thinking that what they had so far accomplished was all too insignificant. They plundered the tents and carried off the produce of those who had been labouring in the neighbourhood and they slew everyone they caught. Only those who took to flight managed to escape. When the rout had become manifest, in fact it only required a brighter day, if somehow it had been possible, to achieve complete success; but when it drifted on into a night battle, they were shot at from the hills and were now surrounded by weapons and arrows which broke off and clung to their bodies. They were deprived by the night of the ability to use their normal tactics in the darkness; nonetheless the heavy infantry advanced against the lighter armed soldiers whose effectiveness lay in fighting at a distance. Thoroughly exhausted, they lost some good men against fresh troops but they drove their enemies out of the area.[37] 113. However who could have withstood their courage, had it been accompanied by reasoning? Though faced with such great obstacles they were prevented by nobody from settling the issue in a better manner. But who would not reckon that the Persians, who had crossed over to conquer others, were clearly worsted, since though they had enjoyed such great advantages, they abandoned their hopes and departed? 114. Whether, therefore, for one person the emperor's superiority in good planning is commended, and he has been demonstrated to be better than friends and opponents alike in his strategy, or whether for another person it is more pleasurable to approve by scrutiny the bare facts; at all events, the Persians quit the camp and started for the pontoon bridge, whereas those of our men who fell conquered with their spirits but renounced their lives, and those who returned did not make the homeward march before they had cleansed the land of the enemy. Nor do I need to add the point that the nature of the terrain caused more damage than the prowess of the enemy, nor that the Persians enlisted the help of their women in the danger, whereas the strongest part of our army did not participate in the battle.[38]

115. Let us define three phases and so consider our judgement: firstly, the period before the battle, secondly, the engagement itself and thirdly, the period of the rout. 116. So then, the enemy accomplished their landing and bridged the river, not by forcing back those who

were pressing against them, but taking their freedom of action from those who had no desire to hinder them. When they had landed and scouted around, they seized what in their judgement were the strongpoints, but not as though suffering a shortage of arms they attacked those who appeared. 117. Up to now they had enjoyed the advantage, but when the armies clashed, instead of standing up to the attackers and fighting it out hand to hand, they began to flee. When they had barricaded themselves within their defensive perimeter, they failed to maintain the defence of the wall but gave up their fortification, and in addition they surrendered the treasure in their tents. Those who were left behind there fell in no order and looked on as the king's son, the successor to the throne, was taken prisoner, flogged, stabbed and, a little later, executed.[39] Indeed if they managed any effective fighting anywhere, what happened was a trick of war, rather than an act of courage.

118. So much for the events of the battle, and as to what happened after it, they did not recover their dead but rushed into flight, broke down the bridges and did not hope even in their dreams to recover the stunning loss. But their king, of brilliant ability and noble in his behaviour until his threats, rent and tore out that head of hair which he would previously adorn; he struck his head frequently and lamented the slaughter of his son, lamented the destruction of his conscripts and wept over his land bereft of its farmers. He resolved to cut off the heads of those who had failed to win for him the success of the Romans. 119. It is not my speech, composed to gratify, which proves this, but their deserters who surrender themselves clearly announce the news. We must accept their word: for they do not delight in false tales of their peril. It is these effects, therefore, that make the victory not doubtful, like the one at Tanagra or, by Heaven, the victory at Oresthis by the Tegeans and Mantineans.[40]

120. However, I can say much more than this, which I think not even the king of the Persians himself would contradict. For it has been admitted by both sides that in the night battle the survivors returned home again. In the circumstances, one of two possibilities must have occurred, either that they were defeated and fled or that they won but nevertheless were wary over the next development. If therefore we suppose the first possibility, clearly the victory lies with us. But if in the night battle, although they gained the advantage, they did not have the confidence to follow up the attack thereafter, then the

emperor's victory becomes much greater. For if they defeated their opponents, but did not stand to face his right hand, then they made it clear, presumably to all, that the emperor's strength lies not in the outcome but rather in his nature.

121. Now it is not that his character is such in war but that in other matters he provides no ground for acclamation, but being so resplendent in arms he is all the more superior in his duties other than in arms, so that we can say he is 'both a good king and a stalwart warrior'. For, if he were seen to be more irascible than the rest, he would not be considered to be better than the others in this regard, but if he took more pleasure in mildness than others, that would be all the more reason for him to surpass them all. 122. Nor again does he suppose that disturbance of one's countenance is befitting for an emperor, but considers that it is appropriate for a state of frenzy and counts it as an affliction, thinking that roughness as regards human society is the behaviour of the tyrant. But he has added easy accessibility in manners to the ruler's share, taking great pride not that he holds the empire together through fear but that he guards it with the affection of the governed. He is adept at giving a response to a favour, and at dealing out pardon for a mistake; he is above emulation and superior to anger, and is master of desire; for he thinks it is his business not to subdue cities but to minister to the sufferings of the soul. A man who is subject to desire he considers should more correctly be called a slave than a master. He is invulnerable with regard to the schedule of the body and does not succumb to ill-timed temper. He brings into the open whatever counsel he himself discovers, and the advice of his close followers he does not belittle with surliness, but in fact he confirms the old saying, that the mark of practical wisdom lies in knowing how to cast one's judgement in favour of the best. He does not declaim at length an empty speech but encompasses the substance of his actions in a conciseness of language. He enrols no one in haste on the list of his close friends, but of those whom he has once enrolled he does not know how to cancel out their names, nor does he exhaust his affection with the passage of time, but he increases his love through familiarity. He has not the least hesitation to run risks for the sake of the just, but is the most unpractised of all in stirring up war for aggrandisement. He is quick to serve a good turn, but slow to take vengeance. He knows how to show mercy to poverty, but not how to indulge envy upon wealth. In the case of those who have committed injustices he

does not search out punishments, but turns them away from their injustices by their emulation of his own person. To such a degree has he exercised prudence that he is embarrassed even by the mention of intemperance; and he stands so far aloof from false swearing that he is pious in keeping his oath also. He rates the failure to accustom the stomach to hunger as close to a lack of manliness. His name has always been inscribed upon the greatest achievements but he has never yet shouted anything aloud. He pays speedy attention to critical moments but does not combine speed with confusion. His confidence in victory does not lie in the multitude of his soldiers, but he expects the better outcome for the man who is aware of piety. There is no omission in the exactness of his preparation but his trust is more in divine favour than in arms for his strength. Never yet has he been beaten back from any undertaking, but he would have taken it very easily even if he had chanced to be baulked. He is neither downcast by grief nor acts meanly on an occasion of great joy, but removes the obvious signs of both and sets his face in a bearing of moderation. He praises the virtues of his associates but with his silence corrects behaviour that is other than it should be. For what is brought under control by others through rebuke, receives amendment from the emperor by his keeping silence, so that he highlights the good in what he praises, whereas in contrast by his silence towards the opposite he remedies the mistake no less effectively. But he avoids the vexation of fault-finding. He does not spend his times of leisure in sleep and ease but has exchanged his repose for the practice of military skills. Nor does he indulge in the licentiousness of the theatre for his amusement but he stimulates his soul for manliness with the spectacle of racing chariots. He is the lightest of all men in mounting a horse, and is more accurate at hitting the target than those praised in Homer for their knowledge of archery. He has brought as much freedom as possible to the lives of his subjects but the measure of their contribution he has revealed as the measure of what is needed. Wherefore having established his government along such lines he has lived with greater authority than he wished, but with greater security than any of the private citizens.

123. However if we were to enumerate the majority of the qualities present in this emperor, we shall be able to mention none of those qualities that belong to his brother. We must indeed turn our account back to the West and attempt in such manner as may be practicable

to pick out brief topics from the many, and briefly to discourse upon those same subjects.

124. So in summary I can indicate the whole by simply declaring this much: that Constans confirmed his equality of nature by the similar conduct of his policy, and he transferred the likeness of his name into a likeness of actions, and caused the actions also to be called brotherly. For just as the one brother checked all the fear spreading from the Persian assault, so this brother compelled the barbarian nations in the West, which had poured around from every direction, to keep the peace. 125. It was then an act of God to ordain an equal government for each brother, but to give each one a different manner to approach government. For the one bridled the neighbouring peoples when they were disturbed, while the other did not permit his empire even to be disturbed; so that whether one took the former as worthy of amazement or considered the second as more brilliant or admired both equally, neither achievement would have escaped the present emperorship.

126. Now I shall say a few words in imitation of Thucydides. For I have not immediately accepted any report without examination nor have I avoided hardship in my quest for the truth and had recourse to what was available, but with difficulty and with the utmost exactitude have I spent my time in the project, and it would not be reasonable to mistrust me.

127. What then are his successes? There is a Celtic race beyond the river Rhine reaching down to the North Sea itself, so well fortified for deeds of war that taking their name from their very practices they are called the Fracti.[41] They are generally called the Franks, but this is a name corrupted by the ignorance of the many. 128. These men surpass all counting in their number, and in the strength of their own multitude they pass beyond hyperbole. For these men a squall upon the sea is no more frightening than upon the land, and the northern cold they find more pleasant than a temperate climate. Their greatest misfortune is a quiet life, and opportunities for wars are the limit of their happiness. And if one were to maim them, they fight on with what is left. If they prevail their pursuit knows no limit, or should it happen that they are defeated, they make the end of their flight the beginning of their attack. They have ordained by law the rewards for folly and the esteem from reckless conduct. They judge peace to be

entirely a state of sickness. 129. Therefore throughout all history those who held the empire on their borders could discover neither the words to persuade them to keep quiet nor the strength of arms to compel them, but they were obliged to stand guard continually night and day to meet their sallies. And they could neither take their food when out of arms nor doff their helmets and relax in security, but they were practically grafted on to their equipment and carried their arms around like the ancient Acarnanians. 130. And the same thing used to happen as on headlands, whenever the sea is driven by changing winds and is roused to a continuous succession of waves. For just as there before the first wave breaks cleanly on the beach, the second one follows quickly and the third one in turn, and this is a continuous process, until the winds cease, similarly the nations of the Fracti also were roused to a frenzy by their love of warfare and would make repeated assaults, and before their first host was properly beaten off, a second army would attack.

131. But even the waves of these Fracti had to cease sometime and to halt their movement for certain. For an emperor appeared who turned their insatiable love of warfare into a desire for peace by no other means than by demonstrating that his own enthusiasm for battles was greater than theirs. Accordingly they no longer dared to join in a trial of combat, but fear sufficed to accomplish the results of the trial. They did not lift their right hands to discharge their spears but held them forth to request a treaty. 132. The proof is as follows. They received officers from us as overseers of their behaviour and, discarding their bestial frenzy, they welcomed human reason. They abandoned their arrogance and honoured the keeping of their oaths. In any case even if the obligation resulting from oaths had not been present they would have loved peace. Thus the inferior is generally brought under control by the superior. 133. And now the emperor has entrusted the observing of their agreements not to the character of the Fracti but to their fear of him, and is determining policy for his whole empire in the cities of Paeonia. Whereas in earlier times the unforeseen movement of the Fracti compelled our leaders to concentrate on them and did not allow them to get to know their empire, but by hearsay alone subjects became familiar to their rulers. If therefore someone is a lover of an easily won victory, let him take his fill of childish play, since there is no one who has not admitted that their slavery resulted from sheer terror. 134. Therefore as to which policy is better, whether to defeat enemies on the move or not

even to allow them to move, let anyone who wishes cast his vote according to his own fortune and nature. Since whichever policy prevails, it belongs to them both. For they boast more in each other's deeds than in their own.

135. And so the Fracti underwent such a yoke of slavery; for slavery to them means not being able to despoil others. But there are also very many other tribes of barbarians attached to us on every side and encircling our empire like wild animals. Some are quite large, others smaller, but they are all equally difficult to defeat. What more could one say about them than that they exceed Homer's catalogue in the number of their nations? 136. In earlier times these men overran and plundered and beset those Romans who neighboured them with an endless series of troubles; and they were confident both in themselves and in league with each other. But when they saw their chief humbled and those who were accustomed to cause trouble being panic-stricken, they were guided by a judgement based on fear and, being chastened by the example, they ended their raids. Yet what on earth might such an emperor have accomplished by entering a trial of strength, who, when merely expected, subdued the most frenzied barbarians?

137. It is not right to pass over in silence his voyage to the island of Britain, because many are ignorant about the island. But the greater the degree of ignorance, the more will be told, so that all may learn that the emperor explored even beyond the known world. I think that his voyage will appear not inferior to the greatest monument of victory. Now Herodotus who investigated beyond what was strictly necessary expressly maintains that the celebrated Ocean does not exist, but says it is a fiction generated by Homer or some other poet and this was how the name was introduced into the poem. While others, who actually believe that the Ocean exists somewhere, become dizzy at the name. But Constans was so far from suffering such a condition that, if he did not investigate and launch a ship, embark and be conveyed and come to anchor in the harbours of Britain, he thought he would be neglecting the greatest of his duties. 138. There is a consideration that provides those who have seen it as witnesses, namely that it is a greater danger to launch a merchant ship upon that sea than to fight a naval battle elsewhere. Such fresh squalls arch the waves up to heaven, and violent winds take them up and carry them out to the boundless ocean. But the greatest danger is

that, whenever the helmsman matches his skill against all the other elements, the sea suddenly sinks away beneath him, and for a time the vessel hangs in mid air above the waves and is seen to rest on uncovered sand. And if the sea sends back the current quickly, it picks up the boat once more and those on board must endure the remaining hazards. But if there is a delay in returning to the sea, the ship gradually sinks as the sand fails to support the weight upon it. 139. The emperor considered none of these risks, or rather, despite being well aware of everything, he did not hesitate. The more he knew of the much vaunted danger, the more he hastened to put to sea. And what is even more remarkable, he did not sit and wait upon the beach until when the fair weather came the ocean would calm the storm, but immediately just as things were, with the winter at its height and everything roused by the season to a peak of fury – clouds, icy chills and surf – without giving prior word to the cities there and without announcing the launch in advance, not wishing to be admired for his purpose before achieving his objective, he embarked a hundred men, so it is reported. He loosed the mooring cables and began cutting through the ocean, and all immediately changed to calm. The ocean flattened its wave and made itself smooth for the emperor's passage, and that usual ebbing of the sea then confuted its law and held on to the land.[42]

140. It did not happen then that while his passage to the island went so calmly, the return voyage turned out differently, but the second went better than the first in keeping with the proverb, so that there can be no dispute that this youthful undertaking was not without the blessing of God. 141. If therefore after the island had rebelled, its inhabitants were holding an uprising, and the empire was being plundered, the news had arrived, and he had been seized with rage on hearing it and had thrown the die for the voyage, to report his act of daring would not have been to the credit of his resolve, but the crisis deriving from the rebels would have taken away the greater part of the glory. But in fact affairs in Britain were settled. He was completely free to enjoy the wonders of the ocean from the land. There was no cause of anxiety compelling him to make the voyage greater than the harm he would have to suffer if he refused the trip. This was the situation and there was no necessity present, or rather there was only one necessity present, in his desire to set his hand to everything. He willingly gave himself over to the greatest dangers,

as though going to suffer the greatest losses if he did not take the greatest risks.

142. While the deeds themselves are amazing, much more so is the reasoning before the deeds. For he is of the opinion that neither will the soul be released from the body before the Almighty wishes for this, nor will it remain with it any longer when He wishes it to be released; nor will anyone live any longer by protecting himself nor for any shorter period by taking risks. Therefore we must use the reasoning of the immortal gods for however long we may live.

143. Why should we mention two or three things spoken or performed with merit, as if his remaining deeds were not equally indicative of wondrous conduct? In order that I may seem neither excessively indifferent nor to be putting my hand to the impossible, I shall neither make mention of everything in sequence nor shall I keep entirely to just a few.

144. His day is spent in action, and his night is the same as his days. There is no room for strong drink, and sober conduct is his usual practice. All who are slothful are most hateful to him, but anyone wide awake is his close friend. He does not himself have bodyguards to protect his person, but he provides the protection from his person for his guards. For whenever he sees them overtaken by deep sleep, he allows them their rest as entirely pardonable, and he himself as though struggling against nature takes a spear and does sentry duty for the imperial quarters. His incessant labour stretches through every season of the year and all occasions. 145. Homer says somewhere referring to the Achaeans: 'since their flesh was not stone or iron'. But if he had chanced to have met this emperor, assuredly he would not have deemed it inappropriate to apply the image of steel to the hardness of his body. For neither is it reduced into weakness by the heat of summer nor does it shrink under winter's cold into numbness, nor is it enticed by the delights of spring into the enjoyment of pleasure, nor is it dragged down by autumn's gifts into luxuriousness. Though it is a type of luxury, a type of feast, to make one's subjects prudent, to frighten foreigners, to be the cause of rivalry in hymns of praise, to add to one's reputation, to give the emperorship distinction rather than take distinction from it, and to spend one's life in adding to the list of improvements, but not in the enjoyment of successes. 146. And so theatres, scurrility and laughter

and every kind of showmanship have been abolished as equivalent to works of pollution, but sobriety, careful meditation, an easy acceptance of toil, a natural disposition to virtue and all suchlike behaviour is promoted first and foremost. All attractiveness of womankind has been subordinated. The man offering bribes is not more honoured than anyone else as a result of his gift, but the man who shows proof of his judgement has become admired more for his goodwill. 147. Every future undertaking is unobservable, but the emperor alone knows beforehand, since he has also decided policy. Nothing is decided upon that is not also put into effect. The alternating speed of his departures and returns baffles the expectations of many. When he is thought to be resident in the imperial quarters he is crossing mountain peaks, and when he is thought to be on the road he is directing policy in the palace. He is supposed to be sailing the sea but actually he is approaching on foot. He is reported to be journeying on foot, but in fact is sailing the ocean out of sight of land. 148. And he carries out so many journeys of this sort without taking along an entourage to assuage his labours nor a host from the army to guard him, but he has found certain men, few in number, whom he has trusted to follow his speed. He has given these men prior instructions to accompany him wherever he leads, as though he himself has sprouted feathers and, fitting his retinue with wings, hastens forth in all directions quicker than you would think possible. 149. And what better could one look for? For when he does not have enemies to fight, he arms himself against wild animals, and when he does not find the occasion for his valour in warfare, he proves his courage against idols. He trains his body in the open sun, and considers that dense shade reduces its users to a state of feebleness. In short he wishes to be called emperor according to the excellence of his virtue rather than according to the better lot of his fortune.

150. In the case of both emperors one might admire the fact that they have tuned the harmony of their soul to be concordant with the mode of their subjects. For good members of the medical profession, who guarantee that title by their skill, have not employed just one type of medicine for all bodies, but observe the difference, and hence discover the appropriate form of medicine. And whenever the unison of both is preserved, then especially the elements of health come together in balance. In exactly the same way an emperorship, which proceeds upon government with understanding, provides a form

appropriate to the condition of the governed. And whether there is need of more bitter or of milder medicines, he will be well aware of the occasion for each. So that if it had occurred to them to exchange their governments with each other, they would assuredly have received also each other's harmony.

151. But although I seem to be speaking of matters of greatest import I am likely not yet even now to have stated the most important. For in former times a spirit of envy had become attached to all emperorships, and those who possessed the inferior provinces would plot against those who had obtained the more important ones, while those who benefited from the more important ones would begrudge those who drew small profits even their inferior positions. But in fact the equal shares of the overall command fed the disorder to an even greater extent, and the law of nature had been judged second to the desire for dominion, and everything related was filled with frenzy against itself. Indeed the greatest of disasters are commemorated as having occurred in the case of emperorships. I think that poets have been inspired by this to exalt the conspiracies even to the vault of heaven. 152. But now all the ancient time has been reversed, and every spiteful eye of envy has been expelled, and an unbreakable bond of friendship unites the souls of the emperors. Their government has been divided by area but is held together by goodwill, and the title of their kinship is confirmed by their deeds. They are so far removed from smarting at each other's prosperity that each withdraws from the first place in favour of the other. Horses and chariots every day, increasing their speed with successions of teams, carry news of each other's thoughts to one another. And each man of those sent out passes through each administration with equal authority. The place where the divisions of the empires are joined is guarded not by the continual presence of armies, but by the immovable strength of trust without guile.

153. What need is there to seek from afar the proof that they own everything in common and are accounted joint rulers by everyone? For the present event itself serves as better evidence than anything. A shared speech for the acclamation of both has been presented and a joint speech has been performed for both; on the grounds that it is not hazardous to admire both equally, but rather that it would not be right not to be equally admiring of them both. 154. Do they not themselves stand sentry for each other instead of envying each

other's good deeds, and were they brought into dangers by those to whom they entrusted power, as is said to have often occurred in the past, when some employed great resources of money and others their generalships for the purpose of rebellion? But even this possibility is to be excluded from the present circumstances. For there is no one who would not accept his own death in preference to becoming vexatious to the emperor who has shown him trust, and there is no one who would not choose to submerge his fortune in the sea rather than become the orchestrator of revolution. 155. And yet those who in the past were celebrated for money enjoyed inferior wealth to men who now are moderately well-off, whereas nowadays those of moderate means live more abundantly than the former emperors, although nevertheless excess of plenty does not incline the will towards boldness. 156. So what is responsible for the former folly and the present good sense? Because at that time the maxim of Demosthenes was effective and the fear of the future was greater than the attendant feeling of favour and confiscations of property overtook the contributions. What happened was like the twists and turns of the Euripus. For the gift would return to the giver with the inflicting of disaster upon the receiver. Accordingly alarm for the future did not allow the recipient to be quiet, but the one hope of safety lay in destroying the donor. By contrast nowadays great wealth flows from the emperors to their subjects, and everywhere security has been linked to reward and those who receive take no greater pleasure in receiving than in keeping possession in safety.

157. There is something else by far more worthy of respect than this which extends its benefit to all. For if one were to ask anyone, what is the most especially grievous for mankind of those sorrows that generally cause distress in the state of captivity, straightaway without any consideration the answer would be the dishonouring of women. This then had not been averted in the earlier emperorships, but just as the collection of tribute had been established among traditional practices, so too the habit of violating women had become a custom. And those who were keeping our enemies in check combined the misfortunes of enslavement with the appearance of freedom. They resembled excellent hounds with regard to the wolves, but they were savage towards the sheep. 158. But now all fear has been removed from marriage, and a sense of security attends the succession of generations with a feeling of confidence. Virtue in character does not prove inferior to a despot's compulsion, but there is no risk in a

woman's beauty flourishing. Every marriage bed over all the land and sea is free from insult as far as these emperors are concerned.

159. Furthermore those involved in farming were abused and though they had little or paltry amounts of produce were compelled to contribute much. And this had occurred through the excessive demands of those appointed earlier to assess the land. There was great want since the contributions were exacting and the land could not supply the requirement. They brought relief for these misfortunes through the precision of secondary commissioners and they put an end to the harm done by the former ones.

160. Why should I speak about farmers or include one by one the classes of those who have prospered? For in short their palaces are left open to the entreaties of everyone from everywhere, and no distinction is drawn between either birth or length of age or quality of fortune for the enjoyment of their generosity. But from their seat on high they command all equally to be of good cheer, since neither youth nor old age nor the contemptible semblance of poverty will be precluded from their joint assistance. Nor even will either an ill-disposed judge or a strong adversary in court damage the cause of justice, but it is easy for the narrator of misfortune to attract compassion.

161. While I am upon this section I was very amazed that they deemed it right to regulate their clemency within the bounds of law, and neither overlooked the victims of injustice by altogether refusing requests nor cooperated with those who dared to cheat, by continuously putting all their trust in them. But since they knew that some men had less by reason of their weakness while others employed their entreaties for deception, in order to compensate the first type with their help and guard against the deceit of the others, they attached the strength of laws onto their clemency, discovering this served as a hindrance to deviousness. And everywhere the result is that the emperors assent to entreaties, but nowhere is the precision of their ordinances harmed by their clemency. 162. In consequence of the same determination they also passed on to the magistrates the resolution of disputes. For when they reviewed it, they found that the strength of the laws was inferior to the imperial authority, but an emperor's soul might give way before the sight of tears. Therefore they were alarmed that if they were moved to pity by prayers and

laments their judgements might have more regard for the spirit of clemency than the letter of the law. And yet what greater act is there than that they, being themselves masters of the laws, should make the laws supreme above themselves? 163. Earlier emperors, when despatching governors to their cities, considered that the most murderous were the best fitted to govern, so that it was not more glorious to destroy more of our enemies than of our subjects. But now while the posture is maintained by the sword, the image of the emperors' gentleness shines forth in the lives of their governors. There is no need of compulsion and murders for the fulfilment of duty, but it suffices to inform the man in charge and immediately afterwards it is completed. 164. By always relieving the earlier governors in their turn they bring into their administrations different men in succession. And with good reason. For if the business of government is burdensome, they do not consider it right that the same men be worn down by a continual burden; whereas if it allows a share in good fortune, they invite many to participate in that fortune. 165. Furthermore they also observed that honours generally benefit good men, and punishments chastise the worthless. They thought that those who spent their energies on punishments were not preventing the growth of wickedness but were cutting down that which was constantly regenerated, and that the practice was like cutting off the heads of the Hydra. But the emperors themselves by gaining early possession of everyone's favour through their own good services, ensured that they will have the employment of the best rather than punish wrongdoers.

166. When therefore there is such great virtue exhibited in our midst, what aspect ought we to consider the greatest of all? Their noble birth or their upbringing? Their sense of justice or the prudence of their characters? Their courage towards their enemies or their harmony one with another? Their humanity towards each individual or their universal wisdom? 167. They did not think to encourage their hopes even towards the greatest of their exploits through resort to divination, not I think because they compared it with what was obvious and found it many times to be inadequate, but because even if it traces the path of the future most precisely, it becomes a hindrance to two qualities, ambition and valour. For with regard to those who will miss their target, if they had foresight divination would prevent them making their eagerness gain control of their fortune, but it immediately makes them cowards by making the worst known in

advance; and those for whom good things lie in store it deprives of their reputation for valour. For they seem to have put their trust more in the prior revelation of the outcome than in their courage. But all those who become good men despite ignorance of their destiny, are remarkable in success and in failure are blameless.

168. If someone were about to make the appropriate calculation of the sum total, in my view let him not examine the bare number of eulogies but let him attribute to each the age of those involved. And perhaps he will find his amazement is greater at the youth of the accomplishers than at the scale of the accomplishments. 169. I think indeed that the very purpose of the creator of the world is now above all being maintained. For when he established the earth, poured forth the sea and extended the rivers, and displayed the position of the islands surrounded by sea, he included everything in this creation – seeds and cattle and in short all that human nature was going to need. However he did not assign everything to every part, but divided the gifts throughout the countries, bringing mankind into partnership through mutual need; and so he reveals commerce, so that he may make common to all the enjoyment of what is produced among a few. 170. This humanitarian scheme, then, which might bring deliverance, had previously been destroyed and ruined, and the plan of social intercourse had been equally prevented by murders, and its architect taken prisoner and thrown down a precipice. The state of the earth was as if it had been split in two. But now what was hitherto separated came together and has been joined, and what so far had been torn apart has been restored to its proper condition. 171. There is one continent, one sea, the islands common to all, the harbours opened up and gates thrown wide. Merchant ships everywhere convey products from all parts and crowd the anchorages. A mutual community has extended through practically all the land under the sun, with some travelling for exploration and others for other reasons, some who cross oceans and others who traverse the continent. Dwellers in the West are observers of the wonders of the Nile while the inhabitants by the Nile gain knowledge of the beauties of the West. There are Phoenicians in the anchorages of Sicily, and Sicilians in turn in the harbours of Phoenicia. The city of Athens has been opened up to the traffickers in logic, and the nation of the Bithynians has become accessible to those desirous to take whatever they want. 172. Why must I deal in minute detail with each case and not rather utter one statement to cover them all? Now the sensible

nations of the world, as though pitching one harmony in chorus, are singing together as their two chorus leaders strike up the tune.

173. And so those who in the past were ending their speeches have generally prayed that they would encounter more good fortune, and they seem to me to have done so quite reasonably, for they were short of more than they had received. But now we can ask for nothing of which we have not long had experience. So this also must be a remarkable feature of the emperors, that they have left us nothing at all to look for.

NOTES
Sam Lieu

1 A principal feature of the oration is the omission of any mention of Constantine II because of his *damnatio memoriae*. Libanius strove, especially through the use of the dual, to give the impression that there were only two royal brothers, Constantius and Constans.

2 Cf. Men. Rhet. 368.15–17: 'Having, as we do, so many blessings from the emperors, it is absurd not to return them our due and proper offering' (trans. Russell and Wilson, p. 77).

3 Cf. Men Rhet. 368.8–14: 'It clearly follows that you should derive the prooemia from the amplification, investing the subject with grandeur on the ground that "it is hard to match" and you "have entered into a contest in which it is difficult to succeed in words"' (trans. cit.). See also Jul., *Or*. I,1a and *Or*. II,54b.

4 Cf. Men Rhet. 368.22–369.2: 'The prooemia of this speech also admit amplifications based on indefinite examples: e. g. as if we were to say, "And as it is impossible to take the measure of the infinite sea with our eyes, so it is difficult to take in the fame of the emperor in words"' (trans. cit.).

5 Cf. Men Rhet. 369.13–17: 'The third idea for the prooemium – remember this precept generally! – should be one that is introductory to the main heading, e.g. in the form of the speaker's uncertainty about the point with which to begin the encomium' (trans. cit., p. 79).

6 Here Libanius makes a major departure from the precepts laid down by Menander (369.18–370,10) in omitting any praise for the *patriae* of the two emperors whereas Julian took the trouble to praise Rome for being the traditional *patria* of Roman emperors. There is no mention of Constantinople, a city which had become the *patria* of Constantius by association, or Illyricum where Constantius was actually born (*Or*. I,5B–6C). Perhaps it is more difficult to eulogise two native cities or, in the case of Constantius, Libanius did not wish to praise a city which had strong associations with Christianity from its very foundation. Flavius Iulius Constantius was born in Illyricum on 7 Aug. 317. Flavius Iulius Constans was born between 320 and 323 and his birthplace is unknown.

7 I. e. Constantius Chlorus. Libanius makes no mention nor even hints at his Claudian descent though it is explicitly mentioned by Julian in both of his orations (I,6D and II,51C). Perhaps the legend had not yet fully taken root in the Greek East, as it is also not found in Eusebius.

8 A *topos* found also in Eusebius, *V. C.* I,14.

9 Strong echo of Eus., *V. C.* I,26,1: 'As he looked on the whole earth as one body and could not fail to see that the capital of the whole world, the seat of government of the Roman empire, was subject to servitude by a tyrant, he presumably wished to leave it first of all to the rulers of the rest of the empire to avenge this, for they were after all senior to him in age.' The main similarities, both topical and verbal, between Libanius' eulogy of Constantine and the *V. C.* of Eusebius are juxtaposed by Petit (1950: 563–64 and 569–71, see also Moreau, 1955: 236–38 who suggests Praxagoras (see above, pp. 7–8) as a possible source for Libanius). Although *verbatim* citations from the *V. C.* are lacking in the oration of Libanius, one cannot rule out the possibility that Libanius used the conveniently panegyrical *V. C.* as a source for his own literary endeavour despite the obviously Christian character of Eusebius' work. Libanius was too good a stylist to borrow from Eusebius without substantially altering the wording of his source. For the most recent discussion see Wiemer, 1994a: 512–14, who argues for the use of the *V. C.* by Libanius.

10 The analogy with Cyrus has already been suggested by Menander Rhetor (371.9) and is also used in the same context by Julian (*Or.* I,10B). Cyrus as the epitome of a good ruler is also cited by Eusebius (*V. C.* I,7,1).

11 No praise was accorded by Libanius to Fausta, the mother of the princes, probably because of the circumstances surrounding her death. Julian, however, managed to praise her without giving any hint of the family tragedy (*Or.* I,9B–D). He even included the brilliant Crispus, the son of Constantine's first wife Minervina and the cause of Fausta's eventual downfall, as one of her sons!

12 The same sentiment is also shared by Julian (*Or.* I,10B) which is contrary to Menander Rhetor (371.3–14) which stresses the need to detail divine signs which occurred at the time of birth and if necessary to resort to invention, as the audience has no choice but to accept the encomium without examination.

13 A *topos* suggested by Menander Rhetor, 371.9–10.

14 On Constantius' training in rhetoric see also Jul., *Or.* I,11C–D.

15 Julian, on the other hand, extols Constantius at some length for acquiring and excelling in the skills of combat not for public display but for military purposes (*Or.* I,10C–11C).

16 Constantius was made Caesar on 8 Nov. 324 at Nicomedia (*PLRE*, i, 226). Constans was made Caesar on 25 Dec. 333 (*ibid*. 220).

17 Constantius was put in charge of the defence of the East in 335 (Jul., *Or.* I,13A) and began raiding expeditions across the Tigris from 336 (Lib., *Or.* XVIII,206–7). He had earlier been sent to Gaul when his brother Constantine II fought on the Danube in 332 (Jul., *Or.* I,12A). Despite the verbiage, Libanius appears ill-informed, compared with Julian, about the careers of the sons of Constantine before 337.

18 Constans was assigned originally to govern Italy, while Constantine II

was assigned to Gaul. Cf. Philost., *H. e.* II,16b, p. 26,21–29. Cf. *BHG* 365,64, p. 585. Opitz.

19 Cf. Jul., *Or.* I, 17Cff. who gives more background detail of the conflict.

20 There were internal reasons why the Sassanians were unable to regain the territories lost to Diocletian. The Shahanshah Narses who signed the treaty in 298/99 died *c.* 302 and was succeeded by Hormisdas II who reigned for about seven years, during which he tried to restore the prosperity of the empire, and was generally loved by his subjects for his gentle and just rule. The same could not be said, however, of Adarnases, his eldest son and successor who was a man of proverbial cruelty. On accession he turned against his two brothers Hormisdas and Shapur: the first he had arrested, the second blinded. His reign was mercifully short as he was soon overthrown by Persian nobles who proclaimed Shapur, his brother who was still unborn at the death of Hormisdas II, as Shahanshah (*c.* 309). Once the news spread outside the empire that the new Shahanshah was an infant, the neighbouring Arab tribes, pressed by hunger, immediately raided Persian territory in large numbers and from many directions. They carried off large amounts of booty without encountering any serious opposition from the Persians. This state of affairs was only reversed after Shapur II came of age and began to prove his mettle as a commander.

21 Not referred to by name in the Greek.

22 This is a proven geological fact. Cf. Dodgeon and Lieu, 1991: 382, n. 32.

23 The export of weapon-grade iron ore to Persia was normally banned by the Roman government. Cf. *Expositio totius mundi et gentium* 22 and Procop., *Pers.* I,19,25–26. Libanius is our only source on the Persian request to have the ban lifted as part of the negotiations before the death of Constantine. In this context it is strange that the affair or 'lies' of Metrodorus, mentioned as the *casus belli*, by Ammianus (XXV,4,23) – a story which is more fully recounted in Cedrenus (i, pp. 516,12–517,15) who had undoubtedly derived it from a reliable pagan source (Praxagoras or Bemarchius?) and which fits well into an account of negotiations concerning custom barriers – should have been omitted. Cf. Dodgeon and Lieu, 1991: 153, Barnes, 1985: 132 and Bleckmann, 1991: 360.

24 Julian (*Or.* I,16D) also praised Constantius for being the only one of Constantine's sons to reach their dying father.

25 Julian, writing after the death of Constans, was more open about the military problems confronting Constantius in the East in 337, especially those caused by the lack of support from his other two brothers (Jul., *Or.* I,18B–C).

26 The use of the singular is deliberate to avoid giving any hint of the fact that Constantius met both his brothers at Viminacium. (See above, pp. **148–49.**) Julian could afford to be more accurate in using the plural (*Or.* I,19B). Neither orator referred to the massacre of Constantine's half-brothers and nephews at Constantinople although both would later provide us with important material for the event. Cf. Jul., *Ep. ad Ath.* 270C and Lib., *Or.* XVIII,10.

27 The swiftness of his return journey to the threatened Eastern frontier is also mentioned by Julian (*Or.* I,20C).

THE SONS OF CONSTANTINE

28 The return of Constantius to the East clearly had a major morale-boosting effect, especially on that of the pro-Roman faction in Armenia. It is indeed odd that the diplomatic manoeuvring in Armenia which features so prominently in Julian is totally absent from Libanius. Cf. Jul., *Or.* I,20D–21A: 'Those of the Armenians who were joined to our enemies immediately changed sides, when you had brought to our territory those responsible for the flight of their country's ruler Tigranes and his son Arsacius, and when you had allowed the exiled [Arsacius?] to return without fear to their native land. Your clemency towards whose who had come over to us and the kindness you showed to the exiled who had returned with their chief, resulted in the former [*sc.* who had gone over to Persia] bitterly deploring their earlier defection, and the others preferring their present luck to their lost power. The fugitives of yesterday [Arsacius?] declared that events had given them a lesson in wisdom. Those who had not changed sides professed themselves rewarded according to their merit. You endowed those who returned [= Arsacius] with such an excess of gifts and honours that they could not be annoyed at the prosperity of their worst enemies, nor regard jealously the privileges justifiably obtained by the latter' (trans. Wright, p. 53).

29 The name of the Persian city is unknown. It may have been a city within the Trans-Tigritanian territories which had been captured by Shapur II in the course of his advance to Nisibis.

30 Julian would later follow the same policy of settling populations of cities he captured *en route* to Ctesiphon in 363 in the Roman empire. The citizens of Anatha, for example, were sent to Chalcis (Amm. XXIV,1,9).

31 I. e. the riots in Constantinople consequent upon the attempts to remove Paulus from his see in 342. See above, pp. **153–54**. Libanius' account of the events in his 'autobiography' (*Or.* I,44) ignores completely the religious dimension and attributes them purely to scholarly rivalry.

32 I. e. the Battle of Singara. For date see above, p. **150**.

33 I. e. the battle fought by the Nemean brook between Corinth and Sicyon about the middle of the summer of 394 B.C. Libanius derived this historical metaphor probably from Demosthenes, *Lept.* 472 – a work well known to Libanius whose *hypothesis* on it is preserved.

34 Cf. Jul., *Or.* I,22B–C where Constantius was praised for his frequent forays across the river (i.e. the Tigris).

35 Cf. Jul. *Or.* I,23D. Singara's strategic importance for the Romans lies precisely in the fact that it was well positioned to learn of Persian attempts to cross the Tigris. Cf. Oates, 1968: 97–99.

36 Julian (*Or.* I, 24C) gives a hundred stades for the distance.

37 A grimmer picture of Roman indiscipline is given by Festus (*Brev.* 27): 'They (the Romans), however, with undefeated strength, an unexpected help against thirst when evening was now pressing on, attacked the Persian camp. They smashed down the defences and seized it and put the king to flight. When they recovered their breath from the battle and gazed in amazement at the water which was discovered with the lights held high, they were overwhelmed by a cloud of arrows since they provided illumination in the darkness to direct the arrow hits with more effect upon themselves.'

38 The Persians probably had a large number of women serving in an auxiliary capacity. This was also remarked on by Zonaras (XII,23) for the army of Shapur I.

39 Confirmed by Julian (*Or.* I,24D).

40 Tanagra (Plato Menexenus 242 a 7) and the battle at Laodicum in Orestheum (Thucydides 4.134) were battles with a dubious outcome.

41 Libanius derives the name 'Phracti' or 'Fracti' from the Greek *pephragmenon* which means fortified or protected.

42 Constans' cross-Channel visit to Britain in the depth of winter (early 343) was certainly unparalleled and may have been designed to take the people in Britain by surprise. It has been suggested that the refortification of the cities in the fourth century was the result of a decision by Constans. (Cf. Salway, 1981: 349.) The extraordinary nature of the journey was also celebrated by the fiercely anti-pagan writer Firmicus Maternus (*De errore* XXVIII,6): 'You (Constans) conquered your enemies; you have extended your authority, and so that greater glory might be added to your virtues, you have changed and scorned the order of the seasons, trampling underfoot the swelling, raging waves of a sea still scarcely known to us, and the Briton trembled before the face of an emperor he did ñot expect' (trans. Ireland, 1986: 145).

FROM CONSTANTINE TO JULIAN

[John the Monk], *Artemii passio* (*The Ordeal of Artemius, BHG* 170–71c, *CPG* 8082)

INTRODUCTION

Sam Lieu

From the revolt of Magnentius to the rise of Julian

The feared civil war between the brothers Constantius and Constans was duly averted by the restoration of the exiled bishops. But in 350 Constantius found himself embroiled in a civil war against the Western armies because of the murder of his brother by agents of Flavius Magnus Magnentius, the *comes* of the Joviani and the Herculiani. He had declared himself emperor on 18 January at Autun and the rebellion found support from commanders who had grown tired of the excesses of an emperor who in later years had, in spite of his arthritis, become indulgent in hunting and the pleasures provided by young 'barbarian' boys (Zos. II,42,2–5 and Zon. XIII,6,1–12). To forestall another rebellion, Constantia, the sister of Constantius, persuaded Vetranio, the elderly *magister peditum* in Illyricum, to declare himself emperor on 1 March (Philost., *H. e.* III,22 and *Cons. Const., s. a.* 350). Constantius who was then in Edessa on the Eastern frontier recognised Vetranio as emperor and placed him in command of the imperial troops on the Danube (Jul., *Or.* I,30B). Vetranio's example was quickly followed by Julius Nepotianus, the son of Constantius' half-sister Eutropia, who declared himself emperor in Rome on 3 June 350; but he was subdued within a month by the forces of Magnentius who had gained controlled of Italy (Zos. II,43,2). Despite the threat of a renewed Persian invasion, Con-

stantius marched west with his main army to face the two usurpers
who were now allied to each other. After much negotiation, Constantius managed to detach Vetranio from the alliance and persuaded
the troops to strip him of the title of Augustus (25 Dec. 350).
(Cf. Jul., *Or.* I,27C, Pet. Patric., frag. 16, *FHG* iv, p. 190, Zos.
II,44,3–4 and Zon. XIII,7,18–20.) Magnentius, who had by now
secured Africa, declared his brother Decentius as Caesar to protect
Gaul. Severe weather conditions now prevented Constantius from
crossing over the Alps for the final contest with Magnentius and,
worried by news he received of Shapur II's plans to renew the
offensive after the unsuccessful third siege of Nisibis in the summer,
Constantius saw no option but to follow the example of Magnentius
in appointing a Caesar to take charge of affairs in the East. As loyalty
to the House of Constantine was now at stake, he proclaimed Gallus
the elder of his two only surviving male cousins as Caesar on 1 March
351 and placed him in charge of the East. Constantius also sent his
long-serving prefect Philippus as envoy to Magnentius to seek peace
but really to spy out his movements and strengths. In a rousing
speech, he nearly succeeded in winning over Magnentius' troops
back to Constantius. A furious Magnentius refused to return him to
Constantius on the grounds that he had abused his powers as envoy
and kept him in custody in which situation he probably remained till
his death (Zos. II,46,2–47,3). (Cf. Jones, 1955: 232.) After initial
skirmishes at Ardana, a major battle between the forces of Constantius and Magnentius was fought at Mursa. It was a pyrrhic
victory for Constantius and his defeated rival withdrew to Aquilea.
The war continued in 352 as Constantius' forces worked their way
through northern Italy and across the Alps in the next year. A battle
at Mons Seleucus in the summer of 353 finally sealed the fate of the
rebellion. Magnentius committed suicide at Lyon on 10 August 353.

The administration of Gallus in the East proved to be both
controversial and short-lived. An aggressive and short-tempered
prince, Gallus inspired fear among the Persians (Philost., *H. e.* III,28
and *AP* 12, trans. below) and suppressed a Jewish rebellion probably
with great brutality (Hieron., *Chron.*, *s. a.* 352). In his insensitive
handling of the urban affairs of Antioch, however, he won himself a
number of powerful enemies at the imperial court. A fearful and
jealous Constantius was forced to have him executed for treason at
the end of 354. (See below, pp. **230–31**.) This left Gallus' half-
brother, Flavius Claudius Julianus, as the only other surviving male
member of the House of Constantine and he was duly proclaimed

Caesar at Milan on 6 Nov. 355, but was dispatched to Gaul to attend to the emergency caused by inroads of the Alamanni who had earlier been 'invited' by Constantius to ravage Roman territory then held by Magnentius in order to keep him occupied on two fronts. Constantius himself conducted a major campaign with conspicuous success against the Limigantes beyond the Danube which had the effect of unsettling tribal settlement patterns and thus weakening the opposition facing Julian. The latter, in a series of brilliantly led expeditions across the Rhine, destroyed the forces of the main Germanic confederacies as well as winning the respect of his troops. (Cf. Amm. XVI,1-XVIII,2, Zos. III,3–7.)

Events in the East took a sudden turn for the worse in 359. Shapur II launched a new and more determined assault against the Roman empire. This time he was advised by a Roman turncoat, Antoninus, to bypass Nisibis and march direct for the Euphrates. The latter was, however, in spate and the Persian army was directed to the north and besieged Amida. The Roman defence was completely disorientated by Persian pickets at Nisibis and various other key points and reinforcements reached Amida more by accident than design. (Cf. Amm. XVIII,5,7–9.) Nevertheless the garrison put up a heroic defence and the city fell after a siege lasting seventy-three days (*ibid*. XIX,1–8). Bezabde, a major city of the trans-Tigritanian territories, and the strategically important Singara also fell to the Persians (*ibid*. XX,6–7). Amida was the 'jewel in the crown' of Constantius' defensive strategy and its fall was a personal blow to Constantius. It was not occupied by the Persians, probably because of the scale of the destruction. After visiting the ruins of the city, Constantius besieged Bezabde which was held by the Persians, but despite the heavy use of artillery, the defence held (*ibid*. XX,11). By now Constantius was desperately short of fighting men in the East and he requested Julian to detach several major elements of the hitherto victorious Rhine army to his aid. The troops, faced with the prospect of being led by a commander who had had little success against the Persians, mutinied at their staging-post at Paris in February (?) 360 and proclaimed Julian Augustus. Faced with the possibility of another civil war, Constantius, who was forced to renew the siege of Bezabde, marched instead to meet Julian with his army, but died of illness at Mopsucrena on 3 November 361, making Julian his heir in his will (*ibid*. XXI,15,3). By the end of the year Julian was welcomed into Constantinople by crowds who cheered him as 'a star which had come to lighten the East' (*ibid*. XXII,9,14, cf. *Pan. Lat*. XI(3),2,3).

(Flavius) Artemius, *dux Aegypti*

During his time in Gaul, Julian was painfully aware of the attempts by those around Constantius to vilify him and to poison the ears of his jealous imperial cousin with news of his victories. Some of these, like the eunuch Eusebius, were also known to be highly corrupt courtiers and unscrupulous administrators. A special court was convened at Chalcedon and many of Constantius' former supporters were tried, found guilty and ordered to be executed. According to Ammianus, it was about this time that (Flavius?) Artemius, *dux Aegypti* under Constantius, was executed on charges of maladministration brought against him by the Egyptians, although Ammianus did not name him specifically as one of those who were tried at Chalcedon (Amm. XXII,11,2). Among the charges brought against him would undoubtedly have been his use of troops against the pagan populace of Alexandria when he ordered the seizure of the famous temple of Serapis. The case highlights one of the key issues confronting Julian in his attempt to revive paganism, namely the return of temple property which had been appropriated by Christians either corporately or individually and the punishment of those who had desecrated the sites. When Constantine went to war against Licinius in 324, he did so on the pretext of a crusade against pagan persecution. Constantine's victory was followed probably by a systematic settling of accounts in which the persecuted took full advantage of recent pro-Christian legislation to exact revenge. This persecution of paganism in the East may explain why the only four known contemporary pagan accounts of the life of Constantine, the lost history of Praxagoras (see above, pp. 7–8), the history of Bemarchius and the relevant sections of the panegyrics on Constantius by Libanius (trans. above, pp. 165–69) and by Julian (see above, p. 18), were all highly adulatory of the emperor. (Cf. Barnes, 1989c: 333–34.) The desecration and appropriation of temple property became widespread under Constantius and Constans. This we can deduce from the number of cases brought by pagans against Christians for the return of either temple-sites or precious building material and decorations under Julian. The despoliation (though not the destruction) of the temple of Serapis was instigated by George of Cappadocia, the Arian appointee of Constantius for the episcopal throne of Athanasius. He was assisted by the soldiers of Artemius, and when the populace heard that Artemius had been executed they turned on George with venomous fury when the occasion arose. This was provided by the discovery, on the site of an erstwhile Mithraeum in Alexandria which was being cleared for the building of a church, of a vast *adytum* which yielded a number of human skeletons. The Christians alleged that these had been used for pagan rites and had them exhibited and paraded through the city in a triumphal procession. The pagan populace armed themselves and attacked the Christians, causing a considerable number of casualties. George himself was executed with deliberate cruelty. The enthusiasm of the pagan mobs did not, however, win the unreserved approval of the new emperor who was concerned about the deleterious effect which rioting had on civic order. In a letter (or edict) addressed to the Alexandrians, Julian ironically questioned them about their reasons for hating George and berated them for not subjecting their complaints against him to the normal course of justice. He mentions in passing the role of the *dux Aegypti* in the despoiling of pagan temples, especially that of Serapis, the most sacred shrine in Alexandria:

> For tell me, by Serapis, for what wrongs were you angry with George? Doubtless you will say that he provoked against you the blessed Constantius, then he brought an army into your sacred city, and the military governor [i.e. Artemius] of Egypt seized the god's most holy shrine, after having taken thence statues and votive offerings and the decoration in the temples. And when you reasonably were displeased and attempted to aid the god, rather the god's possessions, he [i.e. Artemius] dared to dispatch soldiers against you unjustly and unlawfully and sacrilegiously, probably having feared George more than Constantius, who was observing him narrowly, to see if he should behave too moderately and too civilly toward you, but not rather too tyrannically.
>
> (Julian, *ELF* 60 = Soc., *H. e.* III,3,10, trans. Coleman-Norton, 1966,1: 270–71)

Though he died ostensibly the death of a criminal and his role as a religious persecutor was not mentioned in contemporary sources, Artemius was celebrated in Byzantium as saint and martyr (feast day on 20 October). Little was known about his early life and the claim in later sources that he was descended from a noble family is probably spurious. Our oldest and most certain evidence of his role as *dux Aegypti* is a record, on papyrus, of the minutes of a report made to the Oxyrhynchite senate by Eutrygius, formerly a *logistes*, concerning the payment of certain recruits. The *dux*, or commander-in-chief, on visiting the city, had received a complaint from these recruits that they had not had their dues (*POxy.* 1103). He was said to have been a close friend of Constantius and it was in response to the request of the Arianising bishops who gathered at Nicaea in 359 in connection with the Synod of Ariminum and Seleucia that Constantius appointed Artemius as *dux Aegypti*. There is every reason to believe the *AP* that Artemius was closely associated with Constantius and would have shared his imperial patron's pro-Arian views. Once installed in his office in Egypt, he immediately set himself the task of harassing those bishops who remained loyal to the Nicene definition. His attempt to track down the much exiled Athanasius is noted in the index (in Syriac) of the *Festal Letters* of Athanasius:

> XXXI (358–9 A.D.) In this year, Easter Day was on xxviii Pharmuthi; ix Kal. Mai; xxi Moon; Epact xviii; Gods vi; Indict. iii; Coss. Constantius Aug. X, Julianus Caesar III; the governor Faustinus, of Chalcedon, Prefect of Egypt. This Prefect and Artemius Dux, having entered a private house and a small cell, in search of Athanasius the Bishop, bitterly tortured Eudaemonius, a perpetual virgin. On this account no [Letter] was written this year.
>
> (trans. NPNF, p. 505)

The search also took him to the famous Pachomian monastery at Phbow as recorded in the *Vita prima Graeca* of Pachomius:

> And it happened after this, as the holy bishop Athanasius was being sought by the emperor Constantius at the instigation of the enemies of Christ, the Arians, that a certain general by the name of Artemius received authority and was searching everywhere for him. And as a rumour spread, 'Is he not hiding among the monks of Tabennesi, for he loves them?', the duke sailed up for this purpose. As he was sailing up, it happened by chance that Theodore himself was sailing down to visit the monasteries of the brothers near Hermopolis. As he drew near the upper monastery called Kaior, he saw the duke sailing up; the Lord made him understand what was going to happen and he revealed it to the brothers. The brothers wanted to turn back and arrive before him lest he should trouble the brothers in Phbow, but Abba Theodore told them, 'He for whose sake we have come so long a way to visit His servants is able to take

215

care of this affair without there being any grief.' Having said this, he went on to the monasteries.

When Artemius came to the monastery he ordered the army to keep watch around the monastery by night, armed as during war. He himself sat with his lieutenants within the monastery, outside the *synaxis*, having archers standing by him on both sides. Seeing this, the brothers were afraid. But a holy man called Pecos, whom we have mentioned above, exhorted the brothers to keep courage in the Lord. The duke asked through an interpreter, 'Where is your father?' Abba Pecos answered, 'He has gone to the monasteries.' And he said, 'The one who comes after him, where is he?' They showed him Abba Psahref, the Great Steward. And [Artemius] told him privately, 'I have an imperial order against Athanasius the bishop, and he is said to be with you.' Abba Psahref replied, 'He is indeed our father, but I have never yet seen his face. Still, here is the monastery.' After he had searched and not found him, he said to those in the *synaxis*, 'Come, pray for me.' They said, 'We cannot, because we have a commandment from our father not to pray with anyone who follows the Arians' – for they saw with the duke one of the Arians who was acting as bishop – and they left. So he prayed alone. And as he fell asleep in the *synaxis* by day, he woke up with a bleeding nose and was troubled – we do not know for sure what happened to him – and full of fear, he said, 'When that happended to me in the vision, I hardly escaped death with God's mercy.' Thus he withdrew. When Abba Theodore returned and heard these things, he gave praise to God.

(*Vita prima Graeca* 137–38, trans. Veilleux, 1980, i: 395–97)

His main claim to sainthood in Byzantium was undoubtedly the role he played in translating the relics of the Apostles Andrew, Luke and Timothy from lands beyond the Danube to Constantinople during the reign of Constantius, a task which, according to his *passio*, brought him the ducate of Egypt as reward (*AP* 16–18, trans. below, cf. Gaiffier, 1970: 26). His own relics were said to have been translated to Constantinople probably at the beginning of the sixth century by a certain Ariste and deposited in the church of St John the Forerunner in the neighbourhood of the Porticoes of Domninos (*MA* 4, p. 5,3). The church soon became the venue of a major healing cult especially for those suffering from hernia and other diseases which afflict the genitalia or from varix. Our knowledge of this extraordinary healing cult is based mainly on a collection of forty-five short accounts of miraculous cures compiled between 660 and 668 by one or more witnesses. (Cf. Baynes, 1911, 266–67, Delehaye, 1925: 32–38, Janin, 1969: 58 and 433–34 and Magoulias, 1964: 130–43.) The *miracula* are a treasure trove for material on the social and medical history of Byzantium but have little on the life of the saint except that he was 'dux and Augustalis' (*MA* 17, pp. 22–23) i.e. a prefect of Egypt, as the holder of the office was usually regarded as a special representative of the emperor Augustus. It is clear that the cult was already well established (with its own feast day) and well organised (with its own supporters' association) when the *miracula* were compiled. A shorter collection of six *miracula*, published by Papadopoulos-Kerameus with the main collection of the miracula (*MA* pp. 75–79) begins with a brief *encomium* on the martyr (*MA* p. 76,1–13). We learn from this that Artemius was *dux* and *Augustalis* of Alexandria and was honoured by Constantine (*sic*). When Julian the Apostate began to oppress the Christians in Antioch, he went there of his own free will to upbraid the emperor for his misdeeds. For this act of defiance he was subjected to multiple torture to all parts of his body, including being crushed by large boulders. He was finally decapitated.

The earliest extant version of a *vita* or *passio* of Artemius is a short work (= *BHG* 169y.z) which can be dated to the seventh century by its uncouth style and simple story-line. The text of this 'old' *martyrium* was reconstructed by Bidez from two Parisian manuscripts, using later versions of the saint's life as a stylistic control. (Cf. GCS Philostorgius, pp. LXVIII and 166–75.) It incorporates a number of basic elements of the legend surrounding the martyr found in both the accounts of the saint in menologions and in the later and fuller version of the saint's life commonly known as the *Artemii passio*. According to this version, Artemius was a *dux*, the reason for his martyrdom was his objection to Julian's ill-treatment of Eugenius and Macarius, two leading figures of the Church in Antioch, and he suffered death by being pressed by two heavy rocks. After his martyrdom, his remains were taken to Constantinople by a deaconess called Ariste. The place of his martyrdom was Daphne and his feast day is the 20 October.

The *Artemii passio*

Some time before the ninth century, a full-length account of Artemius' secular career and martyrdom was compiled. The authorship of the

Artemii passio (*BHG* 170–71c, *CPG* 8082) is attributed in some manuscripts to a certain John the Monk or John of Rhodes (who is otherwise unknown) and in others to John of Damascus, the great theologian of the eighth century who wrote in Greek in Palestine which was then under Arab rule. The *Artemii passio* is a work of pious fiction as the author, whichever John it was, appears to have little real knowledge of the historical Artemius. However, the hagiographer has embroidered the basic outline of the saint's life as summarised in the 'old' martyrium with substantial *verbatim* borrowings from the now lost Arian Church historian Philostorgius in his attempt to set the hero against an authentic historical background. The hagiographer claims to have consulted Eusebius, Socrates, Philostorgius, Theodoret and many others (§§3–4). Of these, he acknowledges that his debt to Philostorgius is the most extensive as the latter is said to have given a detailed and precise account of the deeds of the martyr. His acknowledgement to Eusebius as his source for the martyr's noble origins and his being honoured by Constantine (§4) is clearly intended to deflect the unwary reader from the fact that there is actually no reference to Artemius in the extant versions of Eusebius' *Ecclesiastical History* or the *Life of Constantine*. The author even made Artemius an eyewitness to the conversion of Constantine. In this the author was following the example of other Byzantine hagiographers in telescoping the events of the fourth century in order to provide a starker contrast between the reign of the first Christian emperor and his apostate heir. Presence at Constantine's vision would have made Artemius at least an octogenarian at the time of his martyrdom. The same desire to link the events of the two reigns in hagiography is also found in the *passio* of Eusignius, who, also martyred under Julian, claimed to have taken part in a 'Persian' campaign early in the reign of Constantine and to have rescued the Emperor from certain death. (See above, p. **143**, n. **13**.) Eusignius, who was said to have been an old man under Constantine, could not have been less than one hundred years old when he was martyred under Julian.

More likely to be historical is his claim that Artemius was a close friend of Constantius (§§5 and 9), as it was undoubtedly due to the patronage of the emperor with whom he shared the Arian faith that Artemius secured his appointment as *dux Aegypti*. But in the *AP* it was the part he played in the transfer of the relics of the saints Luke, Andrew and Timothy to the Church of the Apostles built by Constantius which secured him the command (§§16–18). The events following the death of Constantine, the civil war between Constantine II and Constans and the tyrannical rule of the Caesar Gallus in the East are treated in considerable detail – a reflection, no doubt, of the strength of the lost work of Philostorgius on this period (§§7–15).

Of the martyr's administrative career in Egypt we are told nothing by the *AP* and certainly not anything which could have been inferred from Socrates Scholasticus, one of his alleged sources. The narration focuses instead on the main political events from the death of Gallus to Julian's seizure of power, and the death of Constantius and the punishment of the chief officials and supporters of the former emperor, especially those who might have conspired at the removal of his half-brother Gallus, are given in detail (§§19–22). Artemius was personally summoned to appear before the new emperor who had meanwhile moved court to Antioch in preparation for his campaign against the Persians. His uncle Julian, who preceded him to Antioch, had already set in trend the process of revitalising paganism and the persecution of the faithful (§23). Among those who were arrested were two leading members of the Church of Antioch, Eugenius and Macarius. They were both tortured and exiled after a lively debate in which the saints ridiculed pagan teaching as espoused by the Neo-Pythagoreans and Hermes Trismegistos (§§25–38, omitted from the present translation). At this juncture Artemius arrived at Antioch, not in chains but in the company of his own *comitatus*. He was instantly arrested and stripped of his insignia. When brought before Julian, he was first offered the opportunity to apostasise with the promise of a Praetorian Prefecture and absolution from guilt of complicity in the execution of the emperor's half-brother Gallus (§40). Julian went on to defend his right to rule on the grounds of his royal lineage, but also condemned Constantine as murderer of his wife Fausta, his illegitimate son (Crispus) and his half-brothers (!) (§§42–44). In reply Artemius defended his own innocence, maintaining that he would not have plotted against Gallus who was a Christian (§44). He also launched into a vehement defence of the integrity of Constantine, and accused Constantius and Constantine's half-brothers of his murder. He then claimed to have taken part in the war between Constantine and Maxentius and witnessed Constantine's famous vision before the Battle of the Milvian Bridge (§44) – an event which took place almost half a century before (28 October 312). He rejected out of hand the theosophical arguments which Julian had used to defend his brand of paganism (§47) and urged the Apostate to return to the correct faith (§48). As expected, he was thrown into jail for his defiance (§50). The scene then switches to Daphne, where Julian unsuccessfully tried to revive the famous Oracle of Apollo by removing the bones of the martyr bishop Babylas who was buried in the vicinity. The flames from the sacrifices, however, set the temple alight, causing the permanent destruction of the famous statue of Apollo Musagetes by Bryaxis (Cedren. *Comp. hist.*, i, p. 536,11) and severe damage to the temple (§§51–56). The sections in the *passio* on Julian's visit to Daphne are extremely detailed and are clearly derived from Philostorgius as can be shown by comparison with the relevant parts of Photius' summary (VI,7–9, GCS Philost., pp. 86–94) and with the article on Babylas in the *Suda* (ed. Adler, i, pp. 445.14–446.19) which has also borrowed direct from the now lost full version of Philostorgius' work (cf. Bidez in GCS Philost., pp. LXIX–LXX). The sections furnish a detailed description of Daphne as well as an account of Julian's visit which belongs to a different historiographical tradition from that of the other ecclesiastical sources. This account links the fire with the performance of sacrifice which comes intriguingly close to the explanation which Ammianus (XXII,13,3) passes over as a 'lightly founded rumour'.

The need to underscore the Daphne episode may well be related to the tradition, well established by the seventh century, that Artemius suffered martyrdom at Daphne. Enraged by the events at Daphne, Julian authorised pagans to enter Christian churches and do what they wanted, which led to a number of desecrations (§57). He also commanded Alypius to begin rebuilding Herod's Temple in Jerusalem to disprove the Christian prophecy of its permanent ruin (§58). He then summoned Artemius and placed the blame for the fire on the Christians (§59). To this charge Artemius replied that the fire could only have been divine punishment for the emperor's apostasy. Seeing that Artemius was obviously gloating over his plight, Julian ordered masons and stone-carvers to cut up a large boulder and press Artemius between the two halves (§60). Though the weight of the rock caused his eyes to pop out, Artemius remained alive and even had the strength to proclaim ultimate victory before his persecutor (§§62–63). He was then formally condemned to death by decapitation and one of his final acts was to anathematise the teachings of Arius (§§64–66). After his death, his remains were gathered together by a deaconess of Antioch called Ariste, transferred to Constantinople and placed in the Oxeia. The martyrology then ends with a doxology (§67). However, the historical part then resumes in a manner which suggests that the subsequent woes of Julian were a direct result of his treatment of Artemius. The attempt to rebuild the Temple was hampered first by heavy rain and then fire. Earthquakes also struck a number of other cities (§68). The catalogue of woes reaches a climax with Julian's ill-fated campaign against the Persians which the author of the *AP* recounts in a style which is standard among the Church historians of the fourth and fifth centuries (§69). The narrative goes beyond the death of both Julian and Jovian and to the reigns of Valens and Valentinian. As a final note, the author expresses his regret that Valens was later led astray by the Arians and that Arians like Eunomius (the mentor of Philostorgius!) came to occupy positions of influence (§70).

There is no attempt in the *AP* to associate Artemius with the saint of the healing cult in Constantinople. A link was made, however, in the version of the saint's life in the menologion of Symeon Metaphrastes which is largely derived from the *AP*. In this a note is added to say that Ariste tried to build a church in honour of the martyr but her efforts were unsuccessful (*PG* 115.1212A). According to a seventh-century source, the *Patria Constantinopolitana* of the *illustris* Hesychius of Miletos (revised in the tenth century), the church at Oxeia was not built until the time of emperor Anastasius (591–98) (III,51, pp. 235,21–236,2). It was clearly built as a martyr-church because of the centrality of the vault in its architecture. The body of the saint was said to have lain in a lead coffin (*MA* 33, p. 50,20 and 34, p. 52,29) – a practice which was more common for late Antiquity than Byzantium. (Cf. Mango, 1979: 42.) The cult seems to have declined in popularity after the eighth century as we hear no more of the *martyrion* of Artemius used as a centre of healing after the Iconoclast controversy. (Cf. Mango, 1979: 41.) Despite its importance in Constantinople, the cult remained, however, a largely metropolitan affair. Artemius' name is found in a list of saints whose relics were venerated in a monastery in Rhaidestos (Ligda) founded by Michael Attaliates (11th century) as recorded in his *Diataxis* (1077) but this only demonstrates the link between the monastery at Ligda and its parental foundation in Constantinople. (Cf. Bees, 1920: 384–85.) The last attestation of the saint's relics is to be found in the account of a visit to Constantinople by an English pilgrim in the eleventh century, who noted that the head of the decapitated martyr had been separated from the rest of his relics. (Cf. Ciggar, 1976: 259, §36.)

In the West, Artemius did not find a place in the Roman martyrology until the time of Baronius, which means that he was almost entirely unknown to Latin Christendom throughout the Middle Ages as a saint and martyr. Soon after he was introduced into the calendar of saints, his credentials were questioned by a number of scholars who were aware of his Arian past. Even Battifol, the first modern scholar to study the *AP* critically, surmised that there were originally two Artemii, one an Antiochene martyr and the other the *dux Aegypti* and conveyor of the relics of the Apostles, and at some point the two traditions became merged. (Cf. Battifol, 1889: 253–55. See however Bidez, GCS Philost., pp. LVI–LVII.) This may not seem too far-fetched as Artemius was not altogether an uncommon name. The *vicarius urbis Romae* in the year 359 according to Ammianus (XVII,11,5) was also called Artemius but of him nothing else is known. (Cf. *PLRE*, i, 'Artemius 1'.) The conflicting traditions concerning Artemius the martyr are also reflected in the artistic representation of the saint. He is sometimes portrayed as a noble martyr with a short dark beard like that of Christ. A relief of him in this style was found in an underground chapel of the present Armenian church of the Archangel Michael in Istanbul on the rear wall of a fountain. (Cf. Lehmann, 1920: 382–84.) His military background as *dux et Augustalis* also gave rise to his being depicted as a military saint in the mode of St Mercurius and Niketas the Goth. (Cf. Kazhdan and Ševčenko, 1991: 195.) The pairing of Artemius and Mercurius is also found in a Greek version of a legend concerning the death of Julian the Apostate preserved in the *Ecclesiastical History* of Nicephorus Callistus (X,35, *PG* 96.552). (Cf. Baynes, 1937: 27.) However, if a separate tradition of Artemius as someone other than the detested Arian *dux Aegypti* had existed, the Byzantine hagiographers would have almost certainly exploited it. An important clue to the development of the legend of Artemius, as Brennecke (1988: 129) points out, is the manner in which the execution of an over-zealous Arian official had been transformed into a martyrdom in the *Ecclesiastical History* of Theodoret (III,18,1): 'Artemius was commander of the troops in Egypt. He had obtained this command in the time of Constantine (*sic*), and had destroyed a great many of the idols. For this Julian not only confiscated his property but ordered him to be decapitated.' One can surmise from this that the execution by Julian of Artemius as a zealous enemy of paganism had elevated the victim to the ranks of those who suffered martyrdom under Julian, and his Arianism and his role as the 'hatchet-man' of the hated

THE *ARTEMII PASSIO*

George of Cappadocia had, by the fifth century, been conveniently obscured. This transition to martyr might have taken place first under the reign of the pro-Arian Valens, as it would have been hard to conceive of such a transformation under the more orthodox-minded Theodosius. Such a transformation did not entail the rewriting of his life as Artemius was too unimportant until the success of his cult elevated him to the status of a major medical saint in Byzantium and hence the subject of popular veneration and hagiography. However, anyone who wanted to write a full-scale hagiography of the saint had no choice but to plunge ever more deeply into the murky waters of the history of the Arianizing period of late Roman history which yielded many uncomfortable facts. The author of the *AP* thus had to whitewash on a large scale to produce a laudatory life of the saint, and the product is an alternative history of the period from Constantine to Julian based on the lost Arianising historian Philostorgius, and for this we could not but be thankful.

Editions etc.

The *editio princeps* of the Greek version of the *AP* was published by Angelo Mai in his *Spicilegium Romanum* IV (Rome, 1840), pp. 340–57. Mai's edition was republished with a Latin translation in Migne's *Patrologia Graeca* among the works of John of Damascus (*PG* 96.1252–1320). Substantial parts of the work were critically edited by Bidez for his edition (in GCS) of Philostorgius. The sections excerpted and edited by Bidez fall into two categories: (1) those which closely parallel Photius' summary of Philosotorgius (indicated by 'ad Philost.' in Kotter's edition and in the present translation followed by reference to page and line number of Bidez's edition) and (2) those which are placed in an appendix (indicated as 'in Philost.'). No one who has worked on the *AP* could fail to realise the debt he/she owes to the industry and critical acumen of Bidez. The references to his excellent edition of Philostorgius have therefore been given throughout the translation to enable the reader to make use of the very full references to parallel sources given by Bidez. The present translation is made from the critical edition of the late Bonifatius Kotter (with the permission of the publishers, W. de Gruyter of Berlin) which is based on an examination of all extant manuscripts of the *AP*. To the best of our knowledge, the present translation of the *AP* is the only one into a modern language.

[JOHN THE MONK], *ARTEMII PASSIO*
(*THE ORDEAL OF ARTEMIUS*, BHG 170–71C,
CPG 8082)
translated by Mark Vermes

(= in Philost. 151,5–152,11) A remembrance, or rather an account of
the martyrdom of the saintly and glorious Artemius, great martyr
and miracle-worker, compiled from the *Ecclesiastical History* of
Philostorgius and certain others by the monk John.

(1) I am about to recount the manly virtues of the great and glorious
martyr Artemius and his ordeal, and his nobility which derived from
above and from his ancestors. O holy assembly and chosen people
of God, I call upon the famous martyr himself and the Grace of the
Spirit which obscures him in its protection to assist me in my account
and render help. And I include you in my invocation as I stand in
need of your prayers too, that this undertaking may be easy for me
and free of offence and I may proceed directly with my proposed
account of his martyrdom and his confession of faith.

And as I begin this undertaking let no one find fault with me by
considering the first and ancient commentary upon this remarkable
and famous man. For he who compiled it wrote as the occasion
demanded and as best he could, but affairs at that time were afflicted
by great confusion and disorder. Nor yet was he himself one of those
who are circumspect and particular in the use of language, but a
simple man and plain in style, concerned only with the truth and
aiming to tell the story in any manner whatever and, as the proverb
goes, attaining the holy education of words with the tip of his finger.

(2) (= in Philost. 152,11–153,6) In fact not even I myself am
competent and adequate for the narration of the story, even if my
love of the martyr compels me and rules my reasoning and forces me
on towards the telling. And yet he was praiseworthy for his zeal and
his loyalty to the martyr because he dared even in any manner to set
his hand to an account of his martyrdom, especially when the
impious Apostate Julian had commanded that of those condemned
as martyrs for Christ there should be written neither a memorial
commentary nor any other kind of record (as the earlier emperors
ordained by law), but that the greater number of them should perish
without their defence being published. After this command had
circulated to all regions, those who professed Christ went on being

punished, but according to their prevailing disposition none of the secretaries belonging to the people or of the so-called shorthand writers took any notice of this order. For the Unlawful One was eager to extirpate even the very fame of the martyrs. Therefore some hid themselves away in certain gloomy and unlit places and with difficulty dared to set their hands to these kinds of memorial writings, but went in fear of the emperor's fierce cruelty. And so many tens of thousands of Christians throughout the whole world were destroyed but were honoured with no investigation because of prevailing circumstances; but this did no harm to Christ's champions – the failure to win a memorial. For God recorded their names in heaven and there was no need for memorials among men. But that is enough about these.

(3) (= in Philost. 153,7–19) O holy assembly and chosen people of Christ, sacred nation and royal priesthood, I have encountered many works especially of those who compiled histories and records of the emperors' deeds, and later of those who spent their energy upon the history of the Church; and I have discovered the name of the martyr spread abroad here and there and often mentioned, a man who was conspicuous and famous as all admitted him to be. I did not think to bury this news in the depths of forgetfulness but to bring it into the open and present it to your ears, in that you love Christ and his martyrs, so that the great achievements of the divine martyr might not be shrouded in a few words. And at the same time I was anxious to cheer your ears with the accounts of the history and the recently discovered deeds of courage of the martyr.

(4) (= in Philost. 153,20–154,10) Many writers of histories have made mention of this famous man, including Eusebius called Pamphili,[1] and Socrates of the school of Novatus[2] and Philostorgius,[3] himself a member of the school of Eunomius,[4] and Theodoretus[5] and a good number of others.[6]

Of these Eusebius lived in the times of Constantine the Great and became well known and was the most erudite of the bishops of his day; he introduces the martyr as one who belonged to the Senate and was a notable participant in the highest affairs of the emperor and a most genuine enthusiast for association, or rather friendship, with his son Constantius.[7] For the blessed man seems at no time to have ceased his friendship towards Constantius, which reveals a little the notable high achievements of his nature. But Philostorgius, even if he is a fervent adherent of the school of Eunomius,[8] nevertheless treats the martyr as divine beyond all men, and gave a very thorough and precise account of his deeds, hinting at the nobility belonging to the martyr from earlier times, even before he engaged upon the trials of martyrdom. So I also shall start with the history about him as the writings of the ancients declare.

(5) (= in Philost. 154,11–155,2) The worship of idols had recently come to an end and the deception of demons had been extinguished as a result of the benevolence issuing from our great Lord and Saviour Jesus Christ about the time of the blessed and famous Constantine, the distinguished and pious emperor, the son of Constantius and the blessed Helena. Christ called him back from the vain deceit of idols, by displaying the life-creating Cross in the heavens,[9] and he prevailed over his enemies and the lawless emperors through the force and power of the honoured Cross, and the trumpet horn of the Christians which is beloved by God was raised aloft. The organisation and its increase in strength was through his zeal and faith, and as a result the proclamation of Christ filled the whole world. All the altars of the idols and wooden statues and all the shrines were destroyed, wherever they happened to be upon the earth.[10] But the churches of God were rebuilt, which the Christ-hating wicked emperors had burnt to ashes.

(6) (= in Philost. 155,2–16) After such developments the devil who resents good things could not tolerate such change, but he gathered a storm and tumult through his own shield-bearers. For Arius, who lent his name to the madness, being a presbyter of the Church in Alexandria, drove the Church into terrible confusion by promoting a dogma that was unlawful and full of every kind of blasphemy.[11] For he said that the only-born Son of God, who existed before time, was a creation and foreign from the essence of God the Father. So for this reason the Council of 318 holy fathers gathered at Nicaea and condemned Arius and announced that the Son of God, even our Lord Jesus Christ, was of the same essence as the Father. But the histories of the heathens relate this story, and many of our people have examined it in detail and articulated it clearly. The present occasion will not be appropriate for me to pass my time on these matters, since they require a different and more exacting discussion and examination. But for now I shall relate the first section of his life.

(7) (= ad Philost. II,16a: 26,3–27,21) The emperor Constantine, supporter of Christianity, had passed the thirty-first year of his reign and entered upon the thirty-second, when he learnt that the Persians were mobilising for war against him,[12] and set out from his own city and reached Nicomedia in Bithynia. Here he died following a plot by his own brothers, who handed him a poisonous draught, after a shooting star, so they say, had heralded his death.[13] Constantine had these brothers on his father's side: Dalmatius,[14] Anaballianus[15] and Constantius. For he had been the only son born by Helena to his father Constantius while he was still a private citizen, while by Theodora, the daughter of Maximianus surnamed Herculius, Constantius had other sons: the aforementioned Dalmatius, Anaballianus and Constantius. Constantine had honoured them as Caesars and with the title 'most noble'.[16] Of these Constantius with his lawfully wedded wife gave birth to Gallus and Julian[17] called the Apostate,[18] because he forswore Christ and inclined towards Greek religion. It was Julian who when emperor punished Artemius, the great martyr of Christ and winner of many victories, because of his faith in Christ and his inspired zeal. But all this happened some time later.

(8) Now that I have described the events which had taken place earlier, I shall now turn the account back again to the events which touched upon the martyr. By these I mean by what manner the impious transgressor Julian came to acquire sovereignty over the empire and how Artemius the martyr of Christ ran in the most holy stadium of the Christian confession.

(= ad Philost. III,1a: 29,6–30,7) After the recent death of Constantine the Great, the Roman empire was divided into three administrations, and his sons Constantine, Constantius[19] and Constans[20] shared these between them. And to the first, Constantine,[21] were assigned as his inheritance Upper Gaul and the lands beyond the Alps and the British Isles and as far as the Western Ocean. And to Constans as the last son fell Lower Gaul, that is to say Italy and Rome itself. And Constantius the second of Constantine's sons who was then in charge of the affairs of the Orient and fighting against the Persians,[22] received the allotment of the East. And Byzantium, whose name was changed to Constantinople and New Rome, he made the capital city, and all the territory from Illyricum to the Propontis, such as was subject to the Romans, and Syria, Palestine, Mesopotamia, Egypt and all the islands he made subordinate to his emperorship and administration.[23]

(9) (= in Philost. 155,17–156,6) And the great Artemius accompanied
Constantius on every occasion and business, as his very good friend[24]
and one of those distinguished for virtue and education, and a fiery
devotee of the Christian faith. No one has given us a written record
of his native land and birth, except that he was the thrice-blest
offspring of noble and great ancestors. Wherefore this also has been
recorded about him, that it was he who was ordered by Constantius
to effect the recovery of the holy relics of Christ's Apostles Andrew,
Luke and Timothy,[25] as the proceeding account will explain; but I
shall relate all these things in sequence by following the dates and
setting out the story according to the strict accuracy of the events.

(= ad Philost. III,1a: 30) As has been said then there happened to
be three emperors and each of them ruled his own portion. The first
of them Constantine departed from his own area and came towards
the inheritance of his youngest brother, while Constans was absent
in Rome, and he tried to treat his brother unjustly. And he re-
proached him, although he was not present, on the grounds that there
had been an unfair division of the empire, and that Constans had
appropriated the greatest share of the empire that belonged to him.
But the generals of the province and the guards whom Constans had
appointed said that they could not make any alteration, small or
great, without his approval and agreement; for it was not right.[26] But
Constantine stripped for war and took up arms against a brother who
had done no wrong. And so Constantine fell fighting in war,[27] and
by desiring the share of others he lost even what he seemed to have
under his secure rule.

(10) (= ad Philost. III,1a: 30,20–28) Therefore the people of Constantine defected to Constans and the whole administration of the
West came under that man who had shown no zeal for that; but God
dispensed this justice who said: 'Do not move the boundaries of your
fathers nor fasten upon the furrow of your neighbour.'[28] For the man
who works malice against his neighbour brings destruction upon
himself and invites the justice of God upon his own head. And so
Constans was emperor over the whole of the Western empire, joining
the two inheritances in one unity and bringing together both
portions into one government.

(= ad Philost. III,22a-26a: 49,23–52,34) Not much time elapsed
before Constans inclined towards carousing and drinking sessions
and unusual sexual entertainments,[29] and in an easy-going fashion he
gambled with the whole of his administration, and he danced away

from the grandeur of his emperorship. And so he himself was the subject of a plot by one of his generals, Magnentius, and with his emperorship he also lost his life. When Constans fell, Magnentius governed the empire, and with him Nepotianus and Brettanio received a share in the despotic rule.

(11) When Constantius learnt this from his sister's letters, he set out from the East and came to the West. He met two of them in war and gained victory by force, while Brettanio inclined to his support; when also the sign of the Cross, very large in size and all wondrously revealed, so that it outshone the light of day through the striking force of its radiance, was seen over Jerusalem around the third hour of the day, during the festival called Pentecost; it stretched from the place called the Skull as far as the Mount of Olives, whence the Saviour made His ascension. And so Constantius gained control of the whole empire, being the sole remaining son of Constantine the Great.

(12) Therefore when he gazed upon the size of the empire and felt giddy, inasmuch as he was only human and did not have someone from his family to stand at his side (for neither had a son been born to him nor had any of his brothers been left) he was afraid that another usurper would again rise up against him and challenge his emperorship. He meditated about taking one of his kinsmen to share in his inheritance and assist his emperorship. And this is what he did by promoting Gallus the brother of Julian to be Caesar. Gallus was his cousin on his father's side; for Constantius, the father of Gallus and Julian, was the brother of Constantine the Great. And so Constantius appointed Gallus at Sirmium and gave him as wife his own sister Constantia for the sake of ensuring his loyalty and reliability, and he gave him ministers which he (Constantius) had appointed – for although he was Caesar, Gallus was not allowed his own choice. He appointed Thalassius the Praetorian Prefect and placed Montius in charge of the imperial treasury – men whom it is usual to term quaestors – and at the same time he made Montius a patrician.

(= ad Philost. III 28a: 53,19–26) And Gallus, since he had been sent by Constantius, took a close grasp on affairs in the Orient. The Persians immediately learnt of him and took fright when they ascertained that he was a young man and hot-blooded for action.[30] They no longer made their incursions against the Romans. And while

Gallus was in Antioch in Syria, Constantius settled affairs in the West. At that time more than any other the Roman empire enjoyed a genuine peace when it was guarded by them both. And this was the situation.

(13) (= ad Philost. III,28a: 53,26–55) But Gallus, after putting on the purple of Caesar and now beginning to mount the first steps of the emperorship, did not maintain the same attitude and loyalty which he had exhibited towards Constantius; but he was stern and ungovernable and his anger was implacable. By adopting an importunate spirit and capricious will he overstepped the bounds and slighted the conventions which he had settled with Constantius. His hold upon the government was too imperious and he made his arrangements with great rashness and pretension. As to the ministers which Constantius had sent out with him, the arbitrators of imperial and civil government, namely the Praetorian Prefect Domitianus (for Thalassius had died) and the quaestor Montius, he ordered his soldiers to bind their feet with ropes.[31] This was because they would not obey his authority and assist his unreasonable and ungovernable impulses. He commanded them to be dragged through the marketplace and he slew them both; they were men who were distinguished in rank and had proved themselves superior to every gain and profit. The city bishop gave them a proper burial, showing respect for the unsurpassed quality of their courage.[32]

(14) (= ad Philost. IV, 1a: 56,14–57,28) As soon as Constantius learnt about what had happened, he summoned Gallus to his presence. But Gallus, knowing he was not being called to his own advantage, but reflecting once more that, if he refused to obey, he would necessarily have to declare war and straightaway take up arms against Constantius, chose in preference the part of peace. He sent his wife ahead to appease Constantius and himself went of his own bidding to face the danger. So Constantia set off first, eager to have an early encounter with her brother and to obtain his forgiveness for her husband, so that he would not plot any fatal act against him. She set out on the journey with great enthusiasm and fell ill while in the middle of the journey. She had reached Bithynia and died in a lodging post of that province called Gallicanus.[33] But Gallus, though he considered this unexpected development as a great disaster, nevertheless went further and did not desist from his determined path. But when he reached a city in Noricum called Pytavion,[34] then general

Barbatio was sent from Milan, where Constantius at that time happened to be. Barbatio stripped Gallus of the purple and changing him into a private citizen sent him into exile on an island of Dalmatia.[35]

(15) (= ad Philost. IV,1a: 57,28–58,26) While Gallus was taken under arrest to the island, those who had organised the whole move against him (especially Eusebius the eunuch, who was the Praepositus Cubiculo, and his associates) persuaded Constantius to rid himself of Gallus as soon as possible. Constantius was persuaded and sent men to execute him. And when these men were already well on their way Constantius was once more inclined to mercy and sent by a second courier a letter reprieving Gallus from death. But Eusebius and his associates persuaded the official who was sent not to appear and present the letter before he learnt that Gallus had been destroyed.[36] This is what happened and Gallus died.

(= ad Philost. IV,2a: 59,14–26) Constantius felt anxious about the administration that he might not be able on his own to control the whole empire, especially when the Gauls were being incited all too quickly to support usurpations through their bodily strength and fickleness of mind, whenever the mood took them. He already regretted making away with Gallus, and reasoning that members of his own family were much safer to share the emperorship with him than strangers and foreigners, he sent for Julian the brother of Gallus from Ionia and proclaimed him as Caesar in Milan. He gave to him in marriage his own sister Helena and exchanged pledges. He sent Julian to Gaul to protect that part of the empire. He himself came to Illyricum and resided in Sirmium.

(16) (= ad Philost. IV,3a: 59,26–29) But when he heard that the barbarians beyond the Danube were intending to attack the Roman empire, he set out from Sirmium and travelled to the Danube. He spent a long time on the bank itself and when the bands of barbarians were quiet he marched back into Thrace.

(=in Philost. 156,7–24) When he found himself among the Odrysians, where the emperor Hadrian founded a city and bequeathed his name to the site,[37] he learnt from one of the bishops that the bodies of Christ's Apostles, Andrew and Luke, were actually buried in Achaea, Andrew at Patras and Luke at Thebes in Boeotia.

When the emperor Constantius heard this, he was delighted at the news and cried out aloud and said to his attendants, 'Call Artemius to me.' He was quickly on the spot; Constantius said, 'I rejoice to see you, most God-loving of all men.' And Artemius replied to him, 'O Emperor, may you rejoice in everything and may nothing troublesome ever happen to you.' The emperor said, 'My best of friends, do you seek anything more gracious than the discovery of the bodies of Christ's Apostles?' And the great Artemius said, 'O Lord, who has revealed this treasure to us today, and from what source?' And Constantius said, 'The bishop of Achaea who now presides in Patras.[38] But depart, excellent man, and quickly arrange their removal to Constantinople.'

(17) (= in Philost. 157,1–4) When the great Artemius heard these words from the emperor, he set out along the road to the Apostles, intending to convey their sacred relics to Constantinople.[39]

(= ad Philost. III,2a: 31,13–32,23) And the author of the history has the following remarks about Constantius and the martyr Artemius: it is said about Constantius that not only was he earnest and devoted in his services to God, even though he inclined to the Arian heresy when constrained by the impious and most godless Eusebius bishop of Nicomedia;[40] in other respects indeed he was reasonable and very attentive to decorum and in perfect possession of self-control with regard to his lifestyle and the rest of his behaviour; and indeed with regard to the churches he showed the greatest zeal and his ambition was to surpass by far his own father with his enthusiasm in this respect. He built the greatest church in the city of his father near the Senate, starting from beneath the construction and from the foundations. And in honouring his father's tomb he built there a very large shrine of worship;[41] and he brought back the Apostle Andrew from Achaea, as I said earlier, and transferred him there; and moreover he transferred there Luke the Evangelist also from Achaea and Timothy from Ephesus in Ionia.

(18) (= in Philost. 157,5–20) It was Artemius, one of the best of men, who was ordered to arrange the translation of these saints. As the reward for this service the emperor gave him the administration of Egypt, at the request of the bishops. The author of the history says this about the martyr, as a testimony to him, that even before the trials of his martyrdom he was held in respect by all because of the radiant virtue of his life.

Concerning Luke the following story was related by Anatolius the eunuch,[42] one of those appointed to the emperor's bedroom, who himself experienced in his own case the effect of sanctity. For this Anatolius told how he was badly afflicted with an illness which went beyond the remedies of the doctors. The coffin, in which Luke had been laid, after its bearers had travelled by sea, was just being carried from the sea to the temple,[43] when Anatolius from his devotion got up and joined with its bearers in carrying it so far as his strength allowed, and immediately he was cured of his illness, and the remaining period of his life was extended by quite a few years.

So then Constantius first built the church of the Apostles, even if later Justinian enlarged it to more splendid proportions, and adorned it more magnificently with more valuable timbers. This is the shrine where the bodies of the Apostles now rest, and it is called after them jointly the Church of the Apostles.

(19) So the great Artemius was on his way to Egypt, decorated with the honour of command. (= ad Philost. VI,5a–6a: 72,10–73,13) Constantius set off from Constantinople and journeyed to Syria. And when he reached the great city of Antioch he encamped there and prepared for war against Persia. While he was loitering in the city and readying his army, letters reached him which disclosed the rebellion of Julian. For Julian, as I have revealed earlier at that point in my narrative, had been declared Caesar by Constantius to watch over the West in Gaul; he could not endure any longer to be in the position of Caesar and put on the crown and laid hold upon the more important emperorship. But when he seized control, he no longer thought upon a small scale nor did he feel that he should delay; but wishing to make all Europe (such as was within the Roman empire) subject to his rule, he organised his army and marched through Germany to the Danube. When he had gained the further bank he pushed on through its territories and went unseen by both its prefects, Taurus (so called) in charge of Italy[44] and Florentius who commanded Illyricum.[45] But when he came to Paeonia,[46] he crossed over to the other side of the river and presently held under his control the whole of Illyria and Italy and all the nations as far as the Western Ocean such as were under Roman authority.

(20) (= ad Philost. VI,5a–6a: 73,14–74,15) When Constantius learnt of this through despatches, he was alarmed (naturally enough) and had special fears for Constantinople lest, as Julian also intended, the usurper should get there first and bring the city under his control. He made the utmost haste therefore to take first possession. But

while his army which had been dispersed about the cities of the Orient was being gathered together and making preparations for such a long journey, he gave instructions to the bishops to go ahead and reach Nicaea before him as quickly as possible; for he had thoughts of organising a second synod there, as he was influenced by the impious Arians against the doctrine of shared essence. But when he had crossed Cilicia and had reached the so-called Mopsucrenae, an illness unexpectedly beset him and he was unable to proceed further. And when he realised that he was already in a dangerous condition and would not survive, he sent for Euzoius bishop of Antioch with all speed and gave him leave to baptise him. After being baptised and living on a short while he ended his life there. He was emperor for a full forty years, half of them with his father and the rest on his own.

The army mourned for him and performed the customary practices over him and they placed him in a coffin when they had prepared the corpse with the usual treatment to prevent decomposition. They placed it in a covered carriage and conveyed it to Constantinople, each man accompanying it in his own arms and in the same order in which they had been arrayed by their generals when he was alive.

(21) (= ad Philost. VI,6a-7a: 74,15–75,25) These men reached Constantinople with the body; and Julian attended after arriving from Illyricum and now securely holding the entire empire, since after Constantius' death no one dared to oppose him. When the corpse was being borne into the Church of the Apostles where they were intending to lay it to rest near his father, Julian himself led the bier after removing the diadem from his head. But when they had buried him, he now departed to the palace and again put on the diadem and held control of the government – now he alone had assumed power over the entire Roman empire. Since therefore Constantius was out of his way, he relieved the ferment of his anger upon those who were left and particularly those who through spite had been responsible for the destruction of Gallus. And immediately he beheaded Eusebius the Praepositus Cubiculo because from the start he appeared to have been closely involved in the murder of Gallus through his slanders. And Paulus the Spaniard, who was one of the imperial scribes, he had burnt on the grounds that he had been very virulent towards Gallus. He sent both of these men to Chalcedon and there inflicted on each his particular sentence. And he executed Gaudentius the *dux*

Africae and all others who had reviled Gallus in some way.

(22) (= ad Philost.VI,7a: 25–26) He punished these by letter. Whereas Artemius, the noble defender and martyr of Christ, he punished himself in person and face to face in Antioch, in an inhumane fashion, because of his profession of faith in Christ. He stripped him of his existing powers, unable to bear his freedom of speech and determination. (= ad Philost. VII,1b: 76,15–19) For Julian, as has been shown, when he had taken over the Roman empire, was especially keen to reestablish paganism. So everywhere he despatched letters and gave orders to rebuild their shrines and altars with great zeal and enthusiasm. (= ad Philost.VII,4c, 82,11–17) And he took away all the revenues which Constantine the Great and his son Constantius had assigned to the churches and he consecrated these to the temples of the demons; in place of bishops, presbyters and deacons he established temple attendants and wardens, sprinklers of purifying water and sacrificial officers and carriers of holy baskets and all the titles that pagan nonsense ascribes. These acts and others Julian accomplished in Constantinople.

(23) (= ad Philost. VII,4c: 82,18–30) After this since he had an uncle on his mother's side called Julian, who had rejected the Christian religion to gratify him and who was showing great enthusiasm for paganism, he sent him out to rule the Orient (a position they call Count); he instructed him to damage and destroy the interests of the churches, but everywhere and by every method to increase and revive paganism. And he came to Antioch and by his deeds tried to appear to be more than fulfilling his instructions. He removed as well from all the churches all their treasures such as lay in silver, gold and silken robes, and he also closed the churches to prevent anyone entering in for prayer, and he put bars and bolts on the gateways. So the governor of the Orient did these things in the city of Antioch.

(24) (= ad Philost. VII,4c: 82,31–83,25) But the emperor Julian was still delaying for a time in Constantinople, consolidating affairs there according to how he thought most benefited the interests of his emperorship, and considering and exerting himself as to how he might raise paganism to greater heights. Therefore setting out from Constantinople with his whole army he took the road to Syria. And so he crossed all of Phrygia and descended to its furthermost city called Iconium and turned aside, leaving Isauria behind him.

Crossing over the mountain called Taurus he came to the cities of Cilicia, and drawing close to the travelling station at Issus, he encamped there in imitation of Alexander of Macedon;[47] for at that very place at Issus Alexander also organised his war against Darius the king of Persia, and by defeating him he made the site well known. From there he traversed the Gulf of Issus and came to the city of Tarsus, and thence in hot anger against the Christians to Antioch, threatening their name with total destruction.

(25) When therefore the tyrant had come to Antioch and had encamped by the imperial dwellings, he afforded his violence not a day's rest. There were brought to him as if discredited by some report Eugenius and Macarius who were presbyters of the church in Antioch.[48]

* * *

(35) While these men were being so cruelly punished and suffering the heaviest blows, the blessed and pious Artemius, as has been shown earlier, had been appointed by Constantius governor and Augustalis of all Egypt, and because of his honourable and inimitable management had also received the authority to manage the affairs of Syria. Since he was devoted to the Roman imperial family, and had heard that Julian was emperor and was hastening to wage war in Persia, when he had received a letter instructing him to come to Antioch with his whole army, following his instructions he came to Antioch and with his attendant pomp and bodyguards he stood before the emperor on his platform. This was at the time the Apostate was conducting his inquisition of the holy martyrs.

Artemius said to him: 'O Emperor, why do you so cruelly torture men who are holy and consecrated to God, and force them to abjure their own faith? You should realise that you too are a man liable to the same suffering, with a share in the same type of physical pains, even if God has made you emperor – if in fact it is from God that you have your empire, and not the devil, evil prince of darkness, who has sought you out against us, just as once he sought out and claimed Job, and claimed you in his wickedness, so as to winnow the wheat of Christ and sow a crop of weeds. But his efforts are in vain, for he no longer has the same strength as before. For since Christ came and was raised aloft on the planted cross, the hauteur of the demons has collapsed, their strength has been trampled underfoot and their machinations held in contempt. Do not be deceived, Emperor, or try to find favour with the demons by persecuting the family of Christians, protected by God. (=ad Philost. VII,1c: 77) Understand therefore that the strength and power of Christ are steadfast and invincible; and in any case you yourself have been fully assured of this from the oracular responses which your doctor and quaestor Oribasius has brought you from Apollo in Delphi. And I shall recite the response to you, even if you don't wish it. It goes as follows:

> Speak to the king; the cleverly built palace
> has fallen to the ground. No longer does
> Phoebus have a covering roof, nor the laurel of
> prophecy, nor the babbling spring, and the
> babbling water has been quenched.'

(36) When Julian had heard this speech by the martyr, he was totally astounded, and his anger was more aggravated, like the flame of a fire rekindled when more wood added below revives it. He gave a loud and piercing cry: 'Who is this scoundrel and where does he come from, that has spewed forth such a torrent of oratory before me on my platform?' His troops replied 'It is the Governor of Alexandria, master.' 'Artemius,' said the emperor, 'that villain who arranged a cruel death for my brother?' 'Yes,' they said, 'best of emperors, it is he.' Whereupon Julian said: 'I owe gratitude to the immortal gods and to Apollo of Daphne, because they have exposed to me this criminal who has brought himself here and given himself away.' Then he said: 'The accursed man is to be divested of his authority, and the sinner stripped of his belt, as a penalty for what he has just dared to do. For the murder and bloodshed of my brother, I will appoint his punishment tomorrow, gods willing. For I shall destroy him not with one death, but with thousands and all those that murderers are subject to. For it was no common man but an emperor whose blood he shed, and that when he had suffered no harm from him.'

(37) When the emperor Julian had given these instructions, the holy man was snatched by the bodyguards, divested of his belt together with his authority, placed naked upon the platform and given into the hands of the lictors. They attached ropes to his hands and feet and stretched him in four directions, and beat the martyr's belly and back with ox-hide whips to such an extent that they used four different pairs of thongs on him. One could see an extraordinary and superhuman endurance. For no groan, or cry, or whimper or anything else that men suffer when undergoing torture, was raised

by him, but his expression was unmoved and unchanging. The ground was soaked with blood, and yet the martyr looked as if it was someone else suffering. So all the bystanders were amazed, and even the wicked Julian was astonished at the striking sight. He ordered him to be untied and taken into custody with the other martyrs, while he considered how and by what method and with what sort of death he would deprive the martyrs of their present life.

(38) The martyrs of Christ, as they were taken away into custody, were singing a psalm: 'You have tested us, Lord, and tempered us like silver is tempered. You have brought us into the net, you have heaped afflictions on our backs, you have stood men on our heads. So it remains that we should go through fire and water, so that you may bring us to relief.' When their prayer was finished, great Artemius said to himself: 'See the wounds of Christ have been printed on your body. So it remains that you should surrender your very soul along with the rest of your blood.' And thinking of that verse of scripture,[49] he said: 'See, I have given my back to the whips, and my cheeks to beatings. But what have I undergone, unworthy as I am, any further than my Master did? He too was flayed with whips. His face too took beatings and blows, and He suffered scourging all over His body, and bore a crown of thorns, and His hands were bound behind him, and naked He was fastened to the Cross on account of my sin and transgression – He who knew no sin, and spoke no deceit. Many were the sufferings of my Lord. I in my misery am far from His magnanimity and endurance. So I rejoice and exult, enlightened by the sufferings of my Lord. Imitation of His suffering lightens my load and comparison with my betters softens my pain. I too through Him have been born a Son of God through baptism and the gift of the Holy Spirit, and still more shall I be so through the resurrection from the dead. I give you thanks, Lord, because you have crowned me with your sufferings. But, kind and merciful Lord, guardian of your servants, bring my contest to an end in confession of your name, and do not judge me unworthy of this endeavour, because of the sins that I have committed in this life. For I, Lord, have thrown myself upon your mercies.'

(39) When Artemius had privately made this prayer, he led the way into prison along with the holy martyrs Eugenius and Macarius, and they were handed to the prison guard. And so the martyr of Christ was with the victorious saints Eugenius and Macarius, giving praise

and thanks to God. But when dawn came, the Apostate again ordered the martyrs to stand in the court, and deeming them worthy of no interrogation, other than the great Artemius whom he ordered to be separated from his fellows, he declared the two of them were exiled, and sent them to Oasis in Arabia. There are two places with this name, small Oasis and great Oasis. They are pestilential places, swept by pestilential winds, and none of those who have gone there has survived for even one year, but trapped by deadly illnesses they die there. Having sent the saints Eugenius and Macarius into exile at this place, he ordered the martyrs to be beheaded there. They were executed after forty days, on the twentieth of December. In the place of their execution there was a great miracle. For though the place had no water at all, a spring of water soared upwards which banishes every disease. It still survives to this day and preserves the name of the martyrs.

(40) Julian called the saint Artemius forward and spoke to him: 'Because of your presumption you have forced me to dishonour your race, to disgrace your former high position and to assault your very body. So let yourself be persuaded, Artemius, and come and sacrifice to the gods, especially to Apollo of Daphne, my specially beloved and sacred god; and I shall absolve you of the guilt for the blood of my brother, and restore you to a greater and more honourable status. I shall make you Prefect of the Praetorians and high priest of the great gods, and name you my father, with the second place in my empire, and you will be with me for the remainder of my lifetime and administration. For you know yourself, Artemius, that my brother was slain by Constantius for no good reason, and that envy destroyed him, along with that unholiest of all men the eunuch Eusebius, who wrongly obtained the position of Praepositus Cubiculo which he did not deserve, even though that utterly wicked individual has paid the penalty for his sacrilegious act.

(41) (= ad Philost. II,16: 27,22–29) 'You also know that the position of emperor is more compatible with my family. For my father Constantius was the son of Maximianus' daughter Theodora and my grandfather Constantius. Whereas Constantine was the son of Constantius and Helena, a worthless woman like any other courtesan, and born when he was not yet Caesar, but in the position of a private citizen. So Constantine snatched the empire by boldness of will, and unlawfully killed my father and his two brothers. And his son

Constantius, imitating his father, killed my brother Gallus, even after he had shared most terrible oaths with him. Had we not been saved by the providence of the gods, he wanted to do the same to us, but the gods prevented him, by vouching safety to me in person. Relying on these gods I abjured Christianity and inclined to the Hellenic life. I knew well that the most ancient lifestyle of the Greeks and Romans, employing good customs and laws, speaks directly to the gods who have our confidence from their conduct of affairs.

(42) (= in Philost. 162,19–23) 'For who could be doubtful when he sees the sun riding in heaven and the moon drawn along in a golden chariot? The sun makes our daylight and rouses men to work, and the moon lights up the night and brightens the stars and with unsleeping rays of light urges men to sleep. This is the theology of the Greeks and Romans, Artemius, and with justification and propriety and with fair judgement. For what is more conspicuous than the sun? Or more brilliant than the moon? Or what could be pleasanter and more comely than the dance of the stars? These then the Greeks and Romans worship and revere and have attached their hopes to them; and they call the sun Apollo, and the moon Artemis and the greatest of the stars (which they call the planets) holding the seven zones of heaven, they name one as Cronus, one as Zeus, one as Hermes, another as Ares and the last as Aphrodite. For these gods manage the whole world and everything under heaven is administered by their powers. So men have set up images of them and worship and honour them, and at the same time they invented certain stories for their own amusement. But they do not worship their images as gods, banish the thought! For the more simple and rural sort of people believe this; while those who follow philosophy and have accurately examined the affairs of the gods know to whom to pay their honour and to whom passes the reverence of divine statues.

(43) 'So I call upon your noble nature to join with us and do what is pleasing to us, and to follow the proper Greek religion, and lay hold of the ancient ways and practices. (= ad Philost. II,4b: 14,25–15,29) For Constantine, as you yourself know, who was easily deceived by men and uneducated and proved to be stupid, introduced innovations in religion, and revoked the Roman laws and inclined towards Christianity. This was because he was in fear of his unholy deeds, and because the gods drove him from the flock as accursed, and unworthy of their religion, being steeped in his family's blood. For

he killed his brothers who had done nothing out of place, and his wife Fausta, and his own son Priscus[50] who was a good and worthy man. The gods were disgusted at these unholy crimes and drove him out, and made him wander far and away from their holy and sacred religion, and his cursed and execrable seed and his whole family they obliterated from among mankind. Therefore, my good man, seeing your stability and firmness in all things, I wish you to become a friend in my undertaking and my fellowship, and to share my inheritance, and to join in all of the affairs of the empire. Come here, Artemius, and stand among us men, and forswear Christ, and convert to the ancestral and most ancient and long-standing religion of the Romans and Greeks, and share in the benefits of the gifts made to us by the gods, and become a partner in the highest honours and dignities.'

(44) In response to this speech the martyr of Christ paused and reflected for a little while, and then summoning all his attention and intellect, he replied: 'As regards my religion and faith, O Emperor, I will give you no defence for the moment, though I have at hand proofs of it. With regard to the death of your brother, I will give you my defence, that in no way shall I ever be shown to have harmed his soul, either in deed or word or in so much as a thought, not even if you were to exhaust yourself a thousand times in investigating this. For the truth is immutable. I knew that he was a Christian, pious and just, and an enthusiastic supporter of the laws of Christ. Let heaven be witness, and earth, and the whole chorus of holy angels, and Christ the Son of God, whom I serve with my spirit, that I am innocent of his bloodshed and death, and I brought no help to the unholy men who perpetrated his wrongful murder. For I was not present with Constantius then, but was living in Egypt and spent my time there until this year. This is my defence concerning your brother.

(45) 'As for forswearing Christ and embracing a Greek lifestyle, I will give you this answer, borrowing the reply of the three boys to Nebuchadnezzar: "Your Majesty may be sure that I do not serve your gods, and I will never worship the golden image of your beloved Apollo."[51] (= ad Philost. II,4b: 15,29–17,37) Also, because you insulted the blessed Constantine, the greatest of all emperors, and his family, and called him the enemy of your gods and a maniac, full of murder and steeped in his family's blood, I will make this defence to you on his behalf. It was rather your father Constantius and his brothers that started the wrongdoing, by mixing a poisonous draught

for him and giving him a painful death, when they had suffered no harm from him. Constantine did kill his wife Fausta – and rightly so, since she had imitated Phaedra of old, and accused his son Priscus of being in love with her and assaulting her by force, just as Phaedra accused Theseus' son Hippolytus. And so according to the laws of nature, as a father he punished his son. But later he learnt the truth and he killed her as well, exacting the most righteous penalty against her.

(= ad Philost. I,6: 7,14–23) 'He inclined towards Christ, when He called him from Heaven, when he was fighting his bitter and costly battle against Maxentius. He showed him the sign of the Cross in the middle of the day, shining out more than the sun in brightness, and indicated in Latin writing in the stars his coming victory in the war. I myself saw the sign, being present in the battle, and I read the writing. And also the whole army saw it, and there are many witnesses of this in your army, if you wanted to ask them.

(46) (= in Philost. 163,20–164,11) 'And why do I say this? The prophets from early times made pronouncement of Christ, as you yourself understand quite well. And there are many testimonies of His Advent even from the gods revered by you and the predictions of the oracles, both the Sibylline books and the poetry of the Roman Virgil which you call the Bucolics. And Apollo himself who is admired by you in his prophetic role uttered the following sort of words about Christ. For when asked by his attendants, he answered as follows:

> O wretch among my attendants, would that I had
> not finally and ultimately been asked about the
> prophesied god and the spirit that holds all
> around in a cluster – stars, light, rivers and
> underworld, air and fire – which against my will
> hounds me from this home. But the early morn of
> my tripods has yet been left. Alas, alas groan
> for me, tripods, Apollo has departed, departed,
> since a mortal overwhelms me, a light from heaven.
> He who suffered is God, but Divinity itself
> did not suffer.'[52]

(47) (= in Philost. 163,20–164,11) In reply the transgressor said, 'I think, Artemius, that you did not come into Egypt as a general but as some kind of soothsayer, or rather a buffoon or a begging-priest

and a collector of the fables of hard-drinking old women and ancient stories that have grown old.' And the martyr said, 'You have not properly understood, O Emperor, nor in accordance with your wisdom and virtue. I give you proofs from your own gods and the teachings that are beloved by you, that you may learn the mystery of truth from what is familiar to you. And do not think that I am taking pride in the sayings of the pagans, "for let not the oil of the sinner anoint my head".[53] But caring for the salvation of your soul I leave no stone unturned that you may be persuaded. But it is my belief that, just as Satan blinded Adam of old, the first-formed, through disobedience and the tasting of the tree, so also, Emperor, begrudging your salvation he has stripped you of your faith in Christ. But as for your calling the sun and the moon and the stars your gods, I am ashamed at your profession of ignorance, or rather of poor judgement. Did not Anaxagoras of Clazomenae, clearly your teacher, say that the sun was a red-hot mass and the stars were bodies of pumice-stone and entirely devoid of life and feeling? How therefore, best and most philosophic of emperors, do you yourself address as gods things that are rejected and discredited by your teachers? For I know that you belong to the Platonic school. And Plato was a disciple of Socrates, and Socrates of Archelaus, and Archelaus and Pericles of Anaxagoras. How then, O excellent king, do you address these as gods and above them all hail the sun and swear the imperial oath by it, at the top and bottom of your letters and speeches and in your greetings often say "by the sun"? But why must I labour this point? I do not abjure my Christ, may it never happen! I do not welcome the abominable impiety of the pagans. But I shall remain in the creed in which I was instructed, and I persist in the ancestral traditions, which no era will confound, "even if wisdom has been discovered through consummate wit", to quote something from your poet Euripides.'[54]

(48) At this Julian was dumbfounded and at a complete loss and did not know what to do, amazed at the martyr's great learning and eloquence and his ready defence against everything. So the martyr of Christ said to him: 'Abandon, O Emperor, the dead and departed religion of the Greeks – for it decayed a long time ago – and come over to Christ. He is magnanimous and merciful and accepts your degeneracy.' But it was not possible to resist the impulses of his malevolent spirit, or to recall a soul heading of its own volition at a rush towards destruction.

(= ad Philost. VII,1a: 76,7–14) Julian's heart had long been in labour with paganism after the philosophical company he kept in Ionia with the party attending Maximus, but as long as his brother survived and after him Constantius, he lacked the confidence to reveal his thoughts because of his fear of them. But when these were no longer among men and he himself was now master of the government, then indeed he suddenly and openly laid himself bare and broke out into every kind of enthusiasm for paganism.

(49) Therefore he answered the martyr, 'Since you have reviled my arguments, wicked scoundrel, and have dared to make an attempt to convert me to Christianity, I give you this reward instead of the gifts which I promised.' And so he ordered the martyr to be stripped and his flanks to be pierced through with steel awls hardened in the fire, and his back to be skewered with sharp spikes and split open while he was dragged along on his back. But after these pains had swiftly been visited upon the martyr, he displayed the same steadfastness as before, and as if someone else's body was suffering, and he was a spectator, he seemed to suffer no pain. And so the martyr endured these tortures over many hours and uttered not one cry or groan. Julian clapped his hands and, as though suffering a defeat, rose up from the tribunal and ordered the martyr to be led away again to the prison and that he was to be provided with neither bread nor water nor anything that men take to sustain life. But he himself set out for Daphne, the fairest place in Antioch.

(50) Around midnight as the martyr was praying in prison, Christ appeared to him and said to him: 'Artemius, be a man, and be strong, and do not fear or dread the tyrant. For I am with you to rescue you from every trial and every pain of torture, and I shall crown you in the kingdom of the heavens, and just as you confessed me before men on earth, so shall I confess you before my Father in heaven. So be bold and of good cheer. For you will be with me in Paradise.' When the martyr had heard this from the Lord he was confident, and all night gave praise and thanks to God. He recovered from his blows and wounds, so that not even a bruise appeared on his holy body. He lasted fifteen days without tasting anything at all. For he was nourished by the grace of the Holy Spirit.

(51) (= ad Philost. VII,8a: 86,28–94,19) Julian set off for the suburb of Daphne, as I have already said, preparing sacrifices to Apollo and

expecting to receive oracular responses from him in return.[55] Daphne
is a suburb of Antioch, situated on a plateau within the city's
territory, shaded with every kind of grove as the place is dense with
wood and fruit. For in this location an extraordinary number of every
kind of tree and especially cypress has sprung up, incomparable in
beauty, height and size.[56] Streams of fresh water run everywhere, for
a number of large springs gush out there,[57] with the result that the
city seems to be one of a few with a more than adequate water
supply.[58] The place is very nicely adorned with splendid buildings –
villas, baths and others, constructed both for use and for adornment.
There were temples and statues of various pagan deities and especially that of Apollo which had been worshipped from ancient times.
For it was here that pagan mythology fashioned the incident which
befell the virgin Daphne, and it seems mainly from her that the place
has derived its name.

(52) The statue of Apollo had the following features. His body was
carved out of vine-wood with consummate skill so that its outward
appearance had a coherent unity. The surrounding mantle was gold-
plated and it harmonised in a kind of indescribable beauty with the
parts of his body which were left naked and without gold. The statue
stood with a lyre in its hands and represented a leader of the Muses.
His hair and crown of laurel bloomed in a riot of gold, giving
maximum delight to the beholder.[59] The hollows of his eyes were
filled by two great precious violet stones (hyacinths) in memory of
the boy Hyacinthus of Amyclae. The beauty of the gems and their
size were a permanent and significant ornament to the statue. The
makers of the statue went to extraordinary ends to perfect its beauty,
so that as many as possible might be deceived by it, being ensnared
by the great beauty of its outward appearance into paying it homage.
This indeed was what had happened to Julian: for he venerated it
more than all the other statues, and sacrificed many thousands of
each species to it.

(53) Even though Julian did everything and spared no effort to
procure an oracular pronouncement, there was none, but this statue
and all the others there kept completely silent. He then considered
that he needed the help of the magical art which the pagans call
'*hierurgia*'.[60] He sent for a certain Eusebius who held the greatest
reputation among the pagans for his ability at this, and he ordered
him to render the statue as vital as possible and thereby effective; and

he was to leave out nothing that he considered necessary for this purpose. When he had applied all his tricks and was left with nothing further that he could think of, and the statue had maintained its natural silence in the same way making no more utterance than before, he was then asked by Julian why it was particularly silent even when all their usual tricks had been performed on it. Eusebius said that Babylas was the chief cause of the silence of this statue and of the others, since the gods loathed his corpse lying there in Daphne and for this reason could not endure to visit their shrines. For he did not wish to tell the real reason which he perceived all too well, namely that a superior power had obviously shackled the workings of the demons, especially when the demon masquerading as Apollo had clearly and expressly said, so the story goes, that he was not able to respond because of Babylas.[61]

* * *

(55.13) When Julian learned from Eusebius that this Babylas was preventing the statues from giving utterance, he immediately ordered that the coffin, which was constructed from a large stone, should be moved away from Daphne by those responsible for it and transferred to some far away point of their choice. Immediately, the urban mob poured out of the city as for an important cause and surrounded and began dragging the coffin. It was conveyed as if by some superior force rather than being dragged by men and as it went along it outpaced the enthusiasm of those who were bearing it. Indeed on the same day they carried it further than fifty stades and set it down in the so-called 'Cemetery'. This is a house outside the city which has received many bodies of men from ancient times and of a few who were martyrs for their piety. On that occasion they conveyed the coffin inside it.

(56) As for Julian, he prepared a multitude of victims and offerings so that on the following day he might go up to Daphne with them, hoping that now he would definitely obtain a response from Apollo, if not from the others. As far as he was concerned the entire goal of his enthusiasm and his effort were directed to Apollo since he rather than any other held such an advantage both on account of his oracular skill and because the place, Daphne, was sacred to him; for Julian considered that he rather than any of the other pagan deities would most probably prevail on his own territory. Eusebius and the so-called priests and the throng of temple attendants gathered in a

large crowd to receive the emperor, and they stayed awake around
the statue and exerted themselves in every way, so that when Julian
arrived he would obtain an utterance, since no other excuse was now
left them for a delay. However, in the deep of the night, fire suddenly
fell from heaven and struck the temple, instantly enveloping it on all
sides, and set alight the statue along with the offerings. All was ablaze
and the flames shot up ever higher, when suddenly a great cry broke
out around the temple and an uproar like no other; and although
many were eager to lend their aid, there was no one who could prevail
against the fire. Some ran to the city to inform Julian the Praefectus
Orientis,[62] while the rest of the crowd stood confused and became
spectators of the disaster that had overwhelmed them so unexpectedly. But the fire touched none of the other temples despite the
density and the abundance of woodland growth there, because it fell
only upon the temple of Apollo and consumed it along with its
contents. Consequently, the statue and all its offerings disappeared
completely, and only the mere foundations of the buildings were left
as reminders of the disaster; and even now they can be seen, as clear
proof of the fire sent by God.

(57) When Julian heard what had happened, he was filled with rage
and extremely vexed that the Christians might jeer at the course of
events. He immediately issued orders to drive them out of the great
church and to declare that it was totally inaccessible to them, and
when they had shut if off as securely as they could to confiscate all
its treasures. And he also gave the pagans licence to enter into the
churches of the Christians and do all that they wished. And so when
these orders went out from the impious tyrant Julian, what enormity
of evil was not accomplished? What discordant sound was not
uttered? Men spoke with unrestrained tongues profanities against the
Christian faith and blasphemed Our Lord and God Jesus Christ in
all the cities. (= ad Philost. VII,4a: 80,30–35) For in Sebaste, the
ancient Samaria (by now refounded by Herod and renamed Sebaste)
they brought forth from their tombs the bones of the prophet Elisha
and of John the Baptist and mixing them with the bones of unclean
brutes they burnt them and scattered the dust into the air.

There was a statue of the Saviour in the city of Paneas, magnificently erected by the haemorrhaging woman whom Christ cured,
and set up in a prominent place in the city. After a time it became
well known from the miracle of the grass growing out of it. The
Christians removed it and established it in the sacristy of the church.

This statue the pagans pulled down and they fastened ropes to its feet and dragged it to the market-place until it gradually broke up and disappeared. Only its head was left and was carried off by someone in the confusion raised by the pagans, while they addressed blasphemous and wholly inappropriate words to our Lord Jesus Christ, such as no one had ever heard.

(58) The most lawless Julian himself, of all the impious the most impious, was in exultation and jubilation and took pride when he heard this and issued orders also for the rebuilding of the Jewish temple in Jerusalem. And he expelled the Christians from the city and gave it to the Jews to live in, sending a certain Alypius with dispatch to rebuild the temple.

Julian himself sat on his platform in the place called the Basilica, and ordered the martyr to be brought before him. When the saint was brought forward, Julian said to him: 'To be sure you too have heard, most impious Artemius, of the daring act of those impious Christians like yourself, which they carried out in Daphne in the temple of the saviour Apollo, and how they set fire to his temple together with its offerings, and destroyed the venerable and marvellous statue. But they will not enjoy this mockery and derision of us. For I shall take vengeance for this "seventy times seven"[63] to quote your scriptures.'

(59) Artemius replied: 'I have indeed heard how the anger of God came down as fire from heaven and devoured your god, and burnt all his temple and eradicated it. If then he was a god, why did he not save himself from the fire?'

The Apostate answered: 'It seems that perhaps you too, most unholy man, are jeering and laughing aloud at these events, as if you have obtained some vengeance from your God.' To which the martyr replied: 'Certainly I do, you sinful reprobate, triumph and rejoice and exult at the collapse of the gods worshipped by you. And I delight and relish all the miracles that my Christ works. As for the vengeance for the things that you have done to me, I shall receive that when that unquenchable fire and the everlasting punishment comes upon you. And then not much time will pass before your memory and every trace of it shall be obliterated.' The Apostate replied: 'If you rejoice and take pleasure in these things, impious one, I shall give you an extra dose of the pleasure you long for. But, you unhappy man, I am sparing you through my own goodness, and

I want you to cease from your folly and adopt a sensible view, and come over and worship the immortal gods. For you have been endowed with the greatest respect, and plenty of wealth has been piled up for you from the past and from your ancestors, and the gods have given you many advantages of virtue, even if you have shown yourself ungrateful towards them.'

(60) Artemius replied: 'What madness is this, transgressor, and why do you spend time on these threatening speeches? You allowed the barbarians to revolt, and took up a war against the Persians, through which you shook the whole world, and do you now waste time on me, a servant of the Lord? Pronounce whatever sentence you like on me. For I do not serve your gods, nor do I bow to your orders, but I offer my God every day a sacrifice of praise and confession. Do what you will, evil man.'

When Julian heard this he was infuriated, and he ordered stone-cutters and masons to come to him, and said to them: 'You know the towering rock opposite the theatre which hangs precipitously over the city? Split this rock and place part of it higher up, and put this criminal in between. Then break the chains holding the rock, and let it with its force and weight return to the part it has been split from. And when Artemius is caught in the middle he will be totally squashed to nothing, and his insides will all be flattened. This way he will know whom he is opposing, and against whom he has armed for the fight, and what help he will get from his God, if in fact he can rescue him from my hands.' This order was carried out almost as soon as it was given, and after placing the martyr between the rocks the stone-cutters let go the rock as the tyrant had said. With all its weight it fell headlong and completely covered the martyr's body, and such was the weight that fell on him that as his bones shattered a sound was echoed around of fear and violence, never before heard by human ears.

(61) The saint was compressed and crushed between the rocks, and called out to Christ saying: 'You have uplifted me on a rock and guided me, because you have been my hope, my tower of strength before the face of my enemy. You have set my feet on a rock, and directed my steps. So receive my spirit, only Son of God, you who know my plight, and do not allow me into the hands of my enemies.' For all his insides were ruptured, and the structure of his bones was all shattered, and his eyeballs were knocked from their sockets. But

even so Christ's noble warrior was enduring, like an undented anvil
or a hard stone tougher than any steel. When the saint had lasted
between the rocks for a day and a night, the lawless Julian ordered
the rocks to be pulled apart, expecting that he would be found broken
and crushed and dead. But when the rocks were separated, Artemius
came out walking, though his eyes were out of their sockets and had
left their proper orbits. He was a horrifying sight and a strange
example of the human condition: a man naked, his bones shattered
and their structure crushed, showing the inner arrangement of a
man's body as it came out of its surrounding frame, yet he walked
about and conversed and spoke back to the tyrant.

(62) The accursed Julian saw him and was totally amazed and said to
those present: 'Do you see that strange sight and unnatural example
of human kind? Is Artemius a sorcerer and magician? Isn't this a
phantom and proof of the deceiving demons? Now I believe that
Euripides is wise and possessed of knowledge of many things. He
says this in the *Orestes*:

> There is no word so terrible to say,
> nor any suffering or disaster sent by the gods,
> the burden of which mortal nature may not bear.[64]

'By the immortal and invincible gods, I did not expect, gentlemen,
that this accursed criminal would still be counted among the living.
But now, though his innards are spilling out and his whole frame is
broken, he is moving about and speaking. The gods have preserved
him as a lesson to many men, to be a bogeyman to those who do not
worship their celestial power.' And to Artemius he said: 'See, wretch,
you have lost your eyes, and lost the use of all your limbs. What hope
do you still have left in him in whom you have hoped in vain? Call
upon the goodwill of the gods. Perhaps they will take pity on you,
and not surrender you to the punishments in Hades.'

(63) When the martyr of Christ heard the word 'punishment' he
smiled, and said to the tyrant who lacked all sympathy and pity:
'Your gods will surrender me to punishments? How shall they,
execrable man, escape their own punishment, and be able to bring
help to others? Everlasting fire has been made ready for them, for
them await Tartarus and the worms, and the gnashing of teeth which
will never cease. Along with them you too will be given to the
everlasting and unquenchable fire, to be punished for all time,

because you trampled on the Son of God, and treated as common the venerable blood which He poured out for our sake, and insulted the Spirit of grace in which you were sanctified, and followed pernicious demons. But to me, in return for this small travail and paltry punishment which you have brought upon me, shall be given many rewards and crowns of victory, which shall deck me for the holy marriage when I lie with Christ, and the Lord Christ will garland my head with a crown far greater than the ephemeral one which you wear. But why do I waste words on you, impious wicked tyrant? Stand away from me, most lawless and unholy of all men. Pronounce whatever sentence you like on me, whatever Satan who dwells in your soul inspires you. For I oppose your will, and do not bow to your orders. Do what you will, evil man.'

(64) When the Apostate Julian, God's outcast, had heard this speech from the martyr, he declared this sentence upon him: 'Artemius who has insulted the gods, and has trampled on the Roman laws and ours, and has confessed himself a Christian instead of a Roman and a Greek, and has called himself a Galilaean instead of *dux* and *Augustalis*, we have condemned to the final sentence of death, ordering that his accursed head be chopped off by the sword.'

When Christ's martyr had received this sentence, he left the tribunal with the soldiers leading him away, cheerful and rejoicing, singing hymns and praises to Christ the King. When they reached the place where Christ's martyr was to receive his execution, he said to the soldiers leading him: 'Brothers, I beseech you, give me a short time to pray.' And they said to him: 'Do as your heart wishes.' And the saint turned to the east, and raised his hands to the heavens, and prayed as follows:

(65) 'I give you thanks, Lord and Saviour of those who call upon your name in truth, that you have strengthened me your unworthy servant to tread down the goads of the devil, and to grind down his snares which he laid beneath my feet and to confound the wicked Julian, who skipped away from your sovereignty and attached himself to the devil and those who hate you. He trampled on your holy laws and profaned your divine commandments. I give you thanks, merciful Lord, because you have looked upon my humility, and have not allowed me into the hands of my enemies, but have placed my feet in a broad place and have directed my steps. I give you thanks, only-born Word of the Father, because you have judged

me worthy of the prize of the call above, and of the chorus of your saints, and have ended my life in confession of you, and have shamed those who rose up against me.

'And now I call upon you, Lord, look upon me and upon my humble words, and grant refreshment to your inheritance, because it has grown weak and you have not restored it. For behold your enemies have shouted and those who hate you have raised their head. They have carried out their plan against your people and have plotted against your saints. For they said "Come on, and let us destroy them, and Christ's name shall no longer be mentioned." This is Julian's boast, this is his confidence. This is his threat to your people and to your inheritance on whose behalf you poured out your blood. For behold your altars have been torn down, your sanctuary has been burnt, and the beauty of your house has been obliterated, and the blood of your covenant has been counted as nothing – and all because of our sins and the blasphemies poured out by Arius against you the only-born and your Holy Spirit, when he declared you different from shared essence with the Father, and separated you from His nature, calling you a creation – you the creator of all things – and placing beneath time you who created all eternity. He said this: "There was a time when the Son was not," and the lawless man called you a "Son of will and volition". But that impious man has found the reward for his own mouth and wicked tongue, even if his blasphemies remain, bearing for him the fruit of everlasting and unending punishment.

'But you, magnanimous Lord, suppress the tyranny that is against us, and quell your righteous indignation and anger which we enflamed by provoking you, Lord. Smash the fortresses of idolatry. Crush the altars of the idols, and put an end to the savour of impure blood sacrifices, so that a pure and unbloodied sacrifice may be brought to you in every place in your sovereignty, so that your holy name may be glorified, that of the Father, Son and Holy Spirit, now and for ever and for all ages upon ages. Amen.'

(66) He knelt three times in worship towards the east, and prayed again saying: 'God of God, very God of very God, King of Kings, who dwell in heaven and are seated at the right hand of God the Father who gave you birth, who lived on earth for the salvation of us all, the crown of those who fight piously on your behalf; listen to me your humble unworthy slave, and in peace accept my soul, and give it rest among the saints who from all time have pleased you and

glorified your holy name, that of the Father, Son and Holy Spirit, now and for ever and for all ages upon ages. Amen.'

And then came a voice from heaven saying: 'Artemius, your prayer has been heard, and the grace of healing has been granted to you. Hasten then your course, and complete your ordeal. Come and join the saints, and share the prize which has been made ready for the saints[65] and for all those who have loved the presence of Christ. The lawless emperor shall fall in Persia, as the victim of the impure demons that he worshipped and honoured, obtaining such a reward from them, and another shall be emperor in his place, a true Christian and man of piety, who shall overthrow and destroy all the rites of the idols. The people of God shall be joyful and all the churches shall be freed from idolatry, and a profound peace shall encompass the whole world, and the name of Christ shall be uplifted and magnified from end to end of the world. For idolatry shall no longer raise its head, nor shall Satan have the opportunity to uproot the foundation of the Church. For the gates of Hades shall not prevail against the Church.'

(67) The Blessed man heard these words of the divine voice, and received certain knowledge of future events, and gave thanks to God, full of joy and happiness, and then offered his neck. One of the soldiers came forward and cut off his holy head, the date being the twentieth of October, the sixth day of the week, known as the 'day of preparation'.

His blessed and holy body was requested from the emperor Julian by a woman of faith, called Ariste, a deacon of the Church at Antioch. He granted that it should be given to her. She made a coffin and smeared with myrrh his holy and blessed body, and anointed it with valuable scents and ointments, and laid it in the coffin, and had it carried to the prosperous city Constantinople, placing it in a conspicuous place, since she wanted to build a home worthy of the saintly and great martyr Artemius, and to create a shrine to commemorate his famous martyrdom.

All this was done in Antioch the greatest city of Syria, in the time of the emperor Julian, surnamed the Apostate, when Dulcitius was proconsul,[66] and Salustius prefect,[67] in the place called Daphne, while the Lord and God and our Saviour Jesus Christ reigned over us, to whom be glory and power now and for evermore. Amen.

(68) (= ad Philost. VII,9a: 95,17–96,34) As we said earlier the

Apostate Julian had sent orders to Jerusalem for the rebuilding of the temple of the Jews, which Vespasian and his son Titus had destroyed and burnt along with the city, just as the Lord Christ had predicted concerning it to his sacred disciples: 'No stone shall be left on top of another stone that shall not be destroyed.'[68] The Apostate, wishing to prove false the words of Christ, was very eager to build the temple, and gave instructions that all the expenses of the building should be met from public accounts and monies. So the Jews came running and with great joy began the task, digging the ditch for the foundations with silver buckets and spades. They were about to lay the foundations when a torrential rainstorm came down and filled in the excavation. Lightning and thunder showered down unceasingly for the whole of that night, and there was an earthquake as day drew near, so that many even of those who had stayed out of doors lost their lives. And a fire started in the foundations being dug and burnt to death all those who were caught there. It happened also that some cities fell: Nicopolis and Neapolis, Eleutheropolis and Gaza, and many others. A colonnade at Aelia, that is in Jerusalem, next to the synagogue of the Jews, collapsed and killed many of them. And a fire broke out unexpectedly and destroyed very many Jews. There was darkness in those places and continual earthquakes, causing many deaths in many cities.

(69) (= ad Philost. VII,15a: 100,29–103,22) And Julian set out from Antioch with all his army and marched against Persia. And when he had captured the city of Ctesiphon, he expected after accomplishing a great feat to pass on to other mightier deeds. The accursed emperor did not realise he had been tricked. For having acquired a devilish love of idol-madness and hoping through his godless gods to hold his emperorship for a long time and to become a new Alexander, and to overcome the Persians and to obliterate the name and race of the Christians for all time, he fell victim to his overweening purpose. For he met an aged Persian and was led astray by him on the promise that he would without trouble capture the kingdoms of the Persians and all their wealth; he drew him into the Carmanian desert into roadless regions, ravines and desert-like and waterless areas with all his army. And when he had exhausted them with thirst and hunger and killed off all their horses, the Persian confessed that he had deliberately led them astray so that they might be destroyed by him and he might not view his own native land laid waste by its worst

enemies. Therefore they straightaway cut this man up limb from limb and despatched him to his death.

But immediately in this state of distress they encountered against their will the army of the Persians. A battle took place and while Julian himself was rushing here and there and arranging his men he fell to the spear, so some say, of a soldier; but as others record, to the spear of a Saracen serving with the Persians. But as is the true Christian version and ours, the spear belonged to the Lord Christ ranged against him. For a bow stretched taut from the air suddenly, and launched a missile at him as at a target which driving straight through his flanks wounded him in the abdomen. And he wailed deeply and woefully and thought that our Lord Jesus Christ was standing before him and exulting over him. But he, filled with darkness and madness, received his own blood in his hand and sprinkled it into the air, and when he was about to die shouted out, saying, 'You have won, Christ. Take your fill, Galilaean.' And thus meeting a most hateful death he ended his life after many reproaches upon his own gods.

(70) (= ad Philost. VIII,1a, 6a, 8a: 104,23–27; 107,32–110,14) When the transgressor fell in the no-man's land around the army, Jovian was proclaimed emperor by the army. And making a peace treaty with the Persians, he handed over Nisibis without its inhabitants to the Persians, and departed from there. For the army was being destroyed by hunger and disease. But when he entered on Roman territory he joined the heresy of the supporters of Dissimilar Substance, that is to say the Eunomians. When he reached the province of Galatia, there in a certain place called Dadastana, he suddenly ended his life.

And the population remained without an emperor for forty days, until coming to Nicaea they proclaimed Valentinian. Valentinian proclaimed his own brother emperor on the twenty-fifth of February, after thirty-two days of his own emperorship.

And so when the bishops of the pure and orthodox faith met Valentinian, they requested the convening of a synod. And he answered them: 'God has granted to me to rule over the government of the world, and to you he has given the government of the churches. So I have nothing to do with this matter. Meet wherever you think right and hold your synod.' These were his words then, since his thinking was still orthodox and not yet corrupted. The bishops collected in Lampsacus (which is a city of the Hellespont) and summed up the orthodox dogmas of the Faith. And commending the faith of Lucianus the martyr, they anathematised the doctrine of Dissimilar Substance. And subscribing to the faith earlier laid down by the holy fathers in Nicaea, they sent out to all the churches.

But the emperor Valens was led astray by the heresy of Dissimilar Substance, and bishops began again to be driven out and exiled, when Eudoxius with Aetius, Eunomius and the remaining heretics, who represented the Arian heresy, became the generals.

For this, along with their treacherous inheritance, they won the fitting reward of Hell from Christ, our benevolent Lord. So this is what took place, and let us, who worship the Holy Trinity, give glory to Christ, our true Lord, along with the Father and the Holy Spirit for all ages upon ages. Amen.

NOTES
Sam Lieu

1 I.e. the Church historian Eusebius of Caesarea. He was called Pamphili because he was the intimate friend and devoted admirer of Pamphilus, a presbyter of Caesarea and a martyr. Cf. Barnes, 1981: 199–201.

2 Socrates 'Scholasticus', Church historian and continuator of the *Ecclesiastical History* of Eusebius. He was a known sympathiser of the Novatianists. His *Ecclesiastical History* recounts the riots in Alexandria and cites in full a letter of Julian which mentions the role of the 'governor of Egypt' in the suppression of the riots. (See Introduction, pp. 34–35)

3 On the author of the *AP*'s use of Philostorgius see esp. Bidez, in GCS Philost., pp. XLIV–LVIII, Emmett Nobbs, 1990: 252 and Introduction, pp. 37–38.

4 The execution of Artemius is not mentioned in Photius' summary of the lost *Ecclesiastical History* of Philostorgius. In what form Artemius appeared in the now lost original work of Philostorgius is largely a matter of conjecture. See Introduction, pp. 217–23.

5 Theodoretus, ascetic, Church historian and bishop of Cyr. The brief mention of Artemius in his *Ecclesiastical History* (completed after 428) (III,8,1) is probably the earliest witness to give his despoiling of pagan shrines as the main reason for his execution.

6 The death of Artemius is not mentioned in the extant version of the *Ecclesiastical History* of Sozomen.

7 No reference to Artemius, who flourished several decades after the death of Eusebius (*c.* 340), is found in the latter's voluminous writings.

8 Eunomius (d. 394) was consecrated Arian bishop of Cyzicus in Mysia in 360. He was later banished and recalled under Valens and later banished again under Theodosius. He was a devoted follower of Aetius and his extreme 'Anomoean' position in the Christological controversy earned him many enemies, especially Gregory of Nyssa.

9 See §45 below.

10 An extreme interpretation of Constantine's policy of deliberate neglect towards paganism (cf. Eus., *V. C.* III,51–58). On Constantine's attitude towards paganism see esp. Müller, 1946: 19–25, Bowder, 1978: 80–85, Barnes, 1981: 246–48, Keil, 1989: 196–201 and 216–22. It must be remembered that Constantine was canonised by the Byzantine Church for his championship of Christianity against paganism – hence the need to attribute to him radical anti-pagan policies in order to provide a contrast to the religious policy of Julian. Cf. Linder, 1975: 46.

11 This denunciation of Arius and his teaching helps to mask the awkward fact that the historical Artemius was a fervent supporter of the Arian cause. For full discussion on the attempt by the author of the *AP* to portray Artemius as a champion of the Nicene faith, see Brennecke, 1988: 127–31.

12 The view that Constantine's Persian campaign was a direct response to the aggressive policy of Shapur II apparently wishing to regain lost territories is echoed by Libanius, *Or.* LIX,71 (see above, p. **180.**) See sources cited and trans. in Dodgeon and Lieu, 1991: 155–62. See also Barnes, 1985: 32 for a re-examination of traditional explanations for the outbreak of hostilities in 337.

13 Constantine died on 22 May 337 in Ancyra near Nicomedia while on his way to campaign against Shapur II. The accusation that Constantine was poisoned by his brothers is also found in Zonaras (XIII,4,26) which may have shared the same source (Philostorgius?) as the *AP*. It was probably levelled against them posthumously by Constantine's sons after the 'promiscuous massacre' of 337. Cf. Blockley, 1983: 130, n. 17 and Di Maio, 1977: 246–59. See above, pp. **147–49.**

14 Flavius Dalmatius (*PLRE*, I, Dalmatius 6), son of Constantius I (Chlorus) and Theodora. Consul prior to 333. He was still alive in 335 (Thphn., *Chron.*, A. M. 5827, p. 31,20–22) but may have died before 337. His sons Hannibalianus (*PLRE*, i, Hannibalianus 2) and Flavius Julius Dalmatius (*PLRE*, i, Dalmatius 7) were among those slain in 337.

15 More commonly Hannibalianus (*PLRE*, i, Hannibalianus 1), son of Constantius I and Theodora. He too was probably already dead before 337.

16 Flavius Julius Dalmatius (Caesar 335–37) is here confused with his father Flavius Dalmatius (cos. 333). Hannibalianus, the half-brother of Constantine, was never Caesar. The Hannibalianus who was Rex Regum of the Pontic nations was son of Flavius Julius Dalmatius.

17 Gallus and Julian did not have the same mother. Gallus was born in Massa Veternensis in Etruria in 325 or 326, the son of Julius Constantius (*PLRE*, i, Iulius Constantius 7), the half-brother of Constantine I and Galla (Constantius' first wife, cf. *PLRE*, i, Galla 1), the sister of Vucatius Rufinus and Naeratius Cerealis. In 330 Julius Constantius, after a short stay at Corinth, moved his family to Constantinople, where Galla died. Gallus spent the years 331 to 337 there. Julius Constantius also had another son, older than Gallus, whose death in 337 was recorded by Julian (*Ep. ad Ath*. 270D,3, ed. Bidez) but we are not certain whether he had the same mother as Gallus. Flavius Constantius then married

Basilina (*PLRE*, i, Basilina), the daughter of a Praetorian Prefect of the Orient Julius Julianus (*PLRE*, i, Iulius Iulianus 35). She was still young when she died a few months after the birth of Julian (Jul., *Misop*. 352B).

18 The Greek word παραβάτης is here translated as 'Apostate' although originally it meant 'transgressor'.

19 Flavius Julius Constantius (*PLRE*, i, Constantius 8) was born on 7 Aug. 317, the son of Constantine the Great and his wife Fausta (*PLRE*, i, Fausta 2).

20 Flavius Julius Constans (*PLRE*, i, Constans 3) was born in *c.* 320, the son of Constantine the Great and probably of Fausta.

21 Flavius Claudius Constantinus (*PLRE*, i, Constantinus 3) was born in 317, the son of Constantine the Great. He was probably illegitimate as his mother's identity is not known.

22 Constantius had already been posted by his father before 337 to guard the East against the initial probing attacks of Shapur II and to respond to the events in Armenia. He was based at Antioch at the time of the death of his father. Cf. Julian, *Or.* 1,13B, Festus, 27 (confusion with Battle of Singara in 344?), Thphn., *Chron.* A. M. 5815, p. 20,21–6 and Zon. XIII,4,28. See sources cited and trans. in Dodgeon and Lieu, 1991: 153–54.

23 On the division of the empire after the death of Constantine and the massacre of his sons, see [Aur. Vict], *Epit.*, 41,20 and *Anon. Vales.* 6,35. See discussion and fuller listing of sources in Di Maio, 1977: 259. The source for *AP* on the agreement at Viminacium is clearly Philostorgius as is shown by verbal parallels in Zonaras (XIII,5,2–4) who also used the same source. Cf. Di Maio, 1988: 238.

24 The close friendship of Constantius and Artemius is not attested in contemporary (i.e. 4th and 5th century) sources but can be inferred from the offices Artemius held under Constantius and from the timing of his trial and execution.

25 The discovery of the relics of these saints and their subsequent transfer to Constantinople is Artemius' main passport to fame among hagiographers. (See Introduction, p. **216**).

26 It appears that Constantine II wanted possession of Africa and Italy – part of Constans' share of the empire. Cf. [Aur. Vict], *Epit.*, 41,21 and Zos. II,41. (See above, pp. **148–49**)

27 The decisive battle was fought near Aquileia in 340. Constantine II died of wounds after he had been thrown to the ground by his horse. Cf. Aur. Vict., *Caes.*, 41,22, [Aur. Vict.], *Epit.* 41,21, Hieron., *Chron.*, *s. a.* 340, p. 235, Eutr. X,9,2, Soz., *H. e.* III,2,10 and Ruf., *H. e.* X,16.

28 Proverbs 22,28; Deut. 19,14.

29 Constans is said to have kept young men whom he had acquired either as hostages or by purchase for his sexual pleasure. Cf. [Aur. Vict.], *Epit.* 41,24 and Zos. II,42,1.

30 This accolade to Gallus' bravery most likely goes back to Philostorgius who, like Gallus, was an Arian. Gallus is likely to have made 'what was at least a highly successful demonstration' against Shapur II (Thompson, 1947: 57).

31 The most detailed account of the deaths of Domitianus (PPO) and

Montius the quaestor is given by Ammianus (XIV,7,9–17). The account of Zonaras (XIII,9,11–15) is also worth consulting as it may have been derived from the now lost history of John of Antioch. The source of the *AP* is clearly Philostorgius (Photius) III,28. Constantius, worried by the signs of Gallus' growing independence, sent Domitianus to persuade Gallus to meet the emperor in Italy. According to Ammianus, instead of going immediately to the court of Gallus, the prefect went to the general's quarters and feigned illness to avoid appearing in public or to present himself before Gallus. He did, however, keep Constantius informed of the events in Antioch in reports which were derogatory to Gallus. When he finally appeared before Gallus, he threatened to cut off supplies to the palace unless Gallus immediately presented himself to the emperor. After presenting the Caesar with this ultimatum, Domitianus withdrew once more to his quarters and did not return even though Gallus sent for him several times. Gallus finally had him arrested but this provoked swift action from Montius who assembled the palace guard and informed them that Gallus would be guilty of treason if he persisted with his course of action. Gallus, egged on by his wife, ordered him to be arrested.

32 According to Ammianus' account (XIV,7,15–16) Montius was bound and dragged by the guards to the prefect's residence. They also threw Domitianus down a flight of steps and the two were later beaten to death and their bodies were thrown into a river. The story in *AP* about their bodies being buried by the bishop of the city is at variance with the accounts of both Ammianus (XIV,7,16) and Zonaras (XIII,9,15) which assert that the bodies were thrown into a river. Cf. Di Maio, 1988: 232–33.

33 This information is unique. Both Ammianus (XIV,11,6) and Zonaras (XIII,9,17) merely say that she died *en route*.

34 I.e. Poetovio in Noricum. On the execution of Gallus see also Amm. XIV,11,19–23, Lib., *Or.* XVIII,24, Jul., *Ep. ad Ath.* 270D–271A and Zos. II,55,2–3.

35 Gallus' place of exile and eventual execution is given as Flanona by the Church historians Socrates (II,34,4ff., Hussey) and Sozomen (IV,7,6ff.) while Ammianus (XIV,11,2) gives the impression that Gallus was imprisoned at the town of Istria near Pola. Histria was actually the peninsula in Dalmatia on which the communities of Pola and Flanona were located. Di Maio (1988: 235) rightly points out that the presence of the Danube (Gr. Istros) to the north-east of the region may have confused the historians. *AP* (following Philostorgius) has here once again given precise information.

36 Eusebius' role in frustrating Constantius' attempt to reprieve Gallus at the eleventh hour is not attested in all the main sources (i.e. Amm., Jul., Lib. and Zos.). If true, it would have been a striking omission from Ammianus as it would have clearly demonstrated the amount of power wielded by the eunuchs in court. It is also inconceivable that the careers of those who had tried to hinder the pardon would have been unmolested. Cf. Bowen, 1982: 121–22.

37 I.e. Hadrianopolis Constantius is not known to have been in the area

between the death of Gallus and the arrival of the relics in Constantinople in March 357. The mention of Hadrianopolis seems to point to 359, as the bishop would have then attended the second council of Sirmium. Cf. Mango, 1990: 60.

38 'If there is any truth in this account . . . it shows that the relics in question were far from being widely known' (Mango, 1990: 59–60).

39 On the date of the translation of the relics see esp. Woods, 1991: 287–88 which fully discusses the material from the *AP*.

40 Well-known leader of the Arians who spearheaded the campaign to restore Arius and his followers to the Catholic fold after the Council of Nicaea.

41 Cf. Philost. (Phot.) 3,2, p. 31,1,-32,4 and Zon. XIII,4,28. Another tradition, represented by Eus., *V. C.* IV,59–60, Soz., *H. e.* II,34,4ff. and *Pat. Const.* I,50, pp. 140,9–13, maintains that Constantine built the church of the Holy Apostles and his own mausoleum. See full discussion of the sources in Di Maio, 1977: 252–53 and esp. Mango. 1990: 56–58 who argues that Constantine built his own mausoleum but not the church of the Holy Apostles. The latter which adjoined the mausoleum was the work of Constantius, and the body of Constantine was later moved into the church at the instigation of Macedonius, bishop of Constantinople. On the social significance of the discovery, transfer and installation of relics, see Brown, 1981: 93–96.

42 Nothing else is known about this Anatolius *cubicularius*. Cf. *PLRE*, i, Anatolius (2).

43 The date for the arrival of the relics is given as 3 March 357, by the *Consularia Constantinopolitana*, *s. a.* 357.

44 Flavius Taurus was PPO Italiae et Africae 355–61 (cf. *PLRE*, i, Taurus 3). On hearing of the rebellion of Julian, he tried to collect supplies in Brigantia and the Cottian Alps (Jul., *Ep. ad Ath.* 286b). He fled with Florentius (below) to Constantius (Amm. XXI,9,4 and Zos. III,10,4) and was later condemned to death at Chalcedon.

45 Flavius Florentius was PPO Galliarum 357–60 (cf. *PLRE*, i, Florentius 10). He was at odds with Julian on numerous occasions while the latter was Caesar in Gaul. After Julian was proclaimed Augustus, he fled to Constantius who appointed him PPO Illyrici in succession to Anatolius. When he heard Julian was approaching Illyricum, he fled with Taurus and remained in hiding until the death of the emperor.

46 I. e. Pannonia.

47 The *AP* is our only source which mentions Julian camped at Issus in *imitatio Alexandri* before entering Tarsus. Ammianus (XXII,9,13, see also Lib., *Or.* XVIII,159 and *idem, Ep.* 736,1–2) says that Julian journeyed to Tarsus from Ancyra via the Cilician Gates without mentioning any detour or subsequent visit to Issus which lies on the route *between* Tarsus and Antioch. The desire of the author of the *AP* to maintain this detail from the early version of the saint's martyrdom has undoubtedly contributed to this confusion of geography. Cf. Bidez, GCS Philost., p. L. The imitation of Alexander is an important motif in Roman anti-Persian propaganda. Cf. Anon., *Itinerarium Alexandri*, prolog. (early part of the reign of Constantius, trans. Dodgeon and Lieu,

1991: 176–79). I am grateful to Robin Lane Fox for helpful discussion on this aspect of the *AP* and his kind permission for me to consult his yet unpublished paper: The Itinerary of Alexander: Constantius to Julian.

48 §§25.5–34 which deal with the interrogation and torture of Eugenius and Macarius have been omitted.

49 Isaiah 50,6.

50 I.e. Crispus. The same unusual error is attested in the parallel portion of Photius' summary of Philostorgius (II,3, pp. 14,10–15,1, Bidez) which makes one wonder whether both Photius and the author of the *AP* had consulted the same ms. of Philostorgius in Constantinople. The confusion between Crispus-Priscus, though attested elsewhere, was not a mistake which either Philostorgius or Photius was likely to make. Cf. Bidez, comm. *ad loc.* (p. 14,15–17).

51 Cf. Daniel 3,18.

52 For a detailed commentary on this otherwise unattested citation from the Hermetic writings see Scott and Ferguson, 1936: 241–42.

53 Psalm 140,5.

54 *Bacchae* 203.

55 On the background of Julian's visit to Daphne to revive the oracular cult of Apollo, see esp. D'Alton, 1940: 39–49, Downey, 1961: 387–88 and Lieu, 1989: 46–52.

56 Cf. Lib., *Or.* XI,236: 'and [*sc.* at Daphne] there pours upon the spectator's eyes an arresting brightness, the temple of Apollo, the temple of Zeus, the Olympic stadium, the theatre which furnishes every pleasure, the number and thickness and height of the cypresses, the shady paths, the choruses of singing birds, the even breeze, the odours sweeter than spices, the stately aqueducts, the vines trained to form banqueting halls' (trans. Downey, 1959: 678). The cypress groves at Daphne which symbolised the cult of Apollo became the target for Christian bigotry in the reign of Theodosius, and in 387 (cf. *PLRE*, i, *s. v.* 'Anonymus 61') Libanius (*Or.* I,255) had to protest against a Christian *comes Orientis* who tried to market the timber. Cf. Downey, 1961: 436, n. 127.

57 Cf. Lib., *Or.* XI,240–43 (trans. Downey, *ibid.*: 678).

58 Cf. *ibid.* 244: 'We surpass the beautiful waters of other cities by the abundance of ours, and the abundant waters of other cities by the beauty of ours' (trans. Downey, *ibid.*).

59 Cf. Lib., *Or.* LX, *frag.* 11.

60 *hierurgia* is a generic term for any sacred rite held in the presence of a god, usually embodied in his cult image; used also in connection with the Eucharist in Christian writings.

61 Babylas was a bishop of Antioch who suffered martyrdom in the third century, probably under Decius, but later legends made him the victim of an enraged Philip the Arab who was denied communion by Babylas on account of his guilt in the death of the emperor Gordian (or that of a young royal Persian hostage). For an analysis of the various versions of the legend see Lieu, 1989: 48.

62 Julian, the uncle of the emperor, was Comes Orientis. Errors over his official rank are common in ecclesiastical sources. See references in

PLRE, i, pp. 470–71.
63 Matthew 18,22.
64 *Orestes* 1–3.
65 Reading ἁγίοις *pace* Kotter, p. 241, §66.14.
66 Aelius Claudius Dulcitius was *proconsul Asiae* 361–63. Cf. *PLRE*, i, p. 274.
67 Flavius Sallustius was PPO Galliarum 361–63 but had been Consul Posterior since 1 Jan. 363 with Julian. Cf. *PLRE*, i, pp. 797–98.
68 Cf. Mark 13,2.

BIBLIOGRAPHY

Adams, J. N. 1976. *The Text and Language of a Vulgar Latin Chronicle (Anonymus Valesianus II)*, Institute of Classical Studies Bulletin Supplement 36, London.

Aiello, V. 1992. Constantino, la lebbra e il battesimo di Silvestro, in Bonamente and Fusco (eds) 1992: 17–58.

Arce, J. 1984. *Estudios sobre el emperador Fl. Cl. Juliano (Fuentes literarias. Epigrafia. Numismática)*, Anejos de Archivo Español de Arqueologia 7, Madrid.

Aufhauser, J. B. 1911. *Konstantins Kreuzevision*, Bonn.

Barceló, P. A. 1982. *Roms auswärtige Beziehungen unter der constantinischen Dynastie (306–363)*, Eichstatter Beiträge 3, Regensburg.

Baldini, A. 1992. Claudio Gotico e Constantino in Aurelio Vittore ed *Epitome de Caesaribus*, in Bonamente and Fusco (eds) 1992: 73–89

Barnes, T. D. 1975. Publilius Optatianus Porfyrius, *American Journal of Philology*, 96: 173–86.

Barnes, T. D. 1976a. The Victories of Constantine, *ZPE* 20: 149–55.

Barnes, T. D. 1976b. The *Epitome de Caesaribus* and its Sources, *Classical Philology* 71: 258–68.

Barnes, T. D. 1980. Imperial Chronology, A.D. 337–350, *Phoenix* 34: 160–66.

Barnes, T. D. 1981. *Constantine and Eusebius*, Cambridge, Mass.

Barnes, T. D. 1982. *The New Empire of Diocletian and Constantine*, Cambridge, Mass.

Barnes, T. D. 1983. Two Victory Titles of Constantius, *ZPE* 52: 229–35.

Barnes, T. D. 1984. Constantine's Prohibition of Pagan Sacrifice, *American Journal of Philology* 105: 69–72.

Barnes, T. D. 1985. Constantine and the Christians of Persia, *JRS* 75: 126–36.

Barnes, T. D. 1986. *The Constantinian Reformation*, Crake Lectures 1984, New Brunswick.

Barnes, T. D. 1987. Himerius and the Fourth Century, *Classical Philology* 82: 206–25.

Barnes, T. D. 1989a. Panegyric, History and Hagiography in Eusebius's Life of Constantine, in R. Williams (ed.) *The Making of Orthodoxy: Essays in Honour of Henry Chadwick*, Cambridge: 94–123.

Barnes, T. D. 1989b. Jerome and the *Origo Constantini Imperatoris*, *Phoenix* 43/1: 158–61.

Barnes, T. D. 1989c. Pagans and Christians in the Reign of Constantius, *Entretiens sur l'Antiquité Classique* 34, Fondation Hardt, Vandoueuvres-Genève: 322–37.

Barnes, T. D. 1992. Praetorian Prefects, 337–361, *ZPE* 94: 249–60.

Barnes, T. D. 1993. *Athanasius and Constantius: Theology and Politics in the Constantinian Empire*, Cambridge, Mass.

Barnes, T. D. 1994. The Two Drafts of Eusebius' *Life of Constantine*, in T. D. Barnes, *From Eusebius to Constantine*, Aldershot: XII (first publication, pages numbered separately).

Battifol, P. 1889. Fragmente der Kirchengeschichte des Philostorgius, *RQA* 3: 252–89.

Battifol, P. 1891. *Quaestiones Philostorgianae*, Paris.

Baynes, N. H. 1910. Rome and Armenia in the Fourth Century, *English Historical Review* 25: 625–43. Reprinted in N. H. Baynes (1955). *Byzantium and Other Essays*, London: 186–208. [Cited by page nos of the reprint edn.]

Baynes, N. H. 1911. Topographica Constantinopolitana, *JHS* 31: 266–68.

Baynes, N. H. 1937. The Death of Julian the Apostate in a Christian Legend, *JRS* 27: 22–29.

Beck, H.-G. 1959. *Kirche und theologische Literatur im byzantinischen Reich*, Handbuch der Altertumswissenschaft, XII,2,1, Munich.

Bees, N. A. 1920. Weiteres zum Kult des hl. Artemios, *BNgJ* 1: 384–85.

Bidez, J. 1930. *La vie de l'empereur Julien* , Paris.

Bidez, J. 1935. Fragments nouveaux de Philostorge sur la vie de Constantin, *Byzantion* 10: 403–37.

Bird, H. W. 1984. *Sextus Aurelius Victor: A Historiographical Study*, ARCA Classical and Medieval Texts, Papers and Monographs 14, Liverpool.

Bird, H. W. 1993. *Eutropius: Breviarium*, translated with an introduction and commentary, Translated Texts for Historians 14, Liverpool.

Bird, H. W. 1994. *Aurelius Victor: De Caesaribus*, translated with an introduction and commentary, Translated Texts for Historians 17, Liverpool.

Bleckmann, B. 1991. Die Chronik des Johannes Zonaras und eine pagane Quelle zur Geschichte Konstantins, *Historia* 40: 343–65.

Bleckmann, B. 1992. Pagane Visionen Konstantins in der Chronik des Johannes Zonaras, in Bonamente and Fusco (eds) 1992: 151–70.

Blockley, R. C. 1981 and 1983. *The Fragmentary Classicising Historians of the Later Roman Empire*, 2 vols, Liverpool.

Bonamente, G. and Fusco, F. (eds) 1992. *Constantino il grande: Dall'antichità all'umanesimo*, Colloquio sul Cristanesimo nel mondo antico, Macerata 18–20 Dicembre, 1990, I, Macerata.

Bowder, D. 1978. *The Age of Constantine and Julian*, London.

Bowen, R. F. 1982. *The Emperor Constantius II (A.D. 317–361): A Critical Study*, Ph.D. diss., Leeds Univ., unpublished.

Bowersock, G. W. 1978. *Julian the Apostate*, London.

Braun, R. and J. Richer (eds) 1978. *L'empereur Julien: de l'histoire à la légende (331–1715)*, I, Paris.

Brennecke, H. C. 1988. *Studien zur Geschichte der Homöer*, Beiträge zur historischen Theologie, Tübingen

Brown, P. R. L. 1970. Sorcery, Demons and the Rise of Christianity: From Late Antiquity into the Middle Ages, in M. Douglas (ed.) *Witchcraft Confession and Accusations*, London: 17–45. [Reprinted in P. R. L. Brown, 1972. *Religion and Society in the Age of Saint Augustine*, London: 119–57.]

Brown, P. R. L. 1981. *The Cult of the Saints*, Chicago and London.

Bruun, P. 1953. *Constantinian Coinage of Arelate*, Helsinki.

Bruun, P. 1961. *Studies in Constantinian Chronology*, Numismatic Notes and Monographs 146, New York.

Buck, D. F. 1977. *Eunapius of Sardis*, Ms D.Phil. d6361. Oxford Univ. unpublished.

Buck, D. F. 1988. Eunapius of Sardis and Theodosius the Great, *Byzantion* 58: 36–53.

Burch, V. 1927. *Myth and Constantine the Great*, Oxford.

Burn, R. 1871. *Rome and Campagna*, Cambridge.

Bury, J. B. 1896. Date of the Battle of Singara, *Byzantinische Zeitschrift* 5: 302–5.

Callu, J.-P. 1992. Ortus Constantini: aspects historiques de la légende, in Bonamente and Fusco (eds) 1992: 253–82.

Cameron, A. M. 1983. Constantinus Christianus (review article), *JRS* 73: 184–90.

Cameron, A. M. 1991. *Christianity and the Rhetoric of Empire*, Berkeley and Los Angeles.

Cameron, A. M. and Herrin, J. (eds) 1984. *Constantinople in the Early Eighth Century: The Parastaseis Syntomoi Chronikai*, Leiden.

Chalmers, W. R. 1953. The ΝΕΑ ΕΚΔΟΣΙΣ of Eunapius, *Classical Quarterly* 47: 165–70.

Ciggar, K. N. 1976. Un description de Constantinople traduite par un pèlerin anglais, *Revue des Études Byzantines* 34: 211–67.

Clark, G. 1989. *Iamblichus: On the Pythagorean Life*, Translated Texts for Historians 8, Liverpool.

Coleman, C. B. 1914. *Constantine the Great and Christianity*, Columbia University Studies in History and Public Law 60/1 (Whole series no. 146), New York. [Reprinted also as a separate monograph in 1968].

Coleman-Norton, P. R. 1966. *Roman State and Christian Church*, 3 vols, London.

Coquin, R. G. and Lucchesi, E. 1982. Une version copte de la passion de Saint Eusignios, *AB* 100: 186–208.

Dagron, G. 1974. *Naissance d'une capitale: Constantinople et ses institutions de 330 à 451*, Paris.

Dagron, G. 1984. *Constantinople imaginaire: Études sur le recueil des 'patria'*, Paris.

D'Alton, J. F. 1940. *Selections from St John Chrysostom*, London.

Delehaye, H. 1895. Les Synaxaire de Sirmond, *AB* 14: 396–434.

Delehaye, H. 1925. Les recueils antiques de miracles des saints, *AB* , 63: 1–85 and 305–25.

Demandt, A. 1989. *Die Spätantike: römische Geschichte von Diocletian bis Justinian 284–565 n. Chr.*, Handbuch der Altertumswissenschaft, III/6, Munich.

Den Boer, W. 1972. *Some Minor Roman Historians*, Leiden.

Devos, P. 1982. Une recension nouvelle de la passion grecque BHG 639 de Saint Eusignios, *AB* 100: 209–28.

Di Maio, M., 1977. *Zonaras' Account of the Neo-Flavian Emperors*, Ph.D. diss., Missouri Univ. (Ann Arbor, University Microfilms, 78–914112).

Di Maio, M. 1988. Smoke in the Wind: Zonaras' Use of Philostorgius, Zosimus, John of Antioch and John of Rhodes in his Narrative of the Neo-Flavian Emperors, *Byzantion* 58: 230–55.

Di Maio, M. and Arnold, W. H. 1992. *Per vim, per caedem, per bellum*: A Study of Murder and Ecclesiastical Politics in the year 337, *Byzantion* 62: 158–211.

Dodgeon, M. H. and Lieu, S. N. C. 1991. *Rome's Eastern Frontier and the Persian Wars, 226–363: A Documentary History*, London.

Dölger, F. J. 1913. Die Taufe Konstantins und ihre Probleme, in F. J. Dölger (ed.) *Konstantin der Grosse und seine Zeit*, *RQA* Suppl. 19, Freiburg: 377–447.

Dörries, H. 1954. *Das Selbstzeugnis Kaiser Konstantins*, Göttingen.

Dostálová, R. 1990. Frühbyzantinische Profanhistoriker, in Winkelmann and Brandes (eds) 1990: 156–79. [Reprint of the first part of the author's 'Zur frühbyzantinischen Historiographie von Eunapios zu Theophylaktos Simokattes', *Klio* 69 (1987) 163–80.]

Downey, G. 1938. The Shrines of St. Babylas at Antioch and Daphne, in Stillwell (ed.) 1938: 45–48.

Downey, G. 1951. The Economic Crisis at Antioch under Julian the Apostate, in P. R. Coleman-Norton (ed.) *Studies in Roman Economic and Social History in Honor of Allan Chester Johnson*, Princeton, N. J.: 312–21.

Downey, G. 1959. Libanius' Oration on Antioch (*Oration* XI), *Proceedings of the American Philosophical Society* 103: 652–86.

Downey, G. 1961. *A History of Antioch in Syria from Seleucus to the Arab Conquest*, Princeton, N. J.

Drake, 1976. *In Praise of Constantine: A Historical Study and New Translation of Eusebius' Tricennial Orations*, Berkeley et al.

Drijvers, J. W. 1992. *Helena Augusta: The Mother of Constantine the Great and the Legend of her Finding of the True Cross*, Leiden.

Dummer, J. 1971. Fl. Artemius dux Aegypti, *Archiv für Papyrusforschung* 21: 121–44.

Dvornik, F. 1958. *The Idea of Apostolicity in Byzantium and the Legend of the Apostle Andrew*, Cambridge, Mass.

Eadie, J. W. 1967. *The Breviarium of Festus: A Critical Edition with Historical Commentary*, London.

Ehrhard, A. 1939. *Überlieferung und Bestand der hagiographischen und homiletischen Literatur der griechischen Kirche*, I/3, TU 52, Leipzig.

Ehrhardt, C. 1980. Constantinian Documents in Gelasius of Cyzicus' Ecclesiastical History, *Jahrbuch für Antike und Christentum* 23: 48–57.

Emmett Nobbs, A. 1990. Philostorgius' View of the Past, in G. Clarke (ed.) *Reading the Past in Late Antiquity*, Canberra: 251–63.

Ensslin, W. 1922. Kaiser Julians Gesetzgebungswerk und Reichsverwaltung, *Klio* 18: 104–99.

Errington, R. M. 1988. Constantine and the Pagans, *Greek, Roman and Byzantine Studies* 29: 309–18.

Esbroek, M. van 1982. Legends about Constantine in Armenia, in Th. J. Samuelian (ed.) *Classical Armenian Culture: Influences and Creativity*, Chico: 79–101.

Ewig, E. 1956. Das Bild Constantins des Grossen in den ersten Jahrhunderten des abenländischen Mittelalters, *Historisches Jahrbuch* 75: 1–46. [Reprinted in Hunger, H. (ed.) 1975. *Das byzantinische Herrscherbild*, Wege der Forschung 341, Darmstadt: 133–92.]

Fälschungen 1988. *Fälschungen in Mittelalter: Internationaler Kongress der Monumenta Germaniae Historica, München, 16–19 September 1986, Teil 2, Gefälschte Rechtstexte: der bestrafte Fälscher*, Monumenta Germaniae Historica Schriften 33/2, Hanover.

Fatouros, G. and T. Krischer, 1980. *Libanios, Briefe, Griechisch-deutsch*, Munich.

Festugière, A. J. 1959. *Antioche païenne et chrétienne: Libanius, Chrysostome et les moines de Syrie*, Paris.

Fowden, G. 1991. Constantine's Porphyry Column: The Earliest Literary Allusion, *JRS* 81: 119–31.

Fowden, G. 1994. The Last Days of Constantine: Oppositional Versions and their Influence, *JRS* 84: 146–70.

Franchi De' Cavalieri, P. 1896–97. Di un frammento du una vita di Constantino, *Studi e Documenti di Storia e Diritto* 17–18: 89–131.

Frere, S. S. 1978. *Britannia: A History of Roman Britain*, London.

Gaiffier, B. de 1956. *Sub Juliano Apostata* dans le martyrologie romaine, *AB* 74: 5–49.

Gaiffier, B. de 1970. Les martyrs Eugène et Macaire morts en exil en Maurétane, *AB* 78: 24–40.

Gedeon, M. I. 1900. Δύο παλαιὰ κείμενα περὶ τοῦ μεγάλου Κωνσταντίνου, Ἐκκλησιαστικὴ Ἀλήθεια 20: 253–54, 262–63, 279–80, 303–4.

Gentz, G. 1966. *Die Kirchengeschichte des Nicephorus Callistus Xanthopulus und ihre Quellen*, Nachgelassene Untersuchungen von Günter Gentz, überarbeitet und erweitert von F. Winkelmann, TU 98, Berlin.

Geppert, F. 1898. *Die Quellen des Kirchenhistorikers Socrates Scholasticus*, Studien zur Geschichte der Theologie und der Kirche 3/4, Leipzig.

Gerland, E. 1937. *Konstantin der Grosse in Geschichte und Sage*, Texte und Forschungen zur Byzantinisch-Neugriechischen Philologie 23, Athens.

Gibbon, E., revised by J. B. Bury, 1909. *The Decline and Fall of the Roman Empire*, II, London.

Gladis, C. 1909. *De Themistii Libanii Iuliani in Constantinum orationibus*, Bratislava.

Green, T. M. 1974. *Zosimus, Orosius and their Traditions: Comparative Studies in Pagan and Christian Historiography*, Ph.D. diss., New York Univ. (Ann Arbor, University Microfilms, 74–29,985).

Grégoire, H. 1930–31, La 'Conversion' de Constantin, *Revue de l'Univ. de Bruxelles* 36: 231–72.

Grünewald, T. 1990. *Constantinus Maximus Augustus: Heerschafts-propaganda in der zeitgenössischen Überlieferung*, Historia Einzel-schriften 64, Stuttgart.

Grünewald, T. 1992a. Der letzte Kampf des Heidentums in Rom? Zu posthumen Rehabilitierung des Virius Nichomachus Flavianus, *Historia* 41: 462–87.

Grünewald, T. 1992b. Constantinus novus: zum Constantin-Bild des Mittelalters, in Bonamente and Fusco (eds) 1992: 461–86.

Guidi, I. 1907. Un *BIOΣ* di Constantino, *Rendiconti della Reale accademia dei Lincei, Classe di Scienze Morali, Storiche e Filologiche*, 5th Ser. 16: 304–40 and 637–60.

Günther, R. 1990. Lateinische Historiographie vom 4. bis 6. Jahrhundert, in Winkelmann and Brandes (eds) 1990: 213–23.

Guthrie, P. 1966. The Execution of Crispus, *Phoenix* 20: 325–31.

Habicht, C. 1958. Zur Geschichte des Kaisers Konstantin, *Hermes* 86: 360–78.

Halkin, F. 1958: La passion grecque des Saintes Libyè, Eutropie et Léonis, martyres à Nisibe, *AB*, 76: 293–301.

Halkin, F. 1959a. Une nouvelle vie de Constantin dans un légendier de Patmos, *AB* 77: 63–207.

Halkin, F. 1959b. Les deux derniers chapitres de la nouvelle vie de Constantin, *AB* 77: 370–72.

Halkin, F. 1959–60. La règne de Constantin d'après la Chronique inédite du Pseudo-Syméon, *Byzantion* 29–30: 7–27.

Halkin, F. 1960. L'empereur Constantin converti par Euphratas, and *idem* Les autres passages inédits de la vie acéphale de Constantin, *AB* 78: 5–10 and 11–15.

Hall, S. G. 1993. Eusebian and other sources in Vita Constantini I, in H. C. Brennecke, E. L. Grasmück and C. Markschies (eds) *Logos: Festschrift für Luise Abramowski, Beihefte zur Zeitschrift für die neutestamentliche Wissenschaft*, Berlin: 239–63.

Hanson, R. P. C. 1974. The Circumstances Attending the Death of the Emperor Flavius Valerius Severus in 306 or 307, *Hermathena* 118: 59–68.

Heather, P. J. 1991. *Goths and Romans, 332–489*, Oxford.

Heather, P. J. and Matthews, J. F. 1991. *The Goths in the Fourth Century*, Translated Texts for Historians 11, Liverpool.

Heseler, P. 1935. Neues zur Vita Constantini des Codex Angelicus 22, *Byzantion* 10: 399–402.

Heydenreich, E. 1893. Constantin der Grosse in den Sagen des Mittelalters, *Deutsche Zeitschrift für Geschichtswissenschaft* 10: 1–27.

Heydenreich, E. 1894. Griechische Berichte über die Jugend Constantins des Grossen, in *Griechische Studien Hermann Lipsius zum sechzigsten Geburtstag dargebracht*, Leipzig: 88–101.

Hunger, H. (ed.) 1969. *Joannes Chortasmenos (ca. 1370–ca. 1436–47): Briefe, Gedichte und kleine Schriften*, Vienna.

Huttmann, M. A. 1914. *The Establishment of Christianity and the Pro-scription of Paganism*, Columbia University Studies in History and Public Law 60/2 (Whole series No. 147), New York.

Ioannes, T. 1884. *Μνημεία άολογικά νῦν πρῶτον ἐκδιδόμενα*, Venice. [Reprinted with new introduction by J. Dummer, Leipzig, 1973.]

Ireland, S. 1986. *Roman Britain: A Sourcebook*, London.

Janin, R. 1969. *La géographie ecclésiastique de l'empire Byzantin, première partie: Le siège de Constantinople et le Patriarcat œcuménique, Tome III, Les églises et les monastères*, Paris.

Jeep, L. 1885. Quellenuntersuchungen zu den griechischen Kirchenhistorikern, *Neue Jahrbücher für Classischen Philologie*, Suppl. 14: 53–178.

Jeffreys, E., Croke, B. and Scott, R. 1990. *Studies in John Malalas*, Byzantina Australiensia 6, Sydney.

Jeločnik, A. and Kos, P. 1973. *The Čentur Hoard: Folles of Maxentius and of the Tetrarchy*, Situla 12, Llubljana.

Jones, A. H. M. 1955. The Career of Flavius Philippus, *Historia* 5: 229–33.

Jones, A. H. M. 1964. *The Later Roman Empire*, 3 vols, Oxford.

Jones, A. H. M. 1970 (ii). *A History of Rome Through the Fifth Century*, vol. 2, *The Empire*, London.

Kaegi, W. E. 1975. The Emperor Julian at Naissus, *L'antiquité classique*, 44: 161–71.

Kazhdan, A. 1987. 'Constantin imaginaire': Byzantine Legends of the Ninth Century about Constantine the Great, *Byzantion* 57: 196–250.

Kazhdan, A. 1988. Hagiographical Notes, *Erytheia* 9: 200–5.

Kazhdan, A. and Ševčenko, N. P. 1991. Artemios, *ODB*, I: 194–95.

Keil, V. 1989. *Quellensammlung zur Religionspolitik Konstantins Grossen*, Texte zur Forschung 54, Darmstadt.

Klebs, E. 1889. Das valesische Bruchstück zur Geschichte Constantins, *Philologus* 47: 53–80.

Klein, R. 1977. *Constantius II und die christliche Kirche*, Impulse der Forschung, Darmstadt.

Klein, R. (ed.) 1978. *Julian Apostata*, Wege der Forschung 509, Darmstadt.

König, I. 1987. *Origo Constantini, Anonymus Valesianus, Teil 1, Text und Kommentar*, Trierer historische Forschungen 11, Trier.

Kraft, H. 1955. *Kaiser Konstantins religiöse Entwicklung*, Tübingen.

Kraft, H. 1957. Zur Taufe Kaiser Konstantins, *Studia Patristica* 1 = TU 63, Berlin: 642–48.

Kurmann, A. 1988. *Gregor von Nazianz Oratio 4 gegen Julian: Ein Kommentar*, Schweizerische Beiträge zur Altertumswissenschaft, Heft 19, Basel.

Lehmann, K. 1920. Ein Reliefbild des heiligen Artemios in Konstantinopel, *BNgJ* 1: 381–84.

Lewis N. and Reinhold, M. 1990. *Roman Civilization* II, New York.

Levison, W. 1924. Konstantinische Schenkung und Silvester-Legende, in *Miscellanea Francesco Ehrle: Scritti di Storia e Palaeografia II Per la Storia di Roma* (= Studi e Testi 38) 159–247.

Lieu, S. N. C. (ed.) 1989. *The Emperor Julian: Panegyric and Polemic*, 2nd edition, Translated Texts for Historians 2, Liverpool.

Lightfoot, C. S. 1981. *The Eastern Frontier of the Roman Empire with Special Reference to the Reign of Constantius II*, D.Phil. diss., Oxford Univ., unpublished.

BIBLIOGRAPHY

Linder, A. 1975. The Myth of Constantine the Great in the West: Sources and Hagiographic Commemoration, *Studi Medievali*, 3rd ser. 16/1: 43–95.

Linder, A. 1988. Constantine's 'Ten Laws' Series, in *Fälschungen* 1988: 491–506.

Lippold, A. 1981. Constantius Caesar, Sieger über die Germanen: Nachfahre des Claudius Gothicus? Der Panegyricus von 297 und die *Vita Claudii* der *HA*, *Chiron* 11: 347–69.

Maas, M. 1992. *John Lydus and the Roman Past: Antiquarianism and Politics in the Age of Justinian*, London.

Maas, M. P. 1920. Artemioskult in Constantinopel, *BNgJ* 1: 377–80.

Macmullen, R. 1968. Constantine and the Miraculous, *Greek, Roman and Byzantine Studies* 9: 81–96.

Magoulias, H. J. 1964. The Lives of the Saints as Sources of Data for the History of Byzantine Medicine in the Sixth and Seventh Centuries, *Byzantinische Zeitschrift* 57: 127–50.

Mango, C. 1979. On the History of the *Templon* and the *Martyrion* of St. Artemios at Constantinople, *Zograf* 10: 40–43.

Mango, C. 1985. *Le dévelopement urbain de Constantinople (IVe-VIIe siècles)*, Travaux et Memoires du Centre de Recherche d'Histoire et Civilisation de Byzance, Collège de France, Monographies 2, Paris.

Mango, C. 1990. Constantine's Mausoleum and the Translation of the Relics, *Byzantinische Zeitschrift* 83: 51–61.

Maraval, P. 1985. *Lieux saints et pèlerinages d'Orient*, Paris.

Markus, R. A. 1975. Church History and the Early Church Historians, in D. Baker (ed.) *The Materials, Sources and Methods of Ecclesiastical History*, Oxford: 1–17.

Matthews, J. F. 1989. *The Roman Empire of Ammianus*, London.

Millar, F. G. B. 1969. P. Herennius Dexippus: The Greek World and the Third-century Invasions, *JRS* 59: 12–29.

Momigliano, A. D. (ed.) 1963. *The Conflict between Paganism and Christianity in the Fourth Century*, Oxford.

Momigliano, A. D. 1963. Pagan and Christian Historiography in the Fourth Century A. D., in Momigliano (ed.) 1963: 79–99.

Moreau, J. 1954. *Lactance: De la mort des persécuteurs*, 2 vols, SC 39, Paris.

Moreau, J. 1955. Zum Problem der Vita Constantini, *Historia* 4: 234–45.

Moreau, J. 1971. *Excerpta Valesiana*, Leipzig.

Müller, H. 1946. *Christians and Pagans from Constantine to Augustine*, Part 1: *The Religious Policies of the Roman Emperors*, Pretoria.

Müller-Rettig, B. 1990. *Der Panegyricus des Jahres 310 auf Konstantin den Grossen: Übersetzung und Historisch-philologischer Kommentar*, Palingenesia 331, Stuttgart.

Nixon, C. E. V. 1981. The Panegyric of 307 and Maximian's Visit to Rome, *Phoenix* 35: 70–76.

Nixon, C. E. V. 1983. Latin Panegyric in the Tetrarchic and Constantinian Period, in B. Croke and A. Emmett Nobbs (eds) *History and Historians in Late Antiquity*, Sydney: 88–99.

Nixon, C. E. V. 1987. *Pacatus' Panegyric to the Emperor Theodosius*, Translated Texts for Historians, Latin Series II, Liverpool.

Nixon, C. E. V. 1993. Constantinus Oriens Imperator, Propaganda and Panegyric: On Reading Panegyric 7 (307), *Historia* 42/2: 229–46.

Noethlics, K. L. 1971. *Die gesetzgeberischen Massnahmen der christlichen Kaiser des vierten Jahrhunderts gegen Häretiker, Heiden und Juden*, Ph.D. diss., Cologne.

Norman, A. F. 1965. *Libanius' Autobiography (Oration 1)*, Oxford.

Oates, D. 1968. *Studies in the Ancient History of Northern Iraq*, Oxford.

Obolensky, D. 1988. *Six Byzantine Portraits*, Oxford.

Opitz, H. G. 1934. Die Vita Constantini des codex Angelicus 22, *Byzantion* 9: 540–90.

Pack, E. 1986. *Städte und Steuern in der Politik Julians: Untersuchungen zu den Quellen eines Kaiserbildes*, Collection Latomus 194, Brussels.

Paschoud, F. 1971. *Zosime: Histoire nouvelle, I (Livres I et II)*, Paris.

Petit, P. 1950. Libanius et la 'Vita Constantini', *Historia* 1: 562–82.

Petit, P. 1955. *Libanius et la vie municipale à Antioche au IVe siècle après J.-C.*, Paris.

Petrikovitz, H. von 1960. *Das römische Rheinland: archäologische Forschungen seit 1945*, Arbeitsgemeinschaft für Forschung des Landes Nordrhein-Westfalen, Geisteswissenschaften 86, Cologne and Opladen.

Petrikovitz, H. von 1978. *Rheinische Geschichte*, I: *Altertum*, Düsseldorf.

Piganiol, 1932. *L'empereur Constantin*, Paris.

Pohlkamp, W. 1983. Tradition und Topographie: Papst Sylvester I. (314–335) und der Drache vom Forum Romanum, *RQA* 78: 1–100.

Pohlkamp, W. 1984. Kaiser Konstantin: der heidnische und der christliche Kult in den Actus Silvestri, *Frühe Mittelalterliche Studien* 18: 357–400.

Pohlkamp, W. 1988 Privilegium ecclesiae Romanae pontifici contulit: Zur Vorgeschichte der Konstantinischen Shenkung, in *Fälschungen* 1988: 413–90.

Pohlkamp, W. 1992. Textfassungen, literarische Formen und geschichtliche Funktionen der römischen Silvester-Akten, *Francia* 19: 115–96.

Portmann, W. 1988. *Geschichte in der spätantike Panegyrik*, Frankfurt.

Portmann, W. 1989. Die 59 Rede des Libanios und das Datum der Schlacht von Singara, *Byzantinische Zeitschrift*, 82: 1–18.

Potter, D. S. P. 1990. *Prophecy and History in the Crisis of the Roman Empire. A Historical Commentary on the Thirteenth Sibylline Oracle*, Oxford.

Previale, L. 1949. Teoria e prassi del panegirico bizantino, *Emerita* 17: 72–105.

Ridley, R. T. 1982. *Zosimus, New History: A Translation with Commentary*, Byzantina Australiensia 2, Melbourne.

Rochow, I. 1990. Chronographie, in Winkelmann and Brandes, (eds) 1990: 190–201.

Rodgers, B. S. 1980. Constantine's Pagan Vision, *Byzantion* 50: 259–78.

Rubin, Z. 1982. The Church of the Holy Sepulchre and the Conflict between the Sees of Caesarea and Jerusalem, in L. I. Levine (ed.) *Jerusalem Cathedra* II, Jerusalem and Detroit: 79–105.

Salway, P. 1981. *Roman Britain*, Oxford History of England IA, Oxford.

Schlumberger, J. 1974. *Die Epitome de Caesaribus: Untersuchungen zur heidnischen Geschichtschreibung des 4. Jahrhunderts n. Chr.*, Vestigia XVIII, Munich.

Schlumberger, J. 1982. Die verlorenen Annales des Nicomachus Flavianus: ein Werk über Geschichte der römischen Republik oder Kaiserzeit?, *Bonner Historia Augusta Colloquium 1982–83*, Bonn: 302–29.

Schneider, A. M. 1934. Die Brotvermehrungskirche von Et Tabgah am Genesareth-See, *Collectanea Hierosolymitana* 4, Jeruslaem.

Schneider, A. M. 1941a. Zur Baugeschichte der Geburtskirche in Bethlehem, *Zeitschrift des Deutschen Palästina-Vereins* 64: 74–91.

Schneider, A. M. 1941b. Zur Datierung der Vita Constantini et Helenae, *Zeitschrift für Neutestamentliche Wissenschaft und die Kunde der Alteren Kirche* 40: 245–49.

Schreckenberg, H. 1990. *Die christlichen Adversus-Judaeos-Texte und ihr literarisches und historisches Umfeld (1.–11. Jh.)*, Frankfurt.

Scott, R. 1994. The Image of Constantine in Malalas and Theophanes, in P. Magdalino (ed.) *New Constantines: Rhythm of Imperial Renewal in Byzantium, 4th–13th Centuries*, Aldershot: 57–71.

Scott, W. and Ferguson, A. S. 1936. *Hermetica: The Ancient Greek and Latin Writings which Contain Religious and Philosophic Teachings Ascribed to Hermes Trismegistus, vol. IV, Testimonia*, Oxford.

Seager, R. 1983. Some Imperial Virtues in the Latin Prose Panegyrics: The Demands of Propaganda and the Dynamics of Literary Composition, in F. Cairns (ed.) *Papers of the Liverpool Latin Seminar*, IV, Liverpool: 129–65.

Seeck, O. 1906. *Die Briefe des Libanius zeitlich geordnet*, Leipzig.

Seeck, O. 1911. *Geschichte des Untergangs der antiken Welt* IV, Stuttgart.

Seeck, O. 1919. *Regesten der Kaiser und Papste für die Jahre 311 bis 476 n. Chr.*, Stuttgart.

Ševčenko, N. P. 1991. Menologion of Basil II, *ODB* II: 1341–42.

Sievers, R. 1868. *Das Leben des Libanius*, Berlin.

Simon, J. 1924. Note sur l'original de la passion de Sainte Fébronie, *AB* 42: 66–76.

Smith, R. B. E. 1986. *Studies in the Religious and Intellectual Background of Julian the Apostate*, D.Phil. diss., Oxford Univ., unpublished.

Stillwell, R. (ed.) 1938. *Antioch-on-the-Orontes, II, The Excavations 1933–36*, Princeton, N. J.

Syme, R. 1974. The Ancestry of Constantine, *Bonner Historia-Augusta-Colloquium 1971*, Bonn: 237–53. [Reprinted in R. Syme, 1983. *Historia Augusta Papers*, Oxford: 63–79.]

Taft, R. F. and Ševčenko, N. P. 1991. Synaxarion, *ODB* III.

Thompson, E. A. 1947. *The Historical Work of Ammianus Marcellinus*, Cambridge.

Tolstoi, J. 1926. Un poncif arétologique dans les miracles d'Asklepios et d'Artemios, *Byzantion* 3: 53–63.

Vogt, J. 1963. Pagans and Christians in the Family of Constantine the Great, in Momigliano (ed.) 1963: 38–54.

Warmington, B. H. 1974. Aspects of the Constantinian Propaganda in the *Panegyrici Latini, Transactions of the American Philological Association* 104: 371–84.

Weis, B. K. 1973. *Julian: Briefe, Griechisch-deutsch*, Munich.

Westerhuis, D. J. A. 1906. *Origo Constantini Imperatoris sive Anonymi Valesiani pars prior*, Groningen.

Whittaker, C. R. 1994. *Frontiers of the Roman Empire: A Social and Economic Study*, Baltimore.

Wiemer, H.-U. 1994a. Libanius on Constantine, *Classical Quarterly*, n.s. 44/2: 511–24.

Wiemer, H.-U. 1994b. Libanius und Zosimos über den Rom-Besuch Konstantins I. im Jahre 326, *Historia* 43/4: 470–94.

Wilbur, D. N. 1938. The Plateau of Daphne: The Springs and the Water-system, in Stillwell (ed.) 1938: 49–56.

Wilken, R. 1983. *John Chrysostom and the Jews*, Berkeley.

Wilkinson, J. 1971. *Egeria's Travels*, London.

Winkelmann, F. 1962. *Die Textbezeugung der Vita Constantini des Eusebius von Caesarea*, TU 84, Berlin.

Winkelmann, F. 1964. Die Beurteilung des Eusebius von Cäsarea und seiner Vita Constantini im griechischen Osten, in J. Irmscher (ed.) *Byzantinische Beiträge*, Berlin: 91–119. [Reprinted in Winkelmann, 1993: XV.]

Winkelmann, F. 1966. *Untersuchungen zur Kirchengeschichte des Gelasios von Kaisareia*, Sitzungsberichte der Deutschen Akademie der Wissenschaften, Klasse für Sprachen, Literatur und Kunst Jahrgang 1965, Nr. 3, Berlin.

Winkelmann, F. 1973. Ein Ordnungsversuch der griechischen hagiographischen Konstantinviten und ihrer Überlieferung, in J. Irmscher and P. Nagel (eds) *Studia Byzantina* II, Berlin: 267–84. [Reprinted in Winkelmann, 1993: XII.]

Winkelmann, F. 1978. Das hagiographische Bild Konstantins I. in mittelbyzantinischer Zeit, in V. Vavřínek (ed.) *Beiträge zur byzantinischen Geschichte im 9.–11. Jh.*, Prague: 179–203. [Reprinted in Winkelmann, F. 1993: XIV.]

Winkelmann, F. 1987. Die älteste erhaltene griechische hagiographische Vita Konstantins und Helenas (*BHG* N. 365z, 366, 366a), in J. Dummer (ed.) *Texte und Textkritik: Eine Aufsatzsammlung* (= Texte und Untersuchungen 133), Berlin: 623–38. [Reprinted in Winkelmann, 1993: XIII.]

Winkelmann, F. 1990. Kirchengeschichtswerke, in Winkelmann and Brandes (eds) 1990: 202–12.

Winkelmann, F. 1993. *Studien zu Konstantin dem Grossen und zur byzantinischen Kirchengeschichte*, ed. W. Brandes and J. F. Haldon, Birmingham.

Winkelmann, F. and Brandes, W. (eds) 1990. *Quellen zur Geschichte des frühen Byzanz (4.–9. Jahrhundert), Bestand und Probleme*, Amsterdam.

Woods, D. 1991. The Date of the Translation of the Relics of SS. Luke and Andrew to Constantinople, *Vigiliae Christianae* 45: 286–92.

Zecchini, G. 1993. *Ricerche di storiografia latina tardoantica*, Rome.

INDEX OF SOURCES

GENERAL INDEX

Athanasius of Alexandria 151–53;
    Festal Letters 215
Athens: schools of rhetoric 154–56
Attaliates, Michael 221
St Augustine: *City of God* 5
authority 172–73

Babylas: fire at Daphne temple 246;
    Julian removes bones from
    Daphne 220
Barbatio 231
Barnes, T. D.: *Constantine and
    Eusebius* 32
basilikos logos 98, 159–61, 163
Bassianus 41, 45
Battifol, P. 222
Baynes, N. H. 32
Beetham, Frank: translation of the
    anonymous *Life of Constantine*
    106–42
Bemarchius 9, 100, 157, 213
Bethlehem 137
Bezabde 212
Bibliotheca Hagiographica Graeca
    100–6
Bidez, J. 217, 223
breviaria see epitomes
Britain 79; blessed and happy
    81–82; Constans voyages to
    196–97
Bructeri tribe 64–65, 83–84
bull: revival converts Helena 28
Byzantium *see also*
    Constantinople: Constantine
    captures 126–27
Byzas 126

Caesares (Julian) 105
De Caesaribus (Victor) 41
Caligula 75
Callistus, Nicephorus:
    Ecclesiastical History 102
Calocaerus 2, 48
Cambyses 176
Cana, Galilee 137
Capernaum 136
Cassiodorus 36
Cassius Dio, Cocceianus 25, 29
de'Cavalieri, Franchi 103

Cedrenus, Georgius 25
Chortasmenos, John (Ignatius of
    Selymbria) 105
Christianity *see also* Arianism:
    Constantine changes Empire 2,
    48, 119; Constantine's support
    for Arians 6; historians on
    Constantine 32–38, 72–76; Julian
    persecutes 225; law cases of
    persecution of pagans 213–14;
    legislation for 125; Licinius
    makes mischief against 125–26;
    pagans gain access to churches
    247–48; persecution 116, 225;
    Persian 35
Chronica (Dexippus) 1
Chronicle (Theophanes) 24–25,
    101–2
Chronicon paschale (anonymous)
    24
Chrysanthus, Bishop 131–32
Chrysostom, John 24, 99
Church of the Apostles 233, 234
chyrsargyron (sales tax) 22
Cibalae, Battle of 41, 45
City of God (St Augustine) 5
Claudius II (Gothicus) 43, 68–70,
    75, 108
Constans, Flavius Julius 3, 141,
    193–94; anti-paganism 213;
    arrogance towards Constantius
    150–51; Athanasius at court
    152–53; campaign against Franks
    194–96; character 198–99;
    Constantine II advances on
    territory 228; debauchery
    228–29; division of empire 227;
    education 172–73; and father
    171–75; joint rule with
    Constantius II 199–205; oration
    by Libanius and Julian 162;
    'promiscuous massacre' 337
    147–49; revolt of Magnentius
    210; sympathy with Nicaean
    Christians 151; voyage to
    Britain 196–97
Constantia (daughter of
    Constantine) 48, 210, 229, 230
Constantia (sister of Constantine)

campaign 181–84; 'promiscuous massacre' 337 147–49; rebellion of Julian 233; revolt of Magnentius 210–12; scourge of pagans 9; strategy and battle against Persians 188–92; sympathy for Arians 151–52, 153

Crispus 4–5; baptised by Sylvester 122; conquers Amandus 47; and Constantine's conversion 18; Constantine's grief 17–18; leadership 42; legislation for Christians 125; made Caesar 46; murder 219, 240–41; name linked to Claudius 69; *Panegyrici Latini* 67; Zosimus on 16–17

crosses: Constantine builds three 138–40; Constantine's vision 31–32, 117–18, 127, 226, 242; miracle cure 134; vision over Constantius' battlefield 229

Cyprus 48

Cyril of Jerusalem 34

Cyropaedia (Xenophon) 97, 98

Cyrus 170, 176

Dalmatius (brother of Constantine) 111, 227

Dalmatius the Younger 3, 48, 116; 'promiscuous massacre' 337 147–49; treachery 141

Daphne: fire at temple 244–47

Darius 176, 179

Dexippus 9; *Chronica* 1

Dio Cassius *see* Cassius Dio, Cocceianus

Diocletian, Gaius Aurelius Valerius: abdication 41, 115; co-rule with Maximianus 40; education of Constantine 7; and *Origo Constantini* 43; persecution of Christians 107; persecutions 27–28; plot against young Constantine 111–12; prefers gardening to ruling 63, 65; security of empire 21

Diophantus 155

disease 27–28

Dodgeon, M. H.: translation of *Oratio* LIX (Royal Discourse Upon Constantius and Constans) **164–205**

Domitianus the Praetorian Prefect 230

Domitius Alexander: claim to title of Augustus 65

Donatio Constantini 27

Ecclesiastical History (Callistus) 102

Ecclesiastical History (Eusebius) 33, 98–99; attacked for Arianism 30; source for Zonaras 26

Ecclesiastical History (Sozomen) 35

Ecclesiastical History (Theodoret) 222

Epiphanius 36, 155

Epitome de Caesaribus (anonymous) 4–5, 41; Eunapius as source 10, 11–12

Epitome (Eutropius) 41

Epitome (of Roman) history (Zonaras) 25–31, 32

epitomes 2, 4–6 *see also* under titles

Eudoxius 256

Eugenius 217, 219, 238–39

Eumenius: *Panegyrici Latini* 67; silence on Claudius 69

Eunapius of Sardis 41; anti-Constantine stance 11; on Constantine's love of flattery 20; on founding of Constantinople 29; on Libanius 155, 156–57, 157; *Lives of the Sophists* 9–11, 155; version of Constantine's conversion 18; and Zosimus 12

Eunomius 37, 221, 225, 226, 256

Euphratas 104, 105

Euphrates, Bishop 153

Euripides 243; *Orestes* 250

Eusebius, priest at Daphne 245–47

Eusebius of Caesarea 225; Arian leanings 30; on Constantine's vision 73–74; on Diocletian's abdication 115; *Ecclesiastical History* 19, 33, 98–99; Evagrius refers to 23; *Life of Constantine* 34, 35, 97–99; no references

expedition against Maximinus
Daia 123–24; portrayal in *Origo
Constantini* 44–47; sympathetic
treatment 33; varying
viewpoints on 15–16; Zonaras
on 26
Life of Aurelian (Nicomachus) 6
Life of Constantine (anonymous)
106–42; editions 106;
introduction 99–106
Life of Constantine (Eusebius) 35,
97–99; shortcomings in
biographical information 98,
99–100
Lives of the Sophists (Eunapius)
9–11, 155
Livy (Titus Livius) 6
Logothetes, Symeon
(Metaphrastes) 101, 103;
Artemius 221
Lucianus the martyr 256
Lucifer of Cagliari 151
St Luke 216, 218–19, 228, 231–33
Lydus, Joannes 23

Macarius, Archbishop of Jerusalem
133, 134–35, 138, 217, 238–39;
death 219
Maccabeus, Judas 31–32
Macedonius, *de facto* Patriarch of
Constantinople 152
Magnentius, Flavius Magnus
210–12, 229
Mai, Angelo 223
Malalas, Joannes 24
Marcellus of Ancyra 151
Martinianus 47
Mary Magdelene 136
Massilia (Marseilles) 71–72, 88–89
Mauricius 140
Maxentius 8; claim to title of
Augustus 65; conflict with
Constantine 25; death 45, 118;
defeat in *Panegyrici Latini* 67; in
Origo Constantini 44–45;
resentment at Constantine's
illegitimacy 15; violence and
harshness 7; wickedness
according to the anonymous

Life 116–19, 123, 138–39
Maximiana (mistakenly
Constantine's first wife) 27
Maximianus Herculius 7–8, 8;
abdication 41, 115; claim to title
of Augustus 65; co-rule with
Diocletian 40; death 65–66, 72,
115–16; helps Maxentius 44; not
happy in retirement 63–64;
Origo Constantini 43;
Panegyrici Latini 85–86;
persecution of Christians 107;
plot against Constantine 72,
111–12; villain of the panegyric
70–72
Maximinus Daia: claim to title of
Augustus 65; and Constantine's
ambition 14–15; death 124;
expedition against Licinius
123–24; made Caesar 44; named
Caesar instead of Maxentius 63
Menander Rhetor of Laodicea
159–60, 162
St Menas 129
Merogaise tribe 65, 83
Mestrianus 46
Metaphrastes *see* Logothetes,
Symeon
Metrophanes, Patriarch of
Constantinople 29–30, 133, 138
Minervina: mother of Crispus 42
miracle cures 216–17
Mithras: emperors restore
Mithraeum at Carnuntum 65;
Mithraeum in Alexandria 214;
Sol and Apollo 75
St Mocius 129
Momigliano, A. D. 39
Mommsen, Th. 42
Mons Seleucus 211
Montius 229, 230
Moreau, J. 42
De mortibus persecutorum
(Lactantius) 33, 41, 100
Mount of Olives 135
Mount Tabor 136
Müller-Rettig, B. 77
Mursa 211
Musonius, Bishop 131–32